The
Unspoken
Dialogue

The Unspoken Dialogue
An Introduction to Nonverbal Communication

Judee K. Burgoon

Thomas Saine
The University of Florida

Houghton Mifflin Company
Boston

Dallas Geneva, Illinois Hopewell,
New Jersey Palo Alto London

Printed in the U.S.A.

Library of Congress Catalog Card Number:
77-078913

ISBN: 0-395-25792-1

Part and chapter illustrations by Edith Allard.

Credits

Howard Cosell. Passages from *Cosell*. Reprinted
with permission of Playboy Press from *Cosell* by
Howard Cosell. Copyright © 1973.

Joseph Heller. Passage from *Catch-22*. Copyright ©
1955, 1961 by Joseph Heller. Reprinted by permission of Simon & Schuster, Inc., and of Joseph Heller
and Jonathan Cape.

To Michael, in the hopes that having his name
associated with this book will prompt him to
read it with enthusiasm
and
To Karen, in justification for all the nights I've
spent with Judee

Contents

Preface

Although a relatively new area of inquiry, the study of nonverbal behavior is somewhat addictive. There is something both satisfying and intriguing about exploring the body and how it is used as a medium of communication. The study of nonverbal communication invites an appreciation of the idiosyncracies and complexities and contradictions of human action. Every book represents a vision. *The Unspoken Dialogue* is our vision of a new way of looking at a fascinating subject area.

Traditionally, scholars have taken a somewhat "anatomical" approach to nonverbal behavior, studying first the voice, then the hands, the eyes, the use of time, the use of artifacts, and so on, breaking the nonverbal act down into component codes that are treated independently. But we all know that any piecemeal approach is a misrepresentation of how people communicate. For example, when we attempt to communicate emotions to another person, we integrate cues from various parts of the body to convey our meaning. The body is simply not an amalgamation of unrelated parts. To study it as such is to miss much of the meaning of nonverbal communication.

The vision that directs this book is to emphasize the communicative nature of nonverbal behavior—to focus not on separate codes, but on the ways in which such behaviors combine to fulfill certain communicative functions. Thus, our vision has been to take a *functional* approach to the study of nonverbal communication.

It has occurred to us that most courses taught under the rubric of Speech Communication share a common investigative goal: the assessment of how messages function for people. To this end, we investigate information transfer, persuasion, decision making, cohe-

sion, social solidarity, and impression formation. Why? Because these (among others) are the functions performed by speech. They are also the functions fulfilled by nonverbal behavior. So we have conceived of a text (and a course) that would focus *not* on dissecting each nonverbal code but instead on suggesting how the codes interact to satisfy important communication functions. While this approach may seem unfamiliar in the area of nonverbal communication, we are convinced that it is the most coherent way of viewing the area and the approach that most clearly parallels the perspective of many other communication courses. During three years of using this perspective, we have seen that our students find it an exciting way of integrating knowledge about nonverbal communication and a useful complement to information gleaned from other courses.

One of the difficulties in studying and teaching nonverbal communication is that concepts and research findings alike range from very simple and intuitive observations on the one hand to highly sophisticated and complex variable relationships on the other. This makes it difficult to keep a text at one level or the other. So instead of trying to force simplicity on what are relatively sophisticated concepts, we decided to let the nonverbal literature dictate the level of the book. Consequently, some chapters are more demanding than others. But even at the freshman level, it is important to develop an appreciation of the complexity of ideas. To offer readers at every level an indication of the wealth of research and thought that is available to support the principles presented, we have cited what we feel to be relevant and seminal works in each area of investigation. The complete citations, which appear at the end of each chapter, should provide interested students with a base for further reading and investigation. For more advanced students, the book attempts to raise important issues regarding the testability of ideas, to acquaint students with basic theories, and to provide some insight into the research methodologies used to study nonverbal communication.

As is true of most texts, many people left their mark on this enterprise, and we would like to recognize them for their respective contributions. First, we wish to thank sincerely those who aided and abetted us with their criticisms, suggestions, and encouragement. A number of students, notably Don Stacks, spent many hours reading portions of the manuscript and offering us their reactions. Two other students, Martie Parsley and Marshall Cohen, invested innumerable hours taking photographs. Many colleagues, too, generously sent photos to us. We wish to thank them once again for the interest they showed. Finally, Edward Mabry, who made valuable recommendations on the final version of the manuscript, deserves special thanks. We won't forget the vacation time he gave up for us.

Our gratitude also goes to the several official reviewers of the manuscript: Peter Andersen of West Virginia University, Roy Berko of Lorain County Community College, John Boyd, Joyce Hocker Frost of the University of Montana, Robert Smith of Wichita State University, Mary Jeanette Smythe of the University of Missouri, and John Wiemann of the University of California at Santa Barbara. At best, the reviewers helped us sharpen or reshape our thinking; at worst, they gave us another opportunity to have a good argument.

Last, two special people deserve mention: Michael, whose attitude toward this content area made writing this text a more challenging task but whose continued supportiveness and humor made it a more enjoyable one; and Karen, master critic and speller, who cannot remember when we were not working on the book.

J. B.
T. S.

The
Unspoken
Dialogue

I

The Components of Nonverbal Communication

Nonverbal communication is a widely publicized topic and one that has captured the interest of the American public. Everyone is talking about nonverbal communication. It is a fascinating subject that directly relates to all of us.

The talk has spawned an enormous amount of knowledge and speculation and a lot of misconceptions as well. This book aims at helping you understand nonverbal communication by separating the knowledge from the misconceptions. We have divided the text into two parts. Part I introduces the basics. In Chapter 1, we define nonverbal communication and tell how it compares to verbal communication. Chapter 2 examines a variety of ways to study the subject. Chapters 3 and 4 describe what we call *codes* and tell how these codes are used and how effective they are as vehicles of communication. In Chapter 5, we focus on individual differences in the use of nonverbal cues, for example, how males and females differ in their use of nonverbal messages and how racial and ethnic background influences usage. These chapters should provide a foundation for understanding Part II, which looks at the various kinds of messages that can be expressed through the combined nonverbal codes.

One of the more enjoyable aspects of studying nonverbal communication is watching real people interacting. We have interspersed throughout the chapters some suggestions for mini-experiments that you can carry out on your own. Treat them as your personal version of *Candid Camera*. The research projects we discuss should also offer ideas about observations you can make.

In addition, we have introduced a way for you to test your sensitivity to nonverbal messages. Each chapter opens with a short true–false quiz and a list of key concepts. By the end of the chapter, you should be able to answer correctly all the questions in the quiz and define the concepts. Keep a record of your score on the quiz before and after reading the chapter to check your progress as an informed nonverbal communicator.

1

1

What Is the Unspoken Dialogue?

Test Your Sensitivity

True or False?

1. Everything we do communicates to other people.
2. Our nonverbal communication patterns are inherited primarily from the apes.
3. The vocabulary of nonverbal communication is limited and clearly recognized by everyone.
4. When a nonverbal message contradicts a verbal one, adults tend to believe the nonverbal one.
5. The main purpose of nonverbal messages is to reveal emotions.
6. Nonverbal communication can do everything that verbal communication can do and more.

By the end of the chapter, you should know the correct answers to all six questions and understand these concepts:

- communication
- differences among communication, information, and behavior
- issues involved in defining nonverbal communication
- nonverbal communication
- functions of nonverbal communication
- comparison of verbal and nonverbal communication as to:
  origins
  neurophysiological processing
  coding system
  language capacity
  message characteristics
- relative importance of nonverbal communication

It was 11:55 A.M. on April 30, and Benjamin Crowninshield Bradlee, 51, executive editor of the Washington Post, chatted with a visitor, feet on the desk, idly attempting to toss a plastic toy basketball through a hoop mounted on an office window 12 feet away. The inevitable subject of conversation: Watergate. Howard Simons, the Post's managing editor, slipped into the room to interrupt: "Nixon has accepted the resignations of Ehrlichman and Haldeman and Dean," he said. "Kleindienst is out and Richardson is the new attorney general."

For a split second, Ben Bradlee's mouth dropped open with an expression of sheer delight. Then he put one cheek on the desk, eyes closed and banged the desk repeatedly with his right fist. In a moment he recovered. "How do you like them apples?" he said to the grinning Simons. "Not a bad start."

Bradlee couldn't restrain himself. He strode into the Post's vast fifth-floor newsroom and shouted across the rows of desks . . . to Woodward . . . "Not bad, Bob! Not half bad!" Howard Simons interjected a note of caution: "Don't gloat," he murmured, as Post staff members began to gather around. "We can't afford to gloat!" Then, addressing the visitor, "The White Hats win."[1]

Thus James McCartney, a national correspondent, chronicled the reactions at the Washington *Post* to the Watergate resignations. McCartney's description captures the significance of the event not so much through the actual words he uses as through the nonverbal imagery the passage evokes. Note some of the details he uses to make the event vivid. Bradlee's initial actions, his physical appearance, and his office equipped with a basketball hoop tell us something about him. His body cues—the facial expressions, the desk pounding, the incongruous position of his cheek to the desk, his stride to the newsroom—reveal his attitude and the emotional pitch of the situation. Even time and voice cues are brought into play through the shift in the time element from relaxation to rapid activity and the vocal contrasts of shouts and murmurs. All of these are nonverbal messages that make the verbal narrative come alive for the reader.

We have chosen to label such communicative elements that go beyond the words themselves the *unspoken dialogue*, a phrase that comes from a quotation attributed to Dag Hammarskjold, the former secretary general of the United Nations: "What happens during the unspoken dialogue between two people can never be put right by anything they say." His perceptive observation underscores the importance of the nonverbal side of communication. Successful interaction with the world around us depends greatly on our ability to express ourselves nonverbally and to understand the nonverbal messages of others.

In infancy, our first and only means of communicating needs and receiving reassurances is through nonverbal signals; even after we have mastered verbal language, nonverbal messages continue to permeate all our interpersonal transactions. We actively employ

mini-experiment

Have a nonverbal party. During the first half, no one is allowed to talk. People may communicate only nonverbally. (Vocal sounds such as laughing, grunting, and humming are permitted so long as no meaningful words are used.) Notice which forms of nonverbal communication people seem to prefer. During the second half of the party, people are permitted to talk. Question people on how they felt about using only nonverbal communication and how effective they thought it was. You might also notice how verbal communication changes the tone of the party.

such messages to add color to what we say. They are the fine print and the hidden meaning where words are inadequate. We use them to carry sympathy, advice, innuendo, and punishment where words are inappropriate; to display feelings, attitudes, and reactions where words are unnecessary. With caressing touches, tender voices, and smiling faces, we speak love and are loved. With body movements, we tell a stranger that we would like to get acquainted. We signal disbelief merely by raising an eyebrow. We can encourage someone to talk longer or like us more simply by moving closer. We can command obedience by wearing a uniform.

We are also constantly receiving nonverbal messages from every direction. Family life is infused with them—they form a fundamental part of each family's unique communication system. The classroom bombards us with them—the actions of teachers, the reactions of other students, and the physical environment itself all tell us what is expected of us. Social relationships depend on them—friendships begin, grow, and end with the help of nonverbal messages, and conversations are regulated by them. Even in our leisure time, we are dogged by Madison Avenue's barrage of appeals. Vance Packard's popular book *The Hidden Persuaders* is rife with examples of the clever tactics used to manipulate our behavior as consumers. Even something as trivial as the color of a soap wrapper can be used to elicit a response.

It should be apparent that nonverbal messages have an impressive influence on every facet of communication. Researchers have gone so far as to make estimates of just how important such messages are in the total process of communication. Ray Birdwhistell, one of the pioneers of nonverbal research, believes that less than 35 percent of the social meaning in a situation is conveyed verbally, the rest nonverbally. Albert Mehrabian, another well-known expert, claims that 93 percent of all meaning is transmitted nonverbally. We shall comment on that estimate later, but it should be clear that whatever the percentage, the unspoken dialogue has to be reckoned with if one is to understand communication at all.

To begin our exploration of the unspoken dialogue, we need to start with the basics: definitions.

Definitions

Definitions are critical to understanding what is meant by *nonverbal communication*. They not only create a common vocabulary but also reveal what is or is not to be included for study. We think that, as students of nonverbal communication, you should both know the definition that we'll use and be acquainted with the major issues involved in arriving at that definition. We begin with the term *communication* itself.

Communication

Communication is a slippery concept because people use the word in such a variety of ways. They talk about communicating with pets and communicating with oneself. Computers communicate with satellites, and communication is what comes out of a television set. We have chosen to limit this text to communication that takes place between two or more people. That rules out talking to yourself and to animals.

Even within these limits, there is still much controversy over definitions. Most scholars agree, however, that communication is a *dynamic process*, that it involves creating *shared meaning*, and that meaning results from *sending and receiving messages* via *commonly understood codes*. Our system of verbal language is one such code. In this text, we shall examine seven nonverbal codes based on body movements, physical appearance, the voice, touch, space, time, and artifacts.

Information and Behavior

Another way of clarifying what is meant by communication is to contrast it with information and behavior. People frequently make the mistake of calling anything that is informative *communication*. Few people would claim that the sun has communicated with us when we see sunlight and conclude that it is daytime. Yet when people observe living things and draw the same kinds of inferences, they often want to call the information they have gathered communication. From our point of view, *information is any stimulus in the environment that an individual may interpret and use to guide behavior*. In other words, it is anything that reduces our uncertainty and allows us to make predictions about the world around us. By contrast, communication implies a message that takes the form of a recognizable code and is transmitted from one person to another. Information doesn't require the presence of another person; communication does. Information doesn't require any active or intentional behavior on the part of the carrier or interpreter of the information; as we shall see shortly, communication does. Thus, while all communication is informative, only some information is communication. Communication is thus a subset of information. The leaves turning brown inform us that fall is approaching, red spots on a patient's body inform a doctor that the patient may have measles, and *Popular Mechanics* informs its readers how to repair a carburetor; but only the last is communication—a message between two people involving some degree of intent and active encoding or decoding.

Similarly, many forms of behavior are informative, but only some of them qualify as communication. *Behavior* can be defined as *any actions or reactions performed by an organism*. Behavior differs from communication in that it can take place without others observing it, responding to it, or understanding it. Sleeping and eating are behaviors that also

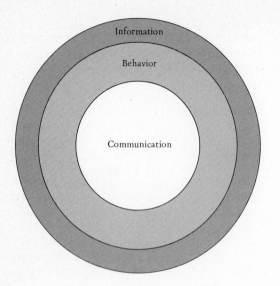

Figure 1.1   Relationships among communication, behavior, and information

inform us about the organism engaging in them, but those behaviors would rarely be classified as communication. (An exception is the spouse who purposely goes to sleep in the middle of an argument. That *is* a message.) The point is that, while communication is informative and frequently takes the form of active behavior, not all information and behavior are communication. Rather, communication can be viewed as a subset of behavior, which in turn is a subset of information. Figure 1.1 illustrates the relationship.

This perspective reduces to a manageable level the number of things that qualify as communication and allows us to clarify what we mean specifically by *nonverbal* communication.

Nonverbal Communication

Edward Sapir once claimed that nonverbal communication is "an elaborate code that is written nowhere, known to none, and understood by all."[2] We wish it were that simple.

Unfortunately, people have such diverse impressions of what is included that everything from extrasensory perception to footprints to biorhythms has been labeled nonverbal communication. Our question is: How broadly should nonverbal communication be defined? If you scratch yourself or spill ketchup on your shirt, is that nonverbal communication? For those who take a broad view, both examples would be. Many people feel that any attribute or behavior—sneezing, being overweight, wearing tennis shoes— qualifies because others may react to it or interpret it. Those who take a narrower view feel that, if you call almost anything communication, you make communication more difficult to study and thereby reduce the possibility of discovering general principles.

We find the information/behavior/communication distinction useful in this regard. If sneezing, scratching, and spilling take place in the absence of other people, they are clearly not communication. If such actions, along with such traits as being overweight, are regarded merely as information about your phys-

Figure 1.2 What do you think is being communicated by the gesture in this picture? Turn the page for the answer.

Behaviors have to have a commonly recognized meaning in the society.

ical state, much as one notices that a tree has bark and produces blossoms, they are still not communication. But if someone thinks that you are sending a message with your appearance and actions (such as communicating that you are anxious or signalling that you want to be considered athletic), then they may be considered communication.

The definition of nonverbal communication can be further refined by addressing some related issues. There is no right or wrong position on these issues. We simply want to introduce some of the alternatives and the implications they carry and then explain our preference.

major issues of nonverbal communication

Signs Versus Symbols If Albert stamps his foot and Martha takes it as a sign that he's angry, is that communication? If Shirley always rubs her nose when she's happy, can Lloyd say she is communicating happiness to him the next time she rubs her nose? These two questions relate to the issue of whether nonverbal communication must be symbolic or whether signs also qualify. Some scholars

distinguish signs from symbols by saying that *signs* are natural parts of what they signify while *symbols* are arbitrarily assigned representations. Smoke is a sign of fire, but the word *smoke* is a symbol for the thing. From a different point of view, symbolic communication must involve "(a) a socially shared signal system, that is, a code, (b) an encoder who makes something public via that code, and (c) a decoder who responds systematically to that code."[3] In other words, if the behavior is not overt, has no meaning shared among observers, and does not produce a predictable response, it is only a sign, an inference made by an observer rather than a message sent by an encoder.

Whichever approach is taken to understand the concept *sign,* they both rule out as communication idiosyncratic behaviors, those behaviors that are unique to the individual. Thus Shirley's nose rubbing would not be considered communication because nose rubbing is not commonly accepted as a representation of happiness. More likely it would be interpreted by those who were not acquainted with Shirley

Figure 1.3 As you can see, the gesture was not a communicative gesture at all. Our hero has just thrown a ball in from left field. This simple example points out the distinction between behavior and communication. (Meg and Dick Leschack)

as a sign that she has a cold or that her nose tickles.

If the criteria of shared meaning and systematic responses are also imposed on the definition of communication (many scholars do not want to be that restrictive), that still leaves open the question of whether nonarbitrary, commonly understood cues should be included. Return to the foot-stamping example. We would expect most people to identify a vehement foot stamp as denoting anger. Yet such a behavior is not truly symbolic since it is not an arbitrarily chosen representation of anger. Rather, it is a natural response that frequently accompanies an expression of frustration. In this particular example, we do not know whether Albert is stamping just to release his own tension or whether he's stamping to tell Martha that he is angry with her. If the latter interpretation is correct, the act could be defined as communication, even though it is more a sign than a symbol, because both Martha and Albert regard it as a message. It also takes the form of a socially recognized signal.

We believe it is reasonable to interpret such actions as communication. There are many nonverbal behaviors, such as gestures and postures, that arise naturally out of the emotions they signal, yet have strong communicative value. We are therefore willing to include both signs and symbols in our definition, so long as they have socially shared meaning.

Intent An equally sticky issue is whether nonverbal cues must be intentional and who decides what is intended. One approach to communication, called a *source orientation*, argues that only those messages that are intentionally sent by their source should be classified as communication. In other words, the source determines what is intentional. Another approach, called a *receiver orientation*, holds that anything a receiver thinks is intentionally sent should be considered communication. This broader view allows accidental behaviors to be included so long as someone thinks they are intentional. Random behaviors that are recognized as such are ruled out with this approach. For example, wearing ragged blue jeans would not be a nonverbal message if people knew that your jeans were your total wardrobe; it might become one if someone thought you were trying to communicate a casual, nonconforming attitude. We prefer the receiver-oriented perspective because we believe that most people engage in a lot of unintentional nonverbal behavior that others interpret as intentional. We would like to include such behaviors for study along with those that are clearly intentional.

(3) _Consciousness_ Some people see consciousness as part of intent; they say that intentional behaviors are conscious ones and vice versa. Others believe that an active subconscious, without conscious awareness, sends intentional messages and interprets the messages of others as intentional. Psychoanalysis, for instance, makes this assumption. A therapist may conclude that if you cross your leg away from him or her, you are unconsciously revealing your unwillingness to communicate. Similarly, you may subconsciously pick up a fleeting expression of insincerity from someone without knowing consciously what makes you distrust that person. Whether such out-of-awareness behaviors qualify as communication is open to question. We do know that through hypnosis people are able to remember things they were never previously aware of, which suggests that we record mentally much more than we recognize.

For our purposes, we will include in our definition those behaviors that someone is aware of, whether it be the sender, the receiver, or an outside observer. (Remember that the behaviors still have to have a commonly recognized meaning in the culture.) This allows us to study such things as pathological communication and instances of insensitive communicators who send out lots of negative messages to each other but can't put their finger on what's bothering them about the other.

(4) _Feedback_ The last issue is whether or not nonverbal communication must be received and acknowledged through some form of feedback, or response. Many definitions of communication include feedback as one of the requisite characteristics. Certainly no one would dispute that when a receiver reacts to a sender's nonverbal message, communication has occurred; but what if the receiver doesn't react? For those who claim that "you cannot _not_ communicate," the answer is easy: no reaction is in itself a message. But no reaction could just as easily mean that the person never got the message; with nonverbal messages it often isn't easy to tell. Furthermore, people may not notice or react to an expression or gesture at the time but may recall it later. We have all at one time or another paid so much attention to the verbal level of communication that we overlooked some important nonverbal cues, only to have them creep into our awareness afterward. Sometimes such cues become meaningful only in the light of subsequent events, as when a depressed friend drops out of school. Not until he or she has left do the early signs become clear.

We don't have the final answer on the issue of feedback. Rather than be restrictive, we prefer to include in nonverbal communication behaviors that are not immediately responded to, with one stipulation: there must at least be a potential for response. If the receiver is physically unable to receive the message (say, too far away to see a smile) or does not understand the code, there has been no communication. Such messages may be labeled _communication attempts_, indicating effort on the part of the source to communicate but failure on the part of the receiver to recognize the message.

Now that we have covered some of the major issues, we are ready to offer our working definition. We consider _nonverbal communication to be those attributes or actions of humans, other than the use of words themselves, which have socially shared meaning, are intentionally sent or interpreted as intentional, are consciously sent or consciously received, and have the potential for feedback from the_

Table 1.1 Criteria for a Definition of Nonverbal Communication

Feature	Is It Necessary for Nonverbal Communication?
Human encoder	Yes
Human decoder	Yes
Separate sender and receiver	Yes
Socially shared coding system	Yes
Symbolic	No
Intentionally sent	No, if interpreted as intentional by receiver
Interpreted as intentional	No, if intentionally sent
Consciously sent	No, if consciously received and intentional or interpreted as intentional
Consciously received	No, if consciously and intentionally sent
Observable feedback	No
Potential for response	Yes

receiver. It should be apparent from the definition that both signs and symbols are included, as are unconscious or unintentional messages that are interpreted as intentional and unconsciously received messages that are intentionally sent. The definition rules out (1) nonhuman sources or receivers, (2) intrapersonal communication, (3) idiosyncratic behaviors, (4) communication attempts that are not received, and (5) behaviors that are neither consciously recognized nor interpreted as intentional by the parties involved. As a quick reference, we have put in Table 1.1 a summary of the issues involved in defining communication and our position on those issues.

With the definitions out of the way, we are ready to begin exploring how nonverbal communication operates in relation to verbal communication—how they work together, how they are similar, and how they differ.

Relationship of Nonverbal and Verbal Communication

Authorities have identified at least six ways in which nonverbal communication works in conjunction with verbal messages.

1. *Redundancy.* Nonverbal cues can be used to say the same thing that is being said verbally. When we tell people that we are pleased with them, we smile to repeat our message. At a noisy hamburger stand, we may hold up two fingers while we yell our order. This built-in repetition increases the accuracy of the communication interchange.

2. *Substitution.* Sometimes, rather than say something aloud, we signal it nonverbally. Rather than tell a friend we are sorry about her misfortune, we may pat her on the shoulder. At the movie theater, we may simply hold up four fingers when asked how many tickets we want. When we are angry, we may simply walk away instead of trying to verbalize our feelings. Because of the richness of nonverbal imagery, it is often more effective to substitute a nonverbal cue for its verbal counterpart: obscene gestures have their impact in part because of the visual images they create. The substitution of nonverbal cues can also increase the efficiency of communication. A nonverbal message frequently can be conveyed much more rapidly than a verbal one (see Fig. 1.4), and two or more messages can be delivered at one time. Consider the child who wants an advance on an allowance. All the while the verbal case is being pleaded, the face, posture, and voice present a supplicant, endearing pose, topped off by an affectionate hug. The use of several nonverbal modes also allows us to convey things we might find hard to say. Imagine the first date between two shy teenagers. They could spend an entire evening discussing the weather before verbally expressing their attraction to each other. How much easier to move close together, to smile, and to touch.

Figure 1.4 Substitution. Gestures, postures, and facial expressions may effectively replace a verbal message. (Harvey Stein)

3. *Complementation.* A function related to substitution is complementation. We often use nonverbal cues to supplement or modify what is being transmitted verbally. The nonverbal elements simply add more details, but in this case the details are neither identical to, nor a replacement for, a verbal message. They serve to expand on the message being conveyed. A good example is the person who reports an accident he or she has witnessed. While telling the narrative, the individual animatedly re-creates the scene through gesture, posture, and voice. All these elements make the story more vivid. They also reveal how that individual feels about the accident. Similarly, when we are asked to reprimand someone or pass along bad news, our nonverbal cues may reveal that we are reluctant to undertake the task. The nonverbal complement is generally important in clarifying both the verbal message itself and the nature of the relationship between speaker and receiver.

4. *Emphasis.* Often we use nonverbal cues to accentuate or punctuate what we are saying verbally. Vocalic elements are especially useful for this purpose. We may moderate our pitch or rate of speaking to emphasize a point. Gestures are also commonly used for this purpose. When Nikita Khrushchev pounded his shoe on the table at the UN, he underscored his message. Groucho Marx perfected his eyebrow-raising and cigar-flicking routine to punctuate the long pauses following his suggestive remarks. In fact, much humor is dependent for its success on the use of nonverbal elements. Timing, posture, and facial expressions all may be used to emphasize the punch line.

5. *Contradiction.* Another nonverbal function that is used for humor and more serious purposes is contradiction. We may frequently use nonverbal cues to send messages that conflict with the verbal message (see Fig. 1.5). Sarcasm depends on just this contrast. The vocal inflection signals that the verbal message means the opposite of what it says. Don Rickles has perfected the use of contradic-

tion in his comedy routines. Not only does his voice drip with sarcasm; even his facial expression displays it. Contradiction may also be used for more subtle and serious purposes. On a job interview, we may signal with our body that we are very interested while our words are more cautious. When we are angry or hurt by someone, we may say, "Nothing is the matter," while our voice and body cry out that something *is* bothering us. At other times, we unsuccessfully coordinate the nonverbal with the verbal so that our nonverbal behaviors accidentally contradict our verbal statements. How many times have people admired something you created or claimed to agree with you, when you were absolutely certain that their opinion was the opposite? Chances are, they did not do a very good job of masking their true feelings; their nonverbal behaviors gave them away. This passage from *Catch-22* illustrates such nonverbal betrayal:

Aarfy seemed a bit unsettled as he fidgeted with his pipe and assured Yossarian everything was going to be all right. . . . "I only raped her once," he explained.

Yossarian was aghast. "But you killed her, Aarfy! You killed her!"

"Oh, I had to do that after I raped her," Aarfy replied in his most condescending manner. "I couldn't very well let her go around saying bad things about us, could I?"

"Aarfy, are you insane?" Yossarian was almost speechless. "You killed a girl. They're going to put you in jail!" . . .

"Oh, I hardly think they'll do that," Aarfy replied with a jovial chuckle, although his symptoms of nervousness increased. He spilled tobacco crumbs unconsciously as his short fingers fumbled with the bowl of his pipe. "No, siree. Not to good old Aarfy." He chortled again. "She was only a servant girl. I hardly think they're going to make too much of a fuss over one poor Italian servant girl when so many thousands of lives are being lost every day. Do you?"

All at once he looked sick. He sank down on a chair in a trembling stupor, his stumpy, lax hands quaking in his lap. Cars skidded to a

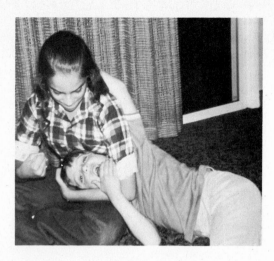

Figure 1.5 Nonverbal cues often contradict verbal cues. Here the smiles betray the threatening gestures and the readily imaginable verbal threats.

stop outside . . . and police whistles screeched. Voices rose sharply. Aarfy was green. He kept shaking his head mechanically with a queer, numb smile and repeating in a weak, hollow monotone that they were not coming for him, not for good old Aarfy, no siree, striving to convince himself that this was so even as heavy footsteps raced up the stairs. . . . Then the door to the apartment flew open, and two large, tough, brawny M.P.'s with icy eyes and firm sinewy, unsmiling jaws entered quickly, strode across the room, and arrested Yossarian . . . for being in Rome without a pass.[4]

6. *Regulation.* The final function nonverbal elements perform is regulating communication interactions. Through our nonverbal behaviors, we can govern when a person talks, how long she or he holds the floor, and even the topics discussed. Or we can use nonverbal signals to gain control of the communication ourselves. We can prevent others from interrupting us and can assure their attention. The regulatory function of nonverbal communication is so important that an entire chapter of this text is devoted to it.

While these six functions illustrate some important facets of nonverbal communication, they imply to some people that nonverbal messages are subordinate to verbal communication. In fact, some people have even defined nonverbal communication as only those other-than-verbal messages that take place in the presence of a verbal message. We see nonverbal communication as much broader in scope than merely clarifying and amplifying the verbal stream. We are interested in studying all those functions that nonverbal communication can perform, with or without the presence of a verbal message. We shall, therefore, be looking at such functions as the communication of emotions, the development of interpersonal relationships (known as relational messages), manipulation of one's self-presentation, and the manipulation of others, in addition to the regulatory function already mentioned. These are some primary purposes of communication in general and are ones to which nonverbal messages are particularly relevant.

A closer examination of the similarities and differences between verbal and nonverbal communication will reveal that the two do not always operate the same way or to the same degree in performing such functions. Sometimes verbal expression is more appropriate or influential; sometimes the nonverbal cues predominate. We can gain a better understanding of the domain of each by looking at some of the major areas of comparison. We shall limit our-selves to the five most significant and interest-ing dimensions: origins, neurophysiological processing, code characteristics, language characteristics, and message characteristics.

Origin: Nature or Nurture?

One highly controversial question regarding human behavior in general is whether behav-ior is dictated by a person's genetic make-up or acquired through environmental and cultural influences. The issue relates to nonverbal com-munication in that, to the extent that the signal system is innate, it becomes a universal lan-guage, a code that can be understood by all cultures; to the extent that it is learned, it is similar to verbal language in its structures, its functions, and its stages of acquisition within a culture.

It is generally recognized that much of our verbal system is learned. Nothing inborn dic-tates that we call a cow a cow rather than a flute. Language must be learned by each gener-ation. This is not to say that nature plays no role. Two writers on nonverbal communica-tion, Abne Eisenberg and Ralph R. Smith, Jr., say:

mini-experiment

Go to a zoo and take pictures of the mon-keys and apes at play, grooming, nurturing (in the case of mothers), feeding, and fight-ing. Then look for photographs in books and magazines of humans in the same situ-ations. See if you can find similarities in the expressions and postures.

We know that the capacity for language is innate, for all human beings display a predis-position to use a language composed of dis-crete sounds linked together by syntactical rules. Regardless of the culture in which he is raised, a child learns to use language in the same chronological sequence as all other chil-dren. For instance, he will utter sentences at the same age in all cultures.[5]

Many linguists believe that the underlying structure of language itself (called *deep struc-ture*) is innate. A recent discovery of a fascinat-ing process called synesthesia also suggests that there is some innate influence on lan-guage. *Synesthesia* is the ability to hear in color. Synesthetic people get mental color im-ages when they hear certain words and sounds. The same sounds typically produce the same colors for people in all cultures (high pitches produce white or bright colors and low pitches produce dark colors). After studying one hundred languages and dialects, Lawrence Marks concluded that many words such as the names of colors are labeled not arbitrarily but in a fixed, evolutionary pattern based upon this sound–color association.[6] The sounds in the word conjure up the color associated with the thing that is named.

For the most part, though, language must be acquired through learning. The vocabulary, the correct sounds, and the rules for stringing sounds and words together differ from culture to culture and must be taught to infants and nonnatives alike.

With nonverbal communication, the relative roles of nature and nurture are not as clear-cut. Some scholars argue that all nonverbal behav-iors are inborn while others claim that they are totally culture bound. Those who support the former position offer as evidence similarities between human and lower primate behavior and examples of universal (cross-cultural) expressions (see Fig. 1.6). The human-to-ani-mal comparisons have produced some supris-ing similarities between human displays and those of apes, monkeys, and chimpanzees. For instance, there is a parallel in laughter and

Figure 1.6

smiling. The broad smile and wide-mouth laugh in humans closely resemble the silent bared-teeth and relaxed open-mouth displays in primates.[7] Ethologists have also found analogues for human behavior among other species.

These comparisons are all based on the assumption that such similarities establish the evolutionary character of behavior. They draw on Darwin's theory of natural selection by suggesting that behaviors are retained in the human repertoire because they have *survival value*. Presumably, those behaviors that are useful become a permanent part of the communication system while the ones that are nonfunctional in terms of survival disappear eventually, leaving a largely universal signal system. Anthropologists who have looked for such universal behaviors have found many examples. One is the eyebrow flash—a quick, often unnoticed raising of the eyebrows. This behavior is a common friendly greeting signal in most cultures. Figure 1.7 illustrates the expression in several different countries. Many emotional displays are also expressed in the same manner across cultures. Such behaviors are taken as proof of the innateness of nonverbal communication.

Those who hold the opposing view, that nonverbal behavior is a function of environmental influences, offer examples of cultural differences to support their case. There are numerous examples of the same behavior having different meanings in different countries and different behaviors having the same meaning. For instance, a belch after dinner is rude in our country, polite in others. Americans and Europeans point with the forefinger; many Africans and Asians point with their lips. The variety of differences that exist is given as evidence that behaviors cannot be innate since they are not universal.

Probably the truth lies somewhere in between. It is possible that many of our facial expressions, gestures, glances, spacing, and touch behaviors have biological roots, but that each culture has modified and adapted them and added other communicative elements. The eyebrow flash is a case in point. In Japan, for example, its use has been suppressed as immodest while in our culture, it has taken on additional meaning such as being a cue of approval or a flirting signal. For whatever reason, the behavior has remained an intrinsic part of human behavior patterns, but each culture has learned different meanings for it. It

What Is the Unspoken Dialogue?

Figure 1.7 Facing page: The eyebrow flash. (From I. Eibl-Eibesfeldt, "Similarities and Differences Between Cultures in Expressive Movements," in R. A. Hinde, ed., *Non-Verbal Communication*, Cambridge: Cambridge University Press, 1972)

seems reasonable that much nonverbal communication can be explained in the same manner. Basic patterns may have an evolutionary base while their specific manifestations and variations may be culturally determined. It is also likely that many nonverbal cues are strictly learned and have their origin in the idiosyncrasies of the culture from which they are derived. Many gestures and vocal inflection patterns fall into this category.

If one accepts the combined heredity–environment explanation for the origin of nonverbal behaviors, the study of nonverbal communication becomes very complex. Discovering which messages have universally understood meaning and which ones follow culture-bound rules can be a challenging undertaking. It also means that nonverbal communication may be more powerful than verbal communication in certain circumstances—for example, in the signalling of aggressive intentions—while verbal communication may work more successfully in others—such as when the culturally prescribed meaning of the nonverbal gesture is ambiguous (as in the case of the head nod, which has multiple interpretations).

Verbal communication, then, appears to be more a product of nurture while nonverbal communication appears to be a product of nature and nurture combined.

Neurophysiological Processing

Recent advances in scientific technology have significantly affected the way in which scholars look at human behavior. One result has been an effort to reduce behavior to quantifiable physical and physiological activities. Recent research has introduced the intriguing notion that verbal and nonverbal communication differ in the ways in which they are neurophysiologically processed.[8]

In the past, the workings of the mind have been a mystery. Researchers have been perplexed by the fact that brain lesions impair the ability to speak but not the ability to interpret nonverbal messages. New techniques have enabled scientists to explore such phenomena by tracing how various stimuli are processed by the brain. Those who study disturbances from brain lesions have concluded that there are different neural pathways for verbal and nonverbal stimuli.[9]

The bulk of research suggests that verbal stimuli are usually processed initially by the left side of the brain, while many nonverbal stimuli are processed by the right side.[10] (This holds only for right-handed people; for left-handers, hemispheric dominance isn't so pronounced.) Doreen Kimura, who has done a significant amount of investigation in this area, has found that the left side of the brain is dominant in the auditory perception of spoken language and the visual recognition of verbal stimuli whereas the right side controls understanding of certain nonspeech sounds, visual and tactile discrimination, and visual recognition of quantities. This discovery fits nicely into the theory of a left–right dichotomy for verbal and nonverbal stimuli. However, Kimura has also found that the left hemisphere controls free movement during speech—what we call gestures. Other researchers have found that rhythmic vocal patterns and meaningful speech are processed by the same side.[11]

What this means is that certain stimuli that have been traditionally regarded as nonverbal are processed by the left side while others are processed by the right. As yet, no clear-cut conclusion is possible as to where the stimuli are initially received. It is also important to point out that, to date, the research has focused primarily on the initial reception of the stimuli. Scientists still have little knowledge of where the stimuli are *interpreted* as messages, when such stimuli take the form of messages, and where nonverbal *encoding* takes place. It is possible that hemispheric dominance affects only the initial reception of stimuli and that, once the signals are decoded or encoded as messages, they are handled like verbal communication. These issues and others are discussed in more detail in Chapter 2. Our conclusion is that, at present, it is not possible to distinguish between verbal and nonverbal communication on the basis of neurophysiological processing.

Coding Systems: Analogic Versus Digital

A third distinction that is frequently made between verbal and nonverbal communication is based on the type of coding system. Verbal communication is regarded as a digital system while nonverbal communication is viewed as predominantly analogic. A *digital* system is one that is composed of *finite, discrete, arbitrary* units; an *analogic* system is *infinite, continuous,* and *natural.* The grading system used in many schools is a good example of a digital system. Usually there are only five possible grades (a finite set), which are clearly distinguishable from one another (that is, they are discrete). The system is arbitrary; there could just as easily be fourteen different grades. Our verbal language system is considered a digital system because it consists of a limited number of units strung together according to cultural rules. The vocabulary is largely arbitrary as are the grammar and syntax. The units of any verbal language are also distinguishable from one another. We can tell one sound from the next, one word from the next, one sentence from the next, and so forth.

By contrast, an analogic system is a form of analogy; it closely resembles what it represents. Thus, the units and the relationships among units cannot be arbitrary but are determined by the nature of what is being coded. A stick drawing as a representation of a person is an example. The arms, legs, and head have to be in the right place and follow the human form in their shape. An analogic code must

also have an infinite continuum of values, such that each merges into the next just as the colors of the spectrum blend into each other. Nonverbal communication is considered to be largely analogic because many of the cues have these properties. Facial expressions are natural outgrowths of the emotions they reveal; a threatening gesture is inherently related to the message it conveys in that it foreshadows the larger act. Neither has a clear-cut beginning or end, and both can be enacted with infinite variation without altering the basic message. Many people consider nonverbal communication to be the more potent message system because of the analogic value of nonverbal codes. However, with nonverbal messages there is also the possibility of greater confusion.

Language Characteristics

A fourth way in which nonverbal communication has been compared to verbal communication is the degree to which it qualifies as a language system. There are at least four features of language that offer points of contrast between verbal and nonverbal communication: degree of rule structure, self-reflexiveness, tense capacity, and ability to reference the negative.

Rule Structure   Every language has a complex set of rules that govern the construction and interpretation of words, phrases, and sentences. English, for example, is one of the most complex of languages. Let us consider whether nonverbal codes are also governed by rules. Those who take a linguistic approach to nonverbal communication believe that they can identify the basic units, or vocabulary, of nonverbal communication and the rules for combining them. We shall discuss some of their efforts in later chapters. Others, such as Randall Harrison, author of a textbook on nonverbal communication, believe that nonverbal codes do not have the degree of structure and sophistication that verbal language has. As Harrison explains:

Not all nonverbal codes share the complex, multilevel structure of language. In particular, it is often difficult to find the counterpart of the phone or phoneme, discrete elements which do not have meaning in themselves but which can be combined in various ways to produce other meaningful symbols. Similarly, jumping a level, many nonverbal codes do not seem to have the complex rules of syntax which in verbal language produce a sentence. [12]

So far, research has not produced a clearly identifiable and unanimously accepted dictionary of nonverbal cues, nor have the experts established a consistent set of rules for combining and ordering components. For instance, there is no catalogue of cues that signal availability or a sure-fire combination of behaviors that represent loneliness. We suspect that, at some point in the future, it will be possible to identify what behaviors carry the same meaning as others and the underlying rules for combining signals. For the time being, perhaps the fairest conclusion to draw is that if the nonverbal codes have a rule structure, it is less apparent than that for verbal communication.

Self-Reflexiveness One of the peculiar features of language is that it need not refer to something else; it can talk about itself, as in the sentence, "This statement is false." Simply put, the principle of self-reflexiveness means that we make statements about statements, and more statements about those statements. Thus, language can become further and further removed from the reality being reflected in the first place. Imagine a picture of a television set within the picture of a television set within the picture of a television set *ad infinitum*. Or consider the entrepreneur who invents a spot remover to remove the spots left by spot remover. Similarly with language, Bill can discuss Karen's description of an event and someone else in turn can describe Bill's description.

This self-reflexiveness can go on indefinitely and is not time bound: Bill can comment on Karen's language an hour after her statement.

Nonverbal communication does not seem to have this capacity, or at least does not have it to the same degree. One nonverbal code may comment on the message being given at the moment by another code, but it rarely comments on itself. A possible exception is a person laughing at his or her own laugh. That could be considered self-reflexive, but it seems unlikely that the reaction could extend beyond one level. For most nonverbal cues, it is hard to imagine any kind of extended self-reflexiveness. How, for instance, can one posture comment on a previous one, which is commenting on yet an earlier one? Or how can a message conveyed by how far apart people stand reflect on a distance message transmitted the day before? Because nonverbal communication appears to have limited, if any, ability to make abstractions about itself, it falls short of qualifying as a language system.

Tense Our verbal language system has a built-in system for indicating whether it is referring to past, present, or future events. *Walk* becomes *walked* to show past tense. By contrast, nonverbal communication is limited to the present. It has no unambiguous way of referring to the past or the future. In this respect, then, nonverbal communication is again more limited than verbal communication. It lacks the flexibility of language to indicate time.

Referencing the Negative We are indebted to Kenneth Burke, one of the great scholars of our time, for this last concept. He has called attention to the fact that language can refer to the absence of something; nonverbal communication cannot. To quote Burke, "The essential distinction between the verbal and nonverbal is in the fact that language adds the peculiar possibility of the Negative." [13] We can speak of unfulfilled expectations or the absence of pain, but how does one indicate these nonverbally? The inability of nonverbal communication to express negatives, then, is the fourth way in which it differs from verbal communication in terms of language characteristics.

To summarize, nonverbal communication may be less complex than verbal communication and have fewer rules; it seems to lack self-reflexiveness; it cannot express tense or the negative. These differences in language features affect the types of messages verbal and nonverbal communication can convey and their relative effectiveness as a vehicle for communication.

Message Characteristics

This last area of comparison concerns the general capacity of the verbal and nonverbal channels to act as message carriers. There are four features we wish to consider: type of content, simultaneity of messages, directness of sensory stimulation, and spontaneity.

Type of Content   Many people have contended that nonverbal communication primarily expresses emotions. It is true that many of the nonverbal codes are especially well suited to this purpose. Like other species, we can signal distress, warning, and affiliation nonverbally. The analogic nature of the nonverbal code allows a broad range of expressions— facial, gestural, postural, and vocal—to match emotional states. It often feels more natural to reveal emotions nonverbally than to try to put them into words. However, nonverbal communication is capable of doing much more than just conveying feelings. Part II of this text is devoted to examining many other kinds of messages that can be communicated through nonverbal codes.

There is an important underlying difference between the kinds of content verbal and nonverbal communications carry. Regardless of the primary purpose of a nonverbal message, it usually carries emotional overtones—feelings about oneself and about others—that are not easily separated from the other elements of the message. Verbal communication differs in that the components can be separated. A verbal message may be rational and impersonal, carrying no affective information. A statement about the weather, for instance, does not have to involve feelings.

At another level, verbal messages can be abstract, expository, and argumentative, cogently expressing complex ideas and opinions. Verbal communication can also narrate and can jump forward and backward in time. Because nonverbal communication lacks the language properties of self-reflexiveness, tense differentiation, and expression of the negative, it is restricted in its ability to be expository or narrative except through pantomime. Even then, the reenactment of an event must follow a linear sequence; that is, it cannot shift back and forth from present to past to future. Finally, verbal communication is often necessary to describe something. Nonverbal cues may supply important elaboration but frequently cannot stand alone. Clearly, verbal and non-verbal communication are suited for conveying different kinds of messages.

Simultaneity of Messages   While verbal communication appears to have the edge in breadth of content, nonverbal communication has an offsetting advantage in that it can carry several messages simultaneously. Not only can each code carry different messages, but there can also be multiple messages within a given code. The face may signal affection, attention, and surprise all at the same time; vocal rate may suggest efforts at control, while intensity may communicate anger. Verbal communication has some ability to transmit *metamessages* (what we often mean when we talk about reading between the lines) but not to the same degree. The multiplicity of messages in nonverbal communication means that the combined nonverbal bands can carry more information at a time than can the verbal band.

REUNION—Lena Dimitrova (left) is tearfully reunited with her sister, Mary Christoff, after 63 years of separation. Christoff came to US from Yugoslavia in 1914 and now lives in Syracuse. Her sister flew to New York from Yugoslav town of Bitola.

Directness of Sensory Stimulation   A third factor that contributes to the power of nonverbal communication is its ability to stimulate the senses directly. Facial expressions, gestures, body movements, postures, and physical appearance all impinge upon visual receptors; verbal messages engage the various senses to a lesser degree, for they are mediated by the thought processes. When an individual hears or reads the words, "His eyes burned with anger," the words must be mentally processed and interpreted before reaching the mechanisms that respond to visual stimuli. The impact is weakened, especially if the person has poor visualizing or fantasizing ability (see Fig. 1.8). Consider the difference between seeing on television children burned by napalm and reading about it. With the television version, all the information from the voices and faces is immediately available to stir our emotions rather than having to be conjured up in the mind. In fact, some people feel that television news imposes too much cruelty and bloodshed upon the viewing public. During the Vietnam War, one particularly disturbing news film

zoomed in for a close-up of a South Vietnamese officer who abruptly and without warning shot a Vietcong captive in the head. People who witnessed the incident from their living rooms were undoubtedly much more horrified than those who read about it in the newspaper the next day. The image of the man suddenly slumping to the ground, his blood splattering on the street, could not be captured in words. Similarly, a comedian's act is more entertaining than the written material itself, partly because of the direct sensory stimulation.

Spontaneity   One final message characteristic that contributes to the forcefulness of nonverbal communication is its apparent spontaneity and sincerity. People generally assume that nonverbal behaviors are unconscious and automatic rather than conscious and manipulated and consequently believe that nonverbal messages are more honest and trustworthy. When we give a gift to a friend, we pay more attention to the spontaneous nonverbal reaction than to the verbal *thank you*. While nonverbal expressions can be masked or faked—pathological liars are particularly adept at controlling their voice and face—this reliance on nonverbal indicators is frequently justified. A good illustration comes from a study on crossracial communication conducted by Shirley Weitz. She set up a situation in which whites first reported on a questionnaire their attitudes toward blacks and then interacted with a black in a simulated interview. She found that the true prediction of friendly behavior was not the response to the questionnaire but the rated friendliness of the person's voice. In fact, behavior during the interview often contradicted the subjects' stated attitude.[14] Many blacks wisely choose to rely on the tone of voice as the best indicator of their relationship with whites.

When all of the message features are taken as a whole—the type of content, the simultaneity of messages, directness of sensory stimulation, and perceived spontaneity—it seems that nonverbal messages are generally more powerful than verbal ones. Research supports this conclusion. For example, it has been observed that when verbal and nonverbal messages are in conflict, the nonverbal message is usually believed.[15] (We say *usually* because some research suggests that children are more attuned to verbal messages. One study found that they believed a verbal criticism more than the smile that accompanied it,[16] and another found that 80 percent of their judgment of a teacher's message came from verbal cues.[17]) Second, when the relative impacts of various verbal and nonverbal cues are compared in terms of their contribution to meaning, the nonverbal cues usually prevail. You will recall that Mehrabian went so far as to claim that only 7 percent of the meaning in a situation is transmitted verbally. Actually, his conclusion, which has been widely quoted, was based on a faulty interpretation from an experiment he conducted with Susan Ferris.[18] They taped someone saying the neutral word *maybe* while the vocal tone was varied to be either positive, negative, or neutral. They then matched the

voices with photographs showing facial expressions that were positive, negative, and neutral. All possible combinations were shown to observers, who rated what they thought the actual attitude was. Mehrabian and Ferris concluded that facial expression carried more weight than the voice. But since only one word was used and was never varied, the verbal element never had a chance to modify the meaning.

Although that study didn't conclusively compare verbal with nonverbal cues, Mehrabian conducted another experiment with Morton Weiner in which the verbal cues were varied along with vocal cues. (They paired positive, negative, and neutral statements with positive, negative, and neutral vocal cues. In all, there were nine possible combinations.) Their results showed that the vocal cues influenced a person's judgment of the expressed attitude more than the verbal cues.[19] Another research team expanded the cues under study to include eye contact, body orientation (facing directly or indirectly), trunk lean (leaning forward or backward), and seating distance, and found similar results: observers of a videotaped therapy interview were twice as accurate in interpreting the actual empathy level as were those who only read the verbal message.[20]

Beyond research, personal experience tells us that we frequently rely more heavily on nonverbal cues than on verbal ones to detect the true meaning of a situation. By the time you have reached adulthood, you can recognize the signals of disappointment and defeat in the movements and eyes of those who have lost a competition, even when they tell you that winning isn't important to them. And you have learned to use nonverbal cues to send messages that would be inappropriate at the verbal level. Ray Birdwhistell offers a telling illustration:

Take courtroom procedure, for example. The present system of restricting admissible evidence to exhibits and words still leaves the

mini-experiment

You can test the relative effects of vocal and verbal messages by tape recording the sample paragraph below in several different ways so that each reading alters the meaning. Play each version to a different group of people and have them answer the questions that follow. To assess the meaning that the verbal part alone carries, have some people just read the paragraph and answer the questions. Then compare the answers to see how vocal cues alter the meaning of a verbal message. (You can also test the combined effects of vocal and facial cues by reading the paragraph aloud with accompanying facial expressions.)

The Paragraph:

John arrived at the party a little late. His host Jeff greeted him by saying, "Don't feel bad about being late." John responded, "I got another traffic ticket on the way over." Jeff shook his head as John entered the room. "By the way," said Jeff, "don't miss the movies they're showing in the den. And help yourself to the refreshments over there on the table." As John looked around the room, he noticed an older man on the far side of the room. "I wonder who invited him," he thought. Then an attractive young woman approached John. "Hi, John." "Hi, Sally, it's so nice to see you." He turned to the food and placed some cheese thing in his mouth. "Pretty awful," he thought as he picked up another.

The Questions:

1. How old is John? the older man?
2. Was Jeff angry about John's late arrival?
3. Was John disturbed about his traffic ticket?
4. Is John a reckless driver?
5. What kind of a party was it? What kind of movies were being shown? What kind of refreshments were being served?
6. Did John know the older man? Was he pleased to see him?
7. Was John pleased to see Sally?
8. Is John shy? aggressive? cynical? flirtatious?
9. Did John like the food?

way open for the introduction of nonadmissible ideas and attitudes. The trial lawyer often is a master of the raised eyebrow, the disapproving headshake and the knowing nod. In many cases, these gestures if translated into words, would be inadmissible as evidence. Yet, as presented, they have a definite effect on the judge and jury.[21]

Perry Mason fans would no doubt agree.

While research and personal experience testify to the frequent preeminence of nonverbal messages, it is not always the case that nonverbal messages are attended to more carefully than verbal ones. People tend to be consistent in preferring verbal or nonverbal cues, and there are people who believe verbal cues more often.[22] As we noted earlier, for many types of messages, verbal communication is more effective. Its language characteristics give it flexibility.

Regardless of which code predominates in a given situation, it is apparent that nonverbal codes play a significant enough role in communication to warrant closer study. It is ironic that while children begin receiving training in verbal skills even before kindergarten, nowhere in the educational system is any attention given to nonverbal communication. We hope that this text will help to counteract that deficiency in your own education.

Summary

In this chapter, we have attempted to stress the importance of nonverbal communication in the overall communication process and to note its distinguishing features. Nonverbal communication is differentiated from other forms of information and behavior in that it is the transmission of a message between two or more people, involving intent and consciousness on the part of at least one of the people and having the potential for feedback. Nonverbal communication may perform six functions in relation to verbal communication: redundancy, substitution, complementation, emphasis, contradiction, and regulation. It may also serve several functions on its own. Finally, nonverbal communication can be distinguished from verbal communication on the basis of its origin, the way it is neurophysiologically processed, its coding system, its language characteristics, and its message potential.

Suggested Reading

Birdwhistell, R. "Background to Kinesics." *ETC.*, 13 (1955), 10–18.

Eibl-Eibesfeldt, I. "Similarities and Differences Between Cultures in Expressive Movements." In R. A. Hinde (ed.), *Non-Verbal Communication*. Cambridge: Cambridge University Press, 1972. (pp. 297–314)

Eisenberg, A. M., and Smith, R. R., Jr. *Nonverbal Communication*. New York: Bobbs-Merrill, 1971. (pp. 11–46)

Ekman, P., and Friesen, W. V. "The Repertoire of Nonverbal Behavior: Categories, Origins, Usage and Coding." *Semiotica*, 1 (1969), 49–98.

Harrison, R. P. *Beyond Words*. Englewood Cliffs, N.J.: Prentice-Hall, 1974. (pp. 57–77)

Marks, L. E. "Synesthesia: The Lucky People with Mixed-Up Senses." *Psychology Today*, 9, No. 6 (1975), 48–52.

Mehrabian, A. "Communication Without Words." *Psychology Today*, 11, No. 9 (1968), 53.

Nolan, M. J. "Nonverbal Expressive Behavior in an Integrated Model of Human Communication." Paper presented at the International Communication Association Convention, Montreal, April 1973.

Packard, V. *The Hidden Persuaders*. New York: David McKay, 1957.

Ruesch, J. "Nonverbal Language." *Psychiatry*, 18 (1955), 323–330.

Ruesch, J., and Kees, W. *Nonverbal Communication: Notes on the Visual Perception of Human Relations*. Berkeley: University of California Press, 1956.

Weakland, J. H. "Communication and Behavior—An Introduction." *American Behavioral Scientist*, 10, No. 8 (1967), 1–4.

Wiener, M., Devoe, S., Rubinow, S., and Geller, J. "Nonverbal Behavior and Nonverbal Communication." *Psychological Review*, 79 (1972), 185–213.

Notes

1. J. McCartney, *Columbia Journalism Review* (July–August 1973), p. 8.
2. E. Sapir, "The Unconscious Patterning of Behavior in Society," in D. Mandelbaum (ed.), *Selected Writings of Edward Sapir in Language, Culture and Personality* (Berkeley: University of California Press, 1949), p. 556.
3. M. Wiener, S. Devoe, S. Rubinow, and J. Geller, "Nonverbal Behavior and Nonverbal Communication," *Psychological Review*, 79, No. 3 (1972), p. 186.
4. J. Heller, *Catch-22* (New York: Dell, 1955), pp. 427–429.
5. A. M. Eisenberg and R. R. Smith, Jr., *Nonverbal*

Communication (New York: Bobbs-Merrill, 1971), p. 42.

6. L. E. Marks, "Synesthesia: The Lucky People with Mixed-Up Senses," *Psychology Today*, 9, No. 1 (1975), pp. 48–52.

7. J. A. R. A. M. Van Hooff, "The Phylogeny of Laughter and Smiling," in R. A. Hinde (ed.), *Non-Verbal Communication* (Cambridge: Cambridge University Press, 1972), pp. 207–241.

8. P. A. Andersen, J. D. Garrison, and J. F. Andersen, "Defining Nonverbal Communication: A Neurophysiological Explanation of Nonverbal Information Processing," paper presented at the Western Speech Communication Association Convention, Seattle, November 1975.

9. See J. Ruesch, "Nonverbal Language," *Psychiatry*, 18 (1955), pp. 323–330.

10. See, for example, Andersen et al. (note 8); A. Carmon and I. Nachson, "Ear Asymmetry in Perception of Emotional Non-verbal Stimuli," *Acta Psychologica*, 37 (1973), pp. 351–357; D. Kimura, "The Asymmetry of the Human Brain," *Scientific American*, 228, No. 3 (1973), pp. 70–78. However, there are many exceptions. See, for example, D. Caplan, J. Holmas, and J. Marshall, "Word Classes and Hemispheric Specialization," *Neuropsychologia*, 12, No. 3 (1974), p. 332; M. S. Gazzaniga and R. W. Sperry, "Language After Section of the Cerebral Commissures," *Brain*, 9 (1967), p. 131; H. W. Gordon and A. Carmen, "Transfer of Dominance in Speech of Verbal Response to Visually Presented Stimuli from Right to Left Hemisphere," *Perceptual and Motor Skills*, 42 (1976), p. 1097; J. Semmes, "Hemispheric Specialization: A Possible Clue to Mechanism," *Neuropsychologia*, 6 (1968), p. 11.

11. S. S. Ratliff and H. J. Greenberg, "The Averaged Encephalic Response to Linguistic and Nonlingustic Auditory Stimuli," *Journal of Auditory Research*, 12 (1972), pp. 14–25; G. M. Robinson and D. J. Solomon, "Rhythm Is Processed by the Speech Hemisphere," *Journal of Experimental Psychology*, 102 (1974), pp. 508–511.

12. R. P. Harrison, *Beyond Words* (Englewood Cliffs, N.J.: Prentice-Hall, 1974), p. 73.

13. K. Burke, *Language as Symbolic Action* (Berkeley: University of California Press, 1968), p. 420.

14. S. Weitz, "Attitude, Voice and Behavior: A Repressed Affect Model of Interracial Communication," *Journal of Personality and Social Psychology*, 24 (1972), pp. 14–21.

15. See, for example, M. Argyle, F. Alkema, and R. Gilmour, "The Communication of Friendly and Hostile Attitudes by Verbal and Non-verbal Signals," *European Journal of Social Psychology*, 1 (1971), pp. 385–402; E. K. Fujimoto, "The Comparative Power of Verbal and Nonverbal Symbols," dissertation, Ohio State University, 1971; E. M. McMahan, "Nonverbal Communication as a Function of Attribution in Impression Formation," *Communication Monographs*, 43 (1976), pp. 287–294. A. Mehrabian and M. Wiener, "Decoding of Inconsistent Communications," *Journal of Personality and Social Psychology*, 6 (1967), pp. 108–114. However, the situation may be complicated by whether the components are positive or negative and moderate or extreme in their evaluative contents. See D. E. Bugental, "Interpretations of Naturally Occurring Discrepancies between Words and Intonation: Modes of Inconsistency Resolution," *Journal of Personality and Social Psychology*, 30 (1974), pp. 125–133.

16. D. E. Bugental, J. W. Kaswan, L. R. Love, and M. N. Fox, "Child Versus Adult Reception of Evaluative Messages in Verbal, Vocal and Visual Channels," *Developmental Psychology*, 2 (1970), pp. 367–375.

17. H. Wass, "Pupil Evaluation of Teacher Messages in Three Channels of Communication," *Florida Journal of Educational Research*, 15 (1973), pp. 46–52.

18. A. Mehrabian and S. L. Ferris, "Inference of Attitudes from Nonverbal Communication in Two Channels," *Journal of Consulting Psychology*, 31 (1967), pp. 248–252.

19. A. Mehrabian and M. Weiner, "Decoding of Inconsistent Communications," *Journal of Personality and Social Psychology*, 6 (1967), pp. 108–114.

20. K. F. Haase and D. T. Tepper, "Nonverbal Components of Empathetic Communication," *Journal of Counseling Psychology*, 19 (1972), pp. 417–424.

21. R. Birdwhistell, "Do Gestures Speak Louder Than Words?" *Collier's* (March 4, 1955), p. 56.

22. Fujimoto (note 15); J. G. Shapiro, "Responsivity to Facial and Linguistic Cues," *Journal of Communication*, 19 (1968), pp. 11–17; L. Vande Creek and J. T. Watkins, "Responses to Incongruent Verbal and Nonverbal Emotional Cues," *Journal of Communication*, 22 (1972), pp. 311–316.

2

Approaches to Nonverbal Communication

Test Your Sensitivity

True or False?

1. Body language tells us what is on someone's mind.
2. Nonverbal messages form a language with specific meanings associated with specific movements.
3. Our nonverbal messages are more primitive than our verbal ones.
4. All of us have pretty much the same sensory ability.
5. Psychoanalysts are more interested in verbal than nonverbal behavior as a reflection of an individual's psychological condition.

The study of nonverbal communication is interdisciplinary. Scholars in such fields as linguistics, anthropology, sociology, physical education, physiology, medicine, physics, psychology, and of course speech communication have contributed to our knowledge of the unspoken dialogue. Each discipline fosters its own unique biases about how behavior occurs and what it means. These are called approaches or perspectives. The purpose of this chapter is to introduce you to some of the approaches, their strengths, and weaknesses, to give you an understanding of the variety of research traditions that have culminated in some of the ideas and concepts we shall explore in subsequent chapters.

What Is an Approach?

By the end of this chapter, you should know the correct answer to all five questions and understand these concepts:

- body language approach
- ethological approach
- linguistic approaches
- psychoanalytic approach
- physiological approaches
- functional approach

An *approach* is a way of looking at something. It is a perspective from which a problem or concept or issue can be viewed. A number of persons may observe an event but give widely varying reports of what happened. Their respective approaches or orientations to the event may be sufficiently different that they were led to perceive certain behaviors selectively while selectively avoiding others. For example, several friends watching a football game may bring to the event very different approaches to viewing the sport. One person may watch the movement of the linebackers in order to understand how the play developed, while a second observer may concentrate on the offensive guards; a third person may simply follow the movement of the quarterback or of the football from one player to another. All, in a sense, are *watching* the same event, but they are *seeing* things differently.

Consider the different approaches taken to the solution of a murder by two famous fictional detectives. Captain Edward X. Delaney, the hero and master sleuth of Lawrence Sanders's best-selling mystery, *The First Deadly*

Sin, relies on the wisdom suggested by the principle of Occam's Razor. The reference is to a fourteenth-century philosopher who believed that solutions to problems are cluttered by irrelevant information. Therefore, the most likely solution to a crime is also the most obvious. To Delaney, detective work involves discovering the obvious. Only through the meticulous and thorough search for evidence can Delaney arrive at the truth. By systematically scrutinizing every possible lead, by collecting a wealth of technical information, gradually he perceives an irrefutable explanation of the crime.

Hercule Poirot, Agatha Christie's private investigator, takes an entirely different approach as he seeks a solution to the *Murder on the Orient Express.* Poirot's approach is based on two assumptions. First, all suspects invariably reveal themselves under interrogation. Even the most clever and practiced criminals are drawn toward the truth. Each suspect's testimony can be compared with the statements of others to differentiate fact from fiction. Second, once these statements are compiled, the perceptive detective need rely only on his intellect; the most skilled investigator is the one who uses the mind to construct from testimony an accurate explanation of the crime.

An approach, therefore, is not only a difference in focus; it is a reflection of *priorities.* Your approach, whether it be with regard to football, mysteries, or nonverbal communication, is an indication of what you believe to be important, worthy of attention, and central to the event being observed. For example, in the study of nonverbal communication, it is not uncommon to find a researcher who isolates a certain behavior or part of the body and credits it with having the greatest communicative value. One approach may encourage the study of facial movement, while another stresses the role of voice in communicating meaning.

An approach may also embrace *assumptions* of a more philosophical tone, such as beliefs regarding the nature of humankind, the morality of a behavior, or the capacity of the human being to adapt or respond in a particular environment. There may be implied assumptions regarding the possible causes of behavior or even how meaning is generated in others. An approach biases the observer in interpreting how a behavior communicates. It is a form of risk the observer must be willing to take in order to achieve some understanding of the event in question. In many instances, assumptions are based on a tradition of research that the observer chooses to rely upon. Still, the risk of error is never completely eliminated. For example, research findings might well indicate that a particular behavioral sequence is abnormal in a given context. Can one then classify an individual who behaves this way as abnormal? One's approach or orientation to nonverbal communication may answer such questions and thereby facilitate the interpretation of behavior, but always at a risk.

An approach may specify a *causal* relationship, or a way of viewing the causes of behavior. A researcher may be predisposed to conclude that certain types of behaviors are motivated by a sexual drive or that an act was unconscious. A behavior may be linked to unseen processes (the unconscious, memory, inner feelings of guilt or shame), or it may be viewed as the product of a prior physical act, as when a smile by one communicator is followed by a smile from another.

An approach may also imply a particular *method* of observation. Certain contexts or settings may be essential if the behavior is to be studied in a natural environment. In many cases, the focal behavior may be so microscopic that special equipment (audio tapes, video recording devices, cameras) may be needed. Obviously, an approach that focuses on subtle inflections in the voice as cues to meaning cannot leave measurement entirely to the ear.

In summary, an approach involves a way of

looking at certain aspects of human behavior, priorities regarding what is important and relevant, assumptions about behavior and how they may be interpreted, beliefs about causality, as well as methods for capturing and monitoring the action.

The study of nonverbal communication has resulted in the development of a number of different approaches, some strikingly different, others overlapping. The most common of these are discussed in this chapter: the body language approach, the ethological, the linguistic, the psychoanalytic, the physiological, and the functional approaches. You will find many instances in which two approaches will differ on one point while agreeing on a second. Also, some researchers are associated with more than one approach.

The Body Language Approach

General interest in the study of nonverbal communication has produced a number of popular commercial treatments of the subject. Julian Fast's *Body Language* and Gerald Nierenberg and Henry Calero's *How to Read a Person Like a Book* are probably the best examples of the *body language* (or *anecdotal*) approach. For the most part, these books are *anecdotal* treatments of nonverbal communication. They rely on scenes of body movements or incidents that illustrate how to decipher nonverbal behaviors and discover the inner thoughts and feelings of others. Between the incidents and stories, however, lie some important (although quite controversial) statements about nonverbal communication.

Assumptions

1. *Our inability to read correctly the nonverbal messages sent by others often leads to interpersonal misunderstandings.* Many popular writers have argued that while we are relatively skilled in understanding the verbal communication system, much of our weakness in attempting to understand others lies at the nonverbal level. The body language literature also implies that nonverbal behaviors are not as readable as the verbal. You have to know what to look for and what to discard.

2. *Nonverbal messages are more authentic and reliable than verbal messages.* While both the verbal and nonverbal channels are capable of transmitting a tremendous amount of information in a short period of time, something more real or trustworthy comes through at the nonverbal level. (For an example of how this assumption of the body language approach works, see Figure 2.1.) Fast describes a young woman undergoing psychotherapy who, while confiding in her psychiatrist of her love for a young man, was unknowingly shaking her head as if to indicate that this was not the case. In this respect, the language of the body provides a means of verifying what is being communicated orally. But what is it about nonverbal behavior that makes it so trustworthy?

3. *The body is the messenger of the unconscious.* We have to reach into Freudian psychology for the belief that your unconscious self is the real you. Your conscious behavior is much like a façade, hiding deep-seated fears, anxieties, and desires. Actions of the body, however, are spontaneous, immediate, and involuntary. Each of us, at one time or another, has engaged in some form of deception. Words, so the thinking goes, are the principal tool of deception. The movements of the body, on the other hand, are difficult to monitor thoroughly and, therefore, are all the more difficult to disguise.

4. *The movements of the body make up a language, in which certain movements have specific meanings.* The body is much like a storage chest for nonverbal behaviors, many of which are symbolic (that is, they are representative of ideas, concepts, feelings); a certain

Figure 2.1 Which would you tend to put more faith in: the nonverbal message being communicated by the speaker and his colleague, or the hypothetical verbal message that accompanies the photograph?

"We want this to be a democratic meeting. We're open to any suggestions and comments you may have. Any gripes, too. If you've got questions or need to have a point cleared up as we go along, don't hesitate to break in. And don't worry about time. We're here as long as we can be of service."

stance or facial expression or leg position is considered to represent a specific meaning. Nierenberg and Calero have argued that even such seemingly insignificant acts as rubbing the nose or tugging at the ear mean something. Nose touching or rubbing disclaims nonverbally what is being communicated verbally.[1] Of course, if everyone were to accept at face value this interpretation of nose touching, catching a cold could have serious interpersonal implications. In another direction, Fast points out that there may well be a language of legs that communicates attitudes or emotional states.

5. *Nonverbal messages indicate sexual motives.* You may recall that one of the first widely popularized statements of the body language approach was an article in *Playboy* magazine. The central point of the article was the notion that a woman's posture, arm and leg position, and facial expression could be interpreted as specific sexual messages. Perhaps the best known characteristic of the body language approach is the idea that almost all behaviors are sexually motivated, even though a communicator may be totally unaware of the connection between body movements and what may (or may not) be a conscious sexual orientation toward another individual. This is not to say that body language cannot be used consciously to achieve sexual ends. Sexual desires, especially among strangers, are seldom stated explicitly. The body plays an important role in communicating what one feels but is reluctant to say openly. Smiles, touches, inflections of the voice all fall into this category. These,

however, are probably conscious attempts by the communicator to show sexual interest. There are vast numbers of behaviors through which the body may show a sexual motive, behaviors of which the communicator is unaware. Sexual orientations toward others, whether positive or negative, invariably filter through the conscious attempts to disguise feelings and reactions. A classic example is the reliance on preening behaviors, including the touching of hair, mustache, beard, or lips or the manipulation of clothing, as when a male tugs at his belt or when a woman unconsciously adjusts her bra strap. Although originally the result of learned grooming behaviors, preening is now taken to be an unconscious indicator of a sexual orientation, a way of signalling one's sexual involvement with another. In a passage that typifies the sexual orientation of the body language approach, Nierenberg and Calero identify some of the ways in which women are likely to show sexual interest:

The most common are smoothing or arranging their hair; smoothing their dresses; turning around and looking at themselves in mirrors or glancing side-ways to see their reflection. Others are a subtle rolling of the pelvic section; slow crossing and uncrossing of the legs . . . and caressing the inside of the calf, knee, or thigh. The delicate balancing of a shoe on the toe on one of the feet tells a man, "You're making me feel comfortable in your presence."[2]

6. *There is a high degree of uniformity in the way individuals communicate nonverbal messages.* It is assumed that we are much more alike than we are different, that our nonverbal repertoires are much the same. The minor differences observed in the frequency with which one individual engages in a particular movement can be written off as an idiosyncrasy. An important assumption of the body language approach is the notion that a specific behavior,

given a common context, has much the same meaning and relevance for one individual as for another.

We do not know how this similarity arises, although most of our nonverbal behaviors are thought to be acquired through socialization. That is to say, we are similar because we all have been taught in much the same ways how to use our bodies. A common tradition of information (from such sources as motion pictures, television programs, books, plays) regarding appropriate body movements provides specific models that assist the learning process.

Limitations

There are a number of shortcomings associated with the body language approach.[3] First, the anecdotal nature of much of the material is without sufficient substance to be considered *theoretical.* Occasionally anecdotes are chosen to illustrate a theory; in most cases, however, the short, popular examples of the various uses of body language merely illustrate the kinds of meanings that can be gleaned from nonverbal messages but without providing a systematic, empirically supported explanation for the behavior.

Second, the approach, while attempting to suggest causes for behavior, leaves many questions regarding the antecedents of actions unanswered. It provides no consistent distinction between motivated and unmotivated behaviors nor between conscious and unconscious movements of the body. Without this distinction, behavior cannot be read as the proponents of the approach suggest.

Third, the body language approach, when considered as an observational method for studying nonverbal communication, is fraught with ambiguities. How might an observer go about reading the nonverbal behavior of another person? What do you look for? A hand movement? leg positioning? facial expression?

These specific body positions are nothing more than isolated instances—frozen frames, if you will—in a continuous series of behaviors. An approach that leads you to draw conclusions from a brief moment may be at worst highly misleading; at best, it underutilizes the available data. Such an approach ignores the continuous, repetitive, contradictory, interactive, and imperfect nature of nonverbal communication.

Consider this situation. You are watching one individual speak to another. The first person goes through a series of preening behaviors, simultaneously folding arms in front and clenching both fists; then he relaxes the body and continues the preening. These behaviors, considered as three isolated incidents, are stereotypes to which the body language advocates say specific interpretations can be given. It is possible that, instead of three separate messages, they are, in fact, a single contradictory message, even a pattern of behaviors that has greater interpretative value than any of the specific movements it comprises. We observers have no way of knowing what slice of life to study. Therefore, it is difficult to know the point at which a behavior becomes *symbolic*.

A note of caution is important here. Just because we are treating the body language literature as an approach doesn't mean that it is necessarily a good way of viewing and explaining nonverbal interaction. On the contrary, many scholars are highly contemptuous of the body language approach. And so are we. Many of the assumptions underlying the body language approach directly contradict some of the most profound thinking and most disciplined research on nonverbal communication. Nevertheless, millions of people read the popular literature and jump to conclusions about nonverbal communication that are suspect at best.

If you are interested in reading some examples of the body language approach, you might try the following: *Inside Intuition* by Flora Davis, *Body Talk* by Maude Poiret, *Contact:*

The First Four Minutes by Leonard Zunin, and *Photoanalysis* by Robert U. Akeret.

The Ethological Approach

Ethology is the comparative study of animal behavior. The ethological approach to the study of nonverbal communication focuses on the origins, development, and functions of nonverbal behavior among the various classes of animal life.

Assumptions

1. *The human being represents a level of biological evolution in the animal kingdom.* For the ethologist, it is imperative that man be seen in an evolutionary perspective. Humans, however culturally exalted, share membership with other species as mere biological substrata in the animal world. From the ethological vantage point, evolution is not a negotiable view; it is a fact. The study of human behavior must fit in with certain research guidelines established for the study of other animal forms. Specifically, man must be encountered in a natural environment and observed unobtrusively. The laboratory is clearly not a natural environment.

2. *Nonverbal behaviors are innate.* In the nature—nurture controversy, the ethologist has most strongly and consistently argued that nonverbal behaviors are innate. Charles Darwin's *The Expression of the Emotions in Man and Animals,* published in 1872, is the classic ethological argument for the innate nature of behavior. Darwin's thesis that expressive behaviors (like smiling, laughing, crying) were acquired because of their survival value—their biological usefulness—can be extended to other forms of body movement such as protective responses and locomotion (moving from one place to another). Some theorists have

gone so far as to suggest that certain voice characteristics (irregular breathing patterns, sustained or modified amplification of the voice) to which we do not give a second thought are the relics of a precivilized period, acquired, perhaps by some lower primate, to signal sexual arousal or to warn of danger. For example, some have observed that the *head tilt*, a behavior that is for many species a signal of submission and a means of terminating physical combat, may perform a similar social function among humans, indicating acceptance, openness, and vulnerability.

It is important to recognize that for a behavior to have been acquired for survival purposes does not necessarily mean that the acquiring animal was a human being, nor does it imply that the behavior continues to be instrumental in the preservation of the species. Very few behaviors except language are considered to be distinctively human. It would be more appropriate to consider the human as the biological benefactor of thousands of years and hundreds of species. In many cases, behaviors are retained that, although no longer of survival value, fulfill some social function.

3. *Nonverbal behaviors are response patterns.* Ethologists view any social, communicative behavior on the part of a human being as a response to something in the environment. If we can assume that nonverbal behaviors are responses, then to what do they respond? The ethological approach isolates those events or occurrences in the environment that consistently spark certain behavioral responses within a species. In this respect, the ethologist tends to view the human as a *reactive* creature, paying only superficial attention to the complex reasoning processes underlying much human behavior.

Ethologists have often written about behavioral displays. *Displays* are behaviors that respond to a biological condition in the animal such as fear, sexual arousal, or aggression. Displays are not usually intended as communication (they are not conscious attempts to impart

meaning), although it is obvious that many displays do provide information about a specific animal. For example, a display of plumage by a male peacock is an involuntary response to sexual arousal. Whether or not the display is meant as communication is irrelevant since it does provide information to other peacocks. W. John Smith has argued that displays, although generally unintended, provide information to other members of the species. Among the traditional displays that involve elaborate nonverbal behaviors are those that precede or accompany aggression, play, or escape, permit locomotion, or signal sexual arousal.[4]

4. *Nonverbal behavior predates verbal behavior in human evolution.* Language is clearly one form of behavior that is not the artifact of evolution. John Lyon, in speculating on the origins of language, noted that, from the thousands of languages for which there is documentation, "no sign of evolution from a simpler to a more complex (from a more 'primitive' to a more 'advanced') stage of development can be found. . . ."[5] The same cannot be said for nonverbal behavior. Nonverbal behavior predates verbal behavior. That is, the use of the body as a communication code was developed before language ability. Nonverbal behavior, according to the ethologist, is a more primitive form of communication. Shirley Weitz has pointed out that, "under conditions of extreme stress, humans resort to nonverbal signs, such as screaming or crying with accompanying facial expressions, rather than undertaking a complex verbal analysis of the situation."[6]

Many ethologists are convinced that nonverbal behavior is more primitive than the verbal and that verbal behavior has evolved from nonverbal. Verbal behavior was acquired as a supplement to the nonverbal codes. Exactly how nonverbal behavior influenced the development of language is, however, not known.

5. *Nonverbal behaviors are not species-specific.* It stands to reason that, if humans (and

their nonverbal repertoire) evolved from lower primate forms, then many similarities should be found throughout the animal world (see Fig. 2.2). Much of the ethological approach focuses on the study of *which* behaviors are common to *which* animal groups. Ethologists feel that, by studying the behaviors of other species, we can come to understand more about ourselves and the functions and origins of human action.

Limitations

Criticisms of the ethological approach to the study of nonverbal behavior are, in some cases, almost a century old. They fill texts in many of the social and behavioral sciences and they involve questions of philosophy as well as biology. As one might guess, the reliance of ethology on the acceptance of a theory of man's biological evolution was bound to stir controversy. Even some social scientists who are personally inclined to accept the notion of human evolution are still unwilling to base a study of man's behavior on such a controversial thesis. Still, it is not so much evolutionary theory itself as some other aspects of ethology that have sparked debate. First, most social and behavioral scientists view behavior not as innate but as learned through participation in a specific culture. Many are convinced that people behave as they do because their culture has taught them to behave in ways that reflect the

Figure 2.2 Human territoriality has been compared to the territoriality of other species.

Peter Vandermark/Stock Boston

values of that culture and not because the behaviors have survival value. Critics of the ethological approach point out that, even if behaviors did originally have survival value, they persist today only if they have cultural value, and that the mechanism for transferring the behaviors from one generation to the next is not biological but cultural.

A second criticism of the ethological approach concerns the notion that data on human behavior and information on other primates are interchangeable. Many feel that the human linguistic and cognitive ability place us apart from other animals, and that attempting to explain human behavior through references to the behavior patterns of other animals is meaningless.

Third, the treatment of nonverbal behavior as a more primitive mode of communication than the verbal is strongly disputed, as there is reason to believe that many nonverbal behaviors evolved from spoken language. Specifically, behaviors that have definite verbal parallels (for example, the separation of the index and middle fingers to form the peace sign), gestures used to illustrate what is being referred to verbally (the use of the hands to indicate height of an object or person), and gestures or vocalizations that pace, sustain, or terminate communication (the use of eye contact or head nods to encourage a communicator to continue speaking) are all forms of nonverbal communication developed to assist the act of speaking.

Ira Kirschenbaum, M.D./Stock Boston

The Linguistic Approaches

If the body language approach is responsible for popularizing nonverbal communication among the reading public, linguistic approaches and the surrounding scholarship have done much to legitimize the study of nonverbal communication within the social and behavioral sciences. Many of the concepts and methods of researching and measuring movements of the body are the contribution of a relatively small number of dedicated researchers, referred to here as the *linguists.*

The term *linguistic,* however, is rather misleading. The linguistic approaches are not an offshoot of the academic discipline of linguistics. The term refers to the fact that in many respects the linguistic approaches parallel the various perspectives taken by linguists toward the study of language. The two share many concepts, theoretical goals, and assumptions regarding the symbolic nature of behavior and also share methods of investigating behavior.

As one might suspect, the linguistic approaches are not highly unified. There are actually two separate approaches that, while they share many assumptions, differ on several crucial issues. The differences are sufficiently great that the approaches are discussed under different labels—the *structure-centered* approach and the *meaning-centered* approach.

The Structure-Centered Approach: Assumptions

The *structure-centered* approach is also known as the linguistic–kinesic[7] approach. The two researchers primarily responsible for developing the philosophy of investigation upon which this approach is based are Ray Birdwhistell and Albert Scheflen. The label "structure-centered" suggests the main distinguishing feature of this approach and its major priority as well—the detection of structure in the body movement system. Birdwhistell uses the term *kinesics* to refer to the study of body movement as communication.

Just as language has structural elements and rules for organizing these elements, body movement has basic motions and principles that coordinate their use as communication. The proponents of this approach argue that, in order to understand the process of communicating nonverbally, we must first determine how messages are organized and what the units of organization are. In this respect, meaning and our understanding of meaning are dependent on understanding the structure of nonverbal behavior.

1. *Nonverbal behavior should be approached as a social not psychological phenomenon.* In *Kinesics and Context,* Birdwhistell argues that psychological approaches to nonverbal behavior invariably lead the researcher to focus on problems of little benefit in understanding nonverbal behavior. A psychological perspective leads one to distinguish the behaviors of one communicator from those of another, to investigate individuals, to consider the influences of personality and past developmental differences. A social approach focuses on the interrelationships among people. The basic unit of study is not the individual but the social context; individuals are treated as components in a larger interpersonal system.

Birdwhistell cites the analogy, often attributed to Scheflen, of applying a psychological approach to comprehending a baseball game. Merely describing the behavior of each player provides little insight into the game itself. Only when you begin to appreciate the notion of *team* as a social system with all its interrelationships and organizing rules can you understand the significance of each behavior. The incident and kinesic translation described in Figure 2.3 illustrate not only the detail but the social nature of nonverbal interaction.

2. *Nonverbal behavior serves both an informational and integrational function.* Any

The two soldiers stood in parallel, legs akimbo with an intrafemoral index of 45 degrees. In unison, each raised his right upper arm to about an 80-degree angle with his body and, with the lower arm at approximately a 100-degree angle, moved the arm in an anterior–posterior sweep with a double pivot at shoulder and elbow; the four fingers of the right hand were curled and the thumb was posteriorly hooked; the right palm faced the body. Their left arms were held closer to the body with an elbow bend of about 90 degrees. The left four fingers were curled and the thumb was partially hidden as it crooked into their respective belts.

The driver of the car focused momentarily on the boys, raised both brows, flared his nostrils, lifted his upper lip, revealed his upper teeth, and with his head cocked, moved it in a posterior–anterior inverted nod which in its backward aspect had about twice the velocity of the movement which returned the head and face to the midline and, thus, to driving focus.

Without apparent hesitation the boys right-stepped posteriorly, one of the boys moving in echo following the movement of the other. Facing the retreating car, one of the boys raised his upper lip to expose his teeth, furrowed his forehead, lowered his brows, contracted the lateral aspects of his orbits, and flared his nostrils. His right arm swept from its posteriorly thrust position, on a shoulder pivot, to rest, fist clenched, upper arm across the right half of the body and the lower right arm thrust up and slightly anterior to the body line. The left hand left the belt and the lower arm swept right and upward to meet the descending upper (right) arm. The left hand grasped the right biceps as, fist still clenched, the right arm moved quickly in an anterior–superior thrust in line with his shoulder and the retreating automobile.

The other boy dropped his face into "dead pan," pivoted his right arm at the elbow, flared and straightened his fingers into crooks, and, as the already-hooked thumb crossed the midline of the body in the lower arm's downward sweep, the apex of the thumb made contact with the apex of the nose. Without hesitation the arm completed its sweep across the body and came to rest hanging, palms slightly forward, at his side. The left arm, on an elbow pivot, swept downward and came to rest mirroring the right.

Figure 2.3 A macrokinesic translation. (From Ray L. Birdwhistell, *Kinesics and Context*, Philadelphia: University of Pennsylvania Press, 1970, p. 176.)

communication, whether verbal or nonverbal, may provide *information* to the receiver about the communicator. As each of us comes into contact with strangers, we seek information that will allow us to anticipate their behavior. Initial interaction, then, serves to provide new information—data regarding the individual's interaction with us, his or her personality, behavioral tendencies, feelings, and attitudes. Of course, any single message provides relatively little conclusive information about the individual, but we have a habit of overinterpreting data. We tend to use a specific behavior as evidence of a number of attitudinal and psychological characteristics. In short, we stereotype, and by doing so, we quickly assemble a substantial amount of information upon which to base our own behaviors. Beyond our initial interactions with strangers, the new information provided by nonverbal messages is limited. Consistency is a most human characteristic. Although we may fancy ourselves as unpredictable and mysterious, we are very much transparent. To our friends and companions, the vast majority of the messages we transmit contains little that can be considered novel. Occasionally, a new facet of personality or a new attitude will surface, but most of our actions and reactions are not unexpected.

Integration,[8] although a rather vague term in itself, refers to the second function performed by nonverbal codes—the structuring of a *process of communication*. Communication does not occur by chance. People work together to generate rules that govern and structure the process of communicating. Nonverbal messages contribute to the structuring of the communication process in four ways. First, nonverbal codes may be used to *sustain interaction*. Movements of the body—a simple nod of the head or casual glance in the direction of another—can serve to maintain contact and prevent the premature termination of communication. Second, nonverbal codes can function to *regulate interaction*. All interpersonal encounters are a series of speaking *turns*, governed by rules permitting individuals the opportunity to communicate uninterrupted. The smooth exchange of speaking turns is primarily a function of the nonverbal cues transmitted by the speaker regarding his or her intention to continue speaking or his or her willingness to be interrupted. Third, nonverbal codes *provide continuity* among the contextual changes that take place during interaction. The continuous flow of movements by two individuals conversing with one another is a unifying force.

Imagine, for example, that you have suddenly awakened to find yourself in the midst of what appears to be a heated conflict among friends. A few moments of observation tell you that the discussion is not heated at all; it is merely the enthusiastic debate over political

issues that has been known to accompany a few beers among friends. Had you awakened earlier in the conversation, the continuity of kinesic behaviors across topics of conversation, as issues escalated from bantering over preferred candidates to intense discussion of foreign policy issues, would have provided a clue to the serious but not divisive nature of the verbal communication.

This example suggests a fourth function served by nonverbal behavior. That is, kinesic behavior can *illustrate similarity* among contexts not adjacent in time by bringing to mind similar situations from the past. Kinesic behavior helps us cross-reference contexts.

3. *Nonverbal communication is a continuous, dynamic, ongoing process.* It is important to realize that movements are part of a larger sequence of behaviors. Kinesic behavior is *interdependent*. One behavior may influence subsequent behavior. Furthermore, kinesic behavior is *interactive*. The body movements of one individual influence the actions of another. People respond not only to what others say but to what others do. Investigations that rely on a single moment of behavior or even several brief samples are unreliable indicators of the larger pattern of social interaction at the nonverbal level.

4. *No movement of the body or variation in voice quality is without meaning in a specific context.* It is a common fallacy to assume that the most obvious behaviors have the greatest meaning or are of the greatest communicative value. Every behavior, no matter how microscopic, is significant—although perhaps not by itself—within the greater pattern of body movement; every behavior has value. Another common mistake is the notion that, because a behavior is not linked to a specific meaning, it doesn't have meaning in that context. One must understand that all behaviors may have communicative value.

5. *Each part of the human body can function as a different modality or channel for communication.* It would be misleading to as-

sume that the various parts of the body work together to generate a highly compatible communicative package, with every aspect of the body sending the same or similar messages. The body is a multifaceted source of communication, using a number of different channels to achieve multiple purposes. To look at a friend and comment to another, "That's her mad look," ignores the possibility that a number of varying messages may have been transmitted that may modify the judgment that she is mad. One part of the body or one expression may comment on the message communicated by another part. It is also possible to use one part of the body to communicate with one person while addressing another behavior to another person. In this respect, an individual may interact at a number of levels of meaning.

6. *Although it is a continuous process, nonverbal behavior possesses structure.* The most characteristic feature of the structure-centered approach is its emphasis on the structure or organization of movements into messages that communicate meaning. Scheflen and Birdwhistell in particular are responsible for the notion that behavior parallels language in that the various movements of the body are organized in much the same way that sounds are coordinated to produce words. This does not mean that every nonverbal behavior has a specific verbal counterpart. Birdwhistell has referred to this assumption as the *carrier* temptation, which "assumes that each gesture, whether as gross as a thumbed nose or as tiny as a first-degree right lid droop, has a 'real' meaning just as 'words' are supposed to have. If the investigator succumbs to this, his attention is directed into a kind of 'lexicon' wherein he draws up lists of moves and their meanings only to discover that most human beings are kinesically illiterate and move in improper English."[9] If no movement can be said to have a specific meaning, how do we know when behavior becomes communicative?

The answer to the question is complex and incomplete. The advocates of the structure-centered approach are convinced that there is a hierarchy of behavioral units for nonverbal behaviors, and that levels or patterns of organized body movements exist. The principal task of the structure-centered approach is to "isolate structural meaning."[10]

Birdwhistell attempted to analyze types of movements, beginning with the face, in terms of variations in the ways individuals make a particular movement. He then isolated the variations that altered an observer's interpretation of the behavior. To accomplish this, Birdwhistell relied on slow motion films of spontaneous interaction.

His research reveals that the behavior we refer to as a *head nod* can be broken down into three units sufficiently distinct to alter an observer's interpretation of what is happening. These *kinemes* are the single nod, the double nod, and the triple nod.

By identifying a large number of possible body movements and then grouping together movements that have the same communicative value, Birdwhistell achieved two important goals. First, he constructed a hierarchy of behaviors that indicates rather explicitly the similarities and differences in communicative value of various muscular movements. Second, he created an observational method that allows a highly detailed notation of behavior. One can, in theory, set about the task of describing behavior as it happens, in the order in which it happens, and in whatever detail one wishes to pursue.

While much has been done to develop and refine this hierarchy for classifying nonverbal behaviors, relatively little has been accomplished on a second priority of the structural approach: the identification of rules and operations by which behaviors are organized into larger patterns of meaning. Just as language has rules that govern grammatical structure, so too does nonverbal language suggest implicit guidelines whereby a member of a particular cultural group engages in a series of bodily movements.

7. *The systematic body movements of any group of individuals are a function of the sociocultural system that unifies that group.* The central mechanism for transmitting nonverbal behaviors from generation to generation is culture. This is not to say that biological causes of behaviors do not exist; they are simply viewed by proponents of the structure-centered approach as unworthy of discussion until the evidence indicates otherwise.

The Meaning-Centered Approach:
Assumptions

Paul Ekman, Wallace Friesen, and Paul Dittmann are the scholars most responsible for the meaning-centered approach to the study of nonverbal communication. In contrast to the structure-centered approach, which is primarily concerned with clarifying the hierarchy of behaviors in the body movement system and discovering the rules for coordinating movements, the *meaning-centered* approach is basically a receiver-oriented approach; it studies how people assign meaning to nonverbal messages. How do we decide that a person is happy? What do we look at? The face? The mouth? Do we look for a smile? How do we know that a person is smiling?

Advocates of the meaning-centered approach recognize that there are only the most subtle differences between the way we show *fear* and *surprise.* The two emotions involve the use of many of the same muscles. The differences are difficult to pin down. If you had to determine whether a picture of a person showed fear or surprise, you would probably have little difficulty in making the correct choice even though you might not be able to explain exactly how the expression of one emotion differs from the expression of another. Apparently, guidelines do exist to assist us in determining the meaning of an expression, but they have become second nature to us; we seldom closely inspect an expression to determine what specific facial gestures are involved. The meaning-centered approach determines on what behavioral grounds people distinguish one message from another. There are two features of the meaning-centered approach that distinguish it from the structure-centered view.

1. *The meaning-centered approach focuses on the behavioral cues upon which the recognition of emotion is based.* What are the primary sources of information upon which judgments of emotion are based? Proponents of the structure-centered view have argued that certain behaviors (for example, posture and body shifts) are more important than others in the organization of nonverbal messages. To advocates of the meaning-centered approach, whether or not a particular behavior is central to the structure of nonverbal messages is irrelevant; what *is* important is whether that particular behavior is instrumental in conveying information that will allow a receiver to judge accurately the emotion being expressed. A shift in body posture might signal that a change has occurred in the emotional climate of the conversation; but if it doesn't assist the receiver in determining what the prevailing emotional climate is, then the behavior is of little importance in the *recognition process.*

Research indicates that no single movement or gesture consistently conveys more information than others. There seems to be a different behavioral key—a behavior without which the judgment of emotion becomes highly unreliable—for each emotion. For example, the cheeks and mouth provide indispensable clues for judging disgust, while the brow and forehead are the greatest source of information for judging expressions of surprise.[11]

2. *The meaning-centered approach focuses on specific channels and their characteristics.* Much of the research by Ekman and Friesen has been limited almost exclusively to the face[12] and hands,[13] while Dittmann's work has dealt with the rhythmic relationship between certain movements of the body and the voice.[14]

These researchers have limited the study of nonverbal behavior to a few specific channels thought to be primary sources of information for the receiver.

Studies of the relationships between certain channels have raised an important question: Which behaviors have similar or identical communicative values? In other words, are there some behaviors that we can interchange at will without altering the meaning conveyed to receivers? Dittmann has suggested that some behaviors—in particular, those behaviors he has labeled *listener responses* (things such as head nods, smiles, and such verbal statements as *yeah, uh huh, right*)—that have as their primary function the encouragement of the speaker are interchangeable.[15] Head nods have much the same effect as saying, "That's right." Because of this aspect of his work, Dittmann is thought to represent the extreme of the linguistic approach. Dittmann suggests that many nonverbal behaviors have direct verbal parallels. Most researchers are willing to admit that a number of nonverbal movements have direct parallels, though they do not include smiling, nodding, and shaking the head among them. Dittmann comes the closest of all the linguists to what Birdwhistell referred to as the carrier temptation—the notion that every behavior, no matter how minute, has a meaning in and of itself.

Limitations of the Linguistic Approaches

Although the linguists are divided on some crucial issues, they all admit that they have encountered obstacles that limit the usefulness and appeal of the linguistic approaches. The first problem has to do with their attempt to identify the rules underlying the organization of nonverbal behavior. It is not clear to what extent these rules or principles are consciously or unconsciously employed. If they are unconsciously used, then how and why are they acquired?

The difficulty in using language as an analogue for the structure of nonverbal interaction is that spoken language, with all its rules for grammatical construction, is a conscious venture. The speaker continuously monitors speech patterns for instances of grammatical violations. Although there is no evidence that we consciously assemble sentences before speaking informally, we are retroactively conscious of rules. But how about kinesic behavior? Is there any reason to believe that we are ever aware of our movements in this way?

Birdwhistell admits that there is a second major shortcoming to the linguistic approach. It concerns the relationship of kinesic behavior to language. Birdwhistell's research has shown repeatedly that language and kinesic action are only partially coordinated. He has found no consistent, one-to-one relationship between most movements of the body and language. Furthermore, there seems to be no coordination between the grammatical structure of language and patterns of behavior. This, Birdwhistell has suggested, must be the next important area for future investigation.

The Psychoanalytic Approach

Psychiatrists and clinical psychologists have become increasingly interested in the relationship between psychological disorders and nonverbal behavior. Clinicians have long relied on a knowledge of the behavioral symptoms of maladjustment in diagnosing and treating psychological problems. Sigmund Freud felt that a patient's physical actions were at least as important as verbal actions in communicating the sources of psychological trauma. During formal psychoanalysis, Freud would sit on a chair near the head of the patient's couch so that he could observe all the patient's movements without disturbing his or her thoughts.

From time to time, scholars have taken a

psychoanalytic approach to the study of non-verbal behavior. Among them are Ray Birdwhistell, Norbert Freedman, Howard Leventhal, and Albert Mehrabian, to mention a few. Freudian psychology has been the dominant intellectual force behind the psychoanalytic view of nonverbal communication. According to the psychoanalytic approach, the individual is constantly attempting to outgrow the psychological and physical inadequacies of childhood. Our behavior attempts to compensate for past failures. It is a feeble attempt to absolve ourselves of lingering feelings of guilt and inferiority. This is not a pretty picture of what motivates the human being, but it does lead to some important assumptions about what underlies nonverbal communication.

Assumptions

1. *Nonverbal behaviors are a response to the psychological condition of the communicator.* Every movement of the body, no matter how seemingly insignificant, is a product of the psychological state of the communicator. The communicator is not always aware of the full range of psychological pressures that prompt certain behaviors. Indeed, many actions result from traumas so unpleasant and destructive that we keep them closeted in the unconscious recesses of the mind. Each of us has behaved at one time or another in ways that later embarrassed us, that brought to mind feelings of guilt, frustration, or self-doubt. Many of these experiences are subsequently resolved and ultimately forgotten, removed from both our conscious and unconscious mind. Unfortunately, some of these experiences are not resolved and continue to haunt us. All of these traumas exert pressure on our minds and are reflected in subsequent behaviors.

Psychoanalysts investigate the behavioral symptoms of such conditions as anxiety, frustration, guilt, and the like, searching for the connection between internal psychological states and overt behavior. Felix Deutsch has argued that one relationship between the body and mind is the tension-relieving function that the body performs.[16] Specifically, body postures reflect and provide an outlet for the anxieties that reside in the unconscious.

A second relationship of interest to proponents of the psychoanalytic approach is the connection between speech anxiety and the various movements of the body that accompany attempts at verbal communication. *Speech anxiety* is the fear of communicating that affects some people. Extreme anxiety or reticence prevents an individual from engaging in many of the everyday personal and public encounters that most of us take for granted. Research has shown that highly reticent people exhibit nonverbal behavioral patterns not characteristic of people in general. For example, high levels of anxiety often produce a tensing of certain muscles,[17] considerable finger and hand movement,[18] little eye contact,[19] and a great deal of self-manipulation (using the hand to touch other parts of the body).[20]

2. *Nonverbal behaviors are artifacts of a psychologically primitive past.* People develop language skills over the course of many years. We acquire a mastery of nonverbal behaviors quite early in life. Research has found that the infant develops a wide variety of facial expressions during the first year. Psychoanalysts have tended to view this developmental disparity between the acquisition of language and nonverbal skills as evidence that many nonverbal behaviors are developed as the child's method of coping with the feelings of insecurity and inadequacy that are natural in childhood. Some nonverbal behaviors are treated as artifacts of the prenatal period, behaviors acquired by the unborn child in response to physiological needs.

Psychoanalysts cite the childish nonverbal behaviors to which adults revert under extreme pressures as evidence of the primitive and regressive nature of nonverbal behavior. All of us can recall situations in which extremes of pressure caused a loss of verbal facility, resulting in the substitution of sobbing and anguished cries. Stress seems to bring out the nonverbal child in each of us.

3. *Any serious or consistent violation of cultural norms regarding the frequency, rate, form, or coordination of nonverbal behaviors is a symptom of the psychological abnormality of the communicator.* Much of what we think of as normal behavior depends on cultural standards. Individuals who depart from cultural standards about appropriate uses of the body and voice are considered foreign or abnormal. According to the norms of the predominant culture of the United States, people in our culture who consistently avoid eye contact or violate norms for personal space are thought to be disturbed. The psychoanalytic approach focuses on the relationship of mental illness to atypical nonverbal behavior.

Nonverbal standards for clinical judgments are vague at present. They are, nevertheless, used constantly. An incident involving Ray Birdwhistell, the father of the kinesic method, illustrates the point. As the story goes, Birdwhistell was a visiting lecturer in a large class at a midwestern university. He entered the classroom, stood before the class as if to put his thoughts in order, then walked over to the instructor and informed him that one student in particular appeared to be emotionally ill. Birdwhistell identified the student. To the instructor's surprise (and relief), it turned out that the individual was not a student at all but a patient from a nearby mental hospital.

4. *Disparity between nonverbal and verbal codes is a symptom of the psychological abnormality of the communicator.* In our culture, there are very few occasions when it is socially acceptable and efficient to send messages on one channel that contradict messages transmitted through another channel. Clinicians have long recognized this incongruity in behavior to be evidence of psychological trauma and maladjustment. Emotionally disturbed individuals often lose the capacity to coordinate the body and voice in order to communicate a consistent, coherent message.

Much psychoanalytic investigation has focused on the *double-bind situation*, thought to cause a breakdown in the individual's ability to transmit consistent messages. Interest in the double-bind situation resulted from research on schizophrenia. Researchers noticed that schizophrenic children often come from families in which one or both parents send inconsistent messages. In double-bind situations, messages (either verbal or nonverbal) are directly contradictory. A classic example is the case of the mother who would remind her daughter each school day how important it is to be a good student but would indicate nonverbally her dread of having to remain at home alone all day. The nonverbal message of loneliness was as clear to the child as the encouragement to succeed in school. Whatever choice the child made was offset by equally serious losses.

Children exposed to double-bind situations develop highly equivocal and inconsistent communication habits, reflecting their confusion and helplessness. Under such pressures, schizophrenia is likely to develop.

Limitations

Critics of the psychoanalytic approach have little sympathy for attempts to construct behavioral standards of normality. They recognize that the human being is a versatile and spontaneous creature, capable of radically different behaviors.

Any behavioral criteria for normality must be flexible and resilient. Certainly developmental and cultural differences are stumbling blocks, since we can hardly assume a common standard to apply to all ages or cultural groups.

An equally serious limitation of the psychoanalytic approach concerns the evasive role of consciousness and intent in determining normative nonverbal behavior. Psychoanalysts assume that nonverbal behaviors are authentic reflections of internal traumas. It is difficult to know from one moment to the next which behaviors are consciously enacted and which are unconscious. If a behavior pattern that departs significantly from the norm is the conscious attempt by a communicator to enact a particular role, then it is difficult to classify the individual as abnormal since the action is intentional and specific to the situation.

Psychoanalysts generally give the individual little credit for having control over the actions of the body or being aware of what the body is doing. Of course, we do not always monitor all the movements of the body. Even so, that is not sufficient grounds for assuming the unconscious mind to be the source of behavior. Often, a behavior will be consciously initiated and then ignored as the mind occupies itself with other affairs.

The Physiological Approaches

As with all other animals, the human being's body places limitations on movement. Our muscle structure, our sensory organs, our brain all impose limits on what, how, and when we can communicate. The *physiological approaches* view nonverbal behavior in terms of anatomical constraints and causes and investigate how physiological structure influences our ability to formulate, transmit, and receive information.

The physiological approaches have a legacy of intriguing and sometimes bizarre explorations into the relationship of physical characteristics and nonverbal communication. Phrenology, which flourished during the 1800s, theorized a relationship between bumps on the head and psychological and behavioral patterns. From time to time, evidence emerges suggesting a connection between abnormal chromosome alignment and aggressive, often suicidal, behavior.

Physiological anthropologists have long been interested in crosscultural investigations into the relationship between the physiological structure of the body and nonverbal behavior. Gordon Hewes, an anthropologist interested in posture, has noted over a thousand different postures of which the human being is capable.[21] Only a few are universal to all known cultures. Physiological differences between cultural groups play an important part in determining behavior. For example, the lean muscle structure of many black Africans makes squatting a more comfortable position than for members of many Western cultures, whose bodies suffer from obesity and show a different development of leg, stomach, and torso muscles.

No matter what the approach to nonverbal communication, it is difficult to ignore the role physiology plays in behavior. Most approaches inevitably must face the issue of exactly how much physiological variables should be relied upon to explain an individual's behavior or differences among groups of individuals. If time permitted, we could outline a number of different ways in which body structure and nonverbal communication are interrelated. There are two approaches in particular, however, that have focused attention directly on the function of the body in controlling movement and that deserve discussion: the *sensory approach* and the *neurophysiological approach*.

The Sensory Approach: Assumptions

The sensory approach differs from the neurophysiological approach in that it looks at the communicative functions of the various senses and the ways in which messages are constructed or modified in order to suit the senses. The neurophysiological approach focuses on the ways in which the nervous system, in conjunction with the brain and sensory organs, enables a person to receive nonverbal messages.

1. *Sensory organs differ in both the amount and kind of information each can receive.* The adage that a picture is worth a thousand words suggests that one channel of communication may be able to accommodate certain types of messages more efficiently than other channels. The sense of smell provides relatively little information; yet there would not be much pleasure in a steak dinner if we could not smell

and taste. There are inherent differences between the sense organs in terms of how *complex* a stimulus each can receive. Sight allows one to determine depth, spatial relationships among objects, color, form, and often texture. We tend to think of sight as fairly reliable. Smell, on the other hand, provides extremely limited information, at least to humans (many species of animals have evolved highly refined olfactory senses).

2. *Sensory organs are interrelated.* The human senses do not function independently of one another. Sight influences smell, just as hearing influences sight. There are also internal sensory receptors that we hardly consider but that work together with external receptors to assemble information. Internal receptors, called *interceptors,* make us aware of internal physiological conditions such as pain, tension and fatigue.

3. *Sensory organs screen information.* It is common knowledge that we don't *see* all that we look at. Hower J. Hsia, known for his research on the capacity of eyes and ears to accept information, reported that we hear and see only a fraction of what we are exposed to.[22] How much information we take in is determined in part by the kinds of stimuli available. Some messages are more easily recorded by the senses than are others. The mind and the senses work together to determine which messages are actually received. (As Eisenberg and Smith note, "If a man were fully conscious of the infinite number of stimuli to which he is daily exposed, he would probably die."[23]) In this way, the human system is able to avoid a state of *information overload.*

4. *Individual sensory power influences the nonverbal messages transmitted.* Sight has an important influence on the effect of distance in interpersonal interaction. Extreme distance during face-to-face interaction obscures our vision of many of the subtle actions of the person with whom we are communicating. Extremely close distance poses much the same kind of limitation on our senses. When a person is standing very close to you, much of his or her body is outside your visual field. We tend, when interacting, to place ourselves at a distance that permits maximum vision of others.

The inability of our senses to detect physical warmth and to smell chemical changes in another's body, except in very close contact, renders these receptors of limited usefulness in transmitting and receiving messages.

5. *Individuals may differ significantly in sensory power.* There are dramatic differences among individuals' ability to hear and see, ranging from total absence of these sensory mechanisms to astounding, superhuman capabilities. Loss of the use of one sensory organ places greater dependence on others. The potential power of our senses generally exceeds our capacities. Blind people, for example, tend to develop auditory power two to three times greater than that of seeing people.

Limitations of the Sensory Approach

The major shortcoming of the sensory approach is that it limits the study of how we decode and encode nonverbal messages to the simple issue of what the senses can and cannot do. The psychological state of the communicator has a tremendous amount of control on the senses. Also, the interrelationship of culture and physiological structure makes statements regarding the causes of nonverbal behavior controversial at best. Did limitations in our auditory ability cause the development of norms for speaking distances in our culture, or did the culture evolve norms for speaking distances that then arrested the full development of our auditory ability? Orientals have a greater range of auditory sensitivity than do Occidentals. Is that the result of physiology or culture?

The Neurophysiological Approach: Assumptions

Research on the effects of neurophysiological damage on the ability to communicate has stimulated some interesting notions regarding the nature of nonverbal communication and the differences between the neurophysiological mechanisms that underlie the verbal and nonverbal modes of communication. As we mentioned in Chapter 1, various parts of the human brain are associated with different perceptual, cognitive, and behavioral processes. Peter Andersen, John Garrison, and Janis Andersen recommend using neurophysiological criteria as a means for resolving the issue of what is and what is not nonverbal communication.[24] They recognize that a conceptual fog has long surrounded the term *nonverbal* and that striking differences exist in what different researchers classify as nonverbal. They felt that if neurophysiological criteria could be established to distinguish verbal processes from nonverbal ones, many of the controversies regarding the nature of codes, the various forms of symbolism, and the role of the unconscious could be resolved.

Advocates of neurophysiological approach to the study of nonverbal communication make two provocative assumptions about the nature of nonverbal communication.

1. *Nonverbal and verbal processes are conceptually independent phenomena.* Verbal processes are digital, arbitrary, logical, and linguistic. Nonverbal processes are thought of as analogic, nonlinguistic, and extralogical. A behavior falls into one category or the other. When an individual engages simultaneously in either the transmission or reception of both nonverbal and verbal behaviors, we must assume that two parallel processes—one logical, one extralogical—are in operation. We cannot talk fruitfully of any common cause for both. Different organismic systems facilitate verbal and nonverbal communication.

2. *Differences between nonverbal and verbal processes can be accounted for by the different neurophysiological mechanisms that underlie each.* Advocates of the neurophysiological approach suggest that verbal and nonverbal behaviors can be distinguished by the neurophysiological differences in the way verbally and nonverbally transmitted information

is received and processed. Specifically, as we noted in Chapter 1, nonverbal messages are thought to be processed through the right hemisphere of the brain, while verbal messages are processed through the left hemisphere. In this respect, the task of determining what behaviors should be classified as nonverbal is reduced to neurophysiological criteria.

Not only can conceptual differences between verbal and nonverbal behaviors be traced to neurophysiological mechanisms that distinguish the two; it is also possible to use neurophysiological differences to distinguish among individuals who rely on nonverbally communicated information from those who depend more heavily on verbally transmitted data. Some evidence has been found to support the concept of hemispheric dominance—the notion that individuals can be categorized according to which hemisphere of the brain is the more influential in processing information. People who are "left hemispheric" are referred to as *verbally dominant* and are thought to be biased toward receiving verbally transmitted information. People who are "right hemispheric" are often thought of as visualizers—they rely upon nonverbal cues as a central source for information. Unfortunately, no one knows whether this hemispheric dominance means that one aspect of the brain functions slower than the other, one hemisphere is dependent upon the other (and is, therefore, subordinate), or, as Harrison has suggested, one hemisphere is suppressed to facilitate the most effective operation of the other.[25]

Limitations of the Neurophysiological Approach

Although the neurophysiological approach is appealing because of its apparently simple, straightforward criteria for distinguishing verbal from nonverbal forms of communication, it presents a number of conceptual problems. First, the approach is basically a *reductionist* one—it attempts to reduce relatively complex issues to a single neurophysiological distinction, as if to suggest that other methods or criteria for differentiating the modes of communication are unsound or unclear. Proponents of this approach have not adequately identified the conceptual advantage of basing the distinction between verbal and nonverbal communication on neurophysiological grounds.

Second, this approach focuses on the decoder and the neurophysiological mechanism underlying the reception of messages (as opposed to the transmission of messages) for the distinction between verbal and nonverbal behavior. This is an important departure from previous attempts at defining communication, most of which examine how a message is encoded, not how it is received. We pointed out in Chapter 1 that there has not been much research on the neurophysiological mechanisms underlying encoding. Since much of the research cited to support the neurophysiological distinction between verbal and nonverbal forms of communication has involved tests of reception rather than transmission, the answer remains unclear.

A third problem surrounding the neurophysiological approach has to do with the *degree* to which the right and left hemispheres of the brain perform different functions. Much of the research conducted on brain-damaged people has shown that, while the right hemisphere seems to be more efficient in receiving nonverbal cues, the left hemisphere is also capable of processing nonverbal stimuli, though more slowly and with less accuracy. In other words, the evidence indicates that the right and left hemispheres do not serve mutually exclusive functions; conditions can be created in which the functions are reversed. How much faster or more accurate must the right hemisphere be in processing a given stimulus before we can classify that stimulus as nonverbal? Are some stimuli more verbal than others simply because the differences in the rates at which the two hemispheres process the data are more pronounced?

This raises a fourth question: Are the differential functions of the two hemispheres of the brain *inherent*? Perhaps the right hemisphere processes nonverbally communicated information more rapidly because it has been trained to process that type of information and not because of any inherent neurophysiological superiority of one hemisphere over the other. Recall that brain-damaged individuals have learned to transfer many right hemispheric functions to the left hemisphere, achieving, with training, a satisfactory level of skill. In such cases as these, the use of neurophysiological grounds as a method of resolving what is and what is not nonverbal behavior is unworkable.

The last problem confronting advocates of the neurophysiological approach has to do with defining left hemispheric activity as logical and linguistic and right hemispheric functions as extralogical and nonlinguistic. The assumption is that nonverbal behavior lacks a logically based system of coding rules by which symbols are organized to communicate thoughts. Many of the tasks cited by Andersen and his associates as evidence of right hemispheric involvement in processing nonverbal messages are tasks that may involve linguistic activity. For example, there is good reason to believe that matching colors, although it involves nonverbal stimuli, generates linguistic activity. That is, one looks at the color, generates a semantic label (red, aqua, turnip green) to assist the memory, and then attempts to match it with a color that fits that semantic label. *That* is linguistic activity. If the right hemisphere facilitates color matching, then linguistic activity is associated with the right hemisphere.

The Functional Approach

In the last several years (and predominantly in the disciplines of speech communication and psychology), research has suggested a new approach to the study of nonverbal communication. The phrase *functional approach* seems to capture the major defining feature of the approach. The following statements reflect some of the central assumptions that underlie this focus on the role of nonverbal messages in fulfilling communication functions.

Assumptions

1. *The specific communication function being investigated determines the nonverbal behaviors to be observed.* As you communicate with others, your behavior (both verbal and nonverbal) is directed toward some end— some function or series of functions that justify the behavior. The particular function may be as straightforward as transmitting factual information; it may be as complex as transmitting messages that help to define the relationship between you and another person. Proponents of the functional approach isolate a particular communication function or goal and then examine the kinds of nonverbal behaviors that individuals employ in fulfilling it. Recent research has focused on such functions as initiating and terminating interaction, affiliation, deception, dominance, the formation of interpersonal impressions, and turn taking. Mark Knapp explored the various nonverbal and verbal messages that converge when we terminate a conversation. He calls this the "rhetoric of goodbye."

2. *Every function has situational characteristics.* For every function, there are a number of representative contexts in which appropriate nonverbal and verbal behaviors will naturally and spontaneously occur. For example, we don't study posture at a movie; we don't investigate the nonverbal behaviors associated with lovemaking by staking out the assembly line at the Ford Motor Company. In each situation (the theater and the assembly line), features of the context interfere with the behaviors being observed. A function must be studied in a context that allows for a variety of verbal and nonverbal messages.

3. *The communication context must be interpersonal in nature.* The functional approach is concerned with the role of nonverbal behavior in achieving some interpersonal goal. Although it is possible to look at individual behaviors in isolation—perhaps as the individual reacts to a novel or threatening situation—unless the individual is seen in an interpersonal context, the information gained about the person is hardly applicable to the study of human communication. Indeed, some would question whether the behaviors could be construed as communicative at all.

4. *Communication is an ongoing, dynamic process.* The nonverbal behaviors in which an individual engages to fulfill a specific function do not constitute an isolated event. The functional approach views behavior as continuous. In a short span of time, each of us may move from one function to a second and perhaps even a third, often duplicating and combining functions. No single moment, regardless of how fully it may be described, can reflect the full range of behaviors communicated to achieve some end. The implication is that we have to look at behaviors in terms of the patterns or regularities or trends in the messages sent.

5. *The behaviors initiated to achieve a function occur within a finite time.* As opposed to approaches that take an evolutionary or developmental approach to behavior, the functional approach focuses on a relatively limited time and the behaviors that occur during that period. The assumption is that functions change rapidly. Behavior must be investigated during a time when it is most likely to occur. Most of these periods are self-evident. For example, in order to examine the nonverbal behaviors associated with the initiation of interaction among strangers, you explore the first several minutes of interaction.

6. *A single nonverbal code may serve several functions.* Many approaches recognize the multifaceted nature of nonverbal messages. Any movement of the body or variation in voice can serve to communicate factual information while commenting on a previous message. In groups, more often than not we find ourselves attempting to achieve one goal with

one person and another entirely different goal with another person. We behave in ways that work toward both goals simultaneously.

7. *A single function may involve several nonverbal codes.* Unlike those investigators who devote their attention almost exclusively to a particular region of the body or a specific behavior, proponents of the functional approach assume that a number of different nonverbal codes may be used to accomplish any particular function. We achieve an intimate communication atmosphere not just with our words or hands but with eyes, facial expressions, posture, and many other attitudes of the body and voice.

8. *A single function may involve the coordination of verbal and nonverbal codes.* If the central focus of the functional approach is to explore those behaviors that facilitate the successful performance of some communicative function, then it is difficult to justify the study of one class of behaviors to the exclusion of all others. The functional approach does not deal exclusively with nonverbal behaviors but assumes that most communication requires coordination of both verbal and nonverbal communication in order to achieve the desired objective.

9. *Study of the immediate causes of nonverbal behavior takes precedence over the study of original causes.* The ethological and psychoanalytic approaches share an interest in the original causes of behavior. The former approach studies precivilized life to discover possible architects of behavior, just as the psychoanalyst assumes that much of the individual's behavior is a product of and a response to past traumas. The functional approach views the search for initial causes of behavior to be a hopeless and frustrating venture. It is more important to come to grips with the existing forces that influence our behavior.

Limitations

This most recent addition to the list of approaches to the study of nonverbal communi-
cation avoids many of the problems that handicap the other approaches. It makes no attempt to provide behavioral criteria for judging psychological normality, and it avoids treating nonverbal behavior in purely physiological terms. The functional approach makes no assumption about the parallel between language and the movements of the body.

Even so, there is a serious limitation to the approach in terms of knowing how to isolate a function. If one's communication objectives are constantly changing, then how are we to determine the prevailing function? We could rely on the communicator to reveal to us the underlying motives for behavior, but that is hardly reliable.

Proponents of the functional approach would probably argue that we must recognize the difference between *intended* and *actual* functions of nonverbal behaviors. The functional approach is interested in actual functions, that is, the interpersonal ramifications of action. If we can assume that the actual consequences of nonverbal behavior are somehow observable, then the task of isolating functions becomes less difficult.

mini-experiment

Watch a short excerpt (three or four minutes) from a television program containing sustained interaction between two or more individuals. Soap operas usually provide such scenes. Then try to determine how advocates of different approaches would be likely to analyze such a sample of behavior. What behaviors would the various approaches emphasize? What kinds of nonverbal behavior would be excluded from examination? What kinds of inferences would be drawn from the segment?

Summary

In this chapter, we have explored some of the many approaches to nonverbal communication that you are likely to encounter as you read articles, study experiments, and form your own ideas about what should be studied and how. If no one approach seems adequate for you, then you probably understand some of the problems associated with each. All views include some things and leave others out. What you should consider is whether a particular approach makes some statements about nonverbal communication that seem right to you.

It is important to remember that these approaches are not mutually exclusive. Just because a researcher is identified with the psychoanalytic approach doesn't mean that he or she rejects all assumptions from other approaches. Paul Ekman is one researcher who has contributed to a number of different approaches without making contradictory assumptions. The various approaches to the study of nonverbal communication often overlap. How much they overlap depends on each individual scholar (and student).

In subsequent chapters, we are not going to sell a particular approach. We recognize that some phenomena are best seen with binoculars while others are better viewed through a microscope. The choice is yours. In Part II, we shall identify the functions of nonverbal communication and then explore what we know about these functions. If, for example, you have become attracted to the linguistic approaches, then you may find parts of Chapters 8 and 9 particularly interesting. If, on the other hand, you prefer the ethological approach, then some of the crosscultural studies in Chapter 5 and material on the possible origins of affect displays in Chapter 8 will interest you. Some of the research discussed in Chapter 7 dealing with quasicourtship behavior and findings in Chapter 6 regarding our propensity to develop interpersonal impressions based upon limited nonverbal data derive from the psychoanalytic approach. And the remaining approaches? Well, take a look for yourself.

Suggested Reading

Andersen, P. A., Garrison, J. P., and Andersen, J. F. "Defining Nonverbal Communication: A Neurophysiological Explanation of Nonverbal Information Processing." Paper presented at the annual meeting of the Western Speech Communication Association, Seattle, Washington, November 1975.

Birdwhistell, R. L. *Kinesics and Context*. Philadelphia: University of Pennsylvania Press, 1970.

Eisenberg, A. M., and Smith, R. R. *Nonverbal Communication*. Indianapolis: Bobbs-Merrill, 1971.

Ekman, P. (ed.). *Darwin and Facial Expression: A Century of Research in Review*. New York: Academic Press, 1973.

Fast, J. *Body Language*. New York: Pocket Books, 1971.

Harrison, R. P. *Beyond Words: An Introduction to Nonverbal Communication*. Englewood Cliffs, N.J.: Prentice-Hall, 1974.

Harrison, R. P. "Nonverbal Communication." In I. de Sola Pool, W. Schramm, N. Maccoby, F. Fry, E. Parker, and J. Fein (eds.), *Handbook of Communication*. Chicago: Rand McNally, 1973.

Hinde, R. A. (ed.). *Non-Verbal Communication*. Cambridge: Cambridge University Press, 1972.

Knapp, M. L. *Nonverbal Communication in Human Interaction*. New York: Holt, Rinehart and Winston, 1972.

Mehrabian, A. *Silent Messages*. Belmont, Calif.: Wadsworth, 1971.

Nierenberg, G. I., and Calero, H. H. *How to Read a Person Like a Book*. New York: Pocket Books, 1973.

Scheflen, A. E. *How Behavior Means*. Garden City, N.Y.: Anchor, 1974.

Weitz, S. (ed.). *Nonverbal Communication*. New York: Oxford University Press, 1974.

Notes

1. G. I. Nierenberg and H. H. Calero, *How to Read a Person Like a Book* (New York: Pocket Books, 1973), p. 171.
2. Nierenberg, p. 129 (note 1).
3. See J. H. Koivumaki, "Body Language Taught Here," *Journal of Communication,* 25 (Winter 1975), pp. 26–30.
4. W. J. Smith, "Displays and Messages in Intraspecific Communication," in S. Weitz (ed.), *Nonverbal Communication* (New York: Oxford University Press, 1974), pp. 332–336.
5. J. Lyons, "Human Language," in R. A. Hinde (ed.), *Non-Verbal Communication* (Cambridge: Cambridge University Press, 1972), p. 76.
6. Weitz, p. 12 (note 4).
7. R. L. Birdwhistell, *Kinesics and Context* (Philadelphia: University of Pennsylvania Press, 1970).
8. Birdwhistell, p. 75 (note 7).
9. Birdwhistell, p. 186 (note 7).
10. Birdwhistell, p. 96 (note 7).
11. J. D. Boucher and P. Ekman, "Facial Areas and Emotional Information," *Journal of Communication,* 25 (Spring 1975), pp. 21–29.
12. P. Ekman, W. V. Friesen, and P. Ellsworth, *Emotion in the Human Face* (New York: Pergamon Press, 1972).
13. P. Ekman and W. V. Friesen, "Hand Movements," *Journal of Communication,* 22 (December 1972), pp. 353–374.
14. A. T. Dittmann, "Developmental Factors in Conversational Behavior," *Journal of Communication,* 22 (December 1972), pp. 404–423; A. T. Dittmann and L. G. Llewellyn, "Relationship between Vocalizations and Head Nods as Listener Responses," *Journal of Personality and Social Psychology,* 9 (1968), pp. 79–84; A. T. Dittmann and L. G. Llewellyn, "Body Movement and Speech Rhythm in Social Conversation," *Journal of Personality and Social Psychology,* 11 (1969), pp. 98–106.
15. Dittmann, 1972 (note 14).
16. F. Deutsch, "Analysis of Postural Behavior," *Psychoanalytic Quarterly,* 16 (1947), p. 211.
17. R. Malmo, C. Shagass, and J. Davis, "Electromyographic Studies of Muscular Tension in Psychiatric Patients under Stress," *Journal of Clinical and Experimental Psychopathology,* 12 (1951), p. 45.
18. A. Raskin, "Observable Signs of Anxiety or Distress During Psychotherapy," *Journal of Consulting Psychology,* 4 (1961), p. 398.
19. H. Gilkinson, "Social Fears as Reported by Students in College Speech Classes," *Speech Monographs,* 9 (1942), pp. 141–160.
20. T. J. Saine, M. A. Levine, and G. E. McHose, "Assessing the Structure of Nonverbal Interaction," *Southern Speech Communication Journal,* 40 (Spring 1975), pp. 275–287.
21. G. Hewes, "The Anthropology of Posture," *Scientific American* (1957), pp. 123–132.
22. H. J. Hsia, "The Information Processing Capacity and Modality of Channel Performance," *Audio/Visual Communications Review,* 19 (Spring 1971), pp. 51–75.
23. A. M. Eisenberg and R. R. Smith, *Nonverbal Communication,* (Indianapolis: Bobbs-Merrill, 1971), p. 52.
24. P. A. Andersen, J. P. Garrison, and J. F. Andersen, "Defining Nonverbal Communication: A Neurophysiological Explanation of Nonverbal Information Processing." Paper presented at the annual meeting of the Western Speech Communication Association, Seattle, Washington, November 1975.
25. R. P. Harrison, *Beyond Words: An Introduction to Nonverbal Communication* (Englewood Cliffs, N.J.: Prentice-Hall, 1974), p. 85.

3

Codes I: The Human Body as Message Carrier

Test Your Sensitivity

True or False?

1. The face is capable of producing 20,000 different expressions.
2. Females are more accessible than males to touch by friends of the same sex.
3. There is a common standard of beauty in this country.
4. The biggest factor determining a person's satisfaction with a date is the date's physical attractiveness.
5. You can make a listener tense by speaking in a tense voice yourself.

By the end of the chapter, you should know the correct answer to all five questions and understand these concepts:

- range of possible gestures, facial expressions, and body movements
- kinemes and Birdwhistell's classification scheme
- emblems, illustrators, adaptors, affect displays, and regulators
- factors influencing the use of kinesic cues
- kinesic norms
- communication functions of kinesics
- haptics
- biological, psychological, and sociological needs for touch
- touch norms in infancy and adulthood
- reasons for touch norms
- capabilities and limitations of touch as communication
- importance of physical appearance and physical attractiveness
- standards of beauty
- endomorphic, mesomorphic, and ectomorphic body types
- physical appearance norms
- communication potential of body type, hair, skin, clothing, accessories, and cosmetics
- restrictions on physical appearance as a communication code
- paralanguage
- capacity for differentiation in vocal cues
- difference between voice set, voice qualities, and vocalizations
- dimensions of voice qualities and vocalizations
- different voice types and their associations
- functions of vocal cues in communication
- potential of vocal cues in communication

In Chapter 2, we indicated our preference for taking a functional approach to nonverbal communication. Before we discuss the various functions in detail, we shall introduce you to the different forms nonverbal messages take. We refer to them as *codes*. In this chapter and the next, we shall discuss briefly the nature of the different nonverbal codes—some of their structural features, functions, some of the factors influencing their use, and their general potency in performing various communication functions. In Chapter 5, we shall investigate in more detail the differences in the ways individuals use the codes. The next three chapters, then, are designed to acquaint you with some important terminology and give you a framework within which to view the remaining chapters.

You are no doubt familiar with the meaning of the terms Morse code and secret code. When used in the context of nonverbal communication, *code* means the medium by which a message is carried or the channel through which it is transmitted. An early text on nonverbal communication, written in the 1950s by Ruesch and Kees, broke the codes down into three categories: sign language, action language, and object language.[1] *Sign language* is any type of gesture that replaces specific words, numbers, or punctuation marks. It ranges from a single gesture, such as a peace sign, to the language system of the deaf. *Action language* includes all those other body movements not used as signs, such as walking and sitting. *Object language* embraces any intentional or unintentional display of objects that might serve as statements about their user. Implements, works of art, architectural structures, footprints, even the appearance of the human body are considered evidence of object language. This classification scheme has since been discarded because it is too limited in some ways and too broad in others. It excludes much of what we regard as nonverbal communication today, such as vocal cues and the manipulation of time. Also, the categories group together things that are fundamentally different. Action language, for example, may be taken to include such disparate things as touch, use of space, and physical postures.

A more contemporary system breaks nonverbal communication into categories based on the human senses that are stimulated by or used for transmitting the message. We shall discuss seven such categories: *kinesics* (body movements), *physical appearance*, *vocalics* (the voice), *haptics* (touch), *proxemics* (space), *chronemics* (time), and *artifacts* (environment and objects). The first two codes appeal to the visual sense, the third to the auditory sense, and the fourth to the tactile sense; all four rely on the human body as the medium. Randall Harrison, in his textbook *Beyond Words*, labels them *performance codes*. They will be discussed in this chapter. The remaining three codes, also called *spatiotemporal* and *artifactual* codes by Harrison, use space, time, and tangible materials or objects as their vehicle for transmitting a message. They will be covered in Chapter 4.

Before we go into these codes in detail, a preliminary comment about assumptions is in order. By breaking nonverbal cues into categories, we do not mean to imply that the various codes are all distinctly different from one another in the way in which they operate. Colin Cherry expressed it well: "The human organism is one integrated whole, stimulated into responses by physical signals; it is not to be thought of as a box, carrying independent pairs of terminals labeled 'ears,' 'eyes,' 'nose,' et cetera."[2] The codes interact with one another in stimulating our senses. Neither do we mean to imply that different codes are responsible for different functions. As we said in the last chapter, the functional approach recognizes that the same function can be performed by different cues and the same cue can perform different functions. A pat on the back or a smile can both signal approval; the same pat on the back can also signal comfort.

Placing the codes in separate categories is, therefore, generally a matter of convenience, dictated partly by the fact that, in the past, scholars have treated them as independent entities. We shall explore some of the differences among the codes in their structures and general use before we bring them together again and look at their combined effects in Part II.

Kinesics

Kinesics, a term originating from the Greek word for *movement*, refers to all the forms of body movement, excluding touch, that may act as nonverbal communication. It is what people usually mean when they talk in a popular sense about *body language*. Ray Birdwhistell, one of the primary scholars in the area of kinesics, recognizes eight regions of meaningful activity: total head; face; neck; trunk and shoulders; shoulders, arms, and wrists; hand and fingers; hips, upper legs, lower legs, and ankles; and feet. These eight regions have an astonishing capacity for variations in cues. Just consider these estimates and observations:[3]

1. Pei estimates that communicating man can produce 700,000 different physical signs.
2. Birdwhistell estimates that the face alone is capable of producing 250,000 expressions.
3. Physiologists estimate that the musculature of the face permits over 20,000 different expressions (not as optimistic an estimate as Birdwhistell's but still an impressive figure).
4. In a study of classroom behavior, Krout observed 7,777 distinct gestures.
5. In therapeutic situations, Krout identified 5,000 distinct hand gestures alone that he believed to have verbal equivalents.
6. Hewes has catalogued 1,000 different postures and their accompanying gestures.

The fact that observers have been able to distinguish that many different cues is amazing to us. It demonstrates the human capacity to make extremely minute differentiations among visual stimuli. Trained observers have even been known to recognize variations in head jerk movements of .25 to .20 millimeters. Extracting meaning from all these variations can be an imposing task, particularly as many kinesic cues have no meaning, many are interchangeable in producing a given meaning, and many have multiple meanings.

Suppose you want to signal rejection of another person's ideas. You can do it in a subtle way by rubbing your nose or crossing your arms; or you can be more blatant and turn thumbs down or hold your nose. Whichever gesture you choose, they all have the same basic meaning. Conversely, even apparently specialized gestures and expressions can communicate many meanings, as is illustrated in a Zen parable:

In a temple in the northern part of Japan two brother monks were dwelling together. The elder one was learned, but the younger one was stupid and had but one eye.

A wandering monk came and asked for lodging, properly challenging them to a debate about the sublime teaching. The elder brother, tired that day from much studying, told the younger one to take his place. "Go and request the dialogue in silence," he cautioned.

So the young monk and the stranger went to the shrine and sat down.

Shortly afterward the traveler rose and went in to the elder brother and said: "Your young brother is a wonderful fellow. He defeated me."

"Relate the dialogue to me," said the elder one.

"Well," explained the traveler, "first I held up one finger, representing Buddha, the enlightened one. So he held up two fingers, signifying Buddha and his teaching. I held up three fingers, representing Buddha, his teaching, and his followers, living the harmonious life. Then he shook his clenched fist in my face, indicating that all three come from one realization. Thus he won. . . ." With this, the traveler left.

"Where is that fellow?" asked the younger one, running in to his elder brother.

"I understand you won the debate."

"Won nothing. I'm going to beat him up."

"Tell me the subject of the debate," asked the elder one.

"Why, the minute he saw me he held up one finger, insulting me by insinuating that I have only one eye. Since he was a stranger I thought I would be polite to him, so I held up two fingers, congratulating him that he has two eyes. Then the impolite wretch held up three fingers, suggesting that between us we only have three eyes. So I got mad and started to punch him, but he ran out and that ended it!"[4]

In addition to the enormous variability of patterns common to the United States, there are behaviors in other countries that are unfamiliar to us. For example, some Bolivian Indian tribespeople indicate both anger and joy by slapping the back of the head; and among the Pitta-Pitta aborigines of Australia, men show contempt by biting their beards and women insult each other by protruding the abdomen, exposing themselves, and vibrating their thighs together. Familiar behaviors to which we assign specific meanings may also have different meanings for different peoples. In the 1950s, when then Vice President Richard Nixon made a goodwill tour of Latin America, there was widespread hostility and resentment toward the United States among the Latin American countries. Unwittingly, Nixon added fuel to the fire. At one of his early stops, he stepped off his airplane and flashed the waiting crowds the A-OK sign. The crowds booed, and the newspapers all carried a photograph of the gesture the next day. The reason? In their culture, what Nixon had signalled was "Screw you."

Given the seemingly infinite number of behaviors and possible meanings, the study of kinesics may seem impossible. However, that is not the case. It is possible to reduce the mass of behaviors to a smaller set of manageable categories.

Classifications of Kinesic Behaviors

People have gone about classifying kinesic cues in two basic ways that reflect the two linguistic approaches discussed in Chapter 2. One classifies according to structural similarities and the other according to similarities in function or meaning.

Structure-Centered Approach Perhaps the best-known and most elaborate example of the first approach is Birdwhistell's scheme.[5] As we noted in Chapter 2, Birdwhistell sought to identify discrete, universally used behaviors that act as the building blocks of nonverbal communication. He succeeded in isolating between fifty and sixty behaviors, which he labeled *kinemes*. Here are the thirty-three that apply to the face and head region:

1–3. three head nods: one nod, two nods, or three nods
4–5. two lateral head sweeps: one sweep or two sweeps
6. one head cock
7. one head tilt
8–10. three connective or junctural head kinemes: holding head position, raising and holding head position, lowering and holding head position
11–14. four brow movements: lifted, lowered, knit, or single brow movement
15–18. four degrees of lid closure: overopen, slit, closed, or squeezed
19–22. four nose positions: wrinkled nose, compressed nostrils, bilateral nose flare, or unilateral nose flare
23–29. seven mouth positions: compressed lips, protruded lips, retracted lips, apically withdrawn lips, snarl, lax open mouth, or mouth overopen (all of these are tentative)
30–31. two chin thrusts: anterior and lateral
32–33. two cheek positions: puffed or sucked

Three other movements that may eventually be granted kineme status are the chin drop, lower eyelid movements, and laugh lines. All of the kinemes have corresponding notational symbols, a sample of which appears in Figure 3.1.

Smaller variations may occur within these kinemes (they even have names—*kines* and *allokines*), but they are not considered meaningful. For instance, trained observers once noted as many as twenty-three different eyelid positions among nurses who were interacting, but the observers agreed that only four of the positions made any difference in the message's meaning. Similarly, it probably doesn't matter whether you wink with your left or right eye—the meaning is the same. The importance of being able to reduce the vast number of kinesic behaviors to fifty or sixty categories is that it focuses attention on those behaviors that have widespread use and significance. According to Birdwhistell, many of the variations noted from culture to culture are not different kinemes but merely variations within kinemes. Thus, all cultures can be analyzed by means of the same set of kinemes.

The next stage of analysis is to look at how the kinemes are combined so that they take on wordlike qualities. These are called *kinemorphs*. Kinemorphs are combined, in turn, into classes and complex constructions that have the same properties as sentences. A come-hither facial expression (direct eye contact, slight smile, head tilted downward) coupled with a beckoning gesture would be an example. It is only at the level of kinemorphs and combinations of kinemorphs, then, that the interpretation of meaning becomes possible in Birdwhistell's system. He is more interested in identifying which behaviors and sequences of behaviors are frequently used than in cataloguing the meanings of the behaviors.

Meaning-Centered Approach The other approach to classifying kinesic behaviors is

Figure 3.1   This sample from Birdwhistell's kinesic recording system shows symbols for facial expression. (From *Kinesics and Context,* Philadelphia: University of Pennsylvania Press, 1970, p. 260.)

Symbol	Description	Symbol	Description
—◯—	Blank faced		Out of the side of the mouth (left)
—⌢	Single raised brow; ⌢ indicates brow raised		Out of the side of the mouth (right)
—⌣	Lowered brow		Set jaw
⩔	Medial brow contraction		Smile: tight—; loose o
	Medial brow nods	⊢⊣	Mouth in repose: lax o; tense—
⌢⌢	Raised brows		Droopy mouth
◯◯	Wide eyed		Tongue in cheek
—◯	Wink	⌢	Pout
> <	Lateral squint	⋇⋇	Clenched teeth
>< ><	Full squint		Toothy smile
⋊⋉ A	Shut eyes (closed pause 2 count blink)		Square smile
⋉⋊ B	Shut eyes (closed pause 5 plus count)	◎	Open mouth
⊕⊕	Sidewise look	S◯L	Slow lick of lips
	Focus on auditor	Q◯L	Quick lick of lips
⊗⊗	Stare		Moistening lips
	Rolled eyes		Lip biting
	Slitted eyes		Whistle
⊖⊖	Eyes upward		Pursed lips
—⊖⊖—	Shifty eyes		Retreating lips
	Glare		Peck !
⊖ ⊙	Inferior lateral orbit contraction		Smack !
△s	Curled nostril		Lax mouth
s△s	Flaring nostrils		Chin protruding
ˌ△ˏ	Pinched nostrils		"Dropped" jaw
△	Bunny nose	⊢⋇⊣	Chewing
◭	Nose wrinkle	⋋ ⋌	Temples tightened
⌣	Left sneer	Ɛ Ʒ	Ear "wiggle"
∿	Right sneer		Total scalp movement

evident in the work of Paul Ekman and Wallace Friesen. Together they have created a way of classifying gestures according to what functions they perform.[6] Actually, their categories can be applied to all forms of kinesic behavior. There are five general categories:

1. *Emblems.* Emblems are intentional behaviors that have a direct verbal counterpart and can be substituted for the verbal form without substantially changing the meaning. (The hitchhiker's thumb is an example.) There must be widespread agreement on their meaning within a culture. They are frequently used when verbal communication is in some way restricted, as when signalling across a crowded, noisy room. A number of common emblems are shown in Figure 3.2.

2. *Illustrators.* Illustrators are acts that accompany the verbal stream and are designed to do such things as pictorialize what is being said, aid in phrasing, augment volume, and gain attention. They may complement, contradict, accentuate, or repeat the verbal message and are usually done deliberately. Unlike emblems, they typically do not have a direct verbal equivalent and do not occur in the absence of conversation. They are employed only by speakers and not by listeners. Ekman and Friesen have identified eight overlapping categories of illustrators: *batons* accentuate words and phrases; *ideographs* sketch the direction or path of thought; *kinetographs* represent body action or nonhuman physical action; *pictographs* re-create the shape of what is being referenced verbally; *deictic movements* point to objects, places, or events; *spatial movements* show spatial relationships; *rhythmic movements* depict the timing or rhythm of an event; *emblematic movements* repeat or substitute for words in illustrating a verbal statement.

3. *Adaptors.* Figure 3.3 depicts a gesture that is part illustrator and part *adaptor*. In the adaptor category are behaviors designed to satisfy physical or emotional needs. These are acts usually carried out in private; at least they are rarely intended for an audience. Behaviors such as scratching, masturbating, tugging at underwear, and primping all qualify as adaptors. When such behaviors are performed in private, the need they satisfy is readily apparent; when they are performed in public, they are usually abbreviated and fragmented, sometimes making it difficult to identify their purpose.

Adaptive behavior tends to become more evident when an individual is experiencing some form of stress or discomfort. People may display agressive tendencies against the self by rubbing or squeezing parts of the body. They may reveal physical discomfort by massaging a sore limb or anxiety by chewing on a pencil. Objects such as cigarettes are often used as props in adaptive behavior.

4. *Affect displays.* Affect displays reveal emotions. They may be intentional or unintentional; in fact, many fleeting expressions of feelings occur without the awareness of the sender. Affect displays may complement, contradict, accentuate, repeat, or replace the verbal message. Or they may act independently of any verbal message. A clenched fist may be all that is needed to communicate anger.

Paul Ekman and his associates have developed a technique for applying the meaning-centered approach specifically to facial expressions. Briefly, they divide the face into regions and look for combinations of motions within and across regions that correspond to different emotions. Their approach, along with other features of emotional displays, will be discussed in more detail in Chapter 8, but we wanted to mention the approach here because the method can potentially be applied to other regions of the body and offers an alternative to the Birdwhistell approach.

5. *Regulators.* The last category, regulators, includes all those kinesic behaviors that are used to control the flow and content of an interaction. Such behaviors as head nods and eye movements may serve either to encourage

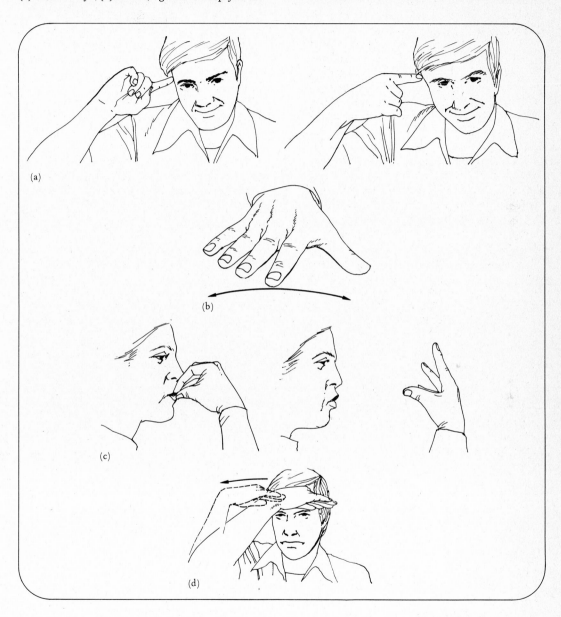

Figure 3.3 An adaptor gesture—holding the cigar—being used as an illustrator.

or discourage further communication. Regulation behaviors appear to be culture-specific. If the appropriate cues are not learned for various cultures, the individual misusing them may be regarded as inept, peculiar, or even rude. Regulatory kinesic cues will be discussed fully in Chapter 9.

Both the Birdwhistell and the Ekman and Friesen approaches are useful in the study of nonverbal communication. We shall call upon both of them as we turn next to identifying kinesic norms.

Kinesic Norms: A Question of Context

By norms, we mean the standard or typical practices within a given group or culture. In this section, we shall look at the kinds of behavior that generally occur and the frequency with which they are used. We shall focus primarily on our culture here; in Chapter 5, we shall look at some crosscultural and individual differences in the use of these cues.

An important point to note is that the choice and meaning of kinesic behaviors, as for all other nonverbal codes, are dependent on the context in which they occur. A facial expression that goes unnoticed in one situation may be highly significant in another; a gesture that is appropriate for one kind of relationship may be totally out of place in another. And the meanings for both the gesture and the face may vary widely from context to context. If you are to determine what behaviors to expect in a given situation and how to interpret them accurately, it is essential that you recognize what norms are operative in that context since they serve to define the context.

The norms in any situation are dictated by a combination of three broad categories of factors: the characteristics of the people (interactants) involved, the nature of the interaction, and environmental constraints.

People Variables Two early writers[7] identified eleven personal characteristics that they believed influence what behaviors are selected and how frequently the behaviors are used.

Most of these characteristics are self-explanatory: personality, sex, racial tradition (including race and culture), age, body deformities, health, metabolic or structural peculiarities, body type, strain or fatigue, transitional emotional states or moods, and special habits springing from special training (such as athletic or dramatic training).

An extremely obese person or someone with arthritis is less likely to use flamboyant gestures, an elderly or tired person is more likely to walk slowly, and an adolescent American female is likely to use stances different from those of her Chinese counterpart. All of the above factors have to be taken into account before we can determine what kinesic patterns an individual will use. Within each of the categories, such as age, sex, and mood, there are some standard patterns; but when all of the factors are combined, there is a great degree of variability from one individual to the next. This makes the task of predicting behaviors difficult. The observer must be extremely sensitive in order to recognize all the factors that contribute to a person's choice of behaviors.

Interaction Variables   These factors relate to the nature and purpose of the interaction. A big consideration is the *definition of the social situation.* Many situations call for artificial, formal behaviors and masking of certain emotions. Our manners at a formal dinner party differ greatly from those at a picnic. A funeral calls for different behaviors than does a bar mitzvah celebration. In essence, the social context dictates what kinesic behaviors are appropriate for the occasion.

A second related consideration is the *purpose* of a given interaction. Even in a generally task-oriented situation, such as a place of business, there can be both social and work-oriented conversations, each calling for a different set of kinesic patterns. It may be acceptable for an auto mechanic to be relaxed and to use a lot of eye contact around the garage manager during a coffee break when everyone is joking around, but a more erect posture and more deferential eye contact may be required when work resumes.

A third factor is *convention* or *fashion.* Until recently, the convention in our culture has been for men to hold doors open for women. Hand clapping is another gesture governed by convention, while holding a cup with the pinkie finger extended is a matter of fashion. Specific conventions and fashions may change rapidly, as is exemplified by the handshake. Many whites think it no longer fashionable to shake hands with a black person in the usual manner, so they attempt (often clumsily) some type of soul handshake.

A final consideration is the *demands of the immediate goal.* Both the nature of the goal and its closeness to attainment affect the repertoire of behaviors selected. For instance, if the goal is delicate labor negotiations, then kinesic cues may be controlled and subtle. If the goal is close at hand (such as the end of a boring task), more frenetic activity is likely.

Environmental Variables   In this category are all those features of the environment that may place constraints on what behavioral patterns emerge. Volume of space, arrangement of furniture, noise, and temperature may have an effect. Seating arrangements that place people far from each other may force them to use more exaggerated gestures, as in the case of a speaker before a large audience. High noise levels may force people to rely on the kinesic rather than the verbal channel to communicate their meaning. Warm temperatures may lead to sluggish movements, cold temperatures to more rapid and clipped movements.

When these different factors are taken into account—the people involved, the nature of the interaction, and the environmental constraints—it is apparent that in all situations, there will be a lot of variability in kinesic patterns. This is not to say that persistent patterns don't occur; but interaction of all the variables makes for a complex result. With this in mind, we turn to an examination of some observable normative behaviors.

Specific Kinesic Norms

Emblems   Paul Ekman has studied emblems in a number of cultures. He reports that the number of emblems appearing in each country varies, ranging from under one hundred among middle-class Americans to over two hundred and fifty among Israeli students. With the exception of emblems that refer to bodily functions (such as eating), there are few emblems that different cultures hold in common. Nonetheless, most cultures have emblems for the same type of message—insults, greetings, departures, interpersonal directions (such as *stop* or *go*), replies (such as *yes* or *no*), and indicators of physical states or emotions.[8] Most cultures have an emblem for suicide, for example, but the gesture differs from culture to culture, largely because the method of committing the act varies.

If we shift to an examination of emblems at a subcultural level, the number of such gestures increases dramatically. Various professions, organizations, fraternities, and secret societies have developed their own unique sets of emblems. At the professional or occupational level, the creation of special emblems is dictated by a need for accurate communication among people working together. Because the gestures are highly specialized, they are unlikely to be understood by anyone outside that occupation. The signal system used in the grain commodities market is a prime illustration. On the floor at the Board of Trade, people must resort to gestures to make their bids. If a person chooses to buy, he holds his palm up and inward; if he wishes to sell, the palm is turned outward. Quantities to be traded are signalled by the number of fingers held vertically, each one representing 5,000 bushels; prices are signalled by horizontally held fin-

gers, each representing ⅛ cent. Equally restricted sign systems have developed among such occupational groups as railroad crews and dock workers.

The gestures common to some other professions have acquired a general use. Take the signals used in radio broadcasting. What does placing the index finger against the throat like a knife mean? What does holding up the thumb and index finger in the form of an *o* mean? What does pointing the index finger to the tip of the nose mean? The first means to stop (literally cut the program off the air), the second means O.K., and the third means *on time* (literally *on the nose*). The fact that most of us know these signs illustrates the carryover effect of many occupational gestures. It is not uncommon for sports-officiating signals or military gestures to be used in other contexts.

Anthropologists have similarly documented the emblematic repertoire of a wide range of cultures and American subcultures. Some of the specific observations will be mentioned in Chapter 5; a description or listing of all the emblems used in the American culture would be tedious if not impossible. The important thing to realize is that every group has a distinct set of such gestures that its members rely on for communication and that understanding those gestures requires knowledge of the specific group using them.

Affect Displays   Around the turn of the century, displays of emotions tended to be stilted because of a development called the *elocutionary movement*. Orators and actors were trained to use a series of stylized gestures, postures, and facial expressions to represent different emotions and attitudes. Figure 3.4 shows two of the standard poses. One of the representative systems was developed by Delsarte in the 1880s.[9] Because he believed that gesture is "the agent of the heart" and that it could be scientifically analyzed, he attempted to identify the primary positions for the head, eyes, eyebrows, nose, lips, torso, and

Figure 3.4   These two poses from the elocutionary movement represent grief (left) and rejection.

limbs and specify their concomitant meanings. For example, the head could be erect, which indicated passivity; it could be inclined laterally away, which showed sensualism; or it could be inclined laterally forward, which indicated affection. Each position had a clear meaning. Dramatists who followed the Stanislavski method of acting similarly had their own "cookbook" of proper movements. From our point of view, these motions seem subjective and artificial, but the people of the time took the theories as gospel because they were labeled scientific. The early silent movies followed the systems very closely. We may find them humorous today, but vestiges of the elocutionary movement's prescription for emotional displays still creep into our modern movies, television programs, and other public performances.

Today emotional displays are less stylized, although the example of television may encourage stereotypic patterns. During an argument, have you ever caught yourself using that familiar wounded look that Hollywood has perfected? Or have you noticed the way children ape their favorite cartoon characters when showing anger or frustration?

Emotions themselves have some universal qualities that lead to a degree of standardization in affect displays. The primary emotions tend to be expressed in a similar manner by all people; that is, people use the same kinemes. Superimposed on these basic displays are some cultural rules about what forms of expression are appropriate for what situations.

mini-experiment

Watch some silent movies or early talkies, then look for examples of the same poses and expressions in today's television soap operas.

For instance, in our culture, the norm is to be exuberant in our show of joy but to be subdued in displays of grief or sadness. It has also been normative in our culture to suppress unpleasant emotions generally; females especially have been expected to maintain a pleasant front. Conversely, males are taught to suppress shows of affection, tenderness, and emotionality in general, except for anger and excitement (as at a football game). It is still taboo for males to cry at sad movies, though such behavior is expected of females. This norm of the unmanliness of showing emotion is undergoing change. As sex roles become less rigid in this society, and more men and women take on some of the characteristics of the opposite sex, we should expect some changes in the norms for emotional displays. The time may come when a female even offers her date a Kleenex during a touching movie.

Illustrators   We know far less about normative patterns concerning illustrators. During the elocutionary period, these gestures were also more stilted and restricted. Textbooks were full of prescriptions about the proper ways to make a speech or public performance. Young seminarians were even chastised for adopting such stances as leaning against a podium or sitting while reading. There seems to be much more flexibility today about what behaviors are acceptable, to the extent that perhaps there are no definitive norms, or at least not ones that can be clearly identified. As for the frequency of use, there are cultural and subcultural differences in the degree to which people rely on kinesic cues to illustrate their verbal messages. For instance, Italians accompany conversation with a great many hand gestures. By contrast, the British use relatively few gestures to illustrate their words.

Adaptors   The primary norm governing these gestures is that of not using them in public. Picking one's ear or scratching one's behind in public is frowned upon. The one exception is certain types of object–adaptor displays—holding cigarettes, bottles, and other objects. It is doubtful that there are culturewide norms regarding these kinds of gestures, but many subgroups set their own preferred patterns. There are still sororities that give lectures to their members on the proper way for a lady to hold and smoke a cigarette. (It should be held by the first two fingers, the elbow of the arm bent so that the cigarette is positioned just above the shoulder.) The stereotypic gangster has his own norm; the cigarette is held between the lips, pointed slightly downward, or between the thumb and forefinger so that it can be effectively hurled at a moment's notice. Here again there is room for more careful observation of the actual norms. An interesting project might be to analyze the fashionable way of manipulating cigarettes, cigars, pipes, beer cans, and the like in a given community. To the extent that such behaviors are approved and prescribed, the community has found acceptable releases for adaptor urges.

Regulators   In Chapter 9, we shall carefully consider regulators that determine what cues we typically use. Here we want to look primarily at the frequency with which various behaviors are used. A review of several studies on eye behavior[10] reveals these conclusions:

1. The normal amount of gazing during an interaction ranges from 28 percent to 70 percent of the time.
2. Under stress conditions, the range broadens to from 8 percent to 73 percent.
3. Individuals are consistent in their typical gaze pattern from one situation to another.
4. Sex, race, and personality affect the amount of eye contact.
5. More gazing is initiated by the listener than the speaker.

We might add to this list a few more conventions of our culture. We consider it impolite to stare at others in this country, so we always try to avoid prolonged eye contact with strangers on the street. You might notice, the next time you are out walking in public, what difficulty people have trying to decide whether to look at each other at all and if so, for how long. If the glance is accompanied by a smile, it is permissible to keep looking; but if the person doing the looking maintains a stone face, the receiver is made to feel very uncomfortable. Another behavior that is still fashionable in some quarters is for women to bat their eyes. Finally, in the United States, it is considered bad form to spend more time looking at other people's dates than at one's own.

From this brief overview of kinesic norms, we can extract a few general statements:

1. Each culture and many subcultures develop a detailed set of emblems that may be used for similar purposes but employ different kinemes. The American set of emblems is one of the smallest.
2. While some of the kinemes for affect displays are universal, each culture has its own rules governing what forms are appropriate in what situations. In our culture, as in most others, there are different norms for males and females. American males are permitted to express a narrow range of aggressive emotions, while females are permitted to express a broad range of affiliative and nurturing emotions.
3. Illustrator norms have not been clearly identified, but the general American culture uses such behaviors in greater moderation than do other cultures.
4. The norm for adaptors directed toward the self is not to display them in public; for adaptors involving the manipulation of an object, the norms are defined at a subcultural level by individual groups.
5. Regulatory cues show wide variability from one individual to another but consistency within an individual. Norms differ according to the sex, race, personality, and listener/ speaker role of the individuals involved and the nature of the social situation.

More specific details about each of these categories of cues will be introduced in Chapters 5, 8, and 9.

The Communication Potential of Kinesics

From all that we have said so far, it should be clear that kinesics is one of, if not *the* most potent of nonverbal codes. In terms of the number of cues that can be used, the possibilities are almost infinite if one considers how many body features can be involved, how much variability there is within any one feature, and how many combinations of features are possible. In terms of decoding, people also have a pronounced ability to make fine discriminations among cues. As for the kinds of messages that can be transmitted, we have indicated that kinesics can perform a tremendous range of functions. All the ones we will cover in Part II rely heavily on kinesic cues. Finally, the research cited in Chapter 1 demonstrates that the kinesic code carries more information for receivers than do other codes. When we give students an opportunity in class to use all the channels except the verbal one to encode a message, they unanimously rely on the kinesic channel alone. The kinesic code is one of the most heavily used and relied-upon means of communicating with others.

Haptics

We are a touch-starved society.
—Desmond Morris

Haptics is the study of touch; it includes both the external and internal sensations we experience. The opening quotation from Desmond

Morris, author of *The Naked Ape* and *Intimate Behavior,* underscores the reason why touch is considered to have such potential for communication: human beings need to touch and be touched. This apparently powerful need has both a biological and sociopsychological basis and can be traced back to infancy.

Touch Needs in Infancy

Biological Value   The biological importance of physical contact begins before birth and is rooted in the need for comfort and protection. The developing fetus receives its first tactile experiences in the womb. The cushion of fluid in the uterus supplies a constant, warm temperature and shelters the fetus from outside forces. The developing infant is pleasantly stimulated by the rhythms and heartbeat of the mother and the rhythms of its own heart and systems. These experiences in the womb allow the infant to develop tactile sensitivity even before birth. The touch sensations are the organism's barometer of its physical well-being.

At birth, the infant is suddenly plunged from that warm, supportive environment into a strange and hostile one. The pressure and temperature of the atmosphere are new; the skin is exposed to the air and foreign objects for the first time; the infant's respiratory system must now take over, which is a new sensation in itself. The newborn is very vulnerable and is totally dependent on others for its protection and comfort, which the mother supplies through physical contact. Her body provides heat, a buffer from impact, nourishment, and a return to the familiar rhythms of the womb. Some feel that the rhythms from the mother's body may help to regulate the infant's internal systems. Doctors have debated the advantages of breast-feeding over bottle feeding for healthy development. In other mammals, all of this physical contact, the licking and nursing and clinging, is essential. Human babies can

survive without continuous close contact (otherwise we wouldn't remove them from their mothers in the hospital), but it appears that some contact is necessary and beneficial. New delivery techniques experiment with keeping the infant with the mother immediately after birth and reducing the trauma of the birth experience by offering maximum contact and maximum simulation of the conditions of the womb.

Communication Value   One thing is certain—contact is necessary as a means of communication between mother and child. Lawrence Frank explains that a baby's sucking is a message to the mother of the child's hunger and that the child learns to respond to the signals of the nipple to satisfy that need.[11] In this manner, the infant associates the mother with satisfaction of basic needs. Similarly, the mother pats and cuddles the child when it is frightened or in pain. Thus the touching between mother and child serves as a communication link through which the infant signals its needs and through which it receives the attention and care that keep its system balanced and healthy.

Psychological Value   Touch also plays a role in psychological development. First of all, a child learns an identity through tactile exploration. Only through touching his or her own body and objects in the environment can the child begin to recognize himself or herself as separate from the rest of the environment. Similarly, the child's awareness of that environment will depend on how much direct tactile exploration is permitted. Children learn spatial dimensions, sizes, shapes, and textures through touching and manipulating things. A child's perceptual learning is therefore dependent on haptic experiences.

The self-explorations that children engage in also contribute to their body images, to whether or not they are comfortable and pleased with their bodies. The associations that children acquire through these early ventures are dependent on how others react to them. Frank says, "The baby begins to communicate with himself by feeling his own body, exploring its shapes and textures, discovering its orifices and thereby begins to establish his body image which, of course, is reinforced or often negated by pleasurable or painful tactile experiences with other human beings."[12] The child who is encouraged to touch his own body and whose touching of others produces pleasurable reactions should develop positive feelings about the human body.

Physical contact is also important to a child's psychological sense of security and well-being. If birth is a traumatic experience and the outside world an alien one, then human contact may be critical to overcoming feelings of fear and isolation. The fact that emotionally disturbed children usually respond well to stroking and rhythmic slapping suggests that this is true. Even adults subconsciously engage in self-touching—patting, rubbing, scratching—when they are disturbed. Touching seems to provide a source of reassurance and comfort. It helps to dispel negative feelings. Tactile stimulation also brings pleasure and self-gratification. This should be apparent to anyone who has ever watched babies explore their hands and feet and coo while patting themselves.

Social Value   The final importance of touch is social in nature. Physical contact appears to be necessary for the development of satisfactory interpersonal relationships. The quality of touch experiences can strongly influence a person's ability to relate to others, to trust them, and to be sensitive to their needs. Psychiatrists have traced many marital problems to a history of inadequate or inappropriate tactile experiences in childhood. Violence and aggression may have the same cause.

A number of studies offer striking demonstration that serious biological, psychological and sociological problems do result when human beings are deprived of touch. Perhaps the most shocking discoveries have come from studies of institutionalized infants. A number of people have found that children who are placed in foundling homes or orphanages develop serious health and behavior problems. They become ill and highly apathetic, often failing to respond to external stimuli. They may bite themselves or bang their head against the crib. Many infants develop *hospitalization syndrome,* a pattern of hysteria and depression that usually ends in death. Around the turn of the century, mortality rates in some homes were close to 100 percent. The children who survived were usually severely retarded and maladjusted. The culprit in all of this? Lack of human contact and sensory stimulation. The infants received so little physical stimulation that they wasted away. Fifty years later, many orphans still exhibit similar symptoms.

While the effects outside the institutional setting may not always be as severe, touch deprivation can still have serious consequences. The well-known Harlow studies of monkeys offer some initial insights.[13] In those studies, the monkeys were separated from their mothers and isolated from other infants. Some were given a wire surrogate mother that supplied food and a cloth mother. Even though the cloth surrogate offered nothing other than soft contact, the baby monkeys would spend hours clinging to it, returning to the wire surrogate only for meals. The behavior pattern was taken as a clear indication of the infant's need for contact with something approximating the warmth and softness of a mother. Monkeys raised in isolation also acquired violent, aberrant behaviors and were later unable to adapt socially. By contrast, those that were raised with other infants but without their mothers acquired necessary social behaviors.

Studies of touch deprivation in humans offer further evidence of debilitating effects. Lack of physical contact in childhood has led to such problems as allergies, eczema, speech difficulties, and learning disabilities in later life.[14]

Based on his examination of 400 primitive cultures including our own, the neuropsychologist James Prescott has concluded there is a strong correlation between lack of physical pleasure and violence: the more pleasure, the less violence and vice versa.[15] Cultures that display a lot of physical affection toward infants have a low incidence of theft, murder, rape, and physical punishment, while those that deny physical pleasure to infants generally have high rates of adult violence.

From all of this evidence, it seems clear that touch experiences are critical during infancy and childhood; but what about their role as we grow older? Is touch still important, or do we outgrow it?

Touch Needs into Adulthood

To some extent, physical contact is supplanted as a means of communication and self-gratification because we learn other ways of communicating messages that we could originally transmit only through touch. Mothers talk and sing to their children while they hold them, comfort them, and reassure them. Slowly the child learns to associate the mother's voice with comfort and security, and eventually learns the words. At the same time, the child is learning his or her own verbal and gestural language systems with which to communicate needs and wants. Thus, touch is slowly replaced by other kinds of communicative signals. The pleasure gained from contact is also partially replaced by other kinds of stimuli that indirectly impinge upon the sense of touch—things like clothing and the rhythms of music. These socially acceptable forms are slowly substituted for self-touching and touching others.

This does not mean that adolescents and adults no longer need or want physical contact. At least in intimate relationships, touch is an integral part of the communication between two people (see Fig. 3.5). Lack of touch is taken as a sign that something is wrong in the relationship. The sex act is seen as the ultimate expression of love and/or desire. The importance of touch in adulthood can be inferred from Prescott's study of body contact practices. He found that those cultures that have little physical contact in infancy may still have low levels of violence if premarital sex is tolerated. In other words, intimate, pleasurable contact in adolescence can counteract the deficit from childhood. Societies that punish premarital sex also exhibit slavery, wife purchasing, fears of castration, theft, exhibitionistic dancing, sexual disabilities, and mutilation and killing of enemies. The restriction of outlets for physical pleasure apparently results in frustration and efforts to seek other forms of stimulation, many of which are counterproductive to the society.

Desmond Morris claims that in our culture we turn to licensed touchers. We pay for the services of those who supply us with the contact we are missing. Hairdressers, barbers, manicurists, masseurs, and masseuses all offer pleasurable touch experiences. Even if the body contact is not the main reason for seeking such services, the body contact is a satisfying by-product that may increase the frequency of our using them. According to Morris, this need for more touch is due to the high degree of alienation our culture has created. As long as man lived in small tribes, everyone knew one another and shared the security of the group; but Western civilization is no longer tribal. The emergence of great urban areas has left us not knowing most of the people we see in a day's time; we do not know whom we can trust, and so we avoid contact with each other. These feelings of uncertainty, isolation, and alienation are aggravated by stress from the excess stimulation that comes from living in urban environments—too many people, too much noise, too little room, too much activity, too few resources. The result is a withdrawal that reduces the opportunities for satisfying

Figure 3.5

touch experiences. Even in the family, children may be deprived of warm, affectionate contact. The alarming rise in alienation that has been documented by sociologists is one possible indication that adults and adolescents in our culture need more touch than they are getting, and the increase in premarital sex is a sign that at least some people are determined to have more pleasurable touch experiences than our culture has previously allowed. The fact that such physical contact is considered improper or immoral by a large portion of the culture raises the question of what the prevailing norms are in our culture.

Touch Norms

Compared to other societies, our culture is restrictive, punitive, and ritualized. Other cultures with different value systems and child-rearing practices have different touch norms. In many, nudity and open physical contact are common, and the seeking of physical pleasure through sexual encounters or masturbation is encouraged rather than punished. In yet other societies, touch is central in the form of scarification rituals, pain endurance tests, and sexual rites of passage. By contrast, touch in any form is minimized in our culture. Nudity causes embarrassment, masturbation is strongly criticized, and affectionate contact with people other than immediate family is frowned upon. Even within the family, there are limitations. Mothers may caress their male children but fathers may not, and fathers must avoid prolonged contact with their daughters. Mothers have been found to touch female children more than male children.[16] There are also rules governing which parts of the body may or may not be touched. The genital regions are to be scrupulously avoided.

In the 1960s, Sidney Jourard conducted a study to find out just which regions are permissible to touch.[17] He divided the body into fourteen regions (ranging from the head to the foot) and asked 300 students to indicate which regions of the body they touched and received touch from parents, same-sex friends, and opposite-sex friends. His general conclusions were that the greatest amount of touch occurred among opposite-sex pairs, and that touch was restricted largely to the head, shoulders, and arms. The taboos against touching the genital and excretory regions were clearly apparent for all combinations except the opposite-sex pairs.

To test whether touch norms had changed in a decade's time, Lawrence Rosenfeld and two of his students repeated the Jourard study in 1975 with 200 new subjects.[18] Their findings are shown pictorially in Figure 3.6. Overall, the new results reveal very few changes from the earlier study. Parents still limit their touching of sons and daughters primarily to the head and arm regions, fathers touch daughters more frequently than sons but touch both in the same general regions, and mothers continue to touch both sons and daughters with about equal frequency but with some differences in the regions most commonly touched. Interestingly, the face region for males receives a high frequency of touch from mothers but very little from fathers, while daughters are frequently touched in the stomach and hip regions by mothers but not by fathers. The patterns for same-sex touching remain constant; males and females report the same body regions to be accessible to touch. The primary change from the 1960s is a significant increase in the percentage of touch to certain body regions from opposite-sex friends: males now receive more in the chest and hip areas than in the past and females receive more in the chest, stomach, hip, and thigh areas. Overall, the body is highly accessible to opposite-sex touching.

While the regions of the body available for touch may be changing slightly, the frequency of touch is not necessarily following suit. Observations made of children in school cafeteria lines revealed that the amount of touching

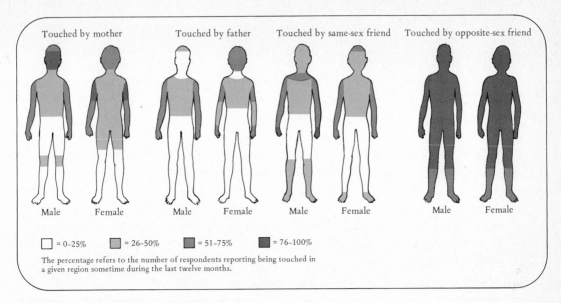

Touched by mother   Touched by father   Touched by same-sex friend   Touched by opposite-sex friend

Male   Female   Male   Female   Male   Female   Male   Female

☐ = 0–25%   ▨ = 26–50%   ▨ = 51–75%   ▨ = 76–100%

The percentage refers to the number of respondents reporting being touched in a given region sometime during the last twelve months.

Figure 3.6   Body regions generally regarded as accessible to touch by others, according to a 1975 survey.

among same-sex pairs declined from the first grade to the sixth grade (except for black children in all-black schools). Furthermore, in integrated schools, only one instance of interracial touching was observed, suggesting that racial touch barriers also remain.[19] Encounter groups have similarly found that people are reluctant to touch one another and feel uncomfortable when they are touched by strangers.[20] A recent effort accurately to measure touch avoidance showed that males are more hesitant to touch members of the same sex, while females are more hesitant to touch members of the opposite sex. Age, religion, and marital status also play a role in touch avoidance: people reduce touch to the opposite sex as they increase in age. Protestants avoid touch more than non-Protestants, and older married persons display an avoidance of touching members of the opposite sex.[21]

We can conclude that the norm in our culture is for limited physical contact to a limited number of body regions. The permissible frequency and locations are dependent on the sex, race, age, religion, degree of acquaintance, and familial ties of the parties involved.

The taboo nature of touch in our culture is ingrained at an early age. Parents discourage infants from touching sex organs by nudging their wandering hands away from their private parts or quickly handing them a toy to keep them occupied in other ways. When children are old enough to understand verbal commands, they are told not to touch Aunt Jennie or Uncle Willie in those places. And when they explore their own genitals, they are told that such behavior is naughty. Guilt, embarrassment, and displeasure in touching the human body are further reinforced by prohibiting children from seeing parents or each other naked. The body must be covered, hidden. That can mean only one thing—there is something shameful about it. The final blow is delivered to little boys when they are told that being manly means not expressing emotions, which translates into suppressing the desire to give or receive affectionate contact.

The prohibitions against touching have both religious and economic overtones. Strains of Puritanism and the Protestant ethic appear in the rejection of pleasure as immoral and sinful. Because most religions in our culture teach that premarital and extramarital sexual relationships are wrong, and because touch carries with it sexual connotations, all forms of touching become restricted. Ann Landers writes that petting should be discouraged because it might lead to sexual intercourse. Teenage girls are warned that no respectable man will marry a woman who has lost her virginity. Thus the pleasure of physical contact is distorted into a sordid affair, and attitudes toward sex and touching are formed that may never be reversed even in the marital relationship.

Besides issues of morality involved in touch, there may also be economic considerations. The value we place on private property may be partly responsible for touch inhibitions. The *don't touch* dictum is applied to things as well as people. We are taught not to touch other

people's property, not to take other children's toys, not to handle Mommy's plants or Daddy's tools. It should not come as any surprise, then, that children become hesitant about all forms of touch and confine their tactile explorations to situations in which they do not expect to be monitored by adults. That kind of secrecy further reinforces the notion that touching is bad. Perhaps that is why people show physiological fear responses when they are threatened by touch from a stranger.

Despite all of the roadblocks that are placed in the way of developing healthy, satisfying tactile behavior patterns, the desire for touch is not extinguished. Our society has responded to the persisting need by sanctioning ritualized touch experiences. Dancing, handshakes, the polite greeting kiss, the slapping ritual in basketball and football huddles are all socially approved examples of physical contact. Our society is full of such touch rituals. However, these socially acceptable forms do not completely satisfy our needs for touching. That may be why people resort to circumventing the system through prostitution and pornography or to developing new subcultures with new rules for behavior, such as religious communes and living together without marriage. The recent rise in popularity of sensitivity groups and the volume of advice coming from medical and psychological experts on the importance of healthy touch experiences forecast a possible change in our haptic norms to greater acceptability of physical contact. Given this possibility and given the already demonstrated significance of tactile stimulation in human development, we turn now to exploring the potency of touch as a communication medium.

The Communication Potential of Touch

The fact that touch has such powerful arousal value and is so central to intimate relationships suggests that it should be a very potent form of communication. Certainly that would be consistent with the commonly held perception of touch. Touch has been associated with the most powerful and mysterious events. The laying on of hands in religious ceremonies is presumed to produce miracles; Christ's healing power came through touch; royalty were always kissed on the hand, and touching even their garment was supposed to bring good fortune; Midas' touch turned everything to gold, and the fairy tale of Rumplestiltskin tells of straw being turned to gold by touching it. We have clearly been taught to associate touch with the most potent of effects.

Does that mean that touch can serve as an effective means of communication? The answer is that it depends on what a touch is being used to convey and what forms the touch takes.

A recent study revealed that when we send touch messages of emotion, we evidently are capable of making fine discriminations. Subjects in the study imagined emotions then tried to express them through a single press of the middle fingers. It is hard to believe that our fingertips carry a great deal of information, but surprisingly the combined horizontal and vertical pressures of the fingers did communicate. Subjects were consistent within themselves in how they encoded the seven passions; and across people, the same pressure patterns were used to express the same emotions.[22]

While fine discriminations are possible in the sending of tactile messages, accurate interpretation is another story. There is little opportunity for variety in transmitting touch messages. The sender can alter the location of touch, the amount of pressure, the duration of contact, the frequency of contact, and the body part used to transmit the message. Compared to the number of features we can vary kinesically, this is a rather limited number. In addition, touch receptors in certain parts of the body are not very sensitive. Have someone place a drawing compass (or two sharp pencils) on your back with the points together and then slowly open it; the compass must be

opened to a considerable degree before you have the sensation of two points on your back.

Consequently, many touch messages we receive are ambiguous. For instance, it can be difficult to distinguish sympathy from love. The type of touch and the location do help to some degree. For example, pats suggest playfulness and touches to the hands are seen as warm. Interestingly, females are more likely than males to differentiate meaning according to location; for males, the type of touch is more meaningful.[23] Generally, though, we have difficulty accurately interpreting touch messages.

Fortunately, touch usually operates in conjunction with other nonverbal cues that help to clarify the message. A facial expression is often all that is needed to know whether a shove is playful or aggressive. By acting as a redundant message itself, touch also aids interpretation of other nonverbal messages. Its arousal value further serves a powerful communication function. More than any other nonverbal mode, touch may arrest the attention of another person and activate the sensory receptors so that the person is receptive to other messages. Beyond its arousal value, touch may play an important part in the communication of affect, in the development of interpersonal relationships, and in the manipulation of others. Thus, despite its lack of specificity, touch is a potentially valuable communication code.

Physical Appearance

I make it a policy never to forget a face but for you I'll make an exception.
—Groucho Marx

Physical appearance, which includes our natural body features, dress, accessories, and cosmetics, is usually the first nonverbal code to have an impact on a relationship. It affects the visual sense and may activate the senses of touch and smell. As the opening quotation suggests, its role in the initial stages of an interaction is particularly important because of the emphasis that we place on physical attractiveness.

Beauty Reigns

If people were given a choice between money and good looks, many would have a hard time making a decision. It has been said that money is power, but so is beauty. Americans today are obsessed with beauty. Cosmetics and fashion are multimillion-dollar industries. We spend great sums of money for products, programs, and secrets to take pounds off or put them on, to eliminate wrinkles, to straighten hair or curl it, to eliminate odors and create new ones, to hold in bulges or push out new ones. Women suffer confining girdles and bras and men stiff collars and neckties to become beautiful people. Senator William Proxmire even went so far as to have hair transplants to cure baldness and Phyllis Diller had a facelift to alter her image. Beauty is definitely big business.

Our obsession with it is nurtured by advertising and Hollywood. Television and motion pictures give us the models for what heroes and heroines should look like. Commercials and advertisements help to perpetuate the stereotypes. When was the last time you saw a fat, slovenly woman or a scrawny, pock-faced man endorsing a product in a magazine ad? Even when "the typical housewife" or "the average workingman" sells coffee or fire insurance, the person is usually neat, clean, and attractive in some way.

The stereotypes for beauty are so ingrained in our culture that, despite physiognomic differences in background, a single standard exists among whites and blacks as to what constitutes a beautiful woman. Researchers showed ten photographs of black women taken from *Ebony* and *Sepia* magazines to fifty white American males and fifty black American males. The subjects reached high agreement on which women were most and least attractive. The photos rated as the most attractive had been identified by a separate panel of judges as being high in Caucasoid rather than Negroid features. When the American sample was compared to a Nigerian sample, the Nigerians showed a more favorable reaction to the Negroid features than had the American subjects.[24] The American preference for the Caucasian facial type indicates the existence of a strong stereotype about female beauty. Lest we be too quick to judge Americans, we should point out that these stereotypic responses are not confined to the United States. A study conducted in Great Britain questioned 4,355 subjects of varying age, sex, occupation, and place of residence and found considerable agreement as to which female faces were pretty.[25] (Interestingly, stereotypes of male attractiveness have received little attention.)

A high level of agreement on what constitutes beauty may exist in every culture, but specific ideals of the beautiful woman or man undoubtedly vary over time and from culture to culture. In the 1880s, after surveying numerous tribes and cultures, Charles Darwin concluded, "It is certainly not true that there is in the mind of man any universal standard of beauty with respect to the human body."[26] While the standards may have varied, the emphasis placed on physical attractiveness throughout the ages has not. Adornment was common as far back as Neanderthal times. The pigment ochre, used to color the body, has been found in burial sites from the mid-Paleolithic era. Since that time, an enormous variety of beautification techniques have developed throughout the world.

Hair has, at various times, been braided, curled, stiffened, frizzed, perfumed, tinted, powdered, cropped short, covered with a wig, and shaved off completely, all in the name of beauty. The African Masai stiffen their hair with cow dung. In some cultures, facial hair has been admired and taken as a sign of status; in others it has been strictly forbidden.

Cosmetics have also had a long history. Face

painting is an ancient art common to some Oriental and African cultures and to certain American Indian tribes. Designs and materials have been as numerous as the cultures that have used them. People have covered their faces with designs of symbolic and ritualistic significance. They have variously accentuated or masked the features and coloring of the face. Occasionally, as is true in American society today, they have striven to achieve a completely natural look. Minerals, herbs, flowers, fruits, vegetables, mud, and synthetics, as well as whale blubber, turtle oil, and other animal products have all been used. Decoration has not been limited to the face. Certain cultures paint the hands and feet as part of their rituals. Perfumes, oils, essences, lotions, powders, and polishes have been used to change the appearance of the body and heighten attractiveness. A recent development peculiar to our society has been the use of deodorants to eliminate natural body odors. (In most other societies, body odors are not only accepted; they are often a source of attraction.)

Like cosmetics and hair fashions, clothing and jewelry have played a significant role in beautification. Numerous volumes have documented the range of styles and materials that have been considered attractive. Today when we see pictures of women in hoop skirts, we regard such styles as an oddity; but the pantsuits and plastic jewelry of our generation would seem strange to women of earlier centuries and different cultures.

Beautification techniques have not been limited to superficial changes. People have gone to great lengths to make the body conform to the cultural standard of attractiveness. Tattooing and scarification have been used to make permanent imprints. People in certain cultures have elongated the lips, ears, and neck, bound the feet, pierced the nose, ears, and mouth, circumcised both boys and girls, and even removed various body parts, all for the sake of status and appearance.

No wonder, then, that with all the ingenuity and energy that has gone into pursuing beauty, our culture is so concerned with it. Some deny that it is important. After all, children are taught that beauty is only skin deep. Recent studies clearly demonstrate, however, that we have yet to rid ourselves of the all-importance of beauty.

A good example is a study of college students that was originally designed to test the degree to which people match themselves up with others whom they judge to be of equal social desirability. The researchers were interested in such factors as personality, intelligence, and social skills. To test their hypothesis, they took advantage of the system of computer dating. A dance was arranged at which dates were supposedly matched according to compatibility. While the freshman participants were picking up their tickets and filling out their preference questionnaires, a panel surreptitiously rated their physical attractiveness. Then, instead of being matched according to their similarities, the students were matched randomly. This was intended to produce all possible combinations of social desirability. When the participants were questioned during the dance and in a follow-up on how they felt about their date, the only factor that predicted satisfaction was not common interests or skills but the attractiveness of the date. Individuals who had initially rated themselves as attractive or popular expected their dates to be attractive and were relatively critical of their dance partners.[27] Other experiments using similar approaches have had the same results.[28]

All of this goes to show what a premium is placed on physical attractiveness and the effect it has on people's perceptions of themselves and others. John Brophy offers a pointed example:

If a portrait of Winston Churchill made in his heyday, in 1940 or 1941 after the Blitz, could be put in front of some intelligent person who possessed no knowledge whatever of who Winston Churchill was, what would he see in that anonymous face? He would see a man in his

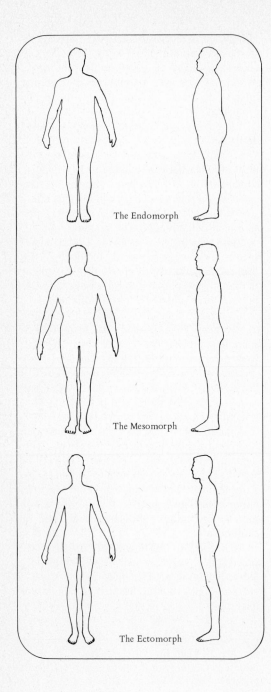

Figure 3.7 Endomorphic, mesomorphic, and ecto-morphic body types.

The Endomorph

The Mesomorph

The Ectomorph

sixties, *with the soft skin and round, dimpling cheeks of a baby, the jaw-line and chin almost lost in fat, eyes and nose both disproportionately small, the mouth richly curved and, probably, holding a cigar, symbol of self-indulgence. From such information how could the observer possibly guess that he was looking at the face of a man who, throughout the worst year of the worst war the world has so far known, held together by his courage a whole beleaguered nation standing alone in arms against tyranny. Churchill's face is a historical fact if ever there was one, but only because history teaches us what to read into it.*[29]

The strong influence physical appearance has on our desire to approach or avoid one another is one reason why it is such an important communication factor.

Physical Appearance: Dimensions and Norms

Physical appearance can convey a tremendous variety of messages. For convenience we shall study two categories of message carriers: the natural elements (the body itself, skin, and hair) and adornments (clothing, accessories, and cosmetics), and we shall look at the current norms within each of these categories.

Natural Endowments Body type is the most prominent natural feature. Bodies can be classified according to their degree of muscularity, height, and weight. Figure 3.7 shows the three main body types. The *endomorph* is soft, plump, short, and round. The *mesomorph* is properly proportioned and athletic, trim, muscular, and average in height. The *ectomorph* has the tall, thin, frail body type. A truly accurate measure of these body types requires measurement techniques not available to the average person. (For instance, researchers have used skinfold calipers to measure subcutaneous fat, have measured the length and density of bones and muscles, and have compared body height to body weight to obtain objective estimates.[30]) You can make a rough estimate of your *somatype* by using a technique employed by early researchers. Assign yourself a score, ranging from a low of 1 to a high of 7, on the degree to which your body fits each of the body types. This means that you will assign yourself three scores, the first for the degree of endomorphy present, the second for the degree of mesomorphy, and the third for the degree of ectomorphy. An extremely thin person would have a score of 1/1/7 while an extremely fat person would score 7/1/1. As a guideline, Chris Evert is about a 3/7/1, Dustin Hoffman is about a 1/6/2, and Don Knotts is a 1/1/7.

The body type norm in this culture doesn't match the preference for muscular men and sleek women. According to physical fitness experts, far too many people in our culture are overweight, tending toward the endomorphic body type. (This body type carries with it some rather negative associations, as we shall see in Chapter 6.) Since the popular notion is that people can control their body weight and physical fitness, body type is viewed as a message about our personality and interest in the way we present ourselves.

A second feature is *skin color*. Though there is a tremendous range of pigmentation, people are usually classified according to the degree to which they have Caucasoid (white), Negroid (brown to black), or Mongoloid (yellowish) coloring. Each culture has definite skin color preferences. Some people claim that the value placed on lighter skin colors in our country is the reason why Chicanos and Puerto Ricans receive less prejudicial treatment than blacks. Ironically, though many white Americans are suspicious of darker-skinned people, they consider a dark suntan attractive. By contrast, women a century ago avoided the sun for fear of freckling and losing their powder-white complexions. One might speculate on whether the change in preferences reflects a change in racial attitudes or will precipitate such a change.

The third feature is *hair*, including body, cranial, and facial hair. For body hair, amount and location are the main considerations. For facial and cranial hair, amount, texture, color, style, and length can all be varied to produce messages. According to a recent survey, females currently prefer hairy-chested men to bare-chested ones. As for facial and cranial hair, any male who wore long hair, a beard, or a mustache during the 1960s and early 1970s is aware of the strong negative reactions they created. During that time, the hair controversy was much discussed. The military's imposition of hair regulations was controversial. Vietnam veterans report that they were given choices of haircuts but they were strongly encouraged to have their hair closely cropped because their commanding officer preferred shorter hair. Combat comfort was cited as the official rationale, but critics claim the true purpose was to reduce individual identity.

Younger men have since conjectured that long hair and beards make them look more attractive and that older men have been jealous. Probably the simplest explanation for the uproar is that the hirsute look was too different from the existing norm—it was a far cry from the flattops and crewcuts of the fifties—and people are always suspicious of new and strange things. The deviant styles were taken as a message of rejection of society's standards. By now the strangeness and hostility seem to have worn off. Commercials picture businessmen with long hair styles, and many men over fifty have acquired sideburns, mustaches, and beards. Hairiness no longer carries the same message. However, as the styles for men change, those at the forefront of change will once again be seen as expressing a challenge to the old ways through the medium of appearance, whether that is their intent or not.

For women, hair has not been so great a communication factor. Women's hair styles have traditionally been more variable, with fewer styles considered deviant. However, hair length, style, and color are still taken as indicators of age, sexual availability, status, and general interest in self-presentation. Consequently, though the range of messages may be more limited, hair is nevertheless a communication vehicle for women.

Adornments   Speculation on why we clothe and beautify our bodies and what these behaviors mean has produced some provocative notions. Lawrence Frank's thesis is that clothing, cosmetics, and jewelry are all designed to stimulate the senses of touch and smell. Western civilization frowns on nudity and touching, so we find ways to experience the sensation of touch vicariously. We attempt to use our appearance as an approach signal. As he puts it,

each cultural group has a conception of the skin and tactile experiences which may or may not be explicitly recognized or stated, but is implied in its prescriptions for covering, exposing, decorating, making and avoiding tactile communication. . . . Thus, admiring glances, indicating approval of the individual's clothing, body arts and grooming, serve as surrogates for invitations to actual tactile contacts. . . . Grooming the skin, bathing of all kinds, anointing, oiling, perfuming the skin,

Figure 3.8   Even casual observation of almost any group of people should convince you that we can communicate attitudes, values, and backgrounds through the clothes we wear. Examine this photo for information presented via kinesics, too. (Norman Hurst/Stock Boston)

plucking hair, shaving, are patterns for modifying communication by the skin, again relying on visual cues to indicate tactual readiness for communication (actual or symbolic).[31]

The notion that clothing is an extension of the skin is not unique to Frank. One early work on the sexual symbolism of clothing even claimed that a man's coat symbolizes body hair.[32]

Among the features of adornment, *clothing* is probably the most meaningful as a communication medium (see Fig. 3.8). Dale Leathers, author of a popular textbook on nonverbal communication, has written, "Our social identity and image is defined, sustained and positively or negatively modified by communication through appearance. For most individuals the major medium of communication by appearance is dress."[33] Clothing as a protest device is a good example. During the Vietnam War, returning veterans often showed their opposition to the war by cutting off the sleeves of their uniforms, sewing rickrack around the edges, and replacing their combat unit insignia with a peace symbol or marijuana patch. Many antiwar protestors also sewed flags on the seat of their pants, an act for which many of them were arrested. At the same time, wearing a flag pin in the lapel was considered patriotic.

The color of clothing itself has been a symbolic message. Red, white, and blue are patriotic colors, while black—often used in armbands to protest various political actions—is a symbol of rejection or mourning.

The communicative power of attire is due in part to its obvious and immediate visual impact and in part to the number of possible variations. Fabric, color, pattern and design, style, neatness, and fashionableness can all be altered. Some efforts have been made to classify different types of clothing, but they have not been very productive. Our guess is that the dimensions of dress most relevant to communication are the degree of formality, choice of colors, the degree to which the outfit is fashionable, and the degree to which it is neat and

mini-experiment

Cut out a series of magazine pictures representing different kinds of dress. (Cut the models' heads off so only the clothing shows.) Ask several people to rate the pictures on attractiveness. At the same time, ask them to identify specifically what they think makes the clothing attractive. Compile a list of the factors. As a follow-up, you may want to try varying some of these factors in your own dress and ask other people to rate your attractiveness. If your initial inquiry was valid, judgments of your appearance should be influenced by the same factors as were judgments of the pictures. (You may even use the results to decide how you want to dress.)

well-fitting. An abundance of research indicates that dress is a significant communication variable, but until people are able to identify exactly what features are most important, we will not know what aspects produce the effects.

As for *dress norms,* they cannot be identified at a cultural level because there is too much variability. People's dress preferences are dictated by their psychological and sociological background. Dress codes are also often established by various jobs and professions. Banks may require female tellers to wear dresses and male tellers to wear suits and ties, while supermarkets may require pants or uniforms for all their employees. Their reasons for legislating certain dress standards could make an interesting study in itself. When our students conducted a survey, they found that most places of employment had formal or informal dress rules, but the employers and employees alike had a hard time explaining the reasons behind them. Often the purpose was couched in terms of safety or creating a positive public image. Since employers dictate their own dress standards, the norms vary from job to job.

Norms for *accessories and cosmetics* are similarly indeterminate, as are the reasons upon which they are based. They do, however, contribute to the communicative effect of physical appearance, as we shall see in later chapters. For instance, something as minor as wearing lipstick can alter the way a woman is perceived. Another cosmetic effect we shall mention later is plastic surgery. Because of the availability of all kinds of beauty aids and accessories (including wigs and contact lenses) and because of the use of plastic surgery techniques, people attribute communicative intent to the way others look. They assume that, since people are able to modify their appearance, they voluntarily choose to look the way they do. This assumption makes appearance a form of communication.

The Communication Potential of Physical Appearance

We have already alluded at several points to the communication capacity of physical appearance cues. In two respects, they have excellent message potential: first because so many features can be varied, and second because of their primacy effect—they are the first cues to be noticed in any interaction. In two other respects, though, physical appearance is restricted as a communication code.

The first limitation involves the notion of intent. While many features such as hair style may be intended as messages, others such as body type are not. Often a receiver will not attribute intent to such features, in which case they are merely information, not communication. However, as we have mentioned, many natural physical features may be regarded as

intentional because of the availability of means to alter them. As a result, we cannot be sure whether a message—and if so, what message—is actually being sent.

The other limitation is that physical appearance cues are more or less frozen during any interaction. Whatever impact they have occurs primarily at the beginning of a conversation. Minor adjustments can be made, such as smoothing the hair, removing glasses, or unbuttoning a shirt; but how we look is basically a fixed element. In terms of the communication functions we shall discuss in Part II, physical appearance gives a first-impression message. It cannot be altered with the dynamics of an interaction. Consider, for example, a woman being tried for murder. She may dress in conservative, modest clothes, wear little make-up, choose a simple hairstyle, and even wear glasses to cultivate a studious look. But if the whole effect leaves the jury unconvinced, other kinds of messages must take over to convey innocence.

Naturally, over the course of a relationship, it is possible to manipulate the appearance. Cher's television popularity has been attributed in part to capturing the public's imagination through her ability to change her appearance. Over time, people can communicate their political preferences, their status, their personality, and their mood for the day by the way they dress and groom themselves. Physical appearance cues, then, derive their main communication value from their strong initial impact and their possibilities for enormous variations during the course of a relationship.

Vocalics

Vocalics includes all stimuli produced by the human voice (other than words themselves) that affect the auditory sense. Everything from sniffs and sneezes to rapid speech, nasality, and singing fall into this category. So do silences and pauses during speech. Many scholars refer to this class of behaviors as *paralanguage* because it is what supports language (*para* meaning *alongside*). We have chosen not to use that label because some people apply it to more than just the voice, using it to cover any kinds of cues that work to clarify the interpretation of language, including all kinesic behaviors. We shall stick with the label *vocalics*.

Dimensions of Vocalics

The earliest and most widely adopted system for classifying vocalic cues was developed by George Trager.[34] He identified three elements to be considered in the study of the voice. The first is *voice set*. Voice set is not vocal behavior itself but rather the background against which vocal stimuli must be judged. It includes the physiological and physical peculiarities of the speaker that help identify that individual's sociological and psychological state. Thus, Trager calls attention to all the nonvoice features that influence our judgment of a voice. The actual vocal features can be grouped into two large classes, *voice qualities* and *vocalization*.

Voice qualities are the general distinguishable elements of the voice that accompany speech. They include all of the following:

1. pitch range (the spread of pitch levels used)
2. vocal lip control (ranging from heavy rasp or hoarseness to degrees of openness)
3. glottis control (thickness of tone quality)
4. pitch control (the sharpness and smoothness of transitions in pitch)
5. articulation control (degree of precision and forcefulness in pronunciation)
6. rhythm control (smoothness or jerkiness of phraseology)
7. resonance (degree of thinness or vibration in the voice)

8. tempo (rate of speaking, faster or slower than the norm)

Vocalizations are very specific sounds or aspects of sounds. They can be broken down into three subcategories:

1. *Vocal characterizers*—things like laughing, crying, giggling, snickering, whimpering, sobbing, yelling, whispering, mumbling, moaning, groaning, whining, breaking, belching, and yawning. Vocal characterizers are, as the label suggests, ways in which a speaking voice can be characterized. A writer might refer to the villain in a novel as having a whimpering or whining voice.
2. *Vocal qualifiers*—the specific acoustic characteristics of intensity, pitch height, and extent. *Intensity* refers to the amount of energy that is expended in making the sound. It is a critical factor in the perception of volume. *Pitch height* is the perceived highness or lowness of the voice. *Extent* is the duration of a given sound. Intensity ranges from overloud to oversoft, pitch height ranges from overhigh to overlow, and extent ranges from clipping to drawl.
3. *Vocal segregates*—sounds that are often referred to as *vocalized pauses* (sounds such as *uh*, *uh huh*, and *sh* that do not qualify as actual words), pauses, coughs, snorts, clicks, and sniffs. These sounds differ from characterizers in that they occur as interruptions of speech rather than simultaneous accompaniments.

Birdwhistell tells a delightful story that illustrates the communicative power of this last category of noises:

My mother's thin-lipped smile, which could be confined to her mouth, when accompanied by an audible input of air through her tightened nostrils required no words—Christian or otherwise—to reveal her attitude. My mother was a sniffer, a great sniffer. She could be heard for three rooms across the house. And, to paraphrase Mark Twain, her sniff had power; she could sniff a fly off the wall at 30 feet. I might even say, she was an irresponsible sniffer, for she always denied her sniffing. When we'd say, "Well, you don't have to sniff about it," she'd respond firmly, "I have something in my passages—and a lady doesn't blow her nose." "Mark my words," she'd say and sniff again.[35]

Because there are so many possible combinations of voice qualities and vocalizations, no two people ever sound exactly the same. Your voice is unique. If you doubt this, consider whether your friends ever have difficulty identifying your voice over the phone. If you have ever listened to a radio program or to a television program without looking at the picture, you probably had no difficulty picking out the voices of well-known people. Rod Serling's voice was unmistakable on commercials, and who could not recognize Barbara Walter's distinctive tones?

Our ability to make such fine discriminations among vocal cues is due to both the large number of elements that define the voice and the extraordinary ranges within these elements that the human ear can distinguish. The possible combinations of the eight dimensions of voice quality are hard to imagine, let alone the combinations of vocalizations. Couple those with the claim that loud speech is one million times as intense as whispered speech, and you have a lot of room for variability!

It is this great variety in voice patterns that has made possible the development of voice prints. Presumably, no two people have the same recorded voice print. Law enforcement agencies have used voice prints to identify criminals. In the state of Michigan, voice prints have been used to apprehend those who make false fire alarm calls and bomb threats. They have even been used to identify a caller who drew a policeman into an ambush with a false alarm. Some specialists in voice analysis are dubious about such uses of voice printing.

They do not believe that the prints can be interpreted as accurately as fingerprints, and they point out that voices can be disguised whereas fingerprints cannot. Even the skeptics, though, do not deny the uniqueness of individual voices and the amazing ability of the human ear to detect minute differences. Perhaps when our technology produces a computer as sensitive as the human ear, we can achieve greater accuracy in voice identification.

Vocal Norms and Standards

In the chapters on regulation, relational messages, affect displays, and manipulation, we shall mention some conversational norms governing specific vocal features—such as length of pauses—in the course of discussing their effects. In general, the concept of norms for separate vocal elements is pretty meaningless in terms of communication. We are more interested in how combinations of features operate. Paul Heinberg has identified a series of voice types based upon some common combinations of voice qualities.[36] Rather than look at norms, he makes a qualitative judgment about which voices are pleasant and unpleasant. The voice quality he considers good and thirteen deviant voice qualities are described below, along with some of the messages they are assumed to convey.

Good voice quality is the result of: sufficient muscle tone in the vocal folds to maintain a highly complex vocal tone at the desired frequency and intensity; positioning of the glottis at the correct vertical level; proper horizontal positioning of the tongue for articulation and audibility; proper use of the nasal cavity; and the right amount of sympathetic resonance. Confusing? Probably the best way to understand what makes a voice good is to consider all the things it is not. Maybe you can identify your own voice quality in the process.

One inappropriate voice is the *breathy*

voice. This is the voice quality that suits the stereotype of mindless women and female movie stars. Too much air escapes through the larynx because of insufficient muscle tension in the vocal folds and poor posture. It is a vocal quality much more common in women than in men. The breathy voice is supposed to connote immorality, stupidity, spinelessness, and lethargy. It also suggests seductiveness in women and homosexuality in men. When used for emphasis, breathiness also conveys softness, awe, lightness, love, passion, and admiration.

A second unacceptable quality is the *tense* voice. This is opposite of the breathy voice. Very little air is expelled, and the vocal folds open and close at a rapid rate. The tense voice often can convey uncooperativeness, emotional insecurity, and bad temper and make the listener tense. When used simply for effect, it can signal anger, rudeness, frustration, or cruelty.

The third voice is the *breathy–tense* voice, which comes from both poor posture and a tense larynx. The person with this voice type is probably perceived as nervous and weak.

The next four voice qualities are all more extreme versions of the tense voice. The *husky* voice sounds like a series of impulses; the *harsh* voice has been likened to the sound of rubbing coarse sandpaper; the *hard* voice has a continuous grating quality; and the *strident* voice sounds like metal hitting metal. The last is highly unusual and often is found in neurotic or psychotic individuals. All the negative characteristics that are attributed to the tense voice apply to these as well.

The eighth quality is the *nasal* voice, produced by too much resonance in the nasal passages. It can even become twangy. The person with this voice may be viewed as dull, lazy, and a whiner. When used for emphasis, this quality conveys repugnance, ugliness, boredom, complaint, and self-deprecation. Its opposite, the ninth voice quality, is *denasality*. This voice most often occurs when people have colds and can't get any resonance in

the nasal cavities. For this reason, it doesn't usually carry a message. However, sometimes people who have nasal voices nasalize some sounds and denasalize others. Then the characteristics associated with nasality apply.

The ninth quality is the *orotund* voice, commonly associated with preachers and politicians. It is the big, full voice that comes from too much resonance in the mouth cavity. Its owner may be viewed as idealistic, authoritarian, or pompous. It can also be used to suggest positiveness, expansiveness, and importance. Martin Luther King, Jr., in his "I Have a Dream" speech, effectively utilized this voice quality.

The next two voice types are related to the level of the glottis. The *flat* voice, which is often perceived as a low monotone, occurs when the glottis blocks out some tone qualities. The *thin* voice, which is often perceived as a high-pitched voice, is produced when the glottis blocks out a different set of tone qualities. In each case, the tones produced are less complex than is considered attractive. The person with a flat voice is assumed to be unemotional and unenthusiastic; the thin-voiced person may be considered immature, insecure, and indecisive. The flat voice, when used for emphasis, can indicate laziness, boredom, or displeasure. The thin voice, used for emphasis, can convey doubt, apology, or weakness.

The final two voice qualities are also opposites. They are the *throaty* voice, which results from moving the tongue upward and toward the back of the mouth, and the *fronted* voice, which results from moving the tongue forward and depressing it. Because the throaty voice forces the lips apart, it is sometimes difficult to understand. The muffled quality it produces may connote stupidity when associated with athletes, or it may connote aristocratic posturing. The fronted voice, by contrast, is very precise and conveys superciliousness, coldness, and disdain. Because British speech tends to employ this clipped pattern, Britishers are often regarded as aloof. When used for effect, throatiness can convey surprise, and frontedness, precision or irritability.

Several of these voice types have been empirically investigated for their communication effects. While not all the results are identical with Heinberg's conclusions, they are generally consistent. Later on, you might want to compare the findings in Chapter 6 on personality stereotypes and in Chapter 11 on the effects of voice features on comprehension to what we have mentioned here.

The Communication Potential of Vocalics

A detailed comparison of vocalizations in humans and a variety of other species, ranging from primates to birds to crickets, reveals that vocalics play an important role in the communication systems of many living beings.[37] For humans, they were probably the first form of communication, and because of the tremendous differentiation possible in both the encoding and decoding of such cues, they have remained a vital component in communication. Vocal cues are important in clarifying and amplifying verbal messages, and they carry important messages on their own as well. In the development of first impressions, they carry a wide range of information, ranging from the speaker's sex and occupation to ethnic background and personality. As interpersonal relationships develop, vocal cues communicate liking and attraction; they reveal status and power. Emotional messages depend heavily on vocal information; interactions are directed and controlled in part by adjustments in volume, rate, intensity, and quality, and impressions are managed through careful use of the voice. Research has also demonstrated that vocal features play a role in determining whether a listener's attitudes and behaviors are changed.

Once again, we must conclude that vocalics is an important nonverbal code. In contrast to haptics and physical appearance, this code is always in operation during a conversation and changes with the dynamics of the interaction. In this respect, it ranks with kinesics as a heavily used and dominant code.

Summary

In this chapter, we have looked at the four codes that rely on the human body as the vehicle for sending messages. In each case, we have identified the important structural features, the dimensions of the code that can be varied for communication purposes, the prevailing norms in our culture, and the general potential of the code as a medium for communication. While all four codes have a normative base and overlapping roles as transmitters of social and behavioral messages, the two codes that emerge as the most structured and the most versatile are kinesics and vocalics; by comparison, haptics and physical appearance are more restrictive in the specificity of their coding and the functions they perform. Consequently, kinesic and vocalic cues are generally the most powerful and widely used communication media. However, haptic or physical appearance messages may become important for certain functions.

In the next chapter, we shall analyze the three remaining codes.

Suggested Reading

Birdwhistell, R. L. *Kinesics and Context*. Philadelphia: University of Pennsylvania Press, 1970.

Birren, F. *Color Psychology and Color Therapy*. New York: McGraw-Hill, 1950.

Birren, F. "Emotional Significance of Color Preference." *American Journal of Occupational Therapy,* 6 (1952), 61–65.

Birren, F. *New Horizons in Color.* New York: Reinhold, 1955.

Burris-Meyer, E. *Color and Design in the Decoration Arts.* New York: Prentice-Hall, 1935.

Critchley, M. *The Lanugage of Gesture.* London: Edward Arnold and Company, 1939.

Darwin, C. *The Expression of the Emotions in Man and Animals.* Chicago: University of Chicago Press, 1965.

Davidson, L. G. "Some Current Folk Gestures and Sign Languages." *American Speech,* 25 (1950), 3–9.

Delaumosne, M. L. *The Art of Oratory, System of Delsarte.* Albany: Edgard S. Werner, 1882.

Ekman, P., and Friesen, W. V. "Hand Movements." *Journal of Communication,* 22 (1972), 353–374.

Ekman, P., and Friesen, W. V. "The Repertoire of Nonverbal Behavior: Categories, Origins, Usage and Coding." *Semiotica,* 1 (1969), 49–98.

Frank, L. K. "Cultural Patterning of Tactile Experiences." In L. A. Samovar and R. E. Porter (eds.), *Intercultural Communication: A Reader.* Belmont, Calif.: Wadsworth Press, 1972. (pp. 200–204)

Frank, L. K. "Tactile Communication." In H. A. Bosmajian, *The Rhetoric of Nonverbal Communication.* Glenview, Ill.: Scott, Foresman, 1971. (pp. 34–56)

Gibbons, K., and Gwynn, T. K. "A New Theory of Fashion Change: A Test of Some Predictions." *British Journal of Social and Clinical Psychology,* 14 (1975), 1–9.

Harrison, R. *Beyond Words.* Englewood Cliffs, N.J.: Prentice-Hall, 1974.

Heinberg, P. *Voice Training for Speaking and Reading Aloud.* New York: Ronald Press, 1964.

Knapp, M. L. *Nonverbal Communication in Human Interaction.* New York: Holt, Rinehart and Winston, 1972.

Luscher, M. *The Luscher Color Test.* New York: Random House, 1969.

Montagu, A. *Touching: The Human Significance of the Skin.* New York: Harper and Row, 1971.

Morris, D. *The Naked Ape.* New York: McGraw-Hill, 1967.

Morris, D. *Intimate Behavior.* New York: Random House, 1971.

Prescott, J. W. "Body Pleasure and the Origins of Violence." *The Futurist* (April 1975), 64–74.

Saral, T. B. "Cross-Cultural Generality of Communication Via Facial Expressions." In D. C. Speer (ed.), *Nonverbal Communication.* Beverly Hills: Sage, 1972. (pp. 97–110)

Trager, G. L. "Paralanguage: A First Approximation." *Studies in Linguistics,* 13, Nos. 1 and 2 (1958), 1–10.

Wolff, C. *A Psychology of Gesture.* New York: Arno, 1972.

Notes

1. J. Ruesch and W. Kees, *Nonverbal Communication: Notes on the Visual Perception of Human Relations* (Berkeley: University of California Press, 1956).
2. C. Cherry, *On Human Communication* (Cambridge: M.I.T. Press, 1957, 1966), pp. 130–131.
3. The actual estimates and related discussion are to be found in R. L. Birdwhistell, *Kinesics and Context* (Philadelphia: University of Pennsylvania Press, 1970); G. W. Hewes, "The Anthropology of Posture," *Scientific American,* 196 (1957), pp. 123–132; M. H. Krout, "An Experimental Attempt to Determine the Significance of Unconscious Manual Symbolic Movements," *Journal*

of *General Psychology,* 51 (1954), pp. 93–120; M. H. Krout, "An Experimental Attempt to Produce Unconscious Manual Symbolic Movements," *Journal of General Psychology,* 51 (1954), pp. 121–152; M. H. Krout, "Autistic Gestures: An Experimental Study in Symbolic Movement," *Psychological Monographs,* 46, No. 4 (1935), pp. 1–119; M. Pei, *The Story of Language,* 2nd edition (Philadelphia: J. B. Lippincott, 1965).

4. R. Sohl and A. Carr (eds.), *The Gospel According to Zen* (New York: New American Library, 1970), pp. 3–4. Originally published in Paul Reps' *Zen Flesh, Zen Bones* (Tokyo: Tuttle, 1957).

5. Birdwhistell (note 3).

6. P. Ekman and W. V. Friesen, "The Repertoire of Nonverbal Behavior: Categories, Usage, and Coding," *Semiotica,* 1 (1969), pp. 49–98.

7. G. W. Allport and P. E. Vernon, *Studies in Expressive Movement* (New York: Hafner, 1937).

8. P. Ekman, "Movements with Precise Meanings," *Journal of Communication,* 26, No. 3 (1976), pp. 14–26.

9. M. L. Delaumosne, *The Art of Oratory, System of Delsarte* (Albany: Edgar S. Werner, 1882).

10. For a summary of related research findings, see P. C. Ellsworth and L. M. Ludwig, "Visual Behavior in Social Interactions," *Journal of Communication,* 22 (1972), pp. 375–403.

11. L. K. Frank, "Cultural Patterning of Tactile Experiences," *Genetic Psychological Monographs,* 56 (1957), pp. 209–225.

12. L. K. Frank, "Tactile Communication," in H. A. Bosmajian (ed.), *The Rhetoric of Nonverbal Communication* (Glenview, Ill.: Scott, Foresman, 1971), p. 37.

13. H. Harlow, "Love in Monkeys," *Scientific American,* 200 (1959), pp. 68–74; H. Harlow and M. Harlow, "The Effect of Rearing Conditions on Behavior," *Bulletin of the Meninger Clinic,* 26 (1962), pp. 213–224.

14. See, for example, J. L. Despert, "Emotional Aspects of Speech and Language Development," *International Journal of Psychiatry and Neurology,* 105 (1941), pp. 193–222; A. Montagu, *Touching: The Human Significance of the Skin* (New York: Harper and Row, 1971).

15. J. L. Prescott, "Body Pleasure and the Origins of Violence," *The Futurist,* 9 (1975), pp. 64–74.

16. V. S. Clay, "The Effect of Culture on Mother–Child Tactile Communication," dissertation, Columbia University, 1966. Clay also found that children receive the most touch during the period of fourteen months to twenty-four months.

17. S. M. Jourard, "An Exploratory Study of Body-Accessibility," *British Journal of Social and Clinical Psychology,* 5 (1966), pp. 221–231.

18. L. B. Rosenfeld, S. Kartus, and C. Ray, "Body Accessibility Revisited," *Journal of Communication,* 26, No. 3 (1976), pp. 27–30.

19. F. N. Willis and G. E. Hoffman, "Development of Tactile Patterns in Relation to Age, Sex and Race," *Development Psychology,* 11 (1975), p. 886.

20. D. N. Walker, "A Dyadic Interaction Model for Nonverbal Touching Behavior in Encounter Groups," *Small Group Behavior,* 6 (1975), pp. 308–324.

21. K. Leibowitz and P. A. Andersen, "The Development and Nature of the Construct *Touch Avoidance,*" paper presented at the Speech Communication Association Convention, San Francisco, December 1976.

22. M. Clynes, "Sentic Cycles: The Seven Passions at Your Fingertips," *Psychology Today,* 5, No. 12 (1972), pp. 58–72.

23. T. Nguyen, R. Heslin, and M. L. Nguyen, "The Meanings of Touch: Sex Differences," *Journal of Communication,* 25, No. 3 (1975), pp. 92–103.

24. J. G. Martin, "Racial Ethnocentrism and Judgment of Beauty," *Journal of Social Psychology,* 63 (1964), pp. 59–63.

25. A. H. Illife, "A Study of Preferences in Feminine Beauty," *British Journal of Psychology,* 51 (1960), pp. 267–273.

26. C. Darwin, "The Descent of Man and Selection in Relation to Sex," in *Great Books of the Western World,* vol. 49, Darwin (Chicago: Encyclopedia Britannica, 1952), p. 577.

27. E. Walster, V. Aronson, D. Abrahams, and L. Rottman, "Importance of Physical Attractiveness in Dating Behavior," *Journal of Personality and Social Psychology,* 4 (1966), pp. 508–516.

28. See E. Berscheid and E. Walster, "Physical Attractiveness," in L. Berkowitz (ed.), *Advances in Experimental Social Psychology,* vol. 7 (New York: Academic Press, 1974), pp. 157–215 for a review of other studies and a discussion of why attractiveness is preferred.

29. J. Brophy, *The Human Face Reconsidered* (London: George C. Harrap and Company, 1962), p. 186.

30. J. B. Cortes and F. M. Gatti, "Physique and Propinquity," *Psychology Today*, 4, No. 5 (1970), pp. 42–44, 82–84.

31. L. K. Frank, 1971 (note 12).

32. E. J. Harnik, "Pleasure in Disguise, the Need for Decoration and the Sense of Beauty," *The Psychoanalytic Quarterly*, 1 (1932), pp. 216–264.

33. D. G. Leathers, *Nonverbal Communication Systems* (Boston: Allyn and Bacon, 1976), p. 96. A similar position is expressed in K. Gibbons and T. K. Gwynn, "A New Theory of Fashion Change: A Test of Some Predictions," *British Journal of Social and Clinical Psychology,* 14 (1975), pp. 1–9.

34. G. L. Trager, "Paralanguage: A First Approximation," *Studies in Linguistics,* 13, Nos. 1 and 2 (1958), pp. 1–12.

35. Birdwhistell, pp. 52–53 (note 3).

36. P. Heinberg, *Voice Training for Speaking and Reading Aloud* (New York: Ronald Press, 1964).

37. W. H. Thorpe, "The Comparison of Vocal Communication in Animals and Man," in R. A. Hinde (ed.), *Non-Verbal Communication* (Cambridge: Cambridge University Press, 1972), pp. 27–48.

4

Codes II: Space, Time, and Artifacts

Test Your Sensitivity

True or False?

1. Like many other species, human beings have a need for their own territory.
2. The primary factor influencing what distance people adopt from one another is whether they like each other.
3. In most cultures, keeping someone waiting more than a half hour is considered rude.
4. People who communicate in unattractive surroundings are more likely to focus on the conversation and develop more positive feelings about the people involved.
5. To produce lively conversations, you should pick a blue-colored room with dim lighting.

In this chapter, we shall look at those means of communicating nonverbally that involve manipulating something besides the human body itself. We shall consider the use of space, time, environment, and objects as nonverbal communication.

Proxemics

The flow and shift of distance between people as they interact with each other is part and parcel of the communication process.
—Edward T. Hall[1]

When is another person too close, too far? How do you feel about someone who takes your chair? When you sit down to talk to friends, where do you sit? What reactions do you have when you walk into a large office in which the person you have come to see is seated behind a massive desk? All of these questions are relevant to the study of *proxemics,* which is how man perceives, structures, and uses space. Everything from how far you stand from other customers in line at a grocery store to how you arrange the furniture in your bedroom is of interest to those who study proxemics.

When we talked about haptics, we emphasized the strong need people have for physical contact. We know that does not mean that we want to touch everybody. For instance, people riding in an elevator always move to make room for new riders rather than touch strangers; and people are resentful when they have to travel in a crowded bus or subway where physical contact is inescapable. During a football game, people are willing to tolerate close contact, but once the game is over, there is a great rush for the exit to escape the crowd. Is there a contradiction here between the need for touch and the desire to avoid it, to maintain some distance?

Probably not. The best explanation is that human beings have two kinds of needs, *affilia-*

By the end of the chapter, you should know the correct answer to all five questions and understand these concepts:

- proxemics
- difference between territoriality and personal space
- types of territories
- factors influencing personal space norms
- reactions to violations of proxemic norms
- communication functions of proxemics
- chronemics
- American concept of time
- psychological time orientations
- biological time systems
- cultural time systems
- communication functions of chronemics
- factors influencing environmental preferences
- dimensions of artifacts
- optimal environmental conditions for communication
- communication potential of objects and environmental features

tive needs and *privacy needs*. At times we want to affiliate with others, to be close; but at other times, we need to have some privacy, to feel that some degree of space is completely ours and inviolate. Our affiliative needs are satisfied by selected individuals—family, friends, people we are attracted to—rather than by strangers. That is why we want contact only with certain people rather than with random individuals. Sometimes we even require distance from the people we like to touch. Our need for privacy is really a need to control the opening and closing of ourselves to others, the freedom to be alone and to restrict access to certain spaces. This need for privacy is reflected in our proxemic behavior and influences the kinds of messages we send through the medium of space. Two primary subcategories of proxemics that arise out of different needs and that can be manipulated as messages are *territoriality* and *personal space*.

Territoriality

Territoriality refers to claiming and defending a geographic territory as one's own. Territories are staked out as a means of protecting the self and providing privacy. Your apartment, house, or room is obviously your territory, and you have the right to defend it against intruders. You may also have some less clearly defined spaces that you treat as your territory. Many students pick out their chair in a classroom and return to it habitually for the rest of the course. Many housewives feel that their kitchen is their territory in the home and resent interference from children, husbands, or well-meaning friends. Their husbands may treat their study, tool shed, or favorite chair in the same way. Because the markers of these territories are either hardly noticeable or totally absent, many people may intrude upon them accidentally, causing distress to the owner because of the social custom that prevents us from asking an invader to leave. If

someone has ever taken your seat in class, you probably just moved to a new one rather than make a fuss. Of course, sometimes the territory is too important to suffer the intrusion in silence.

This territoriality in man has parallels in a wide range of other animal species. The specific patterns of claiming and defending territories differ from birds to lions to dogs, but most species appear to have some territorial instincts. Students of human behavior have been interested in whether man's territorial behaviors are also instinctual. If so, it means that messages of territorial defense or intrusion can be very powerful. Anthropologists have claimed that the ancient ancestors of man were territorial hunters and that this in addition to our history of warfare establishes man's primordial need for territory.[2] The assumption of a biological need for territory has led scientists to investigate the effects of inadequate territory among other mammals with an eye toward the possible implications for humans.

Animal Studies on Crowding One of the best-known studies on overcrowding was made by J. B. Calhoun.[3] He studied what happened to rats when they were confined in a space too small for their population. Everything else in their environment was adequate; they had enough food, water, and air and had social contact with other rats. Nevertheless, the lack of space led to some bizarre behaviors. Female rats changed their nesting and nursing habits, ignored their young, and had many premature births. Infant mortality was high. Male rats attacked each other, engaged in homosexuality, killed and ate the young, or withdrew from each other in fear. Calhoun labeled the general deterioration of their living patterns a *behavioral sink*.

Another revealing study was conducted by John Christian on an island in Chesapeake Bay where he observed overcrowding among Sika deer.[4] Prior to Christian's arrival, the deer population had been increasing rapidly. Though the island supplied adequate food and water to support them, and there were no predators, mysteriously, the deer suddenly began to die in droves. The population dropped from 300 to eighty. When Christian performed autopsies on the deer, he found no evidence of disease; but he did find that their adrenal glands were one-fourth to one-third larger than those of normal deer. After the population tapered off, the adrenal glands underwent a radical reduction in size. Christian concluded that stress from the overcrowded conditions caused the epidemic of deaths. He extended his study of the effects of overcrowding on adrenal activity to mice, dogs, guinea pigs, monkeys, and even man, and concluded that they all respond similarly. Recent field and laboratory studies provide more direct evidence of the effects of overcrowding on humans.

Human Studies on Crowding Several investigations using census data have linked population density to serious health and mental problems.[5] These studies, ranging from midtown Manhattan to inner-city Paris, have found such aberrations as greater crime, tuberculosis, respiratory ailments, mental illness, infant mortality, juvenile delinquency, and suicide in congested locales.

Controlled experiments have also confirmed the detrimental effects of overcrowding on the quality of human life. One series of studies placed pairs of men in confined, isolated spaces similar to a submarine compartment for two weeks. Many found the situation impossible to cope with and terminated the experiment early. Those who stayed displayed strong territoriality and *cocooning* behavior. They marked off their separate spaces and withdrew to them frequently. Many had difficulty getting along with their partner for so long.[6]

Other recent investigations have looked at the effects of dormitory crowding. Researchers at Stony Brook University compared the behaviors of students living in corridor-style dorms, which require daily contact with as many as thirty-three other residents, and those living in suite-style dorms, which impose frequent contact with only the three to five suite mates. Despite the fact that students in both living arrangements had about the same amount of living space, those in the corridor dormitories reported more feelings of crowding, maintained a greater distance from a confederate in an experimental task, felt more uneasy about the possibility of participating in a cooperative task (which usually requires considerable personal involvement), and performed better than suite residents in a competitive task. By contrast, suite residents could tolerate more people in a given space before they experienced crowding; they maintained closer distances to a confederate; and they performed better on cooperative tasks or when working alone.[7] Another dormitory study in a different locale found that students in high-density dorms also had much more negative attitudes about the warmth and friendliness of their fellow residents and the dormitory itself than did those in the lower-density housing.[8]

The fact that crowding has such an impact on people means that it can have important consequences in communication. This is evident from studies of actual interactions. When people find themselves crowded by too many other people, whether on a playground, in a psychiatric ward, or in an experimental laboratory, they respond with asocial behavior.[9] When crowding takes the form of being placed in a small room, males in all-male groups display negative reactions, but females in all-female groups become pleasant and intimate.[10] Daniel Stokols makes the point that it is not the actual room size or number of people in the room that defines crowding but whether one *feels* crowded. If being in a small space doesn't bother you, or if in a cramped social situation you still feel you have the freedom to leave, then you are not really experiencing crowding. It is only if you feel hemmed in with no access to escape that crowding becomes a problem.[11] Carving out territories is one way of reducing the sensation of overcrowding; territories offer a place to retreat to, and they permit control over the space.

Types of Territories   Four general types of territory can be identified, each with a different degree of access.[12] *Public* territory is any locale that is open to all. Public streets, movie theaters, city buses, and parks all fall into this category. The next most accessible type of territory is *interactional*. This is territory designed for social interaction but to which access is restricted to those who have a legitimate right to participate in that interaction. An empty classroom of a public university is a public territory, but when it is filled with students holding class, it is interactional and limited to those who are enrolled. The third type of territory is *home* territory. This is any geographic space, be it grass hut, tent, or mansion, that someone regards as home. Those who live there have the right to control access to it. A person's work space away from home qualifies as home territory. An office or desk is viewed as a private possession not to be violated by others.

One of the authors knew a couple in graduate school who moved into their professor's office. The office was carpeted, had comfortable furniture, a refrigerator, and a bathroom with a bathtub. It was not an unpleasant place to live; but the situation certainly created confusion about whose territory it was. In practice, it gradually worked out that during the day the room belonged to the professor and at night to the students. Everyone became so accustomed to this arrangement that the professor actually began apologizing when he returned to his office at night to work. Fortunately he was very good-natured about the situation and grumbled only occasionally about finding laundry hanging from the ceiling pipes. He was willing to let what was his home territory serve as someone else's home territory in his absence. The only real problem that arose is that the couple's open access led many others to view the office as an interactional territory—a lounge—rather than a private office with restricted availability.

Because of the confusion that sometimes arises about whether a territory belongs to someone, people use various kinds of markers to indicate ownership of a space (see Fig. 4.1). Things like clothing, umbrellas, books, and other personal possessions are frequently used. Even something as simple as a bottle of suntan lotion may effectively tell others that a beach chair belongs to you. It is interesting to note what powerful messages such markers carry. If someone accidentally leaves a newspaper at a cafeteria table, that space may remain unused for the rest of the day.

The final type of territory is *body* territory. This is the human body itself and the space immediately surrounding it. It is the most private territory and is not to be violated except by those select few who are granted that right. Our culture feels very strongly about the integrity of the human body, and we are incensed when it is violated through rape, assault, or murder. Some other cultures do not share that view, at least as far as sexual violation is involved. In fact, men in such cultures may offer their wives and daughters for the pleasure of their guests. Nevertheless, even this practice involves some notion of body territory that is not to be touched except with permission, even if that permission comes from a spouse or parent rather than the person herself. The concept of body territory is closely related to the concept of personal space; in reality, they may be the same thing.

Personal Space

There is an old German fable that goes something like this: Once upon a time, the porcupines gathered together for a little socializing on a cold night. Because of the chill air, they tried to move close together but found that they kept pricking each other with their quills.

So they moved farther apart, but they got cold again. They continued to rearrange themselves until they found a distance at which they could be both warm and comfortable. From that time on, that distance was known as good manners.

We call that distance *personal space*. Personal space differs from territory in that it is not a fixed geographic area but an invisible bubble of space that travels with the individual. This portable bubble surrounding a person is variable in size: it expands and contracts according to the situation. It may be very large when someone is in a strange and hostile environment and may shrink to nothing in the presence of a loved one.

The way we relate spatially to other people appears to be highly normative. That is, social norms govern what distances are to be maintained. These norms are based on a combination of the same three classes of factors that govern kinesic norms: characteristics of the people involved, the nature of the interaction itself, and features of the environment.[13]

People Characteristics　A number of important relationships have been uncovered in this category:[14]

1. *Sex.* Men stand or sit farther apart from each other than do women. Opposite-sex pairs tend to stand or sit closer together than do

Figure 4.1　What territorial markers are present here?

same-sex pairs (although female–female pairs have sometimes been observed to be closer than male–female pairs). A key factor is who is stationary: men and women both approach closer to a seated or standing female than a male.

2. *Age*. People maintain closer distances with peers than with those who are either younger or older than themselves. This holds true even if the older person is a parent.

3. *Race*. People approach members of their own race closer than those of different races. One exception that has been noted is that blacks establish the same distance from a white interviewer as from a black interviewer. There is some evidence that blacks generally prefer more intimate distances for conversation than whites. However, when race is considered in combination with sex, black males in an interview setting have maintained the greatest distance and black females the least, with white males and females falling in between.

4. *Culture*. Norms vary from culture to culture, some societies being classified as *contact cultures* and others as *noncontact cultures*. The culture of the United States, which discourages touch or very close proximity in normal conversation, is a noncontact culture. Our typical distance for conversation is 18 inches to 28 inches.

5. *Status*. The greater the difference in status, the greater the distance.

6. *Familiarity*. People stand farther from strangers than from acquaintances. The least distance is naturally maintained among close friends.

7. *Attraction and liking*. The obvious holds true here. People stand and sit closer to those whom they like.

8. *Personality*. Research has established that different personality types have varying needs for space. For instance, introverts require more space than extroverts. Some intriguing studies of prisoners with violent tendencies have revealed that they need as much as twice the

Figure 4.2

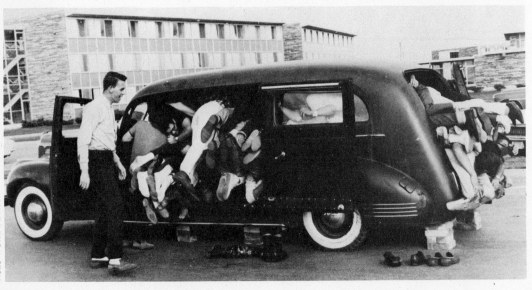

space that nonviolent people require. (This might explain why they become hostile when others approach them at the normative distance; they feel threatened.)

9. *Mood.* A person's psychological state may alter the distance pattern he or she typically adopts. For instance, anxiety leads to increased distance. Emotionally disturbed individuals have been known to adopt deviant seating patterns. Because we are frequently unable to identify another's mood precisely (especially with strangers), this last factor can seriously complicate our ability to predict accurately what distance patterns to expect in a given situation.

Interaction Characteristics   Adding to the complexity of the factors influencing the norms are the features of the interaction itself. Here are the more important variables:[15]

1. *Formality.* The more formal and impersonal the situation or topic, the greater the distance. Edward Hall has proposed a breakdown of personal space that conforms to this aspect of an interaction. He breaks space into four different categories. *Intimate* distance is up to 18 inches and is reserved for the closest of relationships. *Personal–casual* distance ranges from 1½ feet to 4 feet and is used for normal informal conversations. *Social–consultative* distance extends from 4 feet to 12 feet and is used for activities ranging from less personal social conversations to business transactions. *Public* distance is anything beyond 12 feet and is used for public addresses. While the specific distances Hall has attached to each category may be moot, the types of interactions and their order make good sense.

2. *Familiarity with the setting.* One study found that people who are familiar with a room or expect to interact in it in the future maintain closer distances. They appear to personalize the setting, developing a sense of ownership.

3. *Purpose of the interaction.* People tolerate different distances depending upon whether or not they expect to communicate with their immediate neighbors and for what purpose. In a classroom, where attention is usually focused on the front of the room rather than toward one's neighbors, students tolerate intimate distances. When working on a cooperative task or discussion, they remain relatively close. At a table, for instance, they take adjacent or cross-corner seats. When competing on a task, however, they increase the distance, taking opposite seats, which permit some protection from surveillance. Finally, when people are working at tasks that do not require communication or for which they wish to discourage communication, they establish much greater distances. A student reading at a library table, for example, would just as soon not share it and usually attempts to discourage others from invading that territory.

4. *Leadership.* A final interactional consideration is whether a group has a leader or not. If it does, the position taken by the leader often influences the distances others establish. Leaders usually take the most dominant or central positions, the ones that give them the greatest control of the interaction patterns. The distances others adopt from them depend on each person's interpersonal relationship with the leader and other members of the group, their desire to dominate, and the functional constraints of the arrangement of the furniture.

Environmental Characteristics   All the elements of the environment can affect the normative distance. The architectural style of a house or room, the color of appointments, the type of furniture, the temperature, the lighting, the noise level, and even the number of other people present all combine to determine what distance is comfortable. We shall look at just a few of these factors.[16]

1. *Amount of physical space available.* The larger the volume of space available, the closer together people sit or stand. In a large museum

or banquet hall, people place themselves closer together than in a living room. This may be because a large space makes hearing more difficult unless people are close together, or it may be because the availability of space in the immediate environment to which they can retreat makes it less important to increase the distance for conversation.

2. *Population density.* Obviously when the number of people in an enclosed space goes up, the amount of space between people goes down. With the arrival of each new addition, the available space is redivided equally. The presence of many people also increases the noise level, making smaller distances a necessity if people are to hear one another.

3. *Furniture.* The style and arrangement of furniture arbitrarily influence distance. People gravitate to comfortable furniture first, which then dictates what seats others may take. Interior designers suggest that the arc for comfortable conversation in a home is about 8 feet. People therefore choose those seats that best approximate that distance. If the only seats available are either significantly closer or farther than that, people may actually prefer to sit on the floor. Where people have a choice, they will sit across from each other before they will take side-by-side seating up to the point where

mini-experiment

Take someone else's seat in a library, cafeteria, or movie theater while he or she is temporarily out of it. Note the reaction when the person returns. If she or he asks to have the seat back, say you were there first and see how the person responds.

comfortable distance is exceeded; then they will sit side by side. When the furniture includes a table, people will usually take corner-to-corner seating for a square table and adjacent seating for a round table. Of course, the nature of the interaction—whether it is formal or intimate and whether there is a leader or not—can override these normative patterns. For instance, people who are courting will almost always choose the most intimate seating, such as side-by-side on a sofa.

We have said that territoriality and touch reflect two different needs, a need for privacy and a need for affiliation. In any interaction, people strive for the best balance between the two. Usually the norm reflects the position that best satisfies the combined needs of the parties involved. Typically we are unaware of our normative behaviors because they are such well-learned habits. However, when the norms are violated and the equilibrium is destroyed, proxemic behaviors become conscious and attempts are made to restore balance.

Reactions to Norm Violations

People react very strongly to encroachments on their territory or personal space. Some of the best-known studies have been made by Robert Sommer in a library setting.[17] Sommer's researchers singled out people working at a library table by themselves and sat either across from, a few seats away from, or directly next to them. Observers at other tables then watched the reactions of those whose space had been invaded. Responses were relatively consistent. Rarely did people speak and ask the invader to move. Instead, they tried to build barriers between themselves and the intruder by placing books and materials between them (markers), using their body as a barricade, and reorienting their body position away from the intruder. Frequently they pulled their elbows in, shaded their eyes, leaned backward and scratched their head—anything to remove themselves from the invader without appearing to be bothered. Usually the subjects avoided eye contact, but a few glared hostilely at the intruder. After increasing distance and sending cues of irritation, many subjects gave up and took flight. It was clear that people could not tolerate the spatial invasion for any length of time.

Other studies using similar techniques have come up with the same findings.[18] People show signs of anxiety when their space has been invaded and attempt to reduce it by either increasing the physical and psychological distance or retreating completely. Some researchers have verified this anxiety effect through direct physiological measures of the individual whose space is being invaded.[19] In one clever test of this effect, subjects were approached by other people, paper figures, and objects while their galvanic skin response was measured. Approaches were made from the front, the side, and the rear. Reactions were greatest to invasions by other people, with the most reaction coming when a person was approached from the rear. Another experiment similarly found that people comfortably approach much closer to an object (a hatrack) than to another person, which suggests that the presence of people in our immediate environment and not just the loss of space alone makes us anxious.

These findings demonstrate yet another way in which people react to invasions of personal space: they treat others as nonpersons, that is, they treat them as an object rather than a living organism that deserves attention and respect. This reaction is nowhere more evident than in a public elevator. Notice how people behave. They all pretend that there are not living, breathing people standing next to them. They stare at the floor indicator and avoid communication, behaving as if the bodies next to them are mere dummies. Sommer explains why peo-

ple respond this way: "A nonperson cannot invade someone's personal space any more than a tree or chair can."[20] Regarding people in our immediate environment as a chair or hatrack eases tension that a spatial invasion creates; the reaction denies that an invasion is actually occurring. After all, inanimate objects are not a threat. This explains in part why people become uneasy when an occasional good-natured soul breaks the elevator norm and strikes up a conversation. By forcing us to respond to them as people, they make us aware of how vulnerable we are in that confined space and how small the buffer between us is. If New Yorkers had to treat all the people they meet daily on the street as real people rather than as nonpersons, their anxiety level would probably soar. The assignment of nonperson roles to those thousands of strangers allows a person to reduce psychologically some of the stress that already exists from so many forces pushing in on one's meager amount of personal space. (See Figure 4.3.)

While people react negatively to serious encroachments on their personal space, they are also uncomfortable with too much space. Miles Patterson and Lee Sechrest had people conduct interviews at distances ranging from 2 feet to 9 feet. When people interacted at the greater distance, they tried to compensate for it by leaning forward, increasing eye contact, and moving their chairs closer. At the closer distance, the opposite reactions occurred—people tried to increase the distance and reduced eye contact.[21] This supports the notion that we try to achieve some balance between too much and too little space.

The Communication Potential of Proxemics

The effects of inadequate territory and inappropriate personal space patterns demonstrate the power of proxemics in general and its potential as a communication code in specific. A wide range of messages can be communicated through the medium of space. Not only do proxemic and environmental factors combine to regulate the flow of interaction; a person's use of territory and distance can also play a role in the development of interpersonal relationships, self-presentation, and the manipulation of others. Such things as how one marks a territory, whose territory is used to conduct negotiations, and what violations of personal space norms occur can all have message value. We shall look at all these things in the chapters that follow.

Chronemics

You may delay but time will not.
—Benjamin Franklin

Time talks. It speaks more plainly than words. The message it conveys comes through loud and clear. . . . It can shout the truth where words lie.

—Edward T. Hall[22]

Perhaps more than anyone else, Edward Hall is responsible for calling our attention to the

Figure 4.3   Personal space is kept at a minimum in a phone booth. Only the physical barriers and the psychological barrier they provide allow phone-booth users to maintain the pretense of privacy. Would these people feel as comfortable if they were together in an elevator? (Terry McKoy)

communicative power of time. *Chronemics* is the study of how we perceive, structure, and react to time and of the messages we interpret from such usage.

Our concept of time is central to the way we view the world; it colors all of our actions and interactions. In our culture, time is the master and we are its slaves. We play an endless game of beat the clock. We have a strong sense of urgency, a strong feeling that we must move forward into the future.

For Americans, time is a precious resource not to be wasted or taken lightly. We view it as a material object, a commodity: we buy time, save time, spend time, make time. It is seen somehow as a concrete object or container with defined boundaries, as if it had spatial characteristics. It is something we fill. This view of time as something tangible carries over to the ways we mark its passage. We see it as highly divisible: it can be broken down into years, months, days, hours, minutes, seconds, and even milliseconds. When people ask how long they must wait for something, they do not want an approximation such as *before the next full moon;* they want a very specific answer in terms of days or hours or minutes.

The obsession with time in our culture is reflected in the way we schedule our activities and in our consciousness of being off schedule. Every minute must be planned and accounted for. College courses meet for a designated number of minutes and must not deviate from that schedule. Imagine what would happen if a professor simply continued a class until the end of a train of thought and then dismissed students to attend their next class. It would create havoc in the system. Italian television follows this kind of pattern. Programs continue until they are finished; then the next one starts. For American viewers, who are used to each program starting promptly on the hour or half hour, the Italian system seems chaotic and irresponsible if not immoral. But it may not be any crazier than our system that

forces television plots to fit into a precise period or that forces school classes to end even if the teacher is in midsentence when the bell rings. No matter what stage of progress a worker is in on a job, when the lunch whistle blows, the work is abandoned. We are expected to turn our creative energies on and off according to whistles, bells, and time clocks. Those who must daily punch a time clock must neither start nor end their workday too early or too late. The system allows a person neither to donate a few extra minutes some days without pay nor to take a few extra minutes without being docked.

Time is clearly an overriding force in our day-to-day conduct. However, this is not always the case in other cultures and even in American subcultures. Perceptions of time vary enormously across societies. The Sioux Indians, for example, have no words for *late* or *waiting.* The Pueblo Indians do things "when the time is right" and not earlier, and no one can explain exactly what makes the time right. Arab cultures and Oriental cultures have a much vaster notion of time than ours; the present seems inconsequential when seen against the larger scheme of things. We can gain a better understanding of why these significant differences exist by examining time at three different perceptual levels: the psychological, the biological, and the cultural.

Psychological Time Orientations

Joost Meerloo has labeled psychological time *clinical time,* which he defines as "every person's unconscious and partly conscious concept of his personal life span between birth and death."[23] Our concern about death makes us conscious of the passage of time and the way we use it. Perhaps because many Americans fear death, we have come to value time highly. References to the slipping away of time and lost time create strong emotional reactions in us. The lyrics of some popular songs highlight our emotional involvement with time and death; Jim Croce's "Time in a Bottle" and Bob Dylan's "If Tomorrow Wasn't Such a Long Time" are just two of many examples that come to mind. Time is the measuring stick by which we evaluate our successes and pleasures.

Our clinical sense of time is evident in our personal time orientations. People exhibit four different time orientations, each of which implies a different way of relating to self and others.[24] The first is a *past* orientation. The individual with this view is always reliving old times, retelling old incidents. Events are seen as circular—past incidents keep recurring in the present. Old ways of responding are applied to similar new situations. This person takes the old adage about learning from the past seriously. The second type is the *time-line* orientation. The individual with this view sees time as a systematic progression, following a line rather than a circle. The past, present, and future are all well integrated. Unlike the past-oriented person, who views time sentimentally, the time-line person takes a scientific and analytical view of events. The third perspective is the *present* orientation. This is a spontaneous, immediacy-oriented view of events. No integration is needed with the past. Activities are simply enjoyed as they occur and problems handled when they arise. Pleasure comes from the here and now, not from what happened yesterday or may possibly happen tomorrow. The last orientation is toward the *future*. Future-oriented individuals spend much time anticipating what will happen rather than paying attention to what is occurring at the moment. They are interested in speculating on what the future will bring and then relating that to the present.

It should be apparent that these different time orientations affect the ways in which people conduct their lives, which in turn are translated into messages to other people about the values they place on time, on activity, on the past, and on people themselves.

Biological Time Systems

The human body has its own time patterns that are based on natural rhythms. What we often take as random, unpredictable changes in mood or alertness or energy are really due to regular cycles in our psychophysiological system. Everything from our body temperature and metabolic rate to our hearing ability and sleeping habits follow natural rhythms. It is these rhythms, which vary somewhat from person to person, that explain why some people are day people and others night people. The three cycles we know the most about are a *physical* cycle, which averages about twenty-three days, a *sensitivity* cycle, which averages about twenty-eight days, and an *intellectual* cycle, which averages about thirty-three days.

The *physical cycle* involves a person's energy and endurance level. In the first part of this cycle, the individual is highly alert and energetic; in the second half, energy and endurance are at a low ebb. Similarly, the *sensitivity cycle,* which involves our emotional fluctuations, goes through a period of cheerfulness and cooperativeness and then a period of irritability and apathy. The *intellectual cycle* shows the same up-and-down pattern, from peaks in alertness and mental accomplishments to valleys. For all three cycles, the day on which the cycle shifts from positive to negative can be especially critical. For the physical cycle, it means a greater likelihood of having an accident; for the sensitivity cycle, it means a day of hypersensitivity and moodiness; and for the intellectual cycle, it means slow thinking and poor memory.

These cycles influence people's perceptions of time. For instance, when your body temperature is high, time seems to go slowly. Also, these cycles influence the ways in which people use time. The person whose biological clock is set for alertness at night and drowsiness in the morning is often late or slow during the morning hours. Since punctuality is an important nonverbal message, we need to recognize that such messages are not always intentional; we should be aware too of how our behaviors might be interpreted. We know of a university professor who almost never goes to bed before five or six in the morning and then sleeps until noon or later. For people who don't know his idiosyncratic sleeping pattern, his late-afternoon arrival in the office is rather disconcerting. We can only begin to guess what kinds of interpretations are made of it. But those who are aware of his habits simply know not to schedule any early-morning appointments with him.

Our awareness of these cycles, or *biorhythms,* should cause us to think twice about the inferences we draw from other people's behavior. Rather than assuming that something in an interaction itself is causing a person to be moody, creative, or apathetic, we should consider the possibility that his or her behavior may be a reaction to a biorhythm.

Cultural Time Orientations

The cultural time orientation is, of the three, the one most closely related to communication. Each culture has its own way of viewing time, and each has established definite patterns for using time. When these norms are violated, people react strongly and interpret those violations as messages.

Understanding just what the time norms are is not easy because, within each culture, there are actually three different time systems: technical time, formal time, and informal time.[25] *Technical time* has the least to do with communication. It is the precise and scientific way time is measured. It is a nonemotional, logical approach to time. The way in which the space

program tracks time is a technical system. The distinction between a solar, sidereal, and anomalistic year is another example of technical time.

Formal time, by contrast, is the traditional way the culture views time. It is the conscious, formally taught system for measuring time. In our culture, we break time into centuries, decades, years, seasons, months, weeks, days, hours, minutes, and seconds. Our formal calendar has 365 days, our week seven days. We know, of course, that not all cultures use this system. Several, for instance, mete out time according to natural events such as the phases of the moon or the crops in season.

Formal time also includes such things as the way a culture chooses to *order* events, the *cycles* it recognizes, the *values* it places on time, its concept of *duration,* and the degree of *depth* and *tangibility* it assigns to time. Americans see the days of the week as following a fixed order; we are most cognizant of weekly, monthly, and seasonal cycles; we place a high value on time; we judge duration by the clock rather than by natural events; we recognize some depth to time (although not to the degree that, say, the Arabs do); and we see it as something tangible.

These formal concepts are usually learned at an early age. Infants have no sense of time other than their awareness of their own biological cycles. By the age of six, a child has usually learned the days of the week and even that different values are placed on them. Monday through Friday are workdays; Saturday and Sunday are less rigorously scheduled days of leisure, entertainment, and church-going. By the age of eight, most children have learned to tell time by a clock. When they enter school, they gain an awareness of the seasons, especially the distinctions between summer (vacation) and fall and spring (the beginning or end of school). However, most children do not completely master the formal time system until about the age of twelve.

Because our formal time system is deeply rooted in tradition, it evokes strong emotional reactions. The old ways are valued and new schemes seem threatening. A perfect example of the emotional involvement in formal time systems is what happened when Daylight Savings Time was first proposed. A Kansas farmer wrote to his local newspaper to register his strong complaint. He didn't know how anybody else felt about it, but he was violently opposed to Daylight Savings Time because he believed that the extra hour of sunlight would kill his tomatoes.

The third time system is *informal time*. This one is the most difficult to learn and understand because it is loosely defined. It is based on informal practices and is therefore usually not a conscious system. It is hard to say when people learn it. Judging by the behavior of some, there are those who never do. This system can be understood only within a context. It is the system most responsible for our perception of time-related messages.

Take, for example, the concept of *duration*.

mini-experiment

To determine the various informal meanings of punctuality in your geographic area, create a questionnaire that names several hypothetical appointments—such as a doctor's appointment at 10:45, a 7 P.M. dinner date with a friend, a 4:00 meeting with the dean, a 6:30 study date—and asks people at what time they would actually arrive. Sample a variety of people (faculty, students, and others not at the college; males and females; people of high status, people of low status) and note differences in their responses.

In our informal time system, there are eight levels of duration: immediate, very short, short, neutral, long, very long, terribly long, and forever. Now if someone says to you that it will take forever to get through this textbook, what does that mean? What if you are waiting for someone and they tell you they will be ready immediately? Unless you know the individual, the specific situation, and the way the culture usually uses those terms, you will have a hard time guessing what is meant. *Forever* could be anything from two hours to a lifetime, and *immediately* could be anything from one second to twenty minutes. With formal and technical time, labels have a relatively precise meaning. We know exactly what one second is, but used informally, *one second* carries the same ambiguity as *immediately*. Informal time frequently uses the same vocabulary as formal time, leaving a person to wonder what is meant.

One of the most important concepts in our informal time system is *punctuality*. For different situations, the meaning of *on time* varies greatly. For a business appointment, one is expected to show up at the scheduled time or earlier. Arriving even five minutes late requires an apology. Yet for a cocktail party or picnic, it may be perfectly acceptable to show up an hour after the party is supposed to begin. In New York City, an invitation to a party from 5:00 to 7:00 may mean that you are expected to arrive around 6:30 and stay till the party is over; in Salt Lake City, an invitation to dinner at 6:00 generally means that you had better arrive at 5:45.

Because these informal rules are never spelled out, people frequently misjudge situations and send out unintentional messages. One of the most common problems Americans have had abroad is adapting to different time systems. In Latin America, for example, it is not uncommon for people to wait from forty-five minutes to a full day to see an executive with whom they have an appointment. Also, several appointments may be scheduled at once, so that there is no established sequence governing which visitor is seen first. The system is totally incomprehensible to North Americans, who have no tolerance for waiting or going out of turn. Many a business executive has come back to the States feeling that he or she has been subjected to insulting treatment. In a similar vein, many hosts and hostesses have been distressed by dinner guests' showing up forty-five minutes late, long after the soufflé has collapsed and the meat dried out.

Part of the problem with punctuality is that there are two conflicting ways of viewing scheduled times. Some people follow the *displaced point* pattern: they view whatever time is set for something as the ending point. The wife on the displaced point pattern who is supposed to pick up her husband at 6:00 will arrive at or before that time. The person on the *diffused point* pattern views appointed times as approximations and arrives around that time, early or late, though usually within a maximum of acceptable deviation. These two patterns would not create problems if everybody understood which system another intended to follow. Instead, the displaced point wife will probably find herself waiting impatiently at the corner for her diffused point husband, who shows up twenty minutes after the hour. Or a diffused point student who is giving his first apartment-christening party will be frantically trying to clean the place when several guests show up early. We know of one case of a couple showing up two hours early for a party. They were totally unaware that their behavior communicated a message of insensitivity, and they were equally unaware of the nonverbal messages bombarding them in return.

Of course, there are times when people intentionally use punctuality or lack of it as a message. The story is told about Harry Truman, who shortly after assuming the presidency, was visited by a newspaper editor. After the editor had waited forty-five minutes in Truman's outer office, an aide went in to tell the President that the man was becoming very irritated about his long wait. Truman replied, "When I was a junior senator from Missouri that same man kept me cooling my heels for an hour and a half. As far as I'm concerned, the son of a bitch has forty-five minutes to go!"

Other elements in our informal time system that can be equally potent sources of nonverbal messages are *urgency, monochronism, activity,* and *variety.* The timing of events can clearly signal *urgency.* A telephone call in the afternoon is commonplace, but one at 3 A.M. is not. It is an automatic signal of alarm. Similarly, a request for a report in ten weeks' time is nonarousing, but a request to have one ready the same day rings with urgency. Our promptness in completing a task carries the same kind of message.

Monochronism refers to the pattern in our culture of scheduling only one thing at a time. We can communicate that we find a person uninteresting or unimportant by, say, reading the newspaper or doing the laundry while he or she is talking to us. Thus, Americans, accustomed to monochronism, respond negatively to the Latin American *polychronistic* pattern. An American takes being scheduled for an appointment at the same time as other people as a sign that he or she is unimportant.

Activity and *variety* refer to whether or not we are doing something with our time and whether or not there is variation in the activities in which we engage. Americans feel that we must always be doing something lest we communicate that we are unambitious, lazy, and wasting time. Also, Americans must have variety, or else boredom sets in. With variety, time passes quickly. The character Dunbar in *Catch-22* always tries to do boring things simply to make time pass more slowly because he is afraid that time will slip by too quickly. Most Americans prefer that time pass quickly. Lack of variety is seen as a sign of old age and impending death, and variety is taken as a message of health and youthfulness.

Time and Communication

It should be apparent from our discussion of these different levels of perceiving time that there are many ways in which time affects communication and acts as communication. From the amount of time we keep people waiting to the tempo of our daily activities, time is an ever-present, invisible message (see Fig. 4.4). Perhaps because time is such a part of us, it has received very little systematic study other than from an anthropological viewpoint.

We shall attempt, throughout the book, to present what little is known about time in relation to communication.

Artifacts

Three teenagers were wearily winding their way home from a day of exploring some local caves when one of them noticed that his jacket

Figure 4.4

Wide World Photos

was missing. He waved his friends goodbye and retraced his steps. Deep into one of the rarely opened caves, he finally found the jacket and sat down to rest for a moment. Exhaustion caught up with him and he fell asleep. When he awoke, he discovered to his dismay that the entrance to the cave was closed, a practice designed to prevent accidents at night. Trying not to panic, he turned off his now feeble flashlight and sat quietly, expecting his friends to return soon. As time passed and no one came, he became anxious. Fearing a long wait, he divided the remains of his picnic lunch into three small portions to last through the next day and proceeded to eat the first meal. After trying hopelessly to entertain himself and control his fear, he returned to sleep. The cycle of sleeping and eating continued until he had finished the last meal. Just as he began to cry uncontrollably, his friends returned. He sobbed to them that he thought they wouldn't find him and that spending a full day concealed in a cave was intolerable. They were amazed by his story. Only three hours had passed.

This apocryphal story illustrates the strong effect that our environment has on our perceptions and behavior. The dark, enclosed, and cramped features of the cave made the young man feel like a prisoner, causing him to become hysterical in a short period of time. Environmental features and objects, which make up the artifactual code, take advantage of this potency when they are used as a means of communication. Their role as a message system is explained by Ruesch and Kees:

. . . a whole series of situations exists in which people influence, guide, and direct each other by means of signals that are embedded in the material environment. Objects as systems of codification are used pervasively in every walk of life—in business and at home, ranging from household gadgets to articles of furniture. Architectural style, interior decoration and lighting conditions, for example, play significant parts in communication.[26]

As this excerpt suggests, environment and objects communicate in two ways. First, they can serve as implied messages from the designer or user. Shopkeepers create displays to influence consumers; an architectural style may be regarded as a statement by the architect; and an individual's bedroom can be interpreted as a source of information about the person's preferences, interests, and habits. Second, environment and objects can regulate the interactions that happen within their range. People's attitudes and behavior are frequently influenced by their environment. Changes in mood and behavior in turn affect the communication that takes place.

We can see how much surroundings affect people and the way they communicate by looking at some experiments involving an ugly room and a beautiful room.[27] One study used three rooms. The beautiful room was medium sized (11′ × 14′ × 10′) with two large windows, beige walls, carpet, drapes, indirect lighting, and attractive furnishings. The overall impression was of a comfortable study; people described the room as pretty, attractive, and comfortable. The ugly room was cramped (7′ × 12′ × 10′), with two half windows, battleship grey walls, an overhead bulb with a dirty, torn, ill-fitting shade, and disheveled furnishings. The general impression was that it was a janitor's storeroom; it was rated as horrible, repulsive, and ugly. The third room was a large room (15′ × 17′ × 10′) with three windows, grey walls, indirect lighting, and typical office furniture. It had the appearance of being a college professor's office. Students reported to one of the three rooms and were asked to rate photographic negatives of several faces. The environment significantly affected their reactions: subjects interviewed in the attractive room rated the faces much higher on energy and well-being than did those interviewed in the average and ugly rooms. (Surprisingly, ratings in the average room were only slightly higher than those in the ugly room.) The task wasn't the only thing affected; the environment also had pronounced effects on the participants. Subjects and experimenters alike tried to escape from the ugly room by cutting the interview short. The students also responded more negatively to the interviewer in the ugly room and reported that the room produced fatigue, headaches, hostility, irritability, and monotony. By contrast, subjects in the beautiful room found the experience comfortable, pleasant, enjoyable, and energizing, and it made them feel important. In the other studies, in which subjects worked on problem solving and comprehension tasks, results were consistent: people performed much better in attractive surroundings. Given these findings, it is no wonder that people tire of school so easily. Most classrooms we have seen would clearly qualify as ugly environments.

Environmental Preferences

Because physical surroundings, one's environment, can have such an impact on the way people feel and act, people have preferences about where they work and play. Take geo-

mini-experiment

Read Max Luscher's *The Luscher Color Test* (New York: Pocket Books, 1971), which is designed to reveal personality through color preference. The test requires you to rate color swatches in terms of preference. Test yourself and your friends to see if your personality and mood correspond with your color preferences. Also see if geographic background, age, sex, and socioeconomic status influence choices in a manner consistent with the research we have cited.

graphic likes and dislikes, for instance. Sonnenfeld showed fifty slides with varying vegetation, topography, water features, and apparent temperatures to a cross section of people ranging from Eskimos to American college students. He found that, in general, people preferred surroundings similar to their own. There were some sex and age differences. Men preferred a rugged environment; women preferred heavy vegetation and warm temperatures; and young people liked rugged, exotic (unfamiliar) settings.[28] From this study, we can see that preferences are influenced by such personal factors as age and sex and such environmental factors as familiarity and novelty.

Geographic familiarity also influences tastes; it seems to affect color preferences. People who live in southern countries prefer white or bright colors and dark shades close to black in value. People who live in temperate countries generally like greyed or neutral colors instead, except for the occasional use of brilliant colors for a novelty effect. These color preferences may be explained by the experiences each culture has with the shading effect of the sun. In the warm climates, the directness of the sun's rays makes the edges of shadows distinct, whereas in the north, the slanting of the sun's rays causes shadows to blur around the edges. Consequently, people in tropical regions are not familiar with intermediate values and therefore do not care for them in their decorative arts or clothing.[29]

Even within geographic regions, people's color preferences are not uniform. Those who grow up in the West or Midwest tend to prefer warm and neutral-warm colors; those who grow up in green and flat areas have a definite preference for cool and neutral-cool tones; and those who grow up in mountainous areas prefer either bright-cool or neutral-cool colors. Personality differences also affect preferences. Introverts prefer less saturated tones and cool colors such as blue and green while extroverts prefer bright and warm colors. Finally, demographic characteristics make a difference.

Highly educated, older people with a relatively high income and high socioeconomic status prefer subtle, delicate colors with unusual hues and little contrast. Those who are poorly educated, immature, have low income and low socioeconomic status prefer loud colors with variety, high intensity, and high contrast.[30]

In general, the variables that dictate people's clothing choices also affect their environmental preferences. Just as personality and demographic factors affect the style and color of clothing people like, they also affect the kinds of environments people seek out or create. Similarly, an individual's mood at the moment can influence what kind of environment and what color scheme she or he will gravitate toward. Perhaps more important, however, than an individual's personality, mood, age, sex, and familiarity with an environment are the features of the environment itself. The combination of elements in the environment determines whether individuals choose to remain in that environment or escape it, whether they are comfortable in it or anxious, whether they behave socially or antisocially, and whether they communicate successfully or not. It is these same dimensions of artifacts that can be used as message elements.

Dimensions of Artifacts

The first feature of significance is *size* or *volume* of an artifact. This includes both the sizes of objects and the volume of space that remains within the environment. Large objects may dwarf the individual; small objects make a person feel more central in a space. Consider the effects of columns as an example. They usually create a feeling of expansiveness, an awareness of the magnitude of the universe, and a sense of the individual as relatively insignificant. A tall tree, a church spire, or a tower may create such an effect. Small objects, on the other hand, may evoke different responses—perhaps

an awareness of the human responsibility for the creation and care of them. An adult undoubtedly feels different in a kindergarten room with its tiny chairs and tables than in an executive seminar room with a massive table and high-backed chairs.

The relative volume of space also has its effect. Landscape architecture takes this fact into account in the design of space. Figure 4.5 shows some typical activities that might go on in different sized spaces. By your choice of a locale for a conversation, you can communicate what kind of interaction you want to take place. If you invite someone to study with you in an intimate café, your message is that you aren't serious about studying. If you choose to discuss your future relationship with someone at the museum of natural history, chances are you aren't planning a long-term romance.

A second feature is the *arrangement* of elements within an environment. Recall that one of the characteristics of the ugly room is that it was a mess. The lack of orderliness can make people feel anxious or frustrated. Conversely, an aesthetically pleasing arrangement may entice people to linger. Ruesch and Kees offer the example of the arrangement of objects in a shop display affecting buying behavior: "The *arrangement* of similarly shaped objects reinforces or attenuates the impression made by the single object. . . . Buttons, for example, framed on ordered rows as if they were collector's items, suggest plentiful supply, ready availability, specialization; and to some they may hold the promise of expert service."[31]

Furniture can be arranged to dictate various communication patterns. People who want to discourage conversation in their offices place their desk so that their back is to others. Many churches are designed with barriers between seats to prevent people from conversing. Robert Sommer discovered that in many institutions arrangements have a similar effect. Observing the women's ward of a state hospital, he noticed that no one ever spoke to anyone else in the attractive lounge that was provided.

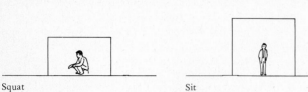

Squat	Sit	Be seated
Eat	Dine	Banquet
Yak	Talk	Converse
Rock n' roll	Fox trot	Waltz
The yodelling three	Light opera	Symphony
Growl at the price of fish	Compare car mileages	Discuss world trade relations

Figure 4.5   The amount of space available is likely to affect the kind of communication that goes on. (From *Landscape Architecture* by J. O. Simonds. Copyright © 1961 by F. W. Dodge Corporation. Used with permission of McGraw-Hill Book Company.)

This seemed especially strange since the elderly and ill usually feel lonely and in need of companionship. Sommer discovered the key to the problem: the chairs were all arranged in neat rows along the walls or in the center facing away from each other. When he changed the arrangement so that chairs faced each other, people began having conversations. Up until that point, the message had been that the seats were not intended for communication but simply for decoration, that the arrangement was not designed for the purpose of interaction but to provide the custodial staff the easiest method of cleaning floors.[32]

A third feature of the environment is the *materials* used—their shape and texture. Roughness or smoothness, softness or hardness, brightness or dullness, apparent depth, and the intricacies of design play upon the visual and tactile senses. As Ruesch and Kees explain,

wood, metal, brick, and textiles produce a variety of anticipation of touch sensations. Wood against wood, metal against brick, a stiffened fabric against a soft and pliable one—all set up "chords" of tactile images that often produce sharp and immediate physical and emotional reactions. Metal may be highly polished or finished with a dull patina; containers may be opaque, translucent, or transparent. Surfaces—whether raised, carved, rough or smooth—when exposed to light reflections, are likely not only to express the moods of those who shaped them, but also to suggest such subtle and abstract manners as interpenetration or merely the simple adjoining of boundaries.[33]

The combination of materials in an environment may seem to invite interaction or discourage it. Soft, plush, heavily textured materials may create a relaxed atmosphere, while hard, bright, or angular objects may create feelings of energy or possibly anxiety. Hotels sometimes purchase hard, uncomfortable chairs for their lobbies simply to discourage people from lingering and chatting there.

A fourth feature of importance is *linear perspective.* By that we mean the lines that are created by walls and objects within a given

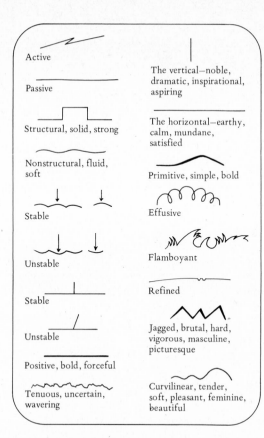

Figure 4.6   Different kinds of lines—in paintings, buildings, rooms, or whatever—can suggest different feelings. (From *Landscape Architecture* by J. O. Simonds. Copyright © 1961 by F. W. Dodge Corporation. Used with permission of McGraw-Hill Book Company.)

space and the relationship of the lines to each other. Flowing, curving lines may create a feeling of relaxation while sharp, jagged, irregular lines may create feelings of tension. A bedroom that is always neat and symmetrical may give you insight into the personality of the individual who sleeps there. At the least, the room creates a different reaction from that of a cluttered room or one decorated in bizarre and asymmetrical patterns. Architects have drawn conclusions about what kinds of lines create what kinds of effects, and they attempt to design spaces accordingly. A sample of the moods that different lines are thought to create is given in Figure 4.6.

A fifth consideration is *lighting and shading*. Low lights tend to create a relaxed, intimate environment in which people want to linger, while extremely bright lights tend to cause fatigue and a desire to escape. Of course, the intensity of the light and its source, whether natural or artificial, make a difference. In general, people seem to prefer moderate intensity and natural lighting, though some enjoy bright sunlight while others shrink from it. On the whole, soft, dim lighting is conducive to social conversation while bright, intense lighting is best for task-oriented communication or activities that do not call for communication. As some interior designers have noted, soft lighting is also more flattering to a woman's make-up, so fluorescent lighting is now sometimes avoided in offices where women work.

Sixth in our list of factors is *color*. Color in the environment has wide-ranging impact, affecting everything from mental abilities to physiological responses.[34] For instance, colors affect sensations of temperature. In one cafeteria, the thermostat was set at what should have been a comfortable level, yet customers kept complaining that the place was cold. An interior designer suggested changing the color of the walls. A simple paint job ended the complaints.

As we noted in the discussion of clothing, color can also reflect or affect moods. How would you feel about studying in a deep purple den? Or taking a class in an all-black room? Or working all day in a bright red cubicle? The colors would definitely influence your feelings, but exactly how you would react is hard to say. In general, blue and green tones are thought to be relaxing; yellows and oranges to be arousing and energizing; reds and blacks to be sensuous; and greys and browns to be depressing.[35] A study that examined the effects of colored lights found that blue and green were associated with feelings of pleasure and coolness; orange and yellow were the most unpleasant and, along with red, the most stimulating; purple created feelings of depression; and red created a feeling of being hot.[36] It is possible that the moods are created in part because the colors trigger physiological responses. Moods also arise from the symbolic value of various colors. Throughout history, different colors have been assigned symbolic meaning. They carry recognizable messages without the need for words. Some of the more common moods and symbolic meanings associated with different colors are presented in Table 4.1.

A seventh element of environments and objects has already been mentioned—*temperature*. Beyond the perceived temperature, actual temperatures can affect interaction. Hot environments lead to hot tempers, as the summer riots of the 1960s showed. Cool temperatures are more conducive to efficient and productive work and calm interactions.

An eighth consideration that operates much like temperature is *noise*. The current concern with noise pollution is testimony to our recognition of the detrimental effects of too much noise. Noise has negative effects both psychological and physiological. However, it is apparent that, in our culture at least, people find silence equally hard to handle. People cannot usually tolerate long silences in conversation. Neither do they like total silence in their work environment. Efficiency experts have been experimenting to find what kind of background noise is the most conducive to work. Many have found music (the right kind of music) to be soothing. Others have experimented with finding the right level of white noise (a low, continuous sound signal such as that created by an air conditioner or fluorescent light) to

Table 4.1   Color in the Environment: Moods Created and Symbolic Meanings

Color	Moods	Symbolic Meanings
Red	Hot, affectionate, angry, defiant, contrary, hostile, full of vitality, excitement, love	Happiness, lust, intimacy, love, restlessness, agitation, royalty, rage, sin, blood
Blue	Cool, pleasant, leisurely, distant, infinite, secure, transcendent, calm, tender	Dignity, sadness, tenderness, truth
Yellow	Unpleasant, exciting, hostile, cheerful, joyful, jovial	Superficial glamor, sun, light, wisdom, masculinity, royalty (in China), age (in Greece), prostitution (in Italy), famine (in Egypt)
Orange	Unpleasant, exciting, disturbed, distressed, upset, defiant, contrary, hostile, stimulating	Sun, fruitfulness, harvest, thoughtfulness
Purple	Depressed, sad, dignified, stately	Wisdom, victory, pomp, wealth, humility, tragedy
Green	Cool, pleasant, leisurely, in control	Security, peace, jealousy, hate, aggressiveness, calm
Black	Sad, intense, anxiety, fear, despondent, dejected, melancholy, unhappy	Darkness, power, mastery, protection, decay, mystery, wisdom, death, atonement
Brown	Sad, not tender, despondent, dejected, melancholy, unhappy, neutral	Melancholy, protection, autumn, decay, humility, atonement
White	Joy, lightness, neutral, cold	Solemnity, purity, chastity, femininity, humility, joy, light, innocence, fidelity, cowardice

mask outside distractions without interfering with the activity taking place within a space.

It is likely that the passage of new federal regulations on noise levels will serve as an incentive for more research into the effects of noise.

A final consideration is the total amount of *sensory stimulation* provided by an environment. This may take the form of activity within the space, movements of objects, or variation among the other dimensions (color, arrangement, and so forth). Studies have found that humans need a certain degree of sensory stimulation from their environment. Recall the evidence about the lack of tactile and visual stimulation on orphans in foundling homes. There the lack of stimulation was frequently fatal. Similarly, animal studies have found that of two environments, the one with greater variation produces more perceptual and behavioral alertness and more capability of adapting to change.[37]

Human beings consciously seek stimulation, not just to relieve unpleasant tensions but because stimulation is pleasing in itself. Environments lacking stimulation may produce dull, apathetic, or restless behavior, while those with a good degree of stimulation may produce feelings of exuberance and energy. Some have speculated that television has heightened our desire for sensory stimulation. We expect things to be presented to us in a multimedia fashion, with lots of auditory and visual variety. Many students are so accustomed to environmental activity that they can't study without the radio or television set. However, it should be noted that stimulation can reach an excessive level. One of the best explanations offered for the problems of city life is that there is an excess of stimulation from noise, traffic, pollution, and people, and that city dwellers are not able to cope with it.

By taking all these features into account, we can begin to see how artifacts can be combined to create different messages. J. O. Simonds has analyzed what reactions we might want an environment to create and what features can

produce them.[38] Figure 4.7 summarizes what combinations of elements can be used to yield eight different messages.

The Communication Potential of Artifacts

It should be clear that environment and objects serve a variety of communication functions. They have symbolic meaning; they can be used to reinforce a particular image; and they can regulate or manipulate the behavior of others. Because there are so many dimensions to be varied, artifacts can produce innumerable messages. Perhaps their most important communication role is in identifying the context and the rules that accompany that context for any kind of interaction. We have stressed throughout this chapter and Chapter 3 the importance of knowing the context before other nonverbal messages can be interpreted. Indeed, the context determines what cues are used and what meaning they carry. We want to close this chapter by examining some sample contexts and the ways in which environmental features define the nature of communication within them.

Artifacts and Specific Communication Contexts

Public Institutions We have already noted that institutions are frequently arranged in a manner that discourages interaction. The arrangements are designed to accommodate such things as the traffic flow of nurses or the custodial staff's tasks. The environment communicates that the institution is designed to promote efficiency rather than to cater to the individual's needs. Drab colors, the lack of texture and variety, and the general antiseptic atmosphere combine to create a dehumanizing environment. The institutional trappings— such things as locks on the doors, arrows on the floors, and well-starched uniforms on the staff—breed conformity and submissiveness.

Tension

Unstable forms. Split composition. Illogical complexities. Wide range of values. Clash of colors. Intense colors without relief. Visual imbalance about a line or point. No point at which the eye can rest. Hard, rough or jagged surfaces. Unfamiliar elements. Harsh, blinding, or quavering light. Uncomfortable temperatures in any range. Piercing, jangling, jittery sound.

Dynamic action

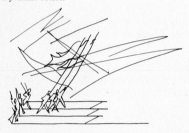

Bold forms. Heavy structural cadence. Angular planes. Diagonals. Solid materials as stone, concrete, wood, or steel. Rough natural textures. The pitched vertical. Directional compositional focus. Concentration of interest on focal point of action—as to rostrum, rallying point, or exit gate through which the entire volume impels one. Motion induced by sweeping lines, shooting lights, and by climactic sequences of form, pattern, and sound. Strong primitive colors—crimson, scarlet, and yellow-orange. Waving flags. Burnished standards. Martial music. Rush of sound. Ringing crescendos. Crash of brass. Roll and boom of drums.

Figure 4.7 Environmental features that can create various moods. (From *Landscape Architecture* by J. O. Simonds. Copyright © 1961 by F. W. Dodge Corporation. Used with permission of McGraw-Hill Book Company.)

Relaxation

Simplicity. Volume may vary in size from the intimate to the infinite. Fitness. Familiar objects and materials. Flowing lines. Curvilinear forms and spaces. Evident structural stability. Horizontality. Agreeable textures. Pleasant and comfortable shapes. Soft light. Soothing sound. Volume infused with quiet colors—whites, greys, blues, greens. *"Think round thoughts."*

Contemplation

Scale is not important since the subject will withdraw into his own sensed well of consciousness. The total space may be mild and unpretentious or immense and richly ornate— so long as the structural forms are not insistent. No insinuating elements. No distractions of sharp contrast. Symbols, if used, must relate to subject of contemplation. Space must provide a sense of isolation, privacy, detachment, security, and peace. Soft, diffused light. Tranquil and recessive colors. If sound, a low muted stream of sound to be perceived subconsciously.

Sensuous love

Complete privacy. Inward orientation of room. Subject the focal point. Intimate scale. Low ceiling. Horizontal planes. Fluid lines. Soft, rounded forms. Juxtaposition of angles and curves. Delicate fabrics. Voluptuous and yielding surfaces. Exotic elements and scent. Soft rosy pink to golden light. Pulsating, titillating music.

Fright

Sensed confinement. A quality of compression and bearing. An apparent trap. No points of orientation. No means by which to judge position or scale. Hidden areas and spaces. Possibilities for surprise. Sloping, twisted, or broken planes. Illogical, unstable forms. Slippery, hazardous base plane. Danger. Unprotected voids. Sharp, intruding elements. Contorted spaces. The unfamiliar. The shocking. The startling. The wierd. The uncanny. Symbols connoting horror, pain, torture, or applied force. The dim, the dark, the eerie. Pale and quavering or, conversely, blinding garish light. Cold blues, cold greens. Abnormal mono-chromatic color.

Gaiety

Free spaces. Smooth, flowing forms and patterns. Looping, tumbling, swirling motion accommodated. Movement and rhythm expressed in structure. Lack of restrictions. Forms, colors, and symbols that appeal to the emotions rather than the intellect. Temporal. Casual. Lack of restraint. Pretense is acceptable. The fanciful is applauded. Often the light, bright, and spontaneous in contrast to the ponderous, dark, and timeless. Warm, bright colors. Wafting, sparkling, shimmering, shooting, or glowing light. Exuberant or lilting sound.

Sublime spiritual awe

Overwhelming scale that transcends normal human experience and submerges one in a vast well of space. Soaring forms in contrast with low horizontal forms. A volume so contrived as to hold man transfixed on a broad base plane and lift his eye and mind high along the vertical. Orientation upward to or beyond some symbol of the infinite. Complete composi-tional order—often symmetry. Highly developed sequences. Use of costly and permanent materials. Connotation of the eternal. Use of chaste white. If color is used, the cool detached colors, such as blue-greens, greens, and violet. Diffused glow with shafts of light. Deep, full, swelling music with lofting passages.

Pleasure*

Spaces, forms, textures, colors, symbols, sounds, light quality, and odors all manifestly suitable to the use of the space—whatever it may be. Satisfaction of anticipations, requirements, or desires. Sequences developed and ful-filled. Harmonious relationships. Unity with variety. A resultant quality of beauty.

Displeasure*

Frustrating sequences of possible movement or revelation. Areas and spaces unsuitable to anticipated use. Obstacles. Excesses. Undue friction. Discomfort. Annoying textures. Improper use of materials. The illogical. The false. The insecure. The tedious. The blatant. The dull. The dis-orderly. Clashing colors. Discordant sounds. Disagreeable temperature or humidity. Unpleasant light quality. That which is ugly.

* It is to be noted that "displeasure" and "pleasure" are general categories, whereas "tension," "relaxation," "fright," and the others mentioned are more specific. With these more specific responses, we can list in more specific detail the characteristics of the volumes designed to induce them. The degree of "pleasure" or its opposite, "displeasure," would seem to depend on the degree of sensed fitness of the volume for its use, and a unified and harmonious development of the plan elements to serve this function. It can be seen that one could therefore experience pleasure and fright simultaneously (as in a fun house) or pleasure and sublime spiritual awe simultaneously (as in a cathedral), and so forth.

Partly because of the artifacts and partly because of the intrinsic nature of institutional activities, hospitals, jails, and other public institutions are considered to be anxiety- and fatigue-producing spaces.

Schools Studies reveal that classroom arrangement can greatly enhance or depress interaction. (We shall discuss this topic in the chapter on regulation.) Despite this fact, most classrooms cling to the old patterns. However, a number of innovations that may affect communication are being introduced in some school systems. One is carpeting—students appear to behave in a more restrained manner when halls and classrooms are carpeted. Another is the windowless classroom, which is supposed to reduce distractions, improve ventilation and heating, and simplify cleaning, though the psychological effects have not been fully explored. Robert Sommer notes that, in his studies, students assigned to windowless classrooms tried to change to another room. One of the problems with such environments is that they separate the individual from "the natural rhythms of movements," affecting time perceptions. Such environments may also be sterile. Most of us like to look outdoors to enjoy the scenery or even just check the weather. One other recent innovation is the elimination of offices for instructors. At Rochdale College in Toronto, planners and educators decided not to have offices for faculty members because offices create expectations that inhibit the type of formal, free interaction they desired.[39]

Bars Bars are one of the few free, non-elitist, non-sophisticated, and non-intellectual meeting places for the average person. A bar is one of the most anxiety-free of environments. It requires none of the propriety involved in visiting someone's home or another more formal setting. This environment, along with the nature of alcohol itself, creates an atmosphere of very free, relaxed communication. According to one writer, bars are open regions: people have the right to engage others in conversation and are obligated to accept overtures from them (or at least not be disturbed by them). While these features are typical of most bars, bars do differ in their clientele. Factors such as decor, lighting, external appearance, location, and the price list influence a person's choice of bars and the kind of activity that takes place. Sommer has found, for instance, that a drab decor attracts a lower-class clientele.[40] Undoubtedly the nature of conversation in such bars differs somewhat from that of a well-appointed lounge attracting upper-class clientele. The presence of scantily clad waitresses also has its effect on the boisterousness of the crowd.

Churches The atmosphere of a church inhibits communication. People typically stop smiling, lower their voices, make greetings brief, and end conversation. Attention is focused on the ceremony and introspection. The influence of this atmosphere is indicated by its effect on workmen. Even when they work in a church on a weekday, they generally behave more reverently than on any other job.

Airports Like schools and hospitals, airports foster fatigue and anxiety. Besides the amount of walking required, and the inherent pressure of having to be somewhere on time, the lack of places to relax contributes to this atmosphere. Airport chairs are designed specifically to inhibit communication and reduce comfort. They are usually made of hard, inflexible, uncomfortable materials and are hooked together in rows set too far apart for conversation. They are designed intentionally to drive people into bars and shops to spend money. There are also no chairs in the bars, to promote high turnover. The result is that there is less intoxication, more profit, and very little intimate or relaxed conversation.

Restaurants   Restaurant decor also influences the amount and intimacy of conversation. If a restaurant owner wants a high turnover, he will use a lot of illumination, little soundproofing, and uncomfortable chairs to reduce intimacy and relaxation. If, on the other hand, he wants people to stay longer, he will use low illumination, carpeting, drapes, padded ceilings, and close seating, all of which create an intimate atmosphere. To accommodate restaurateurs who don't want customers to linger, Henning Larson has designed café chairs that are intentionally uncomfortable.[41]

Offices   The features that make restaurants conducive to communication also make offices conducive to communication. Because of the high illumination common in most offices, and because of the cultural expectations associated with an office, they are not likely to foster intimate conversation; but there is a wide latitude in the nature of communication that may occur. Recognizing this fact, the All Steel Office Equipment Company has begun marketing furniture in terms of its ability to inhibit or encourage various types of communication.[42]

Houses   The home environment significantly influences a person's emotional, intellectual, and personality development, which in turn can influence that individual's communication behavior. Poor housing conditions can lead to pessimism, passivity, inability to adapt to stress, dissatisfaction, and cynicism about people and organizations. Clearly, such an environment does not produce an individual with positive attitudes toward effective performance in communication.

As for research relating specifically to communication in houses, there seems to be a void. What little material there is is conjectural. Goffman determined that bedrooms are generally the location of intimate conversation, though such conversations may be constrained in apartment buildings where the walls are so

thin that the neighbors can hear everything.[43] Goffman's theory is that people, realizing that they can hear their neighbor's conversations, will restrain their own. If our experience with apartment living is any index, Goffman's assertions are questionable.

At home, furnishings and objects set the tone for various activities. Elegant paintings, plush carpet, and rich furniture signal one set of communication expectations; garage-sale decor signals another. The objects used may also create the mood for a social gathering. For example, are guests served food on silver and china or on paper plates? Is the beer, wine, or liquor accessible to all or are beverages served by hired help? Is the food fancy or simple, catered or out of a can? Even the number and location of chairs can make a difference. One way to insure a successful party is to have fewer chairs than guests and to separate the food from the beverages so that people are forced to circulate.

These sample contexts reveal some of the ways in which we can nonverbally direct the content and flow of communication through the use of artifacts. Because different environments carry with them different rules and expectations, all nonverbal messages must be interpreted in the light of these constraints.

Summary

In this chapter, we have examined the role of space, time, and artifacts as communication codes. All three have great message potential because they invoke vital psychological and physiological needs or processes. Since space and time are heavily governed by norms and bound by rules, both conformity to and deviation from what is expected can carry distinct messages. Finally, artifacts are a powerful medium for communication because they have a wide range of dimensions that can be manipulated as messages and because they help define communication contexts.

Suggested Reading

Altman, I. "Privacy: A Conceptual Analysis." *Environment and Behavior,* 8 (1976), 7–29.

Ardrey, R. *African Genesis.* New York: Atheneum, 1961.

Barker, R. G. "On the Nature of Environment." *Journal of Social Issues,* 19 (1963), 17–38.

Beussee, M. P., Ahearn, T. R., and Hammes, J. A. "Introspective Reports of Large Groups Experimentally Confined in an Austere Environment." *Journal of Clinical Psychology,* 26 (1970), 240–244.

Birren, F. *Light, Color and Environment.* New York: Reinhold, 1969.

Birren, F. *New Horizons in Color.* New York: Reinhold, 1955.

Birren, F. *Selling with Color* New York: McGraw-Hill, 1945.

Doob, L. W. *Patterning of Time.* New Haven: Yale University Press, 1971.

Guggenheim, R. "Design of a Behavior Facilitating Environment Through a Deterministic Behavioral Index." In *Annual Studies Seminar on Urban and Regional Research.* Iowa City: University of Iowa Press, 1969.

Hall, E. T. *The Hidden Dimension.* Garden City, N.Y.: Doubleday, 1966.

Hall, E. T. *The Silent Language.* Garden City, N.Y.: Doubleday, 1959, 1973.

Helson, H. *Adaptation-Level Theory: An Experimental and Systematic Approach to Behavior.* New York: Harper and Row, 1964.

Luchiesth, M. *Color and Colors.* New York: Van Nostrand, 1938.

Milgram, S. "The Experience of Living in Cities." *Science,* 167 (1970), 1461–1468.

Mitchell, G. "What Monkeys Can Tell Us About Human Violence." *The Futurist,* 9 (1975), 75–80.

Prescott, J. W. "Body Pleasure and the Origins of Violence." *The Futurist,* 9 (1975), 64–74.

Proshansky, H. M., Ittelson, W. I., and Rivlin, L. G. (eds.). *Environmental Psychology: Man and His Physical Setting.* New York: Holt, Rinehart and Winston, 1970.

Rosenfeld, L. B., and Civikly, J. M. *With Words Unspoken: The Nonverbal Experience.* New York: Holt, Rinehart and Winston, 1976.

Vail, D. *Dehumanizing and the Institutional Career.* Springfield, Ill.: Charles C. Thomas, 1966.

Watson, O. M. *Proxemic Behavior: A Cross-Cultural Study.* The Hague: Mouton, 1970.

Wheeler, L. *Behavioral Research for Architectural Planning and Design.* Terre Haute, Ind.: Wing Miller Associates, 1967.

Notes

1. E. T. Hall, *The Silent Language* (Garden City, N.Y.: Doubleday, 1959), p. 180.
2. See, for example, R. Ardrey, *African Genesis* (New York: Dell, 1970); S. L. Washburn (ed.), *Social Life of Early Man* (New York: Wenner-Gren Foundation, 1961).
3. J. B. Calhoun, "The Role of Space in Animal Sociology," *Journal of Social Issues,* 22 (1969), pp. 46–58.

4. J. J. Christian, "Phenomena Associated with Population Density," *Proceedings of the National Academy of Science,* 47, No. 4 (1961), pp. 428–449.
5. See, for example D. E. Davis, "Physiological Effects of Continued Crowding," in A. H. Esser (ed.), *Behavior and Environment* (New York: Plenum Press, 1971); R. Dubos, *Man Adapting* (New Haven: Yale University Press, 1965), pp.

100–109; D. Stokols, "A Social-Psychological Model of Human Crowding Phenomena," *Journal of the American Institute of Planners,* 38 (1972), pp. 72–84.

6. I. Altman and W. W. Haythorn, "The Ecology of Isolated Groups," *Behavioral Science,* 12 (1967), pp. 169–182.

7. S. Valins and A. Baum, "Residential Group Size, Social Interactions and Crowding," *Environment and Behavior,* 5 (1973), pp. 421–439.

8. L. Bickman, A. Teger, T. Gabriele, C. McLaughlin, M. Berger, and E. Sunady, "Dormitory Density and Helping Behavior," *Environment and Behavior,* 5 (1973), pp. 465–490.

9. See for example, J. Daley, "The Effects of Crowding and Comfort on Interaction Behavior and Membership Satisfaction in Small Groups," paper presented at the International Communication Association Convention, Montreal, April 1973; G. W. Evans and W. Eichelman, "Preliminary Models of Conceptual Linkages Among Proxemic Variables," *Environment and Behavior,* 9 (1976), pp. 87–116; H. M. Proshansky, W. H. Ittelson, and L. G. Rivlin (eds.), *Environmental Psychology: Man and His Physical Setting* (New York: Holt, Rinehart and Winston, 1970); D. Stokols, "A Social-Psychological Model of Human Crowding Phenomena," *American Institute of Planners Journal,* 38 (1972), pp. 72–84.

10. J. L. Freedman, J. Klevansky, and R. R. Ehrlich, "The Effect of Crowding on Human Task Performance," *Journal of Applied Psychology,* 1 (1971), pp. 7–25.

11. Stokols (note 9.)

12. L. M. Lyman and M. B. Scott, "Territoriality: A Neglected Sociological Dimension," *Social Problems,* 15 (1967), pp. 236–249.

13. For a detailed summary of these three categories of norms, see J. K. Burgoon and S. B. Jones, "Toward a Theory of Personal Space Norms and Their Violations," *Human Communication Research,* 2 (1976), pp. 131–146.

14. Support for these relationships comes from J. R. Aiello and S. E. Jones, "Field Study of the Proxemic Behavior of Young Children in Three Subcultural Groups," *Journal of Personality and Social Psychology,* 19 (1971), pp. 351–356; J. C. Baxter, "Interpersonal Spacing in Natural Settings," *Sociometry,* 33 (1970), pp. 444–456; P. R. Connolly, "The Perception of Personal Space Among Black and White Americans," *Central States Speech Journal,* 26 (1975), pp. 21–28; M. Dosey and M. Meisels, "Personal Space and Self-Protection," *Journal of Personality and Social Psychology,* 11 (1969), pp. 93–97; G. W. Evans and R. B. Howard, "Personal Space," *Psychological Bulletin,* 80 (1973), pp. 334–344; R. F. Forston and C. U. Larson, "The Dynamics of Space: An Experimental Study in Proxemic Behavior Among Latin Americans and North Americans," *Journal of Communication,* 18 (1968), pp. 109–116; H. Garfinkel, "Studies of the Routine Grounds of Everyday Activities," *Social Problems,* 11 (1964), pp. 225–250; M. Giesen and H. A. McClaren, "Discussion, Distance and Sex: Changes in Impressions and Attraction During Small Group Interaction," *Sociometry,* 39 (1976), pp. 60–70; J. Gullahorn, "Distance and Friendship as Factors in the Gross Interaction Matrix," *Sociometry,* 15 (1952), pp. 123–134; Hall (note 1); K. B. Little, "Personal Space," *Journal of Experimental Social Psychology,* 1 (1965), pp. 237–247; D. F. Lott and R. Sommer, "Seating Arrangements and Status," *Journal of Personality and Social Psychology,* 7 (1967), pp. 90–94; M. Patterson, "Spatial Factors in Social Interactions," *Human Relations,* 21 (1968), pp. 351–361; M. L. Patterson and D. S. Holmes, "Social Interaction Correlates of the MMPI Extroversion-Introversion Scale," *American Psychologist,* 21 (1966), pp. 724–745; R. F. Priest and J. Sawyer, "Proximity and Peership: Bases of Balance in Interpersonal Attraction," *The American Journal of Sociology,* 72 (1967), pp. 633–649; T. Rosegrant, "The Relationship of Race and Sex on Proxemic Behavior and Source Credibility," paper presented at the International Communication Association Convention, Montreal, April 1973; E. Sundstrom and I. Altman, "Interpersonal Relationships and Personal Space: Research Review and Theoretical Model," *Human Ecology,* 4 (1976), pp. 47–67; H. G. Triandis, E. Davis, and S. Takezawa, "Some Determinants of Social Distance Among American, German, and Japanese Students," *Journal of Personality and Social Psychology,* 2 (1965), pp. 540–551; O. M. Watson, *Proxemic Behavior: A Cross-Cultural Study* (The Hague: Mouton, 1970); O. M. Watson and T. D. Graves, "Quantitative Research in Proxemic Behavior," *American Anthropologist,*

68 (1968), pp. 971–985; F. N. Willis, "Initial Speaking Distance as a Function of the Speaker's Relationship," *Psychonomic Science*, 5 (1966), pp. 221–222.

15. Support for these relationships comes from M. Cook, "Experiments on Orientation and Proxemics," *Human Relations*, 23 (1970), pp. 61–76; J. J. Edney, "Place and Space: The Effects of Experience with a Physical Locale," *Journal of Experimental and Social Psychology*, 8 (1972), pp. 124–135; Hall (note 1); A. Hare and R. Bales, "Seating Position and Small Group Interaction," *Sociometry*, 26 (1963), pp. 480–486; J. K. Heston and P. Garner, "A Study of Personal Spacing and Desk Arrangement in a Learning Environment," paper presented at the International Communication Convention, Atlanta, April 1972; L. T. Howells, and S. W. Becker, "Seating Arrangement and Leadership Emergence," *Journal of Abnormal and Social Psychology*, 84 (1971), pp. 35–44; E. A. Mabry and J. Kaufman, "The Influence of Sex and Attraction on Seating Positions in Dyads," paper presented at the International Communication Association Convention, Montreal, April 1973; G. A. Norum, N. J. Russo, and R. Sommer, "Seating Patterns and Group Tasks," *Psychology in the Schools*, 4 (1967), p. 33; R. Sommer, *Personal Space: The Behavioral Basis of Design* (Englewood Cliffs, N.J.: Prentice-Hall, 1969); R. Sommer, "Studies in Personal Space," *Sociometry*, 22 (1959), pp. 247–260.

16. Support for these relationships can be found in Little (note 14); R. Sommer, "Leadership and Group Geography," *Sociometry*, 24 (1961), pp. 99–110; R. Sommer, "The Distance for Comfortable Conversation: A Further Study," *Sociometry*, 25 (1962), pp. 11–16.

17. Sommer, 1959 (note 15); Sommer, 1969 (note 15).

18. J. C. Baxter, and B. F. Deanovitch, "Anxiety Effects of Inappropriate Crowding," *Journal of Consulting and Clinical Psychology*, 35 (1970), pp. 174–178; N. Felipe and R. Sommer, "Invasions of Personal Space," *Social Problems*, 14 (1966), pp. 206–214; J. D. Fisher and D. Byrne, "Too Close for Comfort: Sex Differences in Response to Invasions of Personal Space," *Journal of Personality and Social Psychology*, 32 (1975), pp. 15–21; P. H. Garner, "The Effects of Invasions of Personal Space on Interpersonal Communication" (thesis, Illinois State University, 1972); M. Patterson, S. Mullens, and J. Romano,

"Compensatory Reactions to Spatial Intrusion," *Sociometry*, 34 (1971), pp. 114–121.

19. M. J. Horowitz, D. F. Duff, and L. O. Stratton, "Body Buffer Zones," *Archives of General Psychiatry*, 11 (1964), pp. 651–656; G. McBride, M. G. King, and J. W. James, "Social Proximity Effects on GSR in Human Adults," *Journal of Psychology*, 61 (1965), pp. 153–157.

20. Sommer, 1969, p. 24 (note 15).

21. M. Patterson and L. Sechrest, "Interpersonal Distance and Impression Formation," *Journal of Personality*, 38 (1970), pp. 161–166.

22. Hall, p. 1 (note 1).

23. J. Meerloo, "The Time Sense in Psychiatry," in J. T. Fraser (ed.), *The Voices of Time* (New York: Braziller, 1966).

24. J. Reinert, "What your Sense of Time Tells You," *Science Digest*, 69 (1971), pp. 8–12.

25. See Hall for a full discussion of these time systems (note 1).

26. J. Ruesch and W. Kees, "Function and Meaning in the Physical Environment," in H. M. Proshansky, W. H. Ittelson, and L. G. Rivlin (eds.), *Environmental Psychology* (New York: Holt, Rinehart and Winston, 1969), p. 146.

27. J. M. Bilodeau and H. Schlosberg, "Similarity in Stimulating Conditions as a Variable in Retroactive Inhibition," *Journal of Experimental Psychology*, 41 (1959), pp. 199–204; A. H. Maslow and N. L. Mintz, "Effects of Esthetic Surroundings: I. Initial Effects of Three Esthetic Conditions upon Perceiving 'Energy' and 'Well-being' in Faces," *Journal of Psychology*, 41 (1956), pp. 247–254; N. L. Mintz, "Effects of Esthetic Surroundings: II. Prolonged and Repeated Experience in a 'Beautiful' and 'Ugly' Room," *Journal of Psychology*, 41 (1956), pp. 459–466; H. Wong and W. Brown, "Effects of Surroundings upon Mental Work as Measured by Yerkes' Multiple Choice Method," *Journal of Comparative Psychology*, 3 (1923), pp. 319–331.

28. J. Sonnenfeld, "Variable Values in Space and Landscape: An Inquiry into the Nature of Environmental Necessity," *Journal of Social Issues*, 2, No. 4 (1966), pp. 71–82.

29. E. Burris and F. Meyer, *Color and Design in the Decoration Arts* (New York: Prentice-Hall, 1937).

30. See, for example, J. P. Guilford, R. Guilford, and W. E. Walton, "Color Preferences of 1,279 University Students," *American Journal of Psychology*, 45 (1933), pp. 322–328; J. H. McInness and J.

K. Shearer, "Relationship between Color Choice and Selected Preferences of the Individual," *Journal of Home Economics,* 56, (1964), pp. 181–187; W. A. Woods, "Some Determinants of Attitudes Toward Colors in Combinations," *Perceptual and Motor Skills,* 6 (1956), pp. 187–194.

31. Ruesch and Kees, p. 146 (note 26).
32. Sommer, 1969 (note 15).
33. Ruesch and Kees, p. 146 (note 26).
34. Bilodeau and Schlosberg (note 27); F. Birren, "Effects of Color on the Human Organism," *American Journal of Occupational Therapy,* 13 (1959), pp. 125–129; F. Birren, *Selling with Color* (New York: McGraw-Hill, 1945); Burris and Meyer (note 29).
35. F. Birren, *Color Psychology and Color Therapy* (New York: McGraw-Hill, 1950); D. C. Murray, and H. L. Deabler, "Colors and Mood-Tones," *Journal of Applied Psychology,* 41, No. 5 (1957), pp. 279–283; L. B. Wexner, "The Degree to Which Colors (Hues) Are Associated with Mood-Tones," *Journal of Applied Psychology,* 38 (1954), pp. 432–435.
36. R. H. Lewinski, "An Investigation of Individual Responses to Chromatic Illumination," *Journal of Psychology,* 6 (1938), p. 6.
37. A. E. Parr, "Psychological Aspects of Urbanology," *Journal of Social Issues,* 22, (1966), pp. 39–45; J. F. Wohlwill, "The Physical Environment: A Problem for Psychology of Stimulation," *The Journal of Social Issues,* 22 (1966), pp. 21–38.
38. J. O. Simonds, *Landscape Architecture* (New York: McGraw-Hill, 1961).
39. D. Lee, "Getting to Rochdale," *This Magazine Is About Schools,* 2 (1968), p. 86.
40. Sommer, 1969 (note 15).
41. H. Bigart, "The Men Who Made the World Move," *Saturday Review* (April 22, 1967), p. 54.
42. Bigart (note 41).
43. E. Goffman, *Behavior in Public Places* (New York: Free Press, 1963).

5

Individual, Subcultural, and Cultural Styles

Test Your Sensitivity

True or False?

1. Arabs view time as a valuable commodity; thus, they abhor idleness and respect promptness.
2. Kissing is one social custom that has relatively the same meaning in all cultures.
3. Females are more accurate than males in sending and receiving facial expressions of emotion.
4. Manic individuals are often characterized by incessant talk, bold and colorful clothing, and wild and exaggerated movements.

By the end of this chapter, you should know the correct answer to all four questions and understand these concepts:

- cultural differences in greetings and other kinesic patterns
- cultural differences in formal and informal time
- contact and noncontact cultures
- reasons for cultural variations
- role signs
- subcultural time patterns: hauley time, Mormon time, street time, short time perspective
- sex differences in eye contact, emotional displays, seating, interruptions, inflection patterns, smiling, touching, and personal space
- androgyny
- schizophrenia and nonverbal correlates
- manic-depressive states and nonverbal correlates
- communication anxiety and nonverbal correlates

One of the obstacles to studying behavior in general (and nonverbal behavior in particular) is that people differ radically in their behavioral repertoires, in their abilities to understand situations, and in their motivations to respond to their immediate environment. People are not just different; they are often so totally different that comparisons are pointless. Fortunately, many of the reasons for these differences are known. A major force contributing to these differences is the prevailing culture. To put it simply, culture provides more than a single form of socialization. Our society offers a variety of different norms for behavior. Depending on your social class, your race, and your sex, you are exposed from childhood to certain standards that mold your actions. Personality, too, increases the possibilities for individual behavior.

Our task of understanding the varieties of human nonverbal behavior is made even more difficult by myths that surround such topics as sex, race, culture, and personality. Stereotypes based upon these factors are particularly insidious because they often label people as being different (which may well be the case) and then attribute a reason for the difference that is totally inaccurate. Stereotypes limit inquiry by oversimplifying differences, by failing to recognize change, and by encouraging us to ignore the wide variety of differences within a given group of people.

As you read this chapter, place aside your personal judgments for the moment and consider a limited sample of data on individual differences. In some cases, the data take the form of stories; in others there are observations by anthropologists and sociologists. Some of the data are the product of experimental research, but in all instances, the findings reflect what is being written in many disciplines about how we differ in our nonverbal communication. In Chapters 3 and 4, we explored some of the norms for the various nonverbal codes. In this chapter, we shall focus on some of the ways in which people differ—specifi-

Figure 5.1

cally by culture, subculture, sex, and psychological condition.

Cultural Differences

Browsing through literature on cultural differences, one is struck immediately by three observations. First, the differences between cultures are endless (see Fig. 5.1). It would be a hopeless task to describe completely how cultures differ. Second, in spite of all that we do know about various groups of people, differences in nonverbal behavior remain a stumbling block to achieving international understanding. LaRay Barna of Portland State University has complained that a problem plaguing courses in intercultural communication is that cultures are often *so* different that individuals have trouble even talking about the differences.[1] Third, the study of intercultural differences is the study of contradictions. Almost any behavior that has a particular meaning or fulfills a specific function in one culture may have a totally different and often opposite interpretation for another group of people. In these next few pages, we shall consider specifically how cultures may differ with respect to *kinesic* behavior, *orientations to time,* and *proxemics.*

Kinesic Behavior

Weston LaBarre, a professor of anthropology at Duke University, has explored crosscultural differences in basic social rituals including many kinesic behaviors.[2] He found that *greeting kinemes* differ noticeably from one culture to another. The Copper Eskimo extend greetings by banging the welcomed party on either the head or the shoulders. Among the Polynesian people, it is customary for men who are strangers to welcome one another by embracing and then rubbing each other's back. And among the peoples of Matavai, friends who have been apart for some time scratch each other's head and temples with the tip of a shark's tooth, often drawing blood.

Likewise, *kissing* as a social custom carries different meanings for various groups of people. In the Orient, kissing is an intimate sexual act and is not permissible in public even as a social greeting or display of friendliness. Among the Tapuya of South America, kisses are exchanged only among the males as a sign of peace.[3]

Gestures showing *derision* or *contempt* vary widely. You may remember from an earlier chapter the example of the Pitta-Pitta women who show contempt by protruding the abdomen and flapping the knees back and forth and the Pitta-Pitta men who make the same point by biting their beard. LaBarre reports several other indications of contempt:

A favorite Menomini Indian gesture of contempt is to raise the clenched fist palm downward up to the level of the mouth, then bringing it downward quickly and throwing forward the thumb and the first two fingers. Malayan Negritos express contempt or disgust by a sudden expiration of breath, like our "snort of contempt." Neapolitans click the right thumbnail off the right canine in a downward arc.[4]

There are also striking cultural differences in *walking behavior* and even, as Figure 5.2 suggests, in sitting behavior. Walking is much more than a comfortable way of getting around. It functions simultaneously to reflect a culture's notion of masculinity and femininity (since often the movement patterns differ for men and women), to indicate formality, and to show time orientation (often through deliberate, rapid movement). European males sometimes seem effeminate to American tourists because when they walk, their posture and hand and arm movements are similar to the female walking pattern in our culture. On the other hand, Orientals often view American women as bold and aggressive because they walk with a longer gait and more upright posture than do Oriental women.

There are also cultural differences in the use of facial and eye expressions. For example, the elders of one African tribe were upset by the teaching practices of a female Peace Corps member in their town. The woman required her students to look her in the eye. In that particular culture, it is not permissible for a child to look an adult in the eye. Unknowingly, the teacher was promoting nonverbal behaviors that violated social custom. Another example, which we have mentioned, is the eyebrow flash (see Fig. 1.7). It is a sign of greeting and recognition in many cultures but is considered immodest and suggestive in the Orient.

The last area of kinesic difference that we shall explore involves emotional displays. There are striking similarities among cultures in the ways in which the face and body are used to communicate affect, but there are important differences as well. Consider the ways in which cultures reflect grief. In Japan, a widow smiles during the burial of her spouse; among some African peoples, bereaved relatives show grief by pulling out their hair; in Ireland, the wake is a time of celebration. Each norm shows us a little about a culture's attitudes toward life, family, and the communication of emotion.

Even though facial expressions are similar in many cultures, each culture modifies the displays and the ways in which they are used. In some cultures, intense emotions are not expressed, while in other cultures, the same emotions are used openly in response to situations that outsiders might consider inappropriate for extremes in emotion.

Often these differences are brought about by the complex of religious beliefs and values that regulates a culture's display of affect.

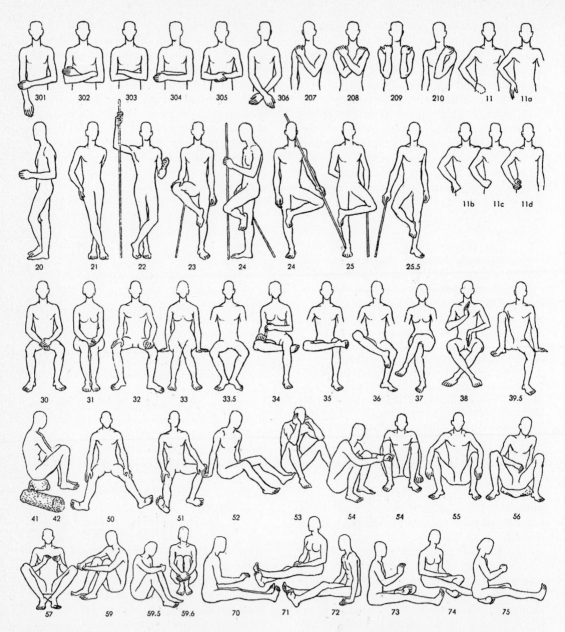

Figure 5.2 Sitting and standing postures differ significantly from culture to culture. The sampling in this figure is from the classification system of Gordon W. Hewes. According to *Scientific American*, in which an article by Hewes appeared, "the figures numbered 301 through 306 (top row on first page) are common resting positions; by contrast, the arm-on-shoulder postures of the next four figures are found mainly among western American Indians. In the next row are variations on the one-legged Nilotic stance, found in the Sudan, Venezuela, and elsewhere. Chair-sitting (third row on first page) spread from the ancient Near East, but the Arabs there have replaced it with floor-sitting postures (fourth and

124 Individual, Subcultural, and Cultural Styles

fifth rows on first page). Sitting cross-legged (top row on second page) predominates south and east of Near Eastern influence. Sedentary kneeling postures (102 to 104) are typically Japanese; sitting with the legs folded to one side (106 through 108) is a feminine trait, a rare exception being the male Mohave Indians. The deep squat (fourth row on second page) is uncomfortable for adult Europeans but replaces the sitting posture for at least a fourth of mankind. The last two rows show various asymmetrical postures." (From "The Anthropology of Posture" by Gordon W. Hewes. Copyright © 1957 by Scientific American, Inc. All rights reserved.)

Chronemics

Around the globe, the differences in the use of and regard for time are fascinating. Generally, cultural time systems differ in two ways: in the use of informal time (ranging from *monochronistic* to *polychronistic* orientations) and in the structure of formal time. As is the case with emotional displays, these cultural differences in regard to time are often a reflection of religious and philosophical differences among people. The following are some examples of the varying treatments of time.

As we noted in Chapter 4, Latin Americans treat time in a polychronistic fashion. They often schedule a number of things to take place at the same time. By contrast, in our culture, time is conceived of as monochronistic, with a separate time for each activity.

The Arabs view time as an endless process. The individual is relatively insignificant—a mere speck in the greater expanse of time. The past is revered. The future and the immediate present are of little concern. Consequently, the individual makes no attempt to structure or control time. A story illustrating the point is attributed to Edward Hall. It tells of two Arab brothers who had been separated for many years. Finally, after many years of searching, one discovered the location of the other brother, phoned him, and agreed upon a meeting place. In time, the one brother arrived at the place and waited in vain for the other to appear. The brother confessed his misery and frustration to an American friend who realized from the man's account that the brothers had failed to name a time to meet. In fact, they hadn't even named a specific year.

The Truk Islanders treat the past as if it were the present.[5] Even their language has no past tense. Thus, past offenses, grudges, and personal traumas are locked in the present. They are treated as if they had just happened. Likewise, a compliment or gift or favor is continually recalled.

In our culture, of course, time is a commodity to be cherished and exchanged and bestowed as if it were tangible. Not so for many other cultures. We have developed very elaborate linguistic and nonverbal means of showing urgency. Waiting is thought of as a waste of time. In such countries as Japan, India, and the Arab nations, and among the Navajo Indians of this country, sitting or waiting is not an idle, unproductive activity but is thought of as constructive.[6]

Northern Europeans, on the other hand, are quite similar to North Americans in their conception of and uses of time. Basically, time is viewed monochronistically, although travelers may notice different values regarding punctuality and differences in what is meant by "being late."

Of course, cultures may also differ with respect to formal time systems. In the following example, Edward Hall notes the modification of formal time used by the Tiv of Nigeria:

The Tiv equivalent of the week lasts five to seven days. It is not tied into periodic natural events, such as the phases of the moon. The day of the week is named after the things which are being sold in the nearest "market." If we had the equivalent, Monday would be "automobiles" in Washington, D.C., "furniture" in Baltimore, and "yard goods" in New York. Each of these might be followed by the days for appliances, liquor and diamonds in the respective cities. This would mean that as you travel about, the day of the week would keep changing, depending upon where you were.[7]

Proxemics

Stories that illustrate just how different cultures are in their preference for personal space seem comical to some. Newspaper reporters and columists are fond of recounting how, at an embassy party, an individual pursued an American around the room trying to achieve a normal interaction distance (one that seems unbearably close for us) as the American backed away to achieve a comfortable distance. This example illustrates the difference between *contact* and *noncontact* cultures. A number of cultures can be classified as *contact cultures* because they exhibit a preference for closeness in everyday interaction. People from Central America, the Arab countries, and India fall into this category. Closeness is important because it allows people to feel the heat radiating from each other's body and to smell the body odors that are a vital aspect of interpersonal relations. Needless to mention, in our culture odor is considered offensive, and extreme closeness is a sign of either intimacy or aggression, depending upon the situation.

In Japan, the desire for closeness has influenced all aspects of family life and reflects a concept of territoriality that is somewhat alien to Westerners. For example, many Japanese dwellings have but a single bedroom. It is a common practice for several members of a family to use one sleeping area. On a cold evening, it is traditional to pile everyone in a circle beneath a single quilt with feet flat against each other as a source of warmth. Houses are seldom compartmentalized to allow for privacy as is the case in this country. (In spite of the mixed sleeping arrangements and public baths, the Japanese strictly adhere to norms that forbid public displays of affection.[8])

Maurice H. Krout has explored the symbolic rituals of various cultures and has formulated an interesting sample of some of the many differences in the ways groups of people use nonverbal messages to achieve similar ends (Table 5.1).[9]

Origins of Cultural Differences

What gives rise to the differences among cultural groups? In previous chapters, we have argued that context is a dominant factor in determining behavior. The point is especially important in considering cultural differences. Just as a single individual finds him- or herself with a cultural context, so too are cultures found within a larger environment. Many sociologists and anthropologists credit this environment with influencing the evolution of cultural norms for behavior. Geography (including terrain and climate), we know, was closely related to early ritual. Changes in the seasons, divisions of labor, marriage, and religion became interwoven influences upon the life style and the daily behavior of people. Certainly the level of industrial development of a people has a great deal to do with nonverbal behavior. It is clear that concepts of time and proximity are in part an artifact of our industrial–technological world.

There is, however, another side to the issue. Some researchers note physiological differences between cultures, arguing that differences in cultural norms are caused by differences in the muscular structure of people.

Subcultural Differences

Much of the research on subcultural differences in nonverbal communication is racial in nature, focusing on normative differences between blacks (usually urban black groups) and whites. Of course, part of the difficulty in interpreting research of this nature stems from the heterogeneity of the black population in this country. A black child raised in the inner city is socialized in a very different way than is a black child raised in a rural environment. Surely, the same is true for white children. What we are left with, more often than not, is little more than a description of black urban norms. The findings are questionable; sometimes provocative; possibly, though not necessarily, factual.

Table 5.1 The Symbolic Rituals of Various Groups

Attitude Expressed	Behavior Pattern	Culture Group
Affection	Embracing and kissing on mouth or cheek	Eur-Americans
	Smelling heads	Mongols
	Rubbing noses	Eskimos and others
	Pressing mouths and noses upon cheek and inhaling breath strongly	Burmese
	Juxtaposing noses and smelling heartily	Samoans
Approval	Smacking lips	Indians (N.A.)
	Back slapping	Eur-Americans
Assent	Elevating head and chin	New Zealanders
	Nodding	Eur-Americans
Derision	Closing fist with thumb protruding between index and middle fingers	European Jews
	Moving one index finger horizontally across the other	Russians, Germans
Humility	Throwing oneself on the back, rolling from side to side, slapping outside of thighs (meaning: you need not subdue me; I'm subdued already)	Batokas
	Bowing, extending right arm, moving arm down in horizontal position, raising it to the level of one's head, and lowering it again (meaning: I lift the earth off the ground, and place it on my head as a sign of submission to you)	Turks and Persians
	Walking about with hands bound and rope around one's neck	Ancient Peruvians
	Joining hands over head and bowing (ancient sign of obedience signifying: I submit with tied hands)	Chinese
	Dropping arms; sighing	Europeans
	Stretching hands toward person and striking them together with mutually synchronized movements	Congo natives
	Extension of arms; genuflection; prostration	Preliterates, European peasants
	Crouching	New Caledonians, Fijiians, Tahitians
	Crawling and shuffling forward; walking on all fours	Dahomeans
	Bending body downward	Samoans
	Permitting one to place his foot on the head	Fundah and Tonga Tabu peoples
	Prostration, face down	Polynesians
	Putting palms together for the other person to clasp gently	Unyanyembans
	Bowing while putting jointed hands between those of other person and lifting them to one's forehead	Sumatrans
Negation (refusal)	Moving arms sideways across the body; shaking head	Eur-Americans
	Throwing head back and making clucking noise with tongue	Turks
	Making smart, quick stroke of the nose with an extended finger on the right hand (if the negation is doubtful, they let the finger linger on the way, but finally rub it across the nose)	Inhabitants of Admiralty Islands

Table 5.1 (Cont.)

Attitude Expressed	Behavior Pattern	Culture Group
Propitiation (of rulers, at graves, at altars)	Extension of arms in making presents	Various peoples
	Kissing feet, hands, garments; uncovering and bowing head	Eur-Americans and others
	Jumping, clapping hands, and even drumming ribs with elbows	Various people
Salutation	Clapping hands (highest form of respectful greeting)	People of Loango
	Clapping hands and drumming ribs with elbows	People of Balonda
	Yielding up one's clothes (as a sign of surrender in salutation)	Assyrians
	Unclothing to the girdle	Abyssinians
	Doffing hat or merely touching it; handshake	Eur-Americans
	Grasping hands and pressing thumbs together	Wanyiika people
	Grasping hands and separating them with a pull so that a snapping noise is made by thumb and fingers	Nigerians
	Engaging in a sort of scuffle in which each tries to raise to his lips the hands of the other; kissing beards	Arabs
	Drawing hands from the shoulder and down the arms to the fingertips of the person greeted, or rubbing hands together	Ainus of Japan
	Blowing into each other's hands or ears	Some preliterates
	Stroking own face with other person's hands	Polynesians
	Smelling each other's cheeks and joining and rubbing each other's noses	Mongols, Malays, Burmese, Lapps
	Snapping fingers	Dahomeans and others
	Silence for a time; then ceremonials varying in complexity	Australian preliterates
Satisfaction	Massaging stomach	Indians (N.A.)
	Striking hands together	Certain peoples, Eur-American children
	Smacking lips; washing hands movement	East-European Jews
Surprise	Gaping mouth, raised eyebrows	Eur-Americans
	Slapping hips	Eskimos, Tlingits, Brazilians
	Lightly tapping nose or mouth	Ainus of Japan
	Pinching cheek	Tibetans
	Moving hand before mouth	Negro Bantus
	Protruding lips as if to whistle	Australian and West African preliterates
Welcome	Spreading arms	Europeans
	No sign of outer expression (when meeting after long separation)	Ainus of Japan, Australian Blackfellows
	Hand clapping	Certain Africans
	Jumping up and down	Natives of Tierra del Fuego
	Weeping	Australian tribes

SOURCE: Maurice H. Krout, "Symbolism," in Haig A. Bosmajian (ed.), *The Rhetoric of Nonverbal Communication* (Glenview, Ill.: Scott, Foresman, 1971), pp. 19–22; and Maurice H. Krout, *Introduction to Social Psychology* (New York: Harper & Row, 1942). Slight modification made by permission.

Kinesic Behavior

The difference in nonverbal behavior between blacks and whites that is perhaps the most difficult to document has to do with body movement. Young blacks have developed a repertoire of stylized movements that are quite different from the movement patterns of their white counterparts. These behaviors are important subjects for discussion because they fulfill important functions for a group of people. These stylized movement patterns are what some have referred to as *role signs;*[10] they signal membership in a subcultural group. Kenneth Johnson, a researcher in ethnic studies at the University of California at Berkeley, has described a number of different mannerisms distinctive of black youths.[11]

1. There is a style of black male walking behavior, called in street jargon the *pimp strut,* which functions as an attention-getting device and serves to exhibit one's masculinity and state one's racial pride, self-confidence, and control.

The young Black males' walk is different. First of all, it's much slower—it's more of a stroll. The head is sometimes slightly elevated and casually tipped to the side. Only one arm swings at the side with the hand slightly cupped. The other arm hangs limply to the side or it is tucked in the pocket. The gait is slow, casual and rhythmic. The gait is almost like a walking dance, with all parts of the body moving in rhythmic harmony.[12]

2. Black conversational behavior is punctuated by the movement of people first toward and then away from the center of a group in a rhythmic, fluid pattern. Whites, on the other hand, remain rather fixed in their distance and body orientation toward other group members.
3. The black *rapping stance*—male positioned at slight angle to female with head tilted to the partner, eye partially closed, with one hand limp at the side and the other hand in the front pocket—is a sign of masculinity and a way of indicating sexual interest.
4. Black females often signal hostility by placing hands on hips with their weight on the heels and with the buttocks extended.
5. During interaction, black listeners will often communicate agreement with a speaker by a movement that involves turning the back to the speaker. It is a way of indicating that the listener is in tune with the speaker; in light moments, the action may be accompanied by laughter.

There has not been much research on *eye behavior.* A couple of studies have shown that white males tend to engage in more eye contact than black males. Furthermore, the evidence indicates that black men engage in the least amount of eye contact when interacting with a white male. One interesting notion about black eye movement comes from Johnson. Johnson suggests that whenever a group of individuals is denied access to verbal channels of communication for expressing feelings of rejection, discontentment, and hostility, they must resort to nonverbal expressions.[13] Ultimately, the nonverbal code is expanded to incorporate subtle new means of indicating disapproval. This is especially true of eye behavior. When blacks use a particular roll of the eyes in talking with whites, Johnson says, "the movement of the eyes communicates all or parts of the message. The main message is hostility."[14]

Proxemics

Teresa Rosegrant, while at Illinois State University, examined both racial and sexual differences in preferences for interpersonal distance.[15] The findings indicated that black males position themselves farther away from others than does anyone else. White males were second in the amount of distance from others, while white females preferred even less distance. Black females showed a preference for the closest interpersonal distance. The findings might well explain some of the difficulties that occur in black–white communication. It may be that whites see the black male as aloof, distant, and possibly hostile because of his preference for greater distance. On the other hand, the black female, with a preference for very close distance, is thought of as aggressive, extroverted, social, and involved. No doubt these impressions based solely on preferences for space could complicate interracial interaction.

Chronemics

As we mentioned earlier, cultures differ dramatically in uses of and feelings about time. The same can be said for many subcultural groups. In Hawaii, the Polynesians live somewhere between two time systems. *Hauley time*—an outgrowth of the life style of the early missionaries in the islands—is very close to our concept of informal time. If you were to hear someone say, "See you at two o'clock hauley time," they mean just that—two o'clock or thereabouts. But if someone were to say "I'll be there at two o'clock Hawaiian time," then something altogether different is implied. *Hawaiian time* is very lax. It means "when you get there."

The Mormon subculture has a very different system. Being even a few minutes late is thought to be inconsiderate. Hence, Mormon communities consider punctuality a virtue. The approved behavior is to arrive early rather than late.[16]

Urban black subculture has a notion of time that is very similar to the concept of Hawaiian time. It is known as *street time*.[17] Like Hawaiian time, street time is a reference to the internal clock of urban blacks. Street time revolves around the activities of the street, not the hours of the clock. When you live on the street, you implicitly know when things are to occur. You know that after work, the men may stop for a few beers. There is no concept of being late. You either make it or you don't. The same is true of working hours. "Work" isn't what happens at eight o'clock; it is what you do once you get to the factory.

No doubt many executives find street time an unmanageable practice. One example in particular comes to mind. The managers in a factory in Detroit were having trouble getting the predominantly black factory workers to start work at the designated hour. Instead of coming in at eight o'clock, the workers would drift in ten or fifteen minutes late each workday. The white executives assumed that the workers were lazy and irresponsible. In reality, the workers were consciously coming in late as a protest against "white man's time." When the two groups got together and discussed the problem, an amicable solution was reached. The workers came in fifteen minutes late and left fifteen minutes late. The clock was punched to the satisfaction of management, and the black workers were able to dictate their time schedule in a small but important way.

In the Detroit example, time was used to make a point. Street time also represents an agenda of activities different from the one that exists in most white communities. John Horton, a sociologist at UCLA, provides the following brief description of activities on the street:

Characteristically the street person gets up late, hits the street in the late morning or early afternoon, and works his way to the set. This is a place for relaxed social activity. Hanging on the set with the boys is the major way of passing time and waiting until some necessary or desirable action occurs. Nevertheless, things do happen on the set. The dudes "rap" and "jive" (talk), gamble, and drink their "pluck" (usually a cheap, sweet wine). They find out what happened yesterday, what is happening today, and what will hopefully happen on the weekend—the perpetual search for the "gig,"

the party. Here peer socialization and rein-
forcement also take place. The younger dude
feels a sense of pride when he can be on the set
and throw a rap to an older dude. He is learn-
ing how to handle himself, show respect, take
care of business, and establish his own
"rep." [18]

On the street, the clock is meaningless. One's sense of timing is tied not to formal time but to the social rhythm of actions in one's peer group. Horton has made the point that street time is very much tied to the flow of money in the black urban community. When money is available, the individual has greater control over activity and is able to structure time by arranging social events. On the other hand, when money is tight, people lose control over time; action dies, and routine sets in.

Of course, street time and the disparity between the time perspective of urban blacks and the structure of time in most white communities presents something of a problem to blacks who are caught between the two worlds. Blacks often refer to lateness among other blacks as *CPT* (colored people's time).[19] When a friend arrives late for a specified appointment, others may chide him for arriving CPT.

mini-experiment

Choose randomly five black males and five black females and an equal number of white males and females to observe. Record clothing styles including colors, formality of clothing, patterns, and so on. Are there differences between either the races or the sexes in your sample? What colors are most preferred by blacks? by females? by whites? by males?

Research has shown that people who are trapped at the lower socioeconomic levels of our society develop concepts of time that are very different from the views of others. Predictably, members of low-income groups acquire a *short time perspective,* which may be defined as a generalized tendency to consider only a brief time period as the context in which behavior choices are made.[20] People with a short time perspective lack an orientation toward the future; they react to the demands of the moment. Many researchers feel that the short time perspective contributes greatly to deviant behavior. Individuals who respond most strongly to immediate pressures are likely to act impulsively without consideration for long-range, possibly negative consequences of their actions.

Sex Differences

The topic of sex differences is one of the hottest controversies in the social sciences today. Traditional assumptions regarding male–female differences are being challenged, and many past and even current research techniques have been criticized as either biased or misleading. Of course, the women's liberation movement has contributed greatly to this discussion. It is by no means, however, the most influential factor. Many social scientists have worked diligently to reappraise the image of women in the social science literature. The following topics represent a collection of research findings on possible differences between men and women in the way they use and respond to nonverbal messages.

Kinesic Behavior

Judging Facial Expressions   The jury is still out on the issue of whether males or females are better at judging emotions from facial

Table 5.2 Percentage of Time Engaged in Eye Contact

	Mutual	Listening	Speaking	Total Time
Males	3.0	29.8	25.6	23.2
Females	7.5	42.4	36.9	37.3

SOURCE: R. Exline, "Explorations in the Process of Person Perception: Visual Interaction in Relation to Competition, Sex, and Need for Affiliation," *Journal of Personality*, 31: 1–20. Copyright 1963 by Duke University Press.

expressions, but available evidence indicates that females are *slightly* better than males in the accuracy of their judgments. Research conducted on children has shown girls to exceed boys consistently. Perhaps the early socialization process for females focuses more on sensitivity than does the process for males. These differences appear to dissipate over time. It is likely that women in our culture are expected to have a heightened sensitivity to certain emotions. There may be certain expressions that males find easier to identify because of their relevance to the performance of the male sex role. Of course, we are speculating here. Still, we may conclude that females have a slight edge in judging facial expressions.[21]

Encoding Facial Expressions There is not much data, but what we do know seems to indicate that females are superior to males in their ability to send certain emotional displays. Specifically, females are better in expressing happiness, fear, love, and anger.[22] Again, this raises speculation that women are socialized to be sensitive to the transmission of these expressions. Thorne and Henley have offered an intriguing hypothesis about the impact of women's superiority in decoding and encoding emotional messages.[23] They have argued that this versatility with emotional cues is actually a social and interpersonal stigma. Because females are adept at sending and re-

ceiving a wide range of cues, they are often thought of as emotional, unstable, and lacking restraint and control. In a sense, this skill has helped perpetuate traditional stereotypes of the female.

Gazing Researchers have explored differences between the sexes in eye contact perhaps more than any other single nonverbal behavior. The differences are as dramatic as, or more dramatic than, those of any other variable. Clearly, females look more at others than do males. Ralph Exline, noted for his research on eye gaze, found that women establish more eye contact than men, including more mutual eye contact, more eye contact while listening, and more while speaking.[24] His findings are summarized in Table 5.2. Over the course of a conversation, females spend approximately 15 percent more time looking at their dyadic partner than do their male counterparts.

Research has also shown that both males and females look more when speaking to a female partner than to a male.[25] Speculation runs that female listeners are generally more attentive, showing more support, interest, and involvement, and thus warranting gaze by a speaker. Some have also noted that the avoidance of mutual eye contact among males may be a function of its intimate, often sexual connotation—a connotation that violates norms regarding appropriate male–male interaction. Such norms may be less restrictive for female–female interaction, or perhaps they do not label eye contact as taboo.

We also know that women prefer, in fact they depend on, visual information about partners more than do men. Research has shown that when women are deprived of the opportunity to see their partner, they report feeling more uncomfortable about the interaction than do males under similar conditions. Females also express greater awareness of being observed by others than do males, perhaps indicating a heightened sensitivity to gaze.[26] Popular opinion holds that there are two groups of people in the world: those who are observers and those who are observed. In other words, some people view others and say, "I wonder what's wrong with him? What made him do that?" Those are the observers. The observed say, "I wonder why he's doing that to me?" The observer never views behavior of another person as a comment on his actions. The observed individual always feels as though even the slightest sign of unhappiness must be aimed at him. Of course this is an oversimplification of the differences between males and females, but there is some evidence to indicate that males tend to develop the perspective of the observer and females that of the observed.

It has also been noted that males exceed females in *staring*, which is generally regarded as a relic from our biological ancestors—a behavior that functions to forestall aggression from other animals.[27] Especially in mixed-sex interaction, the stare of the male typically results in a lowering of the eyes by the female. Henley cited this type of visual interaction as evidence of the submissive cues associated with the contemporary female sex role.[28]

Smiling   In general, women smile more in a wider range of situations than do men. Frieze has argued that the tendency for women to smile even when unhappy—even when it is not appropriate—seems to suggest that women have been trained to present a happy face regardless of the circumstances.[29] Frieze has cited this as evidence of a submissive and acquiescent communication style among females, with the smile used to signal that no harm or threat of ill will is intended. Shulamith Firestone, in *The Dialectic of Sex*, provides an interesting personal commentary:

The smile is the shuffle of the child/woman; it indicates acquiescence of the victim to his own oppression. In my own case, I had to train myself out of that phony smile, which is like a nervous tic on every teenage girl. And this meant that I smiled rarely, for in truth, when it came down to real smiling, I had less to smile about. My "dream" action for the women's liberation movement: a smile boycott, at which declaration all women would instantly abandon their "pleasing" smiles, henceforth smiling only when something pleases them.[30]

Vocalics

Interruptions   Zimmerman and West examined a number of male–male, female–female, and mixed-sex conversations.[31] They found that, in mixed-sex conversations, there were approximately seven times more instances of interruptions of one party by another than in same-sex conversations, observing that "virtually all the interruptions and overlaps are by the male speakers (98% and 100% respectively)."[32] The finding was interpreted as evidence of the tendency of males to dominate mixed-sex interaction, often talking over the speech of the partner or interrupting the female speaker. In response to the interruptions, the women tended not to protest but became silent for noticeable periods of time.

Inflection Patterns   Much of the controversy over how women's speech differs from that of men has focused on differences in inflection patterns and the ways in which certain vocalic features signal dominance or submission. Robin Lakoff has argued that women have been socialized to appear docile, subordinate, and acquiescent.[33] Lakoff has noticed that women tend to use a very different pattern of vocal inflections than do men and that these inflections seriously impair credibility and status and modify the informational value of the message itself. Falling intonation patterns at the end of a phonemic clause are generally associated with declarative statements, commands, and so forth. Rising intonation patterns at the end of a clause tend to indicate questioning, doubt, uncertainty. Lakoff's work has indicated that women's speech shows more instances of *rising* intonation patterns with what is normally thought to be *declarative* statements than does the speech behavior of men. The result, says Lakoff, is that women give the appearance of needing confirmation by others, of not being sure of their own ideas.

Haptics

Research indicates that women touch more and are touched more than males.[34] The evidence also suggests, though, that men tend to initiate touching, while women tend to touch only in response to the advances (touches) of the male.

Curiously enough, much male touching of females is not reciprocated by the female. Thorne and Henley have argued that "nonverbal gestures of dominance and submission often follow this asymmetric pattern: males signal dominance through nonreciprocal touch, with women responding passively or by cuddling to the touch. . . ."[35] Touch itself, then, isn't as important as when one touches and the response of another to being touched.

Proxemics

Personal Space   Men require more personal space than do women, but no one knows why this is the case. Males tend to take greater control over territory, managing property and invading at will the personal space of others more often than do females. There is some evidence to indicate that women prefer more closed and restricted environments.[36] It is not clear whether, as some have argued, this control over space and territory by males is part of an aggressive, domineering pattern of behavior toward women or whether the infringement of a woman's space is invited.

Seating   Not a great deal is known about sex differences in seating preferences. What

we do know is that females have a greater preference for side-by-side seating, while males choose either to face or to be separated from others. In groups, they tend to assume positions associated with leadership (sitting at the head of the table or other central positions in the group). Furthermore, female–female partners sit much closer together than do male–male dyads, but the closest seating is among male–female combinations.[37] (See Figure 5.3.)

Androgyny

Here are some things you should *not* believe about sex differences in nonverbal behavior: Do not conclude that the evidence paints females as strikingly different from males. There are occasional differences. They tend to be relatively subtle. And there is no evidence to indicate that these factors invariably alter the outcome of interaction. Do not assume that the specific causes of sex differences are known. Differences may be the result of cultural prescriptions regarding sex roles (resulting in relatively invariable patterns of behavior); they may be situational responses (males may differ from females in a given situation but only in that situation); they may be the result of biological differences between the sexes. There is some evidence that differences in aggression are due in part to the presence of certain hormones in men that prompt aggressiveness. Do not conclude that these differences are either consistent or stable. The fact of the matter is that sex roles in our culture are in transition, and we can expect that nonverbal behaviors reflecting concepts of masculinity and femininity will change accordingly.

As sex roles have begun to change, the term *androgyny* has come into use. *Androgyny* refers to the combination of what we think of as traditionally masculine and feminine traits in a single individual. An androgynous individual is less restricted by sexual stereotypes than

Figure 5.3 Males tend to converse at greater distances and with more indirect body orientations than do females.

are others. By some estimates, approximately 35 percent of our population is androgynous.[38] If this represents a trend, then we can expect the differences that do exist between the sexes in nonverbal communication to lessen.

mini-experiment

With several unsuspecting oposite-sex partners and several members of the same sex, begin your conversations at a normal distance and gradually begin to move closer. Observe the nonverbal and verbal responses. Do the women respond differently than the men? How do they display their discomfort?

Personality Differences

Much of what is known about the relationship of personality to nonverbal behavior falls into one of two categories of investigation—studies of psychological disorders such as schizophrenia and paranoia and research on personality characteristics such as speech anxiety and introversion. Unfortunately, in both cases the research is filled with anecdotes and case studies that are difficult to interpret. Even when aberrant nonverbal behavior has been studied, it has been only a secondary concern. Table 5.3 capsulizes much of what we know in this area.

Deviant Conditions

Schizophrenia As we mentioned in Chapter 2, there is an interesting relationship between schizophrenia and nonverbal behavior. Schizophrenia has long been thought to be a product of environments in which children are consistently provided with conflicting, ambivalent nonverbal and verbal cues. The individual finds him- or herself in a *double bind,* in which any avenue of action is to some extent wrong. Schizophrenia results when individuals attempt to compartmentalize the dilemmas and contradictions of their world, locking up the memory of their failures and disappointments in one facet of their personality. Schizophrenia does not refer to a *split personality,* as is popularly believed; rather it refers to the development of a new and isolated personality that screens out inconsistent information and permits the individual to perceive things (at least for the moment) as being consistent and harmonic. Schizophrenia takes its toll. Because schizophrenics have no adequate model

for learning consistent patterns of nonverbal behavior, they are never quite able to master the coordinated, coherent, and well choreographed movements that most of us are able to execute. Their actions are spasmodic. They avoid eye contact. Schizophrenics have tremendous difficulty in communicating emotional expressions. Often their tone of voice contradicts facial expression. When they speak, the sentences are often fragmented, incoherent, and without any apparent logical order.[39]

Paranoia The nonverbal signals of paranoia are quite difficult to detect. Psychologists have had much trouble in recognizing the paranoid patient from outward behavior alone.

Table 5.3 Nonverbal Correlates of Psychological Conditions

Condition	Type of Condition	Nonverbal Correlates
Schizophrenia*	Disorder	Flattening of emotions; untidy physical appearance; apathetic mood; rambling, often incoherent speech; jerky and uncoordinated body movements; little attention; little eye contact; inability to communicate emotional cues; long silences
Paranoia*	Disorder	Distortion of feedback; interpreting actions as negative feedback; otherwise capable of normal interaction
Manic states*	Disorder	Hyperactive; wears loud, striking clothes; very confident voice, loud and resonant; talks incessantly; tends to dominate conversation; uproarious laughter
Depressive states*	Disorder	Drab in appearance; somber expressions; shows expressions of unhappiness; flat, low-pitched, monotone voice; relatively inactive; brief verbal exchanges
Hysteria*	Disorder	Exaggerated emotional expressions; use of emotional cues to gain attention
Communication anxiety	Trait/state	Short utterances; many speech errors; tense; heightened finger and hand movement; decreased eye contact
Need for affiliation	Trait-variable	Much eye contact
Extroversion	Trait-variable	Much eye contact; little interpersonal distance
Conceptual abstractness	Trait-variable	Great role playing ability

*Summarized from Argyle, *The Psychology of Interpersonal Behaviour* (Baltimore: Penguin, 1967).

The primary characteristic of paranoia is the distortion of information. Information is consistently viewed in terms of threat and danger. The paranoid individual misreads emotional cues, perceiving criticism directed at him- or herself, exaggerates differences, and often overreacts to joking or kidding by others. The paranoid individual is by no means unable to communicate.[40] In fact, the differences between the normal and paranoid individual are so slight that most of us would attribute the differences to moodiness or the like.

Manic States Manic states are fairly easy to identify. The individual becomes engrossed in a situation, bubbling with enthusiasm, talking incessantly, confidently. Feelings of joy are exaggerated into loud, raucous behavior. In these people, gaiety and humor are not the informal, relaxed moods that serve as a tension release for most of us; they are explosive and almost violent. Noise becomes deafening and feelings are tense. A manic state influences more than one's conversational behavior; it forms a kind of life style that includes extremes of physical activity and boldly colorful clothing.[41]

Depressive States A depressive state is pretty much the opposite of a manic state. A depressive state brings on somber expressions. Emotions are underplayed. The voice becomes a low, flat montone. The individual dresses to reflect the emotions with drab, dark clothing. In contrast to the manic, the depressed individual is relatively inactive, engaging in only the briefest verbal exchanges.[42]

Hysteria Hysteria has come to mean the overintensification or exaggeration of emotional expressions, often manifesting itself in sobbing or crying or some other physical sign of sadness, fear, or despondency. Hysteria can also involve what we tend to think of as positive emotional expressions, such as uncontrollable laughter or what is often referred to as crying for joy. Unlike a manic state, hysteria appears to be uncontrolled. To the individual

prone to hysteria, exaggerated emotional expressions provide a mechanism to gain attention and compassion.[43]

Communication Anxiety Researchers in the field of speech communication have long been interested in the causes, symptoms, and treatment of communication anxiety. Originally, researchers labeled the phenomenon *stage fright,* but it has come to mean something much more than freezing in the presence of large audiences. Communication anxiety can be prompted by almost any situation calling for interpersonal or public communication. Extreme anxiety is referred to as *reticence.* The highly reticent communicator may be totally unable to respond coherently to others in even the most informal situation. When reticents attempt to communicate their utterances are short and fraught with mispronunciations, stutter starts, and hesitations.[44] The communication-anxious individual tends to refuse eye contact and displays nervousness through rapid finger and hand movement. Research has also demonstrated that highly anxious persons prefer greater interpersonal distance during interaction.[45] Close physical distance may have a particularly unnerving effect.

Personality Types

Most other psychological variables are not usually thought of in terms of nonverbal correlates, although occasionally research has found some kind of connection. For example, there is some evidence that *need for affiliation* is related to amount of eye contact. People who have a great need for being affiliated with others give more eye contact than do others.[46] The relationship seems almost intuitive, since eye contact is one means of achieving affiliation and recognition.

What we know about need for affiliation parallels closely the nonverbal correlates of *extroversion.* Highly introverted people tend to require greater distance between themselves and others than do extroverted people. Furthermore, introverts often resist visual interaction as if fearing involvement.[47]

An intriguing psychological variable that may suggest an unusual nonverbal profile is *conceptual abstractness*. Harvey, Hunt, and Schroder have identified four types of conceptual systems ranging from the very concrete to the very abstract. These are the *authoritarian*, the *antiauthoritarian*, the *person-oriented*, and the *information-oriented* systems. A highly concrete system (the authoritarian) tends to process information in dichotomies—things are either black or white, good or bad, right or wrong. Authority legitimizes action; one looks to status to know whether an action has value. At the other extreme of the continuum is the highly abstract, information-oriented individual who is concerned not with the status of a speaker but with the intrinsic value of the message. Things are not black or white; there are gradations of value.[48]

Early in their research program, Harvey and his colleagues conducted a study to determine the extent to which concrete personalities were limited in their ability to portray various roles requiring flexibility and insight into emotions and feelings. They found that the role-playing skills of an individual varied with his or her level of abstractness; the more abstract the personality, the greater the ability to take on roles and portray emotions not actually felt at the time. The authoritarian individuals had a great deal of difficulty in playing any role at all.

The researchers reasoned that one's past experiences influence personality and ultimately one's ability to play roles. For example, children who are not told, "Do this or else," but are provided reasons, shown possibilities, and given behavioral alternatives develop more abstract personalities than do children who grow up in a more rigid and authoritarian environment. The researchers argued that if background influences this ability to play roles, and if there were a way to give a new background to an individual with a concrete conceptual system, then the person's role-playing

ability should improve. Thus, they ran a number of "concrete individuals" through a series of role-playing exercises, at which the subjects failed miserably, and then subjected them to hypnosis. Under hypnosis, the researchers gave the subjects past experiences more suited to an abstract personality. The subjects were awakened and led through the same series of role-playing situations. The differences were amazing. Role-playing abilities improved dramatically. Again under hypnosis, the experiences were removed. The subjects were awakened and led through the exercises again. Their abilities to portray roles were no better than at the outset of the experiment.

What does this research say about psychological differences and nonverbal behavior? First, the study indicates that some individuals experience a great deal of difficulty in expressing emotions they do not feel. These people tend to be thought of as *transparent*. Other people are quite skillful in creating and managing impressions and in fabricating emotions and reactions regardless of their feelings. Second, the study suggests that these may not be the kinds of skills one can practice with any hope of success. One's background seems to contribute in part to role-playing skill; short of hypnosis, nothing much can change one's ability to portray emotions.

Summary

We have tried to provide in this chapter a potpourri of the ways in which people's cultural or subcultural background, sex, and psychological condition can affect their uses of and regard for nonverbal messages. There is convincing evidence that, as people differ in language and dialect, they also differ in their nonverbal behaviors.

Research on sex differences has come to be of more than casual interest because of its relevance to political and social dialogue regarding changing sex roles in this country. While the research has indicated that there are some differences in the nonverbal behavior of men and women, it is difficult to pinpoint the exact causes or understand exactly what implications these differences have for mixed-sex interaction.

Lastly, the research on nonverbal correlates of psychological conditions has shown that any number of psychological variables—from disorders to normal personality traits—can cause abnormal nonverbal behavior. Unfortunately, the differences are often quite subtle and momentary. Even clinical psychologists report difficulty in determining the psychological condition of a patient from nonverbal data alone.

Suggested Reading

Argyle, M. *The Psychology of Interpersonal Behavior.* Baltimore: Penguin, 1967.

Birdwhistell, R. "Masculinity and Femininity as Display." In R. Birdwhistell, *Kinesics and Context.* Philadelphia: University of Pensylvania Press, 1970. (pp. 39–46)

Friedman, R. J., and Katz, M. M. *The Psychology of Depression: Contemporary Theory and Research.* New York: Halsted Press, 1974.

Hall, E. T. *The Silent Language.* Greenwich, Conn.: Fawcett, 1959.

Key, M. R. "Linguistic Behavior of Male and Female." *Linguistics,* 88 (August 1972), 15–31.

Kramer, C. "Women's Speech: Separate but Unequal?" *Quarterly Journal of Speech,* 60 (February 1974), 14–24.

Krout, M. H. "Symbolism." In H. A. Bosmajian (ed.), *The Rhetoric of Nonverbal Communication.* Glenview, Ill.: Scott, Foresman and Company, 1971. (pp. 15–33)

Lakoff, R. "Language and Woman's Place." *Language in Society,* 2 (1973), 45–79.

Mehrabian, A. *Nonverbal Communication.* Chicago: Aldine Atherton, 1972.

Rich, A. L. "Interracial Implications of Nonverbal Communication." In A. L. Rich, *Interracial Communication.* New York: Harper and Row, 1974. (chapter 7)

Samovar, L. A., and Porter, R. E. (eds.). *Intercultural Communication: A Reader.* 2nd edition. Belmont, Calif. Wadsworth, 1976.

Thorne, B., and Henley, N. (eds.). *Language and Sex.* Rowley, Mass.: Newbury House, 1975.

Tompkins, S. S., and Izard, C. E. (eds.). *Affect, Cognition, and Personality.* New York: Springer, 1965.

Notes

1. L. M. Barna, "Stumbling Blocks in Interpersonal Intercultural Communications," in L. A. Samovar and R. E. Porter (eds.), *Intercultural Communication: A Reader* (Belmont, Calif.: Wadsworth, 1972), pp. 241–245.

2. W. LaBarre, "Paralinguistics, Kinesics, and Cultural Anthropology," in L. A. Samovar and R. E. Porter (eds.), *Intercultural Communication: A Reader* (Belmont, Calif.: Wadsworth, 1972), pp. 172–180.

3. LaBarre, 1972, p. 173 (note 2).

4. LaBarre, 1972, pp. 174–175 (note 2).

5. E. T. Hall, *The Silent Language* (Greenwich, Conn.: Fawcett, 1959), pp. 25–26.

6. Hall, 1959, pp. 11, 16, 132–133, 138 (note 5).

7. Hall, 1959, p. 26 (note 5).

8. D. Cathcart and R. Cathcart, "Japanese Social Experience and Concept of Groups," in L. A. Samovar and R. E. Porter (eds.), *Intercultural Communication: A Reader,* 2nd edition (Belmont, Calif.: Wadsworth, 1976), pp. 58–66.

9. See M. Krout "Symbolism," in H. A. Bosmajian (ed.), *The Rhetoric of Nonverbal Communication* (Glanview, Ill.: Scott, Foresman, 1971) pp. 15–33.

10. G. Gordon, *Role Theory and Illness: A Sociological Perspective* (New Haven, Conn.: College and University Press, 1966).

11. K. R. Johnson, "Black Kinesics: Some Non-Verbal Communication Patterns in the Black Culture," in L. A. Samovar and R. E. Porter (eds.), *Intercultural Communication: A Reader* (Belmont, Calif.: Wadsworth, 1972), pp. 259–268.

12. Johnson, p. 263 (note 11).

13. Johnson, p. 263 (note 11).

14. Johnson, p. 261 (note 11).

15. See T. J. Rosegrant and J. C. McCroskey, "The Effects of Race and Sex on Proxemic Behavior in an Interview Setting," *The Southern Speech Communication Journal*, 40 (Summer 1975), pp. 408–420.

16. Hall, 1959, pp. 130, 143–144 (note 5).

17. See J. Horton, "Time and Cool People," in L. A. Samovar and R. E. Porter (eds.), *Intercultural Communication: A Reader,* 2nd edition (Belmont, Calif.: Wadsworth, 1976) pp. 84–94.

18. Horton, 1976, pp. 276–277 (note 17).

19. Horton, 1976, p. 87 (note 17).

20. See, for discussion, R. Jessor, T. D. Graves, R. C. Hanson, and S. L. Jessor, *Society, Personality, and Deviant Behavior* (New York: Holt, Rinehart and Winston, 1968), p. 108.

21. R. Rosenthal, D. Archer, J. H. Koivumaki, M. R. DiMattee, and D. L. Rogers, "Assessing Sensitivity to Nonverbal Communication: The PONS Test," *Divison 8 Newsletter* of the Division of Personality and Social Psychology of the American Psychological Association, January 1974, pp. 1–3.

22. See A. Mehrabian, *Nonverbal Communication* (Chicago: Aldine Atherton, 1972), pp. 141–146.

23. See B. Thorne and N. Henley, "Difference and Dominance: An Overview of Language, Gender, and Society," in B. Thorne and N. Henley (eds.), *Language and Sex* (Rowley, Mass.: Newbury House, 1975), pp. 5–42.

24. R. Exline, "Exploration in the Process of Person Perception: Visual Interaction in Relation to Competition, Sex and the Need for Affiliation," *Journal of Personality,* 31 (1963), pp. 1–20.

25. See P. C. Ellsworth and L. M. Ludwig, "Visual Behavior in Social Interaction," *Journal of Communication,* 22 (1972), pp. 375–403.

26. M. Argyle, M. Lalljee, and M. Cook, "The Effects of Visibility on Interaction in a Dyad," *Human Relations,* 21 (1968), pp. 3–17.

27. L. O'Connor, "Male Dominance: The Nitty-Gritty of Oppression," *It Ain't Me Babe,* June 11–July 1, 1970, pp. 9–11.

28. N. Henley, "Power, Sex, and Nonverbal Communication," In B. Thorne and N. Henley (eds.), *Language and Sex* (Rowley, Mass.: Newbury House, 1975), pp. 184–203.

29. I. H. Frieze, "Nonverbal Aspects of Femininity and Masculinity Which Perpetuate Sex-Role Stereotypes," paper presented at Eastern Psychological Association, 1974.

30. S. Firestone, *The Dialectic of Sex* (New York: Bantam, 1970), p. 90.

31. D. H. Zimmerman and C. West, "Sex Roles, Interruptions and Silences in Conversation," in T. Thorne and N. Henley (eds.), *Language and Sex* (Rowley, Mass.: Newbury House, 1975), pp. 105–129.

32. Zimmerman and West, 1975, p. 115 (note 31).

33. R. Lakoff, "Language and Woman's Place," *Language in Society,* 2 (1973), pp. 45–79.

34. N. Henley, "The Politics of Touch," paper presented at American Psychological Association, 1970.

35. Thorne and Henley, 1975, p. 16 (note 28).

36. Mehrabian, 1972, pp. 20–21 (note 22); Frieze, 1974 (note 29).

37. Mehrabian, 1972 (note 22).

38. S. L. Bem, "Androgyny vs. the Tight Little Lives of Fluffy Women and Chesty Men," *Psychology Today,* 9 (1975), pp. 58–62.

39. M. Argyle, *The Psychology of Interpersonal Behaviour* (Baltimore: Pengiun, 1967), pp. 134–135.

40. Argyle, 1967, pp. 134–138 (note 39).

41. Argyle, 1967, pp. 135–136 (note 39).

42. Argyle, 1967, pp. 136–137 (note 39).

43. Argyle, 1967, pp. 136–137 (note 39).

44. Argyle, 1967, pp. 139–140 (note 39).

45. Argyle, 1967, pp. 138–139 (note 39).

46. Exline, 1963 (note 24).

47. N. A. Mobbs, "Eye Contact and Introversion-extroversion," cited by A. Kendon and M. Cook, "The Consistency of Gaze Patterns in Social Interaction," *British Journal of Psychology,* 60 (1969), pp. 481–494.

48. O. J. Harvey, D. E. Hunt, and H. M. Schroder, *Conceptual Systems and Personality Organization* (New York: Wiley, 1961).

II

The Functions of Nonverbal Communication

Part II introduces you to the functions of the upspoken dialogue by identifying six functions performed by our nonverbal behavior. In the first five chapters, we made the point that the human being is not entirely in control of all the functions performed by the various nonverbal codes. Sometimes our nonverbal behavior controls us. At times, our nonverbal actions are unconscious, or at least spontaneous and unrehearsed. In other cases, we deliberate long and hard over how best to structure a nonverbal message. In the following chapters we explore those functions of nonverbal behavior that are spontaneous and unrehearsed and move in subsequent chapters to the intentional and controlled functions of the nonverbal codes.

In Chapter 6, we look at one of the more spontaneous and automatic functions of our nonverbal behavior—the gleaning of information about others based upon their appearance, movements, voice, and apparel. In Chapter 7, we explore relational messages and how the nonverbal codes comment on our interpersonal relationships, showing liking, status, credibility, and power. Chapter 8, on the communication of emotion, examines how the body, voice, and face allow us to convey and interpret emotions. We discuss some of the problems people encounter in identifying displays of affection and some of the stylistic differences in the ways people communicate emotion. In Chapter 9, we focus on the role of nonverbal cues in the regulation of interaction. How we speak, what we say, when we say it, and to whom we say it all are influenced by a number of relatively subtle nonverbal signals. Chapter 10 explores the presentation of self through the nonverbal codes. Much of what we do nonverbally springs from an attempt on our part to present ourselves to others in a particular way. There are implicit rules regarding how to organize our nonverbal world in order to present a believable, consistent impression of ourselves to others. Last, Chapter 11 takes a look at how we use nonverbal messages to manipulate others, to influence what they learn, what they think, and how they act.

6

First Impressions

Test Your Sensitivity

True or False?

1. First impressions have long-term effects.
2. The voice is a good indicator of age, status, and education.
3. The personality stereotypes associated with different body types are usually inaccurate.
4. People who dress casually are assumed to be politically active.
5. Extremely beautiful women create a highly favorable impression of personality and character.
6. Men with beards are seen as younger and less powerful than clean-shaven men.

A natural starting place for studying the communicative *functions* of nonverbal cues is first impressions, since our first reactions to others supply the framework within which all the other nonverbal functions operate. Those first judgments color our perceptions of everything else that follows. When first impressions are positive, we probably seek further interaction; when they are negative, we attempt to avoid it.

Basic Principles

Men trust their ears less than their eyes.
—Herodotus

Beware, as long as you live, of judging people by appearances.
—Jean de La Fontaine

By the end of the chapter you should know the correct answer to all six questions and understand these concepts:

- principles of first impressions
- factors contributing to physical judgments
- factors contributing to sociological judgments
- factors contributing to psychological judgments
- relative accuracy and consistency of judgments of physical, sociological, and psychological attributes

What happens the first time you meet someone? Chances are, your mind immediately begins searching for information, much like looking for the missing pieces of a puzzle, and then tries to make sense out of the pieces that are assembled. First encounters are full of uncertainty. According to at least one theory,[1] our initial goal is to reduce that uncertainty so as to maintain as much predictability as possible about our environment and the people in it. We do this by looking for clues that may help us develop expectations about how others will act. As a rule, conversation is not a very good source of initial information. When we are first introduced to someone, talk is frequently limited to social amenities and topics such as the weather. We have to rely heavily on nonverbal cues.

To test your own sensitivity to first-impression cues, carefully study the man in the photograph in Figure 6.1, then rate him on the scales below. (To use the scales, for each adjective pair circle the number that best reflects your opinion, a 1 representing a high degree of

Figure 6.1

Unattractive	1	2	3	4	5	6	7	Attractive
Honest	1	2	3	4	5	6	7	Dishonest
Unintelligent	1	2	3	4	5	6	7	Intelligent
Lazy	1	2	3	4	5	6	7	Energetic
Sociable	1	2	3	4	5	6	7	Unsociable
Interesting	1	2	3	4	5	6	7	Boring
Unpersuasive	1	2	3	4	5	6	7	Persuasive
Unfriendly	1	2	3	4	5	6	7	Friendly
Aggressive	1	2	3	4	5	6	7	Meek

the quality on the left and a 7 representing a high degree of the quality on the right. For example, if you think the man is *relatively* intelligent, circle 5 or 6 for that adjective pair; if you think he is *very* honest, circle 1.)

If you are like most people, you probably made your ratings of the man's character fairly readily. The fact that you felt able to make several judgments with very little information illustrates our first point about first impressions: *People develop evaluations of others from limited information.* From a picture alone, you drew conclusions about the man's personality and a host of other personal characteristics. Results of a study involving twelve college students support the thesis that people make wide-ranging judgments from very

little information. The twelve, who were all strangers, were placed in a group and asked to evaluate each other before speaking to one another. With only visual and proxemic information available to them, subjects made judgments about one another on a full range of personality traits. Surprisingly, group members reached as high a degree of agreement among their ratings on such difficult-to-observe traits as bossiness and talkativeness as they did on more superficially apparent features such as tidiness.[2]

We can conclude from this study a second major principle: *First impressions are based on stereotypes.* The students made the judgments they made because they took certain nonverbal cues and used them to form the stereotypes associated with those cues. This is probably what you did in evaluating the photograph in Figure 6.1. The hairstyle, clothing, and skin coloring of the man in the picture may have conjured up stereotypical images such as those frequently presented on television, and these images may have led you to make far-reaching judgments about such things as personality, intelligence, and interests.

It should not be surprising that we form conscious or unconscious stereotypes. Consider the bombardment of nonverbal information that assails the senses and influences judgments. Because too much raw, uninterpreted information can be disturbing, we need some way to classify this abundance of information. Stereotypes offer one system of classification, Take kinesic behavior. Facial expressions, posture, amount of physical acitvity, and even style of walking can influence judgments. Research indicates, for instance, that if you use a lot of gestures and eye contact and smile a good deal, you are likely to be rated favorably by strangers.[3] Proxemic and haptic behavior may also provide clues. How close a person stands to others and whether a person touches others can lead to inferences about everything from cultural background, education, and status to personality and temperament. The cigar-smoking backslapper who puts his arm around your shoulder and pushes his face into yours has to be a used-car salesman, right? At least that's the stereotype. Vocal features add an important dimension. A loud, deep, resonant voice suggests "the politician"; a soft and hesitant one may suggest "the shy, demure female."

Perhaps the most significant factor in the making of initial judgments is physical appearance. Scholars who study the development of interpersonal attraction say that initial impressions are based on *object characteristics*. That is, we initially judge people as we would an inanimate object. Our conclusions are based on what is superficially observable—in most cases, body features and apparel. Thus, our third principle is: *Initial impressions are formed by treating others as objects, judging them on the basis of outward appearances.*

An earlier chapter emphasized the importance of physical attractiveness in our culture. Numerous experiments have found support for the notion that positive attributes are assigned to attractive people.[4] For example, students who were asked to rate yearbook pictures rated the more physically attractive students higher on sexual warmth, responsiveness, sensitivity, kindness, modesty, poise, sociability, extroversion, and interestingness. Even teachers fall into this trap, rating physically attractive children as more intelligent, more successful, and better adjusted socially than plainer students.

The ramifications of these superficial judgments can be serious, because they lead to very subtle forms of prejudice and discrimination. For instance, employment opportunities may be affected. A report on hiring practices has revealed that when the credentials of two male applicants for a job are the same, the taller man consistently gets the job. Mark Knapp, in his textbook on nonverbal communication, reports that male graduates of the University of Pittsburgh who are taller than 6 feet 2 inches have been receiving average starting salaries 12.4 percent higher than those under 6 feet tall.[5] Conversely, fat people have a much harder time than thinner people when it comes to getting jobs, adopting children, and even getting into college.[6]

These particular discriminations probably are not justified. But discrimination based on stereotypes is likely to continue because people place faith in initial impressions. One reason they do so is that initial impressions are often correct. Thus our fourth principle: *Many stereotypic judgments are relatively accurate.* Research on physical appearance, kinesics, and vocalics reveals that people can draw accurate conclusions from such cues about many personal characteristics including sex, age, race, occupation, socioeconomic status, and personality. Coupled with certain haptic, proxemic, and environmental data, these cues provide a wealth of information to shape our impressions. It is no wonder that we often trust our intuitive judgments. Intuition is nothing more than tuning in to all available information, and that information frequently steers us in the right direction.

Take, for example, the man in the photograph in Figure 6.1. Just how accurately did you peg him? Well, if you said he was not particularly attractive physically, most people would agree with that (although attractiveness is largely a matter of personal preference). If you also judged him to be somewhat low in the academic sort of intelligence and less than honest, his history suggests that you were right. You see, he was an Army depot clerk who had only an eighth-grade education and who didn't pass a low-level civil service exam but who managed to win $252,000 on *The $64,000 Question* before the show was exposed as rigged. However, if you rated him as unpersuasive and unaggressive, you would be wrong. After all, he did convince the American public that he was really a whiz. And he was gutsy enough and egotistical enough to claim to be the brightest of all the contestants. So, meek he wasn't. If you made errors in judging the man's personality and social skills, that should underscore the point that even though many of our first impressions are correct, they are not always so nor completely so. Cues can be misleading, and we are all fallible. Our generalization about the accuracy of first impressions is exactly that—a generalization; it does not hold true for all people or all situations or even all characteristics.

The fact that people do make mistakes should be cause for alarm, especially if one is on the receiving end of the faulty judgment. Someone may have decided that you are cold and aloof when you are merely shy and unsure. Conversely, you may have cultivated a friendship with someone who at first appeared to be effervescent and charming, only to discover later that he was all bubble and fizz with no substance. Such faulty impressions may result when important cues are overlooked in initial meetings or when people send messages in first encounters that are inconsistent with their true self. The effects of these faulty impressions can be serious if they cause people to make snap judgments (such as whether to hire someone) or to avoid future encounters. In most cases, further communication does take place, providing additional information. Since these later sources of data have a modifying influence, we can state one additional principle about first impressions: *The effects are usually only short term.*[7] More detailed verbal information, chronemic cues, and environmental and object cues, along with greater information from the kinesic, proxemic, haptic, and vocalic channels, permit a refinement of initial judgments. Stereotypes are replaced with more specific knowledge of the individual. As Allen Dittman argues, strangers begin by relying on the most universally understood channels, but as acquaintance progresses, subcultural and individual modes of communicat-

ing become relevant, and more personal information is revealed.[8] You may judge initially that someone is "a decent sort, maybe not especially interesting," but not until you have talked at length with that person are you likely to uncover his or her specific attitudes about life—and sometimes his or her fascinating opinions and unusual accomplishments. If the additional cues that become available during conversations serve to corroborate the first impression, then their modifying effect may be slight. Even if there is some discrepancy, the first impression may still act as a standard for comparing later actions and statements and may lead to a careful rescanning of both the initial behaviors and the subsequent ones. So, while first impressions tend to lose their importance over time, they still have an impact on the long-term development of interpersonal relationships.

With these basic principles in mind, let us examine more closely what kinds of impressions we form initially and which nonverbal codes are responsible.

Physical Features

The easiest judgments for us to make are about physical characteristics of the individual— age, sex, race, body shape, height, and weight. While it is obvious that we make these judgments based on physical appearance, other kinds of cues, such as vocal qualities and body movements, are also relevant.

Age

Physical Appearance   It seems that we ought to be able to determine a person's age from his or her physical appearance. However, this assumption requires some closer scrutiny. Because of the high premium placed on youthfulness in our culture, industry has supplied us with a glut of products, devices, and techniques for disguising age. Wigs, hairpieces, hair dye, make-up, and padding are all available to take years off the figure, face, and hair. There is also corrective surgery. One author of a nonverbal communication textbook, Dale Leathers, regards this aspect of appearance important enough to warrant devoting an entire section of his text to the effects of plastic surgery. With face lifts, hair transplants, and even fanny-lifts currently in vogue, it is becoming increasingly difficult to estimate the age of many adults. We often cannot distinguish youthful-looking parents from their adult children.

While older people are working hard at looking younger, teenagers typically have the opposite goal in mind—to look older. By adopting hairstyles of those who are slightly their senior, by using make-up or growing beards and mustaches, many teenagers are able to conceal their true age. The only giveaway is the relative softness and youthfulness of their facial features and physique compared to the more angular facial features and full figure of a mature adult. These differences may not be apparent to the casual observer.

In sum, while age can be judged with a degree of accuracy, cosmetic practices can contribute to some error in judgment. We are most successful at making estimates within broad age categories, especially in the infant, pre-teen, and extremely elderly categories.

Clothing choices further compound the situation. Since so many people wear jeans now, it is often hard to tell the college student from the middle-aged parent, worker, or employer. Other fashionable clothing styles appear among almost all age groups from pre-teen to elderly. For instance, at the time of this writing, leisure suits and brighly colored polyester shirts have won acceptance by men and women of all age groups. However, the careful observer may be able to make some age distinctions based on dress. In 1965, a book on the subject of dress stated that young men wear more varied and extravagant clothing than do older men. This may be partly due to the fact that they spend more money on clothes. (Young men supposedly spend twice as much money on clothes as do middle-aged men and three times as much as men aged sixty-five to seventy.) Table 6.1 lists a sample of apparel and accessories that have been suggested by women's magazines of the mid-1970s as communicating age. No doubt some of the items listed in the table will return to popularity among young people as styles change. But the person who wears a preponderance of these styles is probably assumed by most people to be older. On the whole, it is probably safe to conclude that the young are more fashion-conscious than older people and more likely to be dressed in the current styles; this may be the best clothing-related cue of age.

Vocalics   Another means of identifying age is from the voice. Studies have found that listeners can judge the age of a speaker quite accurately from vocal cues alone.[9] For instance, listeners can achieve a high success rate in placing speakers in a twenty-to-thirty, forty-to-fifty, or sixty-to-seventy age range. Our ability to discern age from vocal information is due to the number of vocal features that change with age. One example is pitch level: as we grow older, our pitch level drops.[10] (In very elderly men, pitch may become slightly higher again, although the evidence on this is contradictory.) Rate and flexibility may change. Listen to people in their seventies talk and compare their speed and vocal variation to that of college students. Finally, voice quality appears to change. In a comprehensive study of perceptions of voice qualities (the nasal, breathy, throaty voices, and so forth), David Addington discovered that certain voice qualities convey youthfulness while others suggest maturity.[11] Those perceptions are probably due to actual changes that take place in voice quality at various ages. You can test this for yourself by comparing your voice quality to that of your parent of the same sex and your parents' to their own parents'. You should detect some

Table 6.1 Apparel and Accessories That Reveal Age

Clothes

Women	Men
Straight skirts or full pleated skirts	Straight-legged knit pants that hit above the ankle
Miniskirts	White socks with dark shoes
Sack dresses	Argyle socks
The basic black dress	Grey flannel suits
Cotton housedresses	Sport shirts with alligator emblem
Hose with seams	Flowered cotton shirts
Blouses with roll-up sleeves	Suits with narrow lapels
Coat dresses or dresses with jackets	Baggy pants
Straight-legged pants with elasticized waist	Sleeveless undershirts
	Narrow ties
	Nehru jackets

Prints and fabrics

Women and men

Seersucker	Fake denim
Madras	Lous or "cutesy" prints
Heavy wools	Small-flowered prints
Metallic brocades (for women)	Glen plaids
	Polka dots

Colors

Women and men

Pale pastels	Navy blue
Dark, somber colors	Purples and magentas
White (for shirts and blouses)	Camel combined with grey
Muddy colors	

Accessories

Women	Men
Clutch handbags	Tie tacks
Jeweled-frame eyeglasses	Neck scarves
Single strand of graduated pearls	Penny loafers
Poodle and owl pins	Pointed-toe shoes
Lace handkerchiefs	Hats
Hats	Loose-fitting plaid raincoats
White gloves	Galoshes
Practical shoes	Out-of-date eyeglass frames
Flats	
Rain boots	
Mink-collared coats	

differences beyond those that are due to the uniqueness of your own voice; you should discover that vocal cues reveal age rather accurately.

Kinesics and Proxemics Two other nonverbal codes that may yield supplementary evidence of age are kinesics and proxemics. A person's general posture, frequency of gestures, speed of movement, and apparent energy level are all added indicators of age. We expect straighter posture, greater flexibility, more exuberance, and more expressiveness from the young. Marcel Marceau has done an excellent pantomime on film called *In the Park*, in which he beautifully communicates age through the use of stooped posture, arthritic-looking hand gestures, and a slow, stiff walk. Proxemic cues are less direct. The only way they reveal age is through the distance people maintain in conversation. The smaller the distance, the more likely that one party or both are young; the larger the distance, the more likely that one party or both are old. However, since so many other factors influence distance choices, distance patterns should be used only as corroborating information.

Gender

Physical Appearance While identification of gender from physical appearance cues would not be a problem in a nudist camp, in our culture a person's sex is sometimes as tricky to judge accurately as age. Many a long-haired, clean-shaven, jean-clad male has been mistaken from behind for a female (see Fig. 6.2). (One of our students, who has shoulder-length blond hair, reports that he is invariably called ma'am by gas-station attendants who approach him from the rear.) If males have very delicate features, identification can also be difficult from the front. The same is true for very masculine-looking females. Even people who have a normal male or female build may be difficult to type because of the identical hair

Figure 6.2 Which of the people shown here are males and which are females? (From left to right: male, female, female, male)

and clothing styles for men and women. It appears that the unisex look will be with us for a while and with it a somewhat reduced ability to identify sex from appearance alone.

Vocalics While the movement toward equality between the sexes has had its effect on appearance, it has not changed vocal cues. These still remain a good index of sex. A study that employed over 4000 radio listeners as subjects found that the listeners were very accurate in identifying the sex of various speakers.[12] Other studies, including several informal ones that we have conducted with our students, have found the same thing. Numerous features of the voice are indicative of sex: the average pitch level, inflection patterns, resonance, voice quality and tonal complexity all may distinguish males from females.[13]

Other Cues Beyond physical appearance and the voice, kinesic, proxemic, and haptic cues may aid judgments. As we noted in earlier chapters, males and females differ in the conversational distances they adopt, their walking, sitting, and gesturing patterns, and the amount of touching in which they engage.

Race

Physical Appearance There are specific physical features that we associate with each race, including physiognomy, skin and eye coloring, and hair texture. Most sources define Caucasoid features as very-light-to-brown skin color and fine hair ranging from straight to wavy or curly; Mongoloid features as yellowish-brown-to-white pigmentation, coarse straight black hair, dark eyes with pronounced epicanthic folds, and prominent cheekbones; and Negroid features as brown-to-black skin coloring, tightly curled hair, a broad nose, and thick lips (Fig. 6.3). While most people can be categorized by appearance into one of these three broad groups, many people exhibit a combination of features that makes even this gross categorization difficult. If we attempt to make finer discriminations that take geographic, historic, or ethnic considerations into account, our task is further complicated. If we had to distinguish between, say, Chinese, Aryans, Indians, Japanese, Filippinos, Eskimos, Nigerians, Siberians, Spaniards, and Melanesians, most of us would undoubtedly commit a lot of errors. The melting-pot effect in our country has further blurred racial distinctions. Nevertheless, people commonly make assumptions about racial or ethnic heritage from physical appearance.

That these assumptions are often erroneous is evident from a number of anecdotes reported by people whose appearance defies categorization. For instance, one Jewish woman who has light coloring and light brown hair has on occasion been present in conversations in which slurs against Jews have been made, the offending party obviously being unaware of

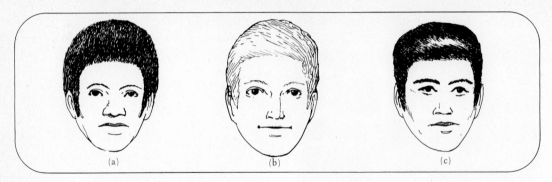

Figure 6.3 Typical facial features of people from within the three main human groups: (a) Negroid; (b) Caucasoid; (c) Mongoloid.

her background. Conversely, a man who is not Jewish has repeatedly been mistaken as being Jewish because of his dark hair and the shape of his nose. One of our black students reports that, for almost an entire quarter, her roommate thought she was Indian, because she has light brown skin and long, wavy black hair.

Vocalics If our batting average for detecting race from appearance cues is not very good, it is not much better for vocal cues.[14] Although one study found that listeners were able to distinguish white from black speakers, an unpublished study reported by Mark Knapp found that people were unable to distinguish racial differences when speakers were from the same neighborhood in Milwaukee. In an effort to verify this result, we conducted our own informal study with our students. We played the recorded voices of eight speakers, only one of whom was black. Very few of the students, including the black students, were able to identify the black speaker, and several mislabeled one of the white speakers as black. However, according to the reports of black students we have spoken with, many blacks believe that they can identify other blacks over the telephone. The key seems to be the degree to which the person speaks with what is commonly called *black dialect*. Both whites and blacks may be able to detect race on occasion, basing their judgments on this characteristic. They are not likely, though, to be very accurate. For other races, detection is even more difficult unless the speaker uses a dialect. We shall treat dialect, however, as a geographic factor.

Body Shape, Height, and Weight

Physical Appearance Here we come to some external features that can be readily identified from visual inspection (except, of course, when people artificially alter their looks with elevator shoes, corsets, and the like or attempt to conceal their shape with loose-fitting clothes). The question is, can these features be identified from other nonverbal cues as well?

Vocalics Several investigations have found that listeners can identify height and general body size for speakers at the extremes of a continuum (in other words, tall or short, skinny or fat).[15] They have more difficulty distinguishing people in the middle ranges. However, if subjects are allowed to match voices with photographs of people, their accuracy increases. Apparently, there is something about a person's voice that fits his or her physical stature.

In summary, what can we say about identifying physical features from nonverbal cues? As would be expected, appearance itself is a pretty fair sign of age, sex, race, and body shape, though not as accurate as we might intuitively expect. Voice is also a good source of information for identifying age and sex, is somewhat accurate for body shape, height, and weight, but is not very accurate for race. Finally, other codes such as kinesics, proxemics, and haptics serve a secondary rather than a primary function and are most useful for determining age, sex, and race.

Sociocultural Features

The category that we label "sociocultural features" includes indicators of a person's sociological and cultural background. Such things as socioeconomic status, education level, occupation, place of residence, ethnic or cultural background, religious and political group membership, and the attitudes that correspond to those groups are all relevant. Physical appearance and vocalics are codes that serve as the chief indicators of these factors. Kinesics, proxemics, and haptics play a much lesser role and, since they have been dealt with in earlier chapters, will not be discussed here.

Socioeconomic Status, Occupation, and Education

Judgments of a person's status, occupation, and educational level are so intricately interrelated that they must be discussed together.

Physical Appearance   An abundance of research has established that dress serves as a good indicator of a person's relative socioeco-

mini-experiment

Tape-record the voices of several people of various ages, sexes, and races. Play the tapes for strangers and see how accurately they can estimate age, sex, and race. To see how people judge you, either have someone else tape-record your voice or call strangers on the telephone and ask them to make the same judgments.

nomic status and, implicitly, degree of education.[16] As many as forty-one relationships have been found to exist between a person's social and psychological background on one hand and interest in and use of apparel on the other hand, which shows there is a strong relationship between an individual's choice of dress and certain sociological features of the individual. That doesn't tell us, however, whether other people make those connections when they observe dress. H. I. Douty attempted to get at this question by conducting a series of studies relating clothing to evaluations of a person. In three of the four studies she conducted, she found that clothing affected judgments of socioeconomic status. In her dissertation research, Mary Lou Rosencranz further established the presence of a strong relationship. She employed a projective technique, in which subjects viewed a series of pictures of incongruously dressed people, such as a woman wearing high heels, a long dress, and gloves among teenagers in bobby socks. Subjects were asked to explain what was going on in the pictures. The results revealed that status attributions were consistently made. Interestingly, those who were most aware of the clothing in the pictures were women of higher status, education, and income themselves.

From these studies, we can conclude not only that our choices of clothing are related to our socioeconomic status but that people recognize the relationship and make judgments accordingly. This means that whether you are trying to buy a car or seeking credit from a local bank, salespeople and loan officers are likely to make snap judgments based on your dress about whether you can afford a major purchase or are a good loan risk. If your dress doesn't meet their standards, you may find yourself ignored or denied help.

Clothing may also signal the degree to which status and social roles differ within a culture. In 1947, Young theorized that "when there are no fixed symbols to mark the social elite in a stratified society, external features of life such as clothes are often used for this purpose."[17] It has been argued that the degree of variability of clothing style in a culture signals the degree to which social roles are well defined. Thus, in a largely middle-class culture such as ours, there is more general similarity in dress than in countries such as India where there are very clear-cut status distinctions. If you have ever traveled in countries where status differences are pronounced, you know that clothing and other features of adornment are a chief means of identifying rank and occupation. For instance, in one Oriental culture, status is signalled by whether the men wear their pants legs down or rolled up around their thighs, the latter being the style worn of necessity by the peasants who work in the muddy fields.

Many cultures further formalize differences in occupation and social position through the use of uniforms or prescribed costumes. In countries ruled by military dictatorships, there is no difficulty identifying the ruling elite—their uniforms are a constant reminder of their status. In our country, we rely frequently on uniforms to set apart various occupations. The policeman's, doctor's, or judge's costume clearly signals professional status. However, in our culture status is not always easily identified by clothing. Michael Harrington attributes this phenomenon to the leveling effect of mass-produced clothing. Here even the poor may appear well dressed, although they may betray their income status by dressing inappropriately for situations outside their subcultural boundaries.[18] For example, a college student may wear a high-school-vintage suit (the only one he owns) to a high-society wedding.

We can summarize the role of apparel in signalling status, education, and occupation by turning to the conclusions drawn by Sybers and Roach, two researchers who reviewed much of the early literature on attire. They note that clothing is clearly a symbol of status, that people are acutely aware of this, and that they rely on apparel as a means of signalling their professional aspirations and personal values. Moreover, they expect others to recognize their status and socioeconomic ambitions from their clothing. Consequently, many believe that if they don't conform to the dress norms for their social level and occupation, their advancement up the ladder will be restricted.[19] This concern about the influence of dress on economic and social advancement is often justified. We have witnessed enough professionally enforced dress codes and conversations about acceptable dress for certain jobs to know that a large number of people take dress as a serious indicator.

mini-experiment

Take a picture of yourself or someone else dressed in relatively formal clothes (a suit for males, a dress for females), then take another picture of the same person dressed very casually. Show each picture to a different sample of people and have them guess the subject's occupation.

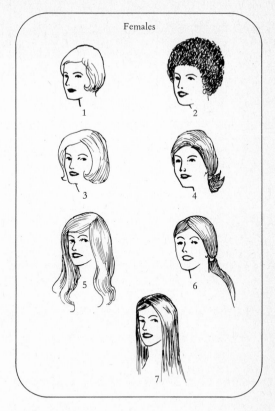

Figure 6.4 Rank order the hairstyles shown in this figure according to their appropriateness for a professional occupation. Do your judgments agree with those of your fellow students? Do you think they would agree with those of personnel directors?

One last aspect of physical appearance that may play a role is hair and beards. An issue of the University of Florida Placement Manual reports the results of a survey among 114 college recruiting officers and managers determining which male hairstyles and beard styles have the most positive effect on hiring decisions. The most favorable ratings were given the moderately short-haired, clean-shaven male. It seems reasonable to conclude that hair- and beard styles also influence the attribution of occupational status to the wearers.[20] Figure 6.4 illustrates several different hair-

styles, hair lengths, and, in the case of males, beard styles. Number 1 among the males is similar to what was rated highest by recruiting officers, numbers 4 and 7 the lowest. (Not all versions were in the study.) You might be interested in seeing how students on your campus respond to the styles and how their answers compare to those of local employers.

Vocalics Vocal cues are responded to in much the same way as appearance. People make judgments about others' education, status, and sometimes even occupation from such vocal features as intonation and inflection patterns, dialect, voice qualities, articulation, fluency, and general style of delivery. In one of the classic studies in the area, Pear asked listeners to distinguish the occupation of nine speakers. Listeners were able to identify occupations with better than chance accuracy. The actor and the minister were especially easy to type. At about the same time, Allport and Cantril conducted a series of six studies, four of which asked subjects to identify the vocation of three speakers. In three of the studies, the identifications were accurate to a significant degree.[21] The occupations represented in those investigations were businessman, actor, and professor. However, a study conducted shortly after that by Fay and Middleton, which required subjects to identify musicians, teachers, preachers, lawyers, and insurance agents, drew slightly different conclusions about the accuracy of judgments of occupation. Although the subjects showed relatively high accuracy in matching voices with occupations, their responses were more consistent with each other than with the truth. In other words, stereotypes associated with certain voice types seemed to be causing the listeners to agree among themselves, though not with consistently high accuracy.[22]

Since those early studies, little research has been conducted to resolve the question of whether occupations are accurately judged or are simply stereotyped from vocal cues. Recent research has instead shifted to examining what types of cues produce different attributions of occupation and how vocal types affect the broader judgments of general status and education level. Barnett Pearce and Forest Conklin suspected that all of these judgments would be influenced by delivery style. They created two versions of a speech, one with a conversational delivery style and one with a dynamic delivery style, and asked listeners to judge the speaker's occupation, economic status, educational attainment, social background, and so on. The subjects rated the speakers who used conversational delivery (which involved a smaller range of inflection, greater consistency in rate and pitch, less volume, and lower pitch) as being better educated, holding a more professional job, and earning a higher income than the dynamic speaker.[23] Similar investigations have found that listeners can effectively identify from vocal cues alone whether speakers are upper, middle, or lower class and whether they have less than a high school education or a college education.[24] Even when speakers try to imitate upper-class speech, listeners can accurately identify their true status.[25] Putting on airs apparently doesn't pay off. In Chapter 7, on relational messages, we shall discuss in more detail those features of delivery that cause a person to be viewed as having high social status. We suspect that these same features are responsible for the judgments of occupation, education, and economic status.

Other Cues Although we have limited ourselves to discussing physical appearance and vocalic cues, there are other nonverbal indicators of social class. One recent development in the area of artifacts is the study of trash. There are those who believe that a person's garbage can reveal much about him or her, including socioeconomic status. You may recall the fuss about reporters rooting through Henry Kissinger's garbage. It is even reported that the Navy department systematically examines the garbage from the Soviet ships to determine the sailors' diet and morale.

Geographic Residence

Physical Appearance It should come as no surprise that certain physical appearance cues reveal what part of the country a person comes from. Cowboy hats are an oddity in the East and North but commonplace in Texas and many western states: many New Yorkers wear dark-colored clothes in the summer, whereas Midwesterners and Southerners prefer whites and light shades; dress is more formal for most occasions along the Eastern seaboard than in the South or West; and new fashions typically appear first on the coasts, commonly emanating from California or New York, then slowly working their way toward the center of the country (although one clothing wholesaler claims that college fashions originate in North Carolina and Virginia).

Vocalics   A better potential indicator of residence or birthplace is the voice—more specifically, dialect. Various geographic regions have distinctive, identifiable dialects. Henry Higgins, in *My Fair Lady,* believed that a person's voice can reveal even the city block where she or he grew up. Many phoneticians in fact are surprisingly accurate in making such judgments. Pear's classic radio study, mentioned earlier, was one of the first efforts to examine the ability of average people to detect geographic background from audio cues alone. He found that his subjects were not very accurate in identifying a speaker's birthplace. He might have obtained better results if he had asked subjects to identify the region the speakers had lived in longest. A more recent study by Nerbonne took that approach. He found that listeners could distinguish whether the speaker was from an eastern, southern or General American dialect region, the latter being what is spoken in most of the country. Of course, this category is extremely broad; subjects might have been hard pressed if asked to be more specific about locale. It is difficult to discern the dialect from a region that has no noticeable accent, such as the Midwest, or an area such as Florida where there is a mix of dialects. You might try your own luck in analyzing where your classmates come from. Consider the stereotypes that you associate with different accents.

Ethnic and Cultural Background

Physical Appearance   We have noted that differences in physical appearance exist from culture to culture, including subcultural

groups. One of the chief ways that sociological and anthropological texts distinguish cultures and ethnic groups is by their clothing and grooming customs and pertinent racial features. That is not to say, however, that the typical observer can accurately identify an individual's nationality or ethnic background from these cues. Accuracy is dependent on the extent to which the person conforms to the normative appearance of his or her group. Those who live in traditional Chinese, Japanese, German, Italian, Mexican–American, Slavic, or other ethnically homogeneous communities and neighborhoods are more likely to exhibit the appearance features associated with that culture than are those who live in more heterogeneous areas. Accuracy is also dependent on the degree to which the common appearance features of a culture are unique and do not overlap those of other cultures. (For instance, traditionally Nordic features are not common in most parts of the world.) If you err in judging what culture a particular person comes from, it may be because the physiognomy, skin color, and dress of the person are similar to those of a different culture. Or perhaps you have not had sufficient experience with other cultures to be skilled at making distinctions.

Vocalics   Our ability to judge cultural and ethnic background from vocal cues is governed by the same kinds of considerations. Each language is associated with certain inflection, rate, and rhythm patterns as well as a set of common vocal qualities. The degree to which an individual exhibits the vocal patterns of the language associated with his or her culture and the degree to which those features overlap other languages will affect how accurately a listener can identify the culture or language. Accuracy will also depend on the degree of familiarity the listener has with a wide range of languages and the particular language in question. Research by Cohen and Starkweather suggests that we are most successful at recognizing the vocal characteristics of our own language. They recorded samples of speech from Chinese, English, German, Italian, and Spanish speakers, then filtered the speeches so that the verbal element was muffled, leaving only the vocalic cues. The (American) subjects who heard the tapes identified the English voice significantly more often than any of the others. The researchers concluded that distinct vocal characteristics associated with each language elicit recognition from native speakers.[26]

The role of vocal cues in cultural identification and the differences between cultures are aptly demonstrated by an excerpt from a book on intercultural communication by Edward Hall and William Whyte, both noted observers of cultural and group behavior:

In the Arab world, in discussion among equals, the men attain a decibel level that would be considered aggressive, objectionable, and obnoxious in the United States. Loudness connotes strength and sincerity among Arabs; a soft tone implies weakness, deviousness. This is so "right" in the Arab culture that several Arabs have told us they discounted anything heard over the "Voice of America" because the signal was so weak!

Personal status modulates voice tone, however, even in the Arab society. The Saudi Arabian shows respect to his superior—to a Sheik, say—by lowering his voice and mumbling. The affluent American may also be addressed in this fashion, making almost impossible an already difficult situation. Since in American culture one unconsciously "asks" another to raise his voice by raising his own, the American speaks louder. This lowers the Arab's tone more and increases the mumbles. This triggers a shouting response in the American—which cues the Arab into a frightened "I'm not being respectful enough" tone well below audibility.[27]

Group Membership and Related Attitudes

The last types of attributions people typically make are those concerning the groups or organizations to which a person belongs—religious, social and political—or the kinds of religious, social and political views they hold. These judgments may be made almost exclusively from physical appearance cues (in addition to verbal cues) and are often based on stereotypes (see Fig. 6.5). In a large-scale study of the inferences observers draw from clothing, Kelley showed drawings of various clothing styles to 410 students and asked them to judge such things as whether the wearer was liberal or conservative, supported or opposed the Vietnam War, was religious or not, and was politically active or apathetic. He found that unconventional dress was associated with the political left, greater activity in politics, and use of marijuana and LSD.[28] Our students, who were interested in these findings, conducted their own versions of the experiment by using magazine pictures of different dress styles for males and females, ranging from very casual (jeans, T-shirts, halter tops) to very formal (suits for men, evening gowns or dresses for women.) The heads were removed so that facial appearance and hair wouldn't influence judgments. People wearing moderately formal or conservative dress were most often thought to belong to a fraternity and to be religious, Republican, and politically active; informal dress was associated with liberality but little political activity, smoking marijuana, and being Democratic. One study also made a comparison by age groups. Interestingly, the younger group (composed of eighteen-to-twenty-five-year-old students) was more influenced in their evaluations by dress differences than was the older (thirty-five and over) group.[29]

What can we conclude from these results? First, it is apparent that people make definite judgments about such sociological considerations as voting preference, political involvement, religious involvement, and group membership. Secondly, stereotyping from appearance seems to be more prevalent among younger people than among older people. Third, some of our traditional stereotypes may

be changing. While in many instances, political and social liberalism or conservatism is assumed to correspond to the degree of formality and conservatism in dress, political activism is associated with more formal dress styles rather than the expected informal dress style. Apparently, jean-clad individuals are assumed to be apathetic toward politics while those who dress in obviously expensive, fashionable clothes are assumed to be politically active. One last important observation is that slight differences in styles can produce different reactions. For example, while religiosity may be associated with somewhat formal clothing, overly formal styles carry a country club image that is contrary to a religious image. Similarly, the fit and stylishness of clothes can affect evaluations.

Psychological Features

In this last category, we shall look at judgments made about personality and mood on the basis of nonverbal cues. Such judgments are again largely stereotypic. Early writers suggested that these judgments about internal processes are less accurate than inferences based on the more external physiological and sociological evidence. It is true that for certain kinds of judgments accuracy declines, but for others a surprising degree of accuracy is possible.

Body Type and Body Attractiveness

Body types are clearly related to personality. Not only do stereotypes exist of the jolly, easygoing fat person and the sensitive and high-strung thin person, but people also describe themselves according to stereotypes. Many traits typically associated with each of the somatypes show up when people rate their own temperament.[30] More surprisingly, they also show up in parents' and teachers' evaluations of children.[31] The commonly found associations are listed in Table 6.2.[32]

Since you have already scored yourself on somatype in Chapter 3, you can test how well these traits conform to your body build. The proportion of qualities that you think apply to you in each column should be roughly equivalent to the degree to which your shape fits into each of the three categories. Suppose you scored yourself as a 4/4/4 on somatype. About an equal number of qualities in each of the three columns should be applicable to you. If you scored yourself a 1/3/7, you should find the most attributes that describe you in the ectomorph column, a few in the mesomorph column and almost none in the endomorph column. The research that has supported these associations has asked subjects to choose among set lists of adjectives. For instance, a person was asked to describe how he or she feels most of the time by choosing three adjectives from a list of twelve or by underlining one word out of three. It was not possible to describe oneself as assertive, relaxed, and tense. If your self-description based on the list of adjectives given did not conform to your body type, perhaps you chose adjectives from one list that were in conflict with ones you chose from another list.

It is also possible that the body-type stereotypes truly don't fit you. After all, they are based on an average, and exceptions always exist. Nevertheless, it is surprising how well they fit most people. Juan Cortés and Florence Gatti, who have done considerable work in the area, report that in studies of college students and convicts, mean temperament ratings have consistently corresponded with mean somatype ratings. They also note that even nursery-school-age and elementary-school-age children show striking conformity in these relationships.[33] The evidence seems clear that more than just a stereotype is involved, that people actually do behave according to the expectations that go with their body type.

Table 6.2 Personality Traits Commonly
Associated with Body Types

Endomorph	Mesomorph	Ectomorph
Affable	Active	Aloof
Affected	Adventurous	Anxious
Affectionate	Argumentative	Awkward
Calm	Assertive	Cautious
Cheerful	Cheerful	Considerate
Complacent	Competitive	Cool
Cooperative	Confident	Detached
Dependent	Determined	Gentle-tempered
Extroverted	Dominant	Introspective
Forgiving	Efficient	Meticulous
Generous	Energetic	Reflective
Kind	Enterprising	Reticent
Leisurely	Hot-tempered	Serious
Placid	Impetuous	Shy
Relaxed	Optimistic	Sensitive
Soft-hearted	Outgoing	Tactful
Soft-tempered	Reckless	Uncooperative
Warm	Social	Withdrawn
	High need for achievement	Low need for achievement
	Nonconforming	Conforming

These findings have caused much speculation as to why clusters of behaviors and personality traits are related to somatype. One line of thought suggests that temperament has physiological determinants and that the genetic, organic, and metabolic processes that produce a certain body type also influence temperament. Thus low metabolism and high blood pressure affect both physical and psychological make-up. An alternative line of thought that makes some sense is that children are responded to according to their appearance—fat and skinny children get negative reactions and teasing; mesomorphs get lots of positive reinforcement because they are more attractive. Research seems to support this view. In the 1950s, Jourard and Secord re-

ported that people's liking for their own body related to whether they thought their parents liked their body.[34]

It seems reasonable to assume that if parents communicate to a child that his or her body type is unattractive, the child develops a poor self-image, which in turn affects personality. Recent research by Ellen Berscheid, Elaine Walster, and George Bohrnstedt confirms that this frequently happens. They produced a body image questionnaire which was responded to by 62,000 *Psychology Today* readers. Of those respondents who had below-average body images, an overwhelming majority reported that they were sometimes or frequently teased as a child by their peers about their appearance, most often for being overweight. Males were made fun of more often than females. Negative feedback about body appearance did not come from peers alone, however. One respondent reported that her mother had pet names for her such as "prune face" and "garbage disposal"; these, she claimed, had more influence on her than anything her peers could say. Negative body images in turn influence self-esteem. Berscheid, Walster, and Bohrnstedt found that only 11 percent of respondents with a below-average body image had an above-average level of self-esteem.[35] A recent Associated Press news report, based on a three-year study of fat people, also revealed that the obese individual is likely to be depressed, anxious, and filled with self-loathing. Seventy percent of the overweight patients studied considered themselves unattractive, and 41 percent avoided looking in mirrors.

Along with the negative feedback that overweight or underweight children receive about their bodies, they also learn what behaviors are expected of them. Fat children are supposed to be lazy and bad at sports; thin children are supposed to be fragile and awkward. Based on the expectations that others signal to these children, and based on the number of rewarding or unrewarding experiences they have, they undoubtedly learn the self-image and personality traits that fit their body type.

Whichever explanation of the causes for the relationship of body build to personality is correct, it is clear that body type is a reliable and powerful indicator of personality. If the second explanation has some plausibility, it also has important implications for communication: it means that body image, personality, and communication are all intricately interrelated. People communicate expectations based on physical shape and approach or avoid others on the same basis. This causes people to adopt the behaviors and communication style that fit their body type. The communication process—both verbal and nonverbal—serves to enforce the cycle, and so the stereotypes are perpetuated.

One interesting counterpoint to the problems associated with having an unappealing body type is that having an attractive physical appearance may also have its drawbacks. We noted in earlier chapters that attractive people generally are considered more desirable and are assigned more favorable attributes; but there are a few areas in which the highly attractive person is perceived negatively. A recent survey reports that outstandingly beautiful women are rated as having more negative personality traits than average-looking women and as being poor risks as wives and mothers.[36] It seems, then, that both extremes of the physical-attractiveness continuum carry negative associations.

Hair and Beards

We commented in Chapter 3 on the obvious stereotyping that is made regarding long hair and beards on males. This stereotyping extends beyond mere judgments about an individual's political beliefs, social attitudes, and group membership to inferences about personality. A study conducted by Freedman in 1969 asked both men and women to describe clean-shaven and bearded men. The men, who were all beardless, described the bearded male as more independent and extroverted; the women described bearded men as more sophisticated, mature, and masculine.[37] More recently, Robert Pelligrini took photographs of men with beards and mustaches. He then had them shave to goatees, photographed them again, had them shave to bare faces and photographed them one last time. When he asked people to rate the photographs, he found a consistent pattern: the more hair on the face, the higher the ratings on masculinity, maturity, self-confidence, dominance, courage, liberality, nonconformism, industriousness, and good looks.[38] The effect of men's hair *length* is less clear. Shorter hair typically is associated with more conservative, traditional personality traits. Whether those are regarded positively apparently depends on the personality of the receiver. We know of no research yet that has given equal time to women, examining the attributions, if any, attached to different female hairstyles or colors. It seems time for somebody to question the commercial claims that blondes have more fun.

Dress and Adornment

Just as clothing and other features of adornment lead to judgments about a broad range of physiological and sociological attributes, they also contribute to numerous personality and mood attributions. In 1963, Aiken attempted to advance our understanding of the interrelationships by administering to a large sample of women a series of eighty true–false questions such as *I see nothing wrong with wearing dresses that have plunging necklines, I like close-fitting, figure-revealing dresses, I try to choose dresses that are like those most women are currently wearing,* and *A new pair of shoes makes me feel like a new person.* Based on the responses, five dimensions of attitudes towards dress emerged—(1) interest in dress, (2) economy in dress, (3) decoration in dress, (4) conformity in dress, and (5) comfort in dress—

which were then related to personality. For example, those who showed great interest in dress were conventional, conscientious, compliant before authority, stereotyped in thinking, persistent, suspicious, insecure, and tense.[39] While the results may be obsolete today, they support the relationship of personality to interest in clothing.

Another study, conducted by Gurel, Wilbur, and Gurel in 1972, showed that the clothing people wear is related to personality. They administered personality tests to people in a coffee house and compared their answers to the kinds of clothes they were wearing. Those who scored highest on conformity were the greasers—people wearing black leather jackets, knit pullovers, and teased or greased hair; those who scored lowest on conformity were the hippies—those who wore old grubby clothes, peace symbols, and beads.[40]

Color preferences are also related to personality. The predominant colors in a person's wardrobe can provide a clue to the individual's personality type. The personality traits that have been found through extensive research to be associated in people's minds with various colors are shown in Table 6.3.

The combination of color and design preferences in clothing is also related to personality. In one investigation, fabric patterns and color preferences were compared to personality traits, physical characteristics, and occupational interests. We might expect our clothing choices to be governed by such things as our hair and skin coloring and our body size (heavy people are persistently advised to avoid large designs and bright colors). However, this was not the case. The only relationships that were significant were those involving personality and job interests. People who preferred small designs were concerned about making a good impression; those who chose less bold prints were modest and conveyed an image of naturalness. Assertive, sociable women preferred deep shades and saturated colors, while submissive, passive women preferred lighter tints.[41]

Table 6.3 Color and Personality

Color	Personality Characteristics
Red	Extroverted, impulsive, stimulating, action-oriented, physical, youthful, athletic, competitive, sensual, dramatic, other-directed, strong sex drive, productive
Blue	Highly educated, cultured, high income, introverted, sensitive to others, respected, steady character, cautious, secure, relaxed, empathetic, loyal, dedicated, normal sex drive, need for contentment
Yellow	Moderately stimulating, intellectual, idealistic, high-minded, attracted to cults, safe friend, theoretical, philosophical, confident, industrious, fitful, future-oriented, difficult to understand, compulsive
Orange	Sympathetic, friendly, extroverted, athletic, active
Purple	Affectionate, pompous, solemn, artistic, good mind, keen wit, observant, verbose, creative, needs discipline, easy to live with, insecure, not cheerful, possible homosexuality and emotional insecurity
Green	Fair, respectable, a joiner, good citizen, sensitive to etiquette and social custom, frank, normal sex drive but not prudish, stable, wants to impress and be recognized, wants to be independent
Black	Vain, sophisticated, worldly, mysterious, wise, revolting against fate, acts hastily
Brown	Earthy, conscientious, shrewd, obstinate, parsimonious, dependable, steady, sensuous, conservative, responsible in love, wants security, may be ruthless
White	Simple, young, decent, venial, flirtatious, likes to be alone

Although we know that clothing, color, and design preferences are actually related to personality, the research we have just cited does not demonstrate whether observers of these features connect them with the correct personality traits. We do not know of any study that has both identified how an individual's clothing relates to his or her personality and determined whether observers accurately identified personality traits from the clothing. Research has, though, looked at specific accessories and adornments and asked respondents what personality traits they associate with them.[42] For example, a 1952 study revealed that when female interviewees wore lipstick, they were rated by their male interviewers as more frivolous, placid, and conscientious, less talkative, and less interested than when they did not wear lipstick; and a 1944 experiment found that people who wore eyeglasses were viewed as more intelligent, dependable, and industrious but not more honest than those who did not wear glasses.

The results of these studies should not be taken as currently applicable. Hamid, for one, found that responses to eyeglasses have changed over the years. In 1968, he conducted a study that led to the following conclusion: people who wore glasses were rated consistently lower on physical attractiveness and sophistication than people who did not and consistently higher on being conventional, shy, and religious.[43] His investigation also looked at the effects of a variety of clothing and other adornment factors. He asked forty-five male and female students to evaluate eight color photographs of female figures selected from magazines. The pictures were all highly similar in terms of facial expression, hair color (blond), and figure. What varied were the styles of make-up, presence or absence of glasses, use of jewelry, type of clothing, neckline, dress color, length of hemline, type of stockings, and shoe color. Subjects were asked to rate the photos on certain dimensions: adjectives used were *sophisticated, shy, snob-*

bish, conventional, immoral, religious, physically attractive, intelligent, and *unimaginative.* All subjects were able to make distinctions among photos on the basis of sophistication, conventionality, intelligence, religiosity, and imagination. The males made additional judgments on morality, shyness, and attractiveness. Specifically, bright colors and high hemlines were associated with being attractive and sophisticated but immoral. Hamid's study makes clear that different features of clothing generate personality judgments, but the accuracy of those judgments has yet to be confirmed.

Vocal Cues

Intuitively, we are all aware of the personality associations conjured up by various voices. Who, for instance, doesn't get a clear image of false bravado from Don Knotts's voice? Beneath the sensuality, Marilyn Monroe's voice seemed to reveal her vulnerability. When we speak to strangers over the phone, we get immediate impressions of their warmth, self-assurance, and patience. Lilly Tomlin's routine about telephone operators is funny in part because it captures the insensitivity and exasperation we have too frequently thought we heard at the other end of the telephone line.

Research on many aspects of the voice has yielded evidence of a significant number of relationships to personality and personality attributions. Mallory and Miller state:

There is a widespread tendency for listeners to attribute specific personality characteristics to an individual on the basis of his speech. Audiences often derive their impressions of a lecturer from the sounds of his voice as well as from the words that he utters. It is customary for personnel managers to be influenced in their decisions by the voices of those they interview. . . . In all these cases there is evidently an implicit assumption that the voice is, to some degree, a reflection of personality. Psychologists recognize this possibility and include various aspects of speech among the "expressive movements" which they regard as vehicles of personality projection.[44]

Studies fall into one of three classes, (1) those that focus on the actual relationship between voice characteristics and personality traits, (2) those that focus on the accuracy of judges in identifying personality traits, (3) those that focus on the perceptions attached to various vocal features. Early research fell primarily in the first two categories. Investigators began by focusing on specific vocal qualities. They found, for instance, that inflection correlated with intelligence and breathiness related to neuroticism, introversion, and submissiveness.[45] In 1934, Allport and Cantril took a different tack. They considered how the total voice related to personality traits and other characteristics. The results of their eight experiments at Harvard formed an important foundation for later research. Based on a total sample of 587 judges, they drew the following conclusions:[46]

1. The voice conveys correct information about inner as well as outer characteristics of personality.
2. Although there is no uniformity in the expression of personality from the voice (that is, certain personality traits are not consistently evidenced by certain vocal features), many features of personality can be determined from the voice.
3. Uniformity among judges exceeds their accuracy in typing personality. In other words, people are more consistent than they are accurate.
4. Stereotypes play an important role: "for the various features of personality there is associated in the minds of judges some preconception of the type of voice to which these features correspond."
5. The more highly organized and deep-seated traits and dispositions are judged more con-

sistently and more accurately than are physique and appearance features.
6. Oversimplification appears to occur: if a voice arouses a stereotype, several personality features are likely to be subsumed under that stereotype.
7. The more information given regarding a speaker, the more accurate the judgment. Judges can better match voices to personality summaries than to specific traits.
8. Accuracy of judgment is dependent on the heterogeneity of the voices and personalities of the speakers. The more similar the speakers, the more difficult to discriminate among them.

Results of two subsequent studies by Fay and Middleton were not completely consistent with Allport and Cantril's conclusions; they found that listeners were not very reliable in their estimates of the intelligence and introversion of a range of speakers who had taken intelligence tests or personality inventories.[47] As a result of these and several other studies that found high consistency among listeners (they typically picked the same answers) but not high accuracy, some researchers concluded that the utility of judging personality traits from the voice is limited.[48] However, Kramer pointed out that rarely has agreement among judges been high when judgments have been incorrect; rather, consistency has occurred either when listeners' judgments were also accurate or when they were completely random. Kramer argued that since many of the personality measures might be faulty and/or the experimental methods used questionable, listeners' judgments might very well be accurate and in fact might be a good measure to use in assessing personality.[49] The implication of these conclusions is that people undoubtedly make subconscious judgments about personality from voice and that they may be more accurate than we realize. The flamboyant person who is privately insecure may actually leak that information through vocal cues.

Table 6.4 Personality Traits Associated with Voice Qualities

	Males	Females
Breathy	Young, artistic	Feminine, pretty, petite, effervescent, high strung, and shallow
Thin	No relationships	Social, physical, emotional, and mental immaturity; high sensitivity; sense of humor
Flat	Masculine, sluggish, cold, and withdrawn	Same as for males
Nasal	Unintelligent, short, lazy, immature, fat, boorish, unattractive, sickly, uninteresting—all socially undesirable traits	Same as for males
Tense	Old, unyielding	Young; emotional, feminine, and high strung; unintelligent
Throaty	Old; realistic, mature, sophisticated, and well-adjusted	Unintelligent, masculine, lazy, boorish, unemotional, ugly, sickly, neurotic, quiet, careless, inartistic, naive, humble, uninteresting, apathetic
Orotund	Energetic, healthy, artistic, sophisticated, proud, interesting, enthusiastic	Lively, gregarious, increased aesthetic sensitivity, proud, humorless

From *Nonverbal Communication in Human Interaction* by Mark L. Knapp. Copyright © 1972 by Holt, Rinehart and Winston. Adapted by permission of Holt, Rinehart and Winston.

Contemporary research has attempted to solve some of the methodological and measurement problems and has once again turned to certain features of the voice as a more fruitful means of understanding personality. David Addington attempted to ascertain what personality traits are perceived from what voice qualities. He trained two male and two female speakers to simulate the breathy, thin, tense, flat, throaty, nasal, and orotund voice qualities and then had four subgroups of raters rate the voices and sixteen subgroups rate the perceived personality characteristics. Table 6.4 shows the traits he found associated with each of the voice qualities for the male and female speakers.[50]

While Addington was interested in a relatively constant feature of the voice, other researchers have examined more variable features of vocal delivery. Markel, Phillis, Vargas, and Howard looked at combinations of loudness and tempo. They recorded 124 voice samples, classified them as loud or soft and fast or slow, then correlated the vocal types with the speakers' responses to two personality measures. The *loud–fast voice* correlated with being self-sufficient and resourceful, expecting the worst of people, and being intrapunitive (blaming oneself for problems). The *loud–slow* voice was associated with being aggressive, competitive, confident, self-secure, radical, self-sufficient, and resourceful; tending toward rebelliousness for its own sake; being low on introspection; and responding to stressful situations with hypochondria. The *soft–fast voice* correlated with being enthusiastic, happy-go-lucky, adventuresome, thick-skinned, confident, self-secure, radical, phlegmatic, composed, optimistic, nonconforming, independent, and composed under stress. Finally, the *soft–slow voice* was associated with being competitive, aggressive, enthusiastic, happy-go-lucky, adventurous, thick-skinned, reckless, and carefree, but withdrawn and introspective under stress.[51] You might want to compare your own voice qualities to the personality features listed to see if they apply to you. Other investigations which have looked at such vocal features as resonance, loudness, pitch, and tempo have found that vocal profiles correlate with personality profiles.[52] In other words, voices are often good indicators of actual personality traits.

More important, however, is how these voice qualities are perceived by listeners. Addington also reported findings on rate and pitch variety. Faster rates increased perceptions of the speakers as animated and extroverted; greater pitch variety made the males appear more dynamic, feminine, and aesthetically inclined and the females more dynamic and extroverted. Two other investigations that carry implications for the rate and pitch variety characteristics are those by Schweitzer and Pearce and Conklin, both of which looked at dynamic and nondynamic delivery (dynamic delivery being more energetic, faster, and having more pitch variety). Schweitzer found that listeners rated the dynamic speaker as significantly less humble, more refined, more aggressive and bold, more energetic, and warmer. However, a series of other personality features (such as modesty, fairness, sincerity) were not influenced.[53] Pearce and Conklin's results closely paralleled Schweitzer's. The dynamic delivery was associated with being tough-minded, task-oriented, assertive, and self-assured while the conversational delivery earned higher ratings on being honest and people-oriented.[54]

From all of this research, we can extract some important principles about personality attributions and vocal cues. First, the voice actually does vary according to personality. Such features as pitch, tempo, rate, inflection, and voice quality are potentially relevant. Second, judges are highly consistent in their perceptions of voices, indicating that stereotypes do exist. Third, judges are frequently accurate in the personality traits they assign to various voice characteristics. Finally, specific features of the voice alter personality perceptions. Already we have some understanding of the personality attributions attached to different voice

mini-experiment

Take pictures of several people dressed as they choose to dress and against the backdrop of their living quarters. Let them select whatever dress, objects, and locale they think best relects their personality. Then tape-record a sample of speech from each one. See if other people are able to match the photos with the voices.

qualities, to changes in variety of rate and pitch, and to dynamic or nondynamic delivery in general. As research in this area continues, we should be able to pinpoint how alterations in specific cues influence personality attributions.

Summary

Throughtout this chapter we have asserted that people rely heavily on nonverbal information to develop their first impressions. That information may or may not be intentional, and the perceptions that result may or may not be accurate, but they are nevertheless important to the initial stages of interaction. The stereotyping that occurs may be useful means of reducing our initial uncertainty about others. Much of the information acquired may also be accurate, particularly if it concerns external characteristics. However, first impressions are usually not permanent. As the relationship progresses, first judgments are modified.

In the next chapter, we shall look specifically at the nonverbal cues that become increasingly important as we define further an interpersonal relationship.

Suggested Reading

Berger, C. R., and Calabrese, R. J. "Some Explorations in Initial Interaction and Beyond: Toward a Developmental Theory of Interpersonal Communication." *Human Communication Research,* 1 (1975), 99–112.

Berscheid, E., and Walster, E. "Physical Attractiveness." In L. Berkowitz (ed.), *Advances in Experimental Psychology.* New York: Academic Press, 1973.

Berscheid, E., Walster, E., and Bohrnstedt, G. "Body Image: The Happy American Body." *Psychology Today,* 7, No. 6 (1973), 119–131.

Cortés, J. B., and Gatti, F. M. "Physique and Propensity." *Psychology Today,* 4 (1970), 42–44, 82–84.

Heidi, G., "These Gestures Shout That You're Getting Old." *New Woman* (July–August 1976), 53–56, 58–59.

Leathers, D. G. *Nonverbal Communication Systems.* Boston: Allyn and Bacon, 1976. (pp. 102–109).

Pearce, W. B., and Conklin, F. "Nonverbal Vocalic Communication and the Perception of a Speaker." *Speech Monographs,* 38 (1971), 235–241.

Roach, M. E., and Eicker, J. B. (eds.). *Dress, Adornment and the Social Order.* New York: Wiley, 1965.

Roach, M. E., and Eicker, J. B. *The Visible Self: Perspectives on Dress.* Englewood Cliffs, N.J.: Prentice-Hall, 1973.

Notes

1. C. R. Berger and R. J. Calabrese, "Some Explorations in Initial Interaction and Beyond: Toward a Developmental Theory of Interpersonal Communication," *Human Communication Research*, 1 (1975), pp. 99–112.

2. R. Barker, "The Social Interrelatedness of Strangers and Acquaintances," *Sociometry*, 5 (1942), pp.176–179.

3. P. V. Washburn and M. D. Hakel, "Visual Cues and Verbal Context as Influences on Impressions Formed After Simulated Employment Interviews," *Journal of Applied Psychology*, 5 (1973), pp. 137–141.

4. E. Berscheid and E. Walster, "Physical Attractiveness," in L. Berkowitz (ed.), *Advances in Experimental Psychology* (New York: Academic Press, 1973); K. Dion, E. Berscheid, and E. Walster, "What Is Beautiful Is Good," *Journal of Personality and Social Psychology*, 24 (1972), pp. 285–290.

5. M. L. Knapp, *Nonverbal Communication in Human Interaction* (New York: Holt, Rinehart and Winston, 1972), pp. 73–74.

6. H. Channing and J. Mayer, "Obesity—Its Possible Effect on College Acceptance," *New England Journal of Medicine*, 275 (1966), pp. 1172–1174.

7. See, for example, J. G. Delia, "Dialects and the Effects of Stereotypes on Interpersonal Attraction and Cognitive Processes," *Quarterly Journal of Speech*, 58 (1972), pp. 285–297.

8. A. Dittman, *Interpersonal Messages of Emotion* (New York: Springer, 1972).

9. G. Allport and H. Cantril, "Judging Personality from the Voice," *Journal of Social Psychology*, 5 (1934), pp. 37–54; P. B. Davis, "An Investigation of the Suggestion of Age through Voice in Interpretative Reading" (M.A. thesis: University of Denver, 1949); G. P. Nerbonne, "The Identification of Speaker Characteristics on the Basis of Aural Cues" (dissertation, Michigan State University, 1967); T. H. Pear, *Voice and Personality* (London: Chapman and Hall, 1931); E. Kramer, "Personality Stereotypes in Voice: A Reconsideration of the Data," *Journal of Social Psychology*, 62 (1964), pp. 247–251.

10. R. E. McGlone and H. H. Hollien, "Vocal Pitch Characteristics of Aged Women," *Journal of Speech and Hearing Research*, 6 (1963), pp. 164–170; E. D. Mysak, "Pitch and Duration Characteristics of Older Males," *Journal of Speech and Hearing Research*, 2 (1959), pp. 46–54.

11. D. W. Addington, "The Relationship of Selected Vocal Characteristics to Personality Perception," *Speech Monographs*, 35 (1968), pp. 492–503.

12. Pear (note 9).

13. See, for example, A. Epstein and J. H. Ulrich, "The Effect of High- and Low-Pass Filtering on the Judged Vocal Quality of Male and Female Speakers," *Quarterly Journal of Speech*, 52 (1966), pp. 267–272; G. Fant, "A Note on Vocal Tract Size and Factors and Non-Uniform F-Pattern Scalings," *Speech Transmission Laboratory Quarterly Progress and Status Report*, 4 (1966), pp. 22–30; H. Hollien, D. Dew, and P. Philips, "Phonational Frequency Ranges of Adults," *Journal of Speech and Hearing Research*, 14 (1971), pp. 755–760; P. H. Ptacek and E. K. Sander, "Breathiness and Phonation Length," *Journal of Speech and Hearing Disorders*, 28 (1963), pp. 267–272; R. Lakoff, "You Are What You Say," *Ms.* (July 1974), pp. 65–67.

14. Knapp, pp. 155–156 (note 5); Nerbonne (note 9).

15. Allport and Cantril (note 9); P. Fay and W. Middleton, "Judgments of Kretschmerian Body Types from the Voice as Transmitted Over a Public Address System," *Journal of Social Psychology*, 12 (1940), pp. 151–162; Nerbonne (note 9).

16. H. I. Douty, "Influence of Clothing on Perception of Persons," *Journal of Home Economics*, 55 (1963), pp. 197–202; A. Hoffman, "Clothing Behavioral Factors for Specified Group of Women Related to Aesthetic Sensitivity and Certain Socio-Economic and Psychological Background Factors," *Journal of Home Economics*, 49 (1957), p. 233; M. L. L. Rosencranz, "The Application of a Projective Technique for Analyzing Clothing Awareness, Clothing Symbols, and the Range of Themes Associated with Clothing Behavior" (dissertation, University of Illinois, 1960). See also M. L. L. Rosencranz, "Clothing Symbolism," *Journal of Home Economics*, 54 (1962), pp. 18–22; M. L. L. Rosencranz, "Sociological and Psychological Approaches to Clothing Research," *Journal of Home Economics*, 57 (1965), pp. 26–29.

17. K. Young, *Social Psychology* (New York: F. S. Crofts, 1947), pp. 419–420.
18. M. Harrington, *The Other America* (New York: Macmillian, 1962), p. 5.
19. R. Sybers and M. E. Roach, "Clothing and Human Behavior," *Journal of Home Economics,* 54 (1962), pp. 184–187.
20. *Placement Manual* (Gainesville, Florida: University of Florida, Fall 1976), pp. 22–23.
21. Allport and Cantril (note 9).
22. P. J. Fay and W. G. Middleton, "Judgment of Occupation from the Voice as Transmitted over a Public Address System and over a Radio," *Journal of Social Psychology,* 23 (1939), pp. 586–601.
23. W. B. Pearce and F. Conklin, "Nonverbal Vocalic Communication and the Perception of a Speaker," *Speech Monographs,* 38 (1971), pp. 235–241.
24. L. S. Harms, "Listener Judgments of Status Cues in Speech," *Quarterly Journal of Speech,* 47 (1961), pp. 164–168; Nerbonne (note 9).
25. D. S. Ellis, "Speech and Social Status in America," *Social Forces,* 45 (1967), pp. 431–451.
26. A. Cohen and J. Starkweather, "Vocal Cues in Language Identification," *American Journal of Psychology,* 74 (1961), pp. 90–93.
27. E. T. Hall and W. F. Whyte, "Intercultural Communication: A Guide to Men of Action," *Human Organization,* 19 (1960), p. 7.
28. J. Kelley, "Dress as Nonverbal Communication," paper presented to the Annual Conference of the American Association for Public Opinion Research, May 1969.
29. Our thanks to Mark Peterson, Linda Saarinen, and Kathy Kazen for sharing their results with us.
30. J. B. Cortés and F. M. Gatti, "Physique and Self-Description of Temperament," *Journal of Consulting Psychology,* 29 (1965), p. 434.
31. R. N. Walker, "Body Build and Behavior in Young Children; II. Body Build and Parents' Ratings," *Child Development,* 34 (1963), pp. 1–23.
32. J. B. Cortés and F. M. Gatti, "Physique and Propensity," *Psychology Today,* 4 (1970), pp. 42–44, 32–34; Cortés and Gatti, 1965 (note 30).
33. Cortés and Gatti, 1970 (note 32).
34. S. M. Jourard and P. F. Secord, "Body-Cathexis and Personality," *British Journal of Psychology,* 46 (1955), pp. 130–138.
35. E. Berscheid, E. Walster, and G. Bohrnstedt, "Body Image: The Happy American Body," *Psychology Today,* 7, No. 6 (1973), pp. 119–131.
36. M. Dermer, "When Beauty Fails" (Dissertation: University of Minnesota, 1973).
37. D. G. Freedman, "The Survival Value of the Beard," *Psychology Today,* 3 (1969), pp. 36–39.
38. R. J. Pelligrini, "Impressions of a Male Personality as a Function of Beardedness," *Psychology,* 10 (1973), pp. 29–33.
39. L. Aiken, "Relationships of Dress to Selected Measures of Personality in Undergraduate Women," *Journal of Social Psychology,* 59 (1963), pp. 119–128.
40. L. M. Gurel, J. C. Wilbur, and L. Gurel, "Personality Correlates of Adolescent Clothing Styles," *Journal of Home Economics,* 64 (1972), pp. 42–47.
41. N. H. Compton, "Personal Attributes of Color and Design Preferences in Clothing Fabrics," *Journal of Psychology,* 54 (1962), pp. 191–195.
42. W. J. McKeachie, "Lipstick as a Determinant of First Impressions of Personality," *Journal of Social Psychology,* 36 (1952), pp. 241–244; G. Thornton, "The Effect of Wearing Glasses upon Judgments of Persons Seen Briefly," *Journal of Applied Psychology,* 28 (1944), pp. 203–207.
43. P. N. Hamid, "Style of Dress as a Perceptual Cue in Impression Formation," *Perceptual and Motor Skills,* 26 (1968), pp. 904–906.
44. E. Mallory and V. Miller, "A Possible Basis for the Association of Voice Characteristics and Personality Traits," *Speech Monographs,* 25 (1958), p. 255.
45. See, for example, C. C. Crawford and W. Michael, "An Experiment in Judging Intelligence by the Voice," *Journal of Educational Psychology,* 18 (1927), pp. 107–114; W. E. Moore, "Personality Traits and Voice Quality Deficiencies," *Journal of Speech and Hearing Disorders,* 4 (1939), pp. 33–36.
46. Allport and Cantril (note 9).
47. P. J. Fay and W. G. Middleton, "Judgment of Intelligence from the Voice as Transmitted Over a Public Address System," *Sociometry,* 3 (1940), pp. 186–191; P. J. Fay and W. G. Middleton, "Judgment of Introversion from the Transcribed Voice," *Quarterly Journal of Speech,* 28 (1942), pp. 226–228.
48. J. Starkweather, "Vocal Communication of Personality and Human Feelings," *Journal of Communication,* 11 (1961), pp. 63–72.

49. E. Kramer, "Personality Stereotypes in Voice: A Reconsideration of the Data," *Journal of Social Psychology,* 62 (1964), pp. 247–251.

50. D. W. Addington (note 11).

51. N. N. Markel, J. A. Phillis, R. Vargas, and K. Howard, "Personality Traits Associated with Voice Types," *Journal of Psycholinguistic Research,* 1 (1972), pp. 249–255.

52. Mallory and Miller (note 44); N. N. Markel, "Relationship between Voice-Quality and MMPI Profiles in Psychiatric Patients," *Journal of Abnormal Psychology,* 74 (1969), pp. 61–66.

53. D. A. Schweitzer, "The Effect of Presentation on Source Evaluation," *Quarterly Journal of Speech,* 56 (1970), pp. 33–39.

54. Pearce and Conklin (note 23).

7

Relational Messages

Test Your Sensitivity

True or False?

1. An observer can judge whether you like someone or not just by watching your eyes.
2. When we are attracted to someone, our posture becomes more relaxed.
3. If a woman turns her wrist outward and begins to stroke it, it means she's not interested in a man.
4. In a conversation, the person who first breaks a silence is usually lower in status.
5. The more status and power a person has, the greater the distance he or she maintains from others.
6. People who have a foreign accent and speak slowly are seen as competent.

A couple sit side by side in the park, their posture relaxed, legs and shoulders touching. She smiles as she looks at the ground; he gazes fondly at her as he brushes her hair back from her face. He leans close to whisper something and takes her hand. As they rise to leave, she gently squeezes his hand.

What conclusions can you draw about these two people? That they are brother and sister? mother and son? salesperson and customer? two strangers who have just met? Probably not. If you are at all sensitive to nonverbal cues, you probably concluded that they are lovers. The cues that influenced your judgment— proximity, touching, facial expressions, and courtship cues—are what we call *relational messages*, messages about the nature of the relationship between people.

In the broadest sense, relational messages may indicate the feelings, personalities, and identities of the people in the communication transaction.[1] In other words, they can involve anything that has to do with how two or more people regard each other, themselves, and their relationship. For instance, in a conversation between Jill and Jasper, Jill may send nonverbal messages to Jasper about her self-concept as an attractive individual, about whether she thinks Jasper is attractive, and about whether she thinks she and Jasper like each other. Jasper may do the same. All of these messages are considered relational because they help to define the overall nature of the relationship. If Jill sees herself as unattractive and Jasper as highly desirable, for example, she may relate to him in a very unsure, unassertive way. Outsiders may similarly recognize Jill's insecurity in the relationship and her need for reassurance. Relational messages, then, may be interpreted by participants in the interaction or by observers of it, so long as someone attributes intent to them.

In the next chapter, we shall explore the ways in which people communicate their emotional feelings. In this chapter, we shall focus exclusively on the ways in which people use

By the end of the chapter, you should know the correct answer to all six questions and understand these concepts:

- relational messages
- inclusion/exclusion
- confirmation/disconfirmation
- affection
- control
- nonverbal variables that signal attraction and liking:
  eyes
  faces and bodies
  voices
  silences
  distance and touch
  physical appearance
- stages of courtship and quasicourtship
- nonverbal variables that signal credibility, status, and power:
  kinesic behaviors
  voices
  time and silences
  distance and touch
  physical appearance
  environment and objects

nonverbal cues to assess the nature of the relationship between themselves and others or those they are observing. We have chosen not to emphasize self-perception in this chapter for two reasons: first, it will be covered indirectly later when we examine how people try to manipulate their nonverbal performances to create certain impressions. Second, because this is a book about communication, we are more interested in the nature of communication transactions and how people regard those transactions than in how they regard themselves. In this chapter, we shall look at such things as attraction, credibility, and power—features of communication that are strictly defined by the relationships between people. We shall attempt to uncover the kinds of nonverbal messages that reveal the nature of a relationship between two people or are perceived to reveal it.

Relational messages may carry four basic kinds of information.[2] First, they may signal *inclusion* or *exclusion*, that is, whether a person is being included in an interaction. Cliques are well known for their obvious signalling of membership. Members dress alike, form tight little conversational circles, and turn their backs on those who don't belong. Such inclusion messages, which are employed with varying degrees of subtlety by all age groups, may also serve as a form of rejection to those who are left out.

Second, relational messages may indicate either *confirmation* or *disconfirmation*. *Confirmational messages* are supportive in nature; they indicate acceptance and support of another's identity and self-perception. Smiling, nodding, and touching are common means of communicating confirmation. *Disconfirmational messages*, on the other hand, provide negative feedback; they fail to support the individual's self-perceptions. The student who receives a raised eyebrow in response to his statement that he is really working hard is receiving a message of disconfirmation. Such messages may also indicate rejection by failing

to grant the other's worth. Always being chosen last for the company bowling league or receiving snickers about the way you dress are examples. Lack of inclusion is also in itself a form of disconfirmation.

Third, relational messages may involve a *control* element, indicating who has the power to define, direct, or dominate the relationship. In the movie *Gone With the Wind*, Scarlett O'Hara unquestionably ran the show with her many suitors. All conversation and all longing glances were directed her way.

Finally, relational messages may involve an *affection* component, indicating the degree to which a person feels emotionally close to another or attempts to express feelings of closeness. The popular notions of *stroking* and *massaging the ego* fall into this category because they are attempts at expressing affection or liking toward another. We may give others strokes with smiles and pleasant voices. These four components of relational messages combine in varying degrees to communicate attraction, liking, credibility, power, and status.

Attraction and Liking

Courtship consists in a number of quiet attentions, not so pointed as to alarm, nor so vague as not to be understood.

—Laurence Sterne

The messages used to communicate attraction and liking are a mixture of inclusion, confirmation, and affection messages. Conversely, disliking and repulsion may express themselves in messages of exclusion, disconfirmation, or lack of affection. Such messages frequently dictate whether communication will even occur, whether it will be pleasurable, and whether it will lead to further interactions. People who are attracted to each other find ways to make contact; those who develop an aversion to one another avoid it.

All of the nonverbal channels may play a role in signalling attraction and liking. Consider this situation:

Bob and Dan arrived at the party just behind Carol. When she saw them, she quickly patted her hair into place, smoothed her clothing, and turned to smile at them. She caught Bob's eye and held his glance for a moment before turning to say hello to Dan. While still speaking to Dan, she brushed up next to Bob. She squeezed Bob's arm gently and said in a soft voice, "It's nice to see you." As they entered the house, Carol hesitantly broke off from the two and joined a group of friends, but she frequently looked in Bob's direction. When he moved toward the group, she became more erect and turned her body to face him while avoiding his eyes. But he went to speak to Dan instead.

"I guess it's really over between Carol and me," he said dejectedly.

"Man, you've got it all wrong," replied Dan. "She's been giving you signals all evening that she still cares."

In this case, Bob was so concerned about his own feelings that he failed to recognize all the nonverbal cues that Carol gave him. She used eye behavior, facial expression, body posture and orientation, vocal cues, preening gestures, proxemic cues, and even touch to communicate her message. Let's look more closely at how each of these cues and others can be used to signal attraction and liking.

Eyes

Eyes have long been recognized as one of the key means of signalling affection and attraction. Literary passages abound on the gazing behavior of people in love or people who are aroused by each other. This passage from Hermann Broch's *The Sleepwalkers: A Trilogy* is typical:

So they smiled frankly at each other and their souls nodded to each other through the windows of their eyes, just for an instant, like two neighbors who have never greeted each other and now happen to lean out of their window at the same moment, pleased and embarrassed by this unforeseen and simultaneous greeting.[3]

People in love are known to spend much time gazing into each other's eyes.[4] When we like someone or are attracted to him or her, we are likely to look at that person for long periods of time, whereas we look less at those whom we dislike.[5] However, you may recall from Chapter 5 that there are some differences in the reponses of men and women: men adjust their eye behavior according to whether they like the other person only while they are listening; women, on the other hand, express attraction through visual behavior only while speaking.[6] Thus, if you are making judgments about whether a man is attracted to someone, you should observe his eye behavior when he is listening; for women, when they are talking.

Along with time spent in gazing, the size of the pupil also influences judgments of attraction and liking. Pupil dilation or constriction is something we cannot consciously control. It occurs without our awareness or intent, yet it can give away our true feelings about someone. When people see something or someone they like, their pupils dilate.[7] In fact, homosexuality has been detected by having people look at pictures of nudes and determining whether observers have greater pupil dilation while looking at photos of males or females.[8] People described as having "bedroom eyes" probably have dilated pupils.

Interestingly, people are attracted to others with dilated pupils. Women in times past played upon this fact. They used the stimulant belladonna to make their pupils larger. Students in our nonverbal communication class were intrigued by the relationship between pupil dilation and attraction, so they conducted a small study. They showed photos of two women, one with constricted and one with enlarged pupils, to male students and asked them to rate the women. The woman with the dilated pupils was rated more sympathetic, happier, more feminine, more naïve, more attractive, more open, younger, and more sexually interesting than the other. It seems reasonable to assume that if we view people with larger pupils as more attractive, and our own pupils dilate when we are attracted to someone, a kind of continuous cycle may be at work when two people find themselves drawn to each other. Through the eyes alone, they may discover that they are interested in each other and at the same time insure that they remain attracted to each other.

Faces and Bodies

Facial and body expressions are also significant carriers of attraction and liking messages. In fact, one study found that the combinations of eye contact, body orientation, trunk lean, and distance in a counselor–client interaction conveyed twice as much information as the verbal message in communicating empathy.[9] In the case of Bob and Carol, Carol signalled her interest by smiling and orienting her body toward Bob to gain his attention. Typically, people who are attracted to one another engage in increased smiling and nodding, lean toward each other, maintain erect posture (but not to the point of being stilted), and orient their bodies toward each other. The behavior of student tutors bears this out. Undergraduates were asked to help children, some described as dull and some as bright. Tutors who thought they were working with a bright child smiled more often, maintained more direct eye gaze, leaned forward more, and nodded their heads more than did tutors working with children said to be dull or children who had not been categorized.[10]

Researchers have noted that people who like each other tend to *mirror* each other's behavior, for example, by adopting similar postures and tension levels.[11] If one person is relaxed, the other becomes relaxed. If one sits with both elbows on a table, the other adopts the same position. Medical professionals have discovered that psychiatrists and nurses achieve the highest degree of rapport with patients when their bodies are in the *upper body mirror congruent* position,[12] that is, when their trunk, shoulders, and arms are in the same configuration as the patient's. Next time you are in a group of people, see if those who feel positive toward each other fall into the same postures. You may also notice that significant shifts in posture away from congruency are often associated with changes in feelings.

We have already mentioned several cases in which our knowledge of relational messages of attraction and liking have come out of a medical setting. People in medicine and related professions (nursing, speech therapy, and so on) have long been aware of the nonverbal cues that their patients or clients give them. One researcher in particular, Albert Scheflen, advanced knowledge significantly when he realized that not only were patients giving signs of attraction to their doctors but doctors were unconsciously sending such signs also. What Scheflen saw in clinical situations was similar to what takes place in normal courtship behavior. Thus, he labeled the patterns *quasicourtship*. To better investigate what was happening in clinical situations, he decided first to get a better understanding of typical courtship cues. In the process of observing, he discovered that the signals appear in almost any interaction—during a class, at a cocktail party, in a psychotherapy session, or at a business meeting. People don't expect all these flirtations to end in sexual relations; they simply find the courtship behavior rewarding in itself. Regardless of age or status or degree of acquaintanceship, people who engage in this quasicourtship behavior go through three basic stages: courtship readiness, positioning for courtship, and actions of appeal or invitation.[13]

Courtship Readiness   The behaviors involved in courtship readiness are the behaviors that precede actual courting. The most common indicator of readiness is increased muscle tone. Posture improves, sagging tummies and behinds are pulled in, even bags around the eyes tend to disappear. People generally appear more alert. In addition, eyes may seem brighter and skin coloring may change. Preening behaviors usually accompany the physiological behaviors. These are the kinds of gestures that we earlier labeled *adaptors* — specifically, those adaptors that are designed to improve our appearance. Men may tug at socks, straighten ties, button jackets, or comb their hair into place. Women may check their make-up, straighten their clothing, and smooth their hair. The next time you are in a public restroom, notice the various kinds of preening that people engage in just before they leave. Or watch people trying on clothes in a department store. They are likely to display a gamut of readiness behaviors, from furtive glances in the mirror to the smoothing of wrinkled underwear. All these behaviors are the same kinds of behaviors we exhibit when we are engaged in quasicourtship or courtship interactions.

Positioning for Courtship   The next stage of the game is getting into the right position. People naturally place themselves in close face-to-face positions for direct and intimate conversation; but they also tend to adopt positions that close others out. They lean toward each other, place chairs in a way that prevents others from joining them, and place arms and legs together so that they become an enclosed unit (see Fig. 7.1). If other people are present, the upper body may be turned to include them politely while the lower body—legs, trunk, and feet—clearly signals exclusion.

Invitations   The last stage of the process involves making implicit appeals to the other person via body language, verbal innuendo, and vocal orchestration. The general notion is to arouse the other individual. You probably already know and have used many of the typical behaviors—things like holding eye contact longer than usual, winking, cocking the head, and increasing the frequency of touch, especially in areas that are usually off limits. For instance, women may begin by casually touching a man on the arm, then progress to a pat on the knee or thigh. Men may first take the liberty of touching a woman's hair or putting an arm around her shoulder. The more serious the courtship, the further and more intimate the touching becomes. There are also several cues that are not as easily recognized. Men may protrude the pelvis, unbutton extra buttons, adopt poses that accentuate their muscles, or catch a woman's eye then slowly appraise her body. Women may slowly and imperceptively

mini-experiment

Go to a discotheque or bar. Isolate several couples for observation. Record the frequency of the various courtship cues and note in what stage of the courtship process the couples seem to be. See if you can guess how intimate the relationship is. Then ask the couples how well they know each other (just met? infrequent dating? living together? married?). You may find that dancing and drinking speed up the courtship process for strangers.

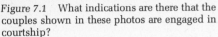 What indications are there that the couples shown in these photos are engaged in courtship?

roll their hips, protrude the breasts, sit with their legs crossed to expose the thigh, turn wrists and palms outward, place a hand on the hip, or stroke the wrist or thigh.

In the case of true courtship, there is, of course, the desire for the relationship to progress to whatever level of intimacy is mutually acceptable and satisfying. Quasicourtship probably serves simply to make the two parties feel attractive and sexually appealing. They rarely intend the interaction to continue beyond flirtation. To ensure that neither party misunderstands the purpose of the courtship signals, additional cues are added as definers. One way of keeping the interactions at a less-than-intimate level is to make the posturing involvement incomplete. People may face slightly in the direction of actual or imaginary others, they may open their arm and leg positions to include others, or they may disengage eye contact to observe or make contact with

others. They may also make the conversation audible to others so that others may feel free to join the conversation, or they may use nods and glances to remind their courtship partner that other people are present, thus invoking social rules of conduct.

The omission of typical cues from the courtship repertoire may also signal that the courtship is not serious. For instance, the ritualistic use of touch and facial expression to convey affection may be absent. Finally, the sheer inappropriateness of a given context may signal quasicourtship. Frequently, male students and female teachers or female students and male teachers unconsciously fall into quasicourtship routines in the process of expressing interest in each other because quasicourtship is such an ingrained pattern for showing liking and approval. If the flirtatious behavior occurs in front of the rest of the class, the context indicates that it isn't serious.

Voices

We have already touched briefly on vocal qualities in mentioning that people use the voice as a signal of courtship. Usually people who are trying to entice or be enticing speak in hushed tones with slurred pronunciation. Men and women both may lower their pitch level to sound more seductive. In less sexually oriented contexts, people expressing liking and attraction use less volume but a lot of pitch and intonation variety to convey enthusiasm. Voice qualities tend to be softer than usual, with more breathiness and less tension. Of course, people who like each other are probably close together, so there is no need for loud, emphatic voices. The quieter tones are also conducive to intimate conversation and self-disclosure.

Silences

Silence is both a vocalic variable, because it is an extended pause, and a chronemic variable, because the length of the silence carries meaning. Silence may carry two opposite meanings. When it follows friendly communication, it can be taken as a sign of a high degree of attraction and comfort in the relationship. There is no need to talk. This may be especially true if communication is continuing at the nonverbal level with facial expression, eyes, touch, and so forth.

However, silence can also be a message of rejection or aversion. We sometimes refuse to speak to someone as a signal of dislike. The absence of conversation preceded by a hostile interaction or no interaction at all is likely to signal intense negative feelings. Even when it is unintentional, the failure to speak to others is often taken as a sign of aversion. Tom Bruneau notes: "Fat persons, dwarfs, very tall persons, crippled persons with mobility problems, blind persons, persons with pronounced speech or hearing disorders, etc., have known nervous silences toward them. Differences in appearance, such as perceived ugliness, dress and color of skin, when different than the situational norm, seem to be greeted by initial silences."[14] The inability of others to make conversation readily with someone who is different is the first clue to that person that she or he is not being accepted or regarded positively. Silence is a powerful way to communicate prejudice.

Distance and Touch

One important way people indicate their liking for another is to move closer to that person.[15] When people have been asked to role play a situation in which they like one another, they typically adopt a closer stance or seating position. When students are asked to identify relationships between individuals in photographs, they invariably conclude that those who are close to each other are friendly. Conversely, people maintain a greater distance from those whom they dislike.[16] People with handicaps or deformities know this well. Other people continually communicate to them that they are in some way offensive by keeping them at a distance.

If distance serves as exclusion and disconfirmation and closeness signals inclusion and confirmation, it might seem reasonable to expect actual physical contact to be the ultimate message of liking and attraction, and the avoidance of touch when touch is expected a powerful negative message. This is apparently the case among married and dating couples. Ernst Beier and Daniel Sternberg, two psychologists, have conducted extensive observations of nonverbal communication among newlyweds. They found that those couples who were happiest with their marriage sat close together and touched each other more often than they touched themselves. By contrast, those who were experiencing conflict created a feeling of distance by crossing their arms and legs (reducing the possibility for touch) and touched themselves more often than they touched their spouse.[17] Parents also communicate affection or coldness to their children by the presence or absence of touch. The acceptable forms of touch may vary from family to family, but the effort to make physical contact is still present among affectionate families. It may even take the form of assisting with each other's grooming. Thus, mothers straighten collars for their sons and fathers pat their daughters' hair. For both siblings and parents, rough play also offers a means of contact. It should be possible to index the degree of affection, warmth, and security in a family by the frequency and ease with which the members hug, kiss, pat, and otherwise touch each other.

While touch appears to be a vital relational message among friends and relatives, it apparently does not perform the same functions of confirmation, affection, and inclusion among strangers, or at least not to the same degree. These were the conclusions of two recent studies that compared touch to other kinds of messages of empathy and warmth.[18] In one investigation, a message of empathy was accompanied either by no touch, by imagined touch (subjects were instructed to imagine being touched), or by actual touch. While actual touch did lead to more positive feelings, empathy was perceived to be even greater when accompanied by no touch or by imagined touch. Another study combined touch and no touch with warm and cold behavior (other kinesic behaviors that signalled warmth or coldness). The researchers found that it was not the presence or absence of touch that made a difference but the presence or absence of other friendly cues. While these studies are not definitive, they do imply that touch is less necessary and useful in communicating attraction and liking among people who are not well acquainted than among friends or relatives. Its main function may be to confirm what other nonverbal cues are already signalling about the degree of attraction in the relationship.

Of course, the obvious avoidance of touch may be a powerful message of repugnance, exclusion, and disconfirmation. Wilbur Watson, who recently observed the frequency of touch in a nursing home, discovered that the staff engaged in much less touching with extremely handicapped patients, even though touch is frequently a necessary part of medical care.[19] Many minorities report similar experiences of people carefully avoiding contact with them. It seems, then, that the explicit avoidance of contact with strangers may be a meaning-laden message.

Physical Appearance

A last nonverbal code that plays an obvious role in signalling attraction and liking is appearance—our grooming habits and choice of apparel. It's hardly earth-shattering to suggest that we can tell others a lot about our feelings toward them by how much effort we put into appearing attractive for them or how appropriately we dress for various occasions. It is doubtful that prospective in-laws would feel warmly toward their daughter's fiancé if he showed up for their first meeting unshaven, bare-chested, wearing dirty, torn jeans. Nor would a funeral party feel that someone in a bizarre and flashy costume was showing much respect.

Credibility, Status, and Power

> By and by a proud-looking man about fifty-five—and he was a heap the best-dressed man in that town, too—steps out of the store, and the crowd drops back on each side to let him come.
>
> —Mark Twain

So far, we have looked primarily at the affection, inclusion, and confirmation components of relational messages. We've seen how we can guess whether people like each other, and how the expressions of affect translate into inclusion and confirmation or exclusion and disconfirmation. In this section we will look more at the element of control in relationships—whether people grant each other credibility, status, and power. We have grouped these three communication effects together and labeled them *control elements* because they work together to establish who dominates and directs a relationship. The individual who is initially viewed as powerful is likely to be granted high status and credibility because of that position of power. We shall focus on the nonverbal cues that are interpreted by participants in or observers of an interaction as indicators of the relative credibility, status, and power of the participants. In later chapters, we shall consider how people intentionally manipulate their nonverbal performance to increase their control over others.

Kinesic Behaviors

The most effective features of the kinesic repertoire are eye behavior, posture, and gestural or body activity. Direct eye contact may be interpreted as a sign of credibility. If a person looks you in the eye when he or she says something, you are likely to assume that the person is being honest with you and knows what he or she is talking about. When people avert their eyes, we usually assume either that they are keeping something from us, in which case we find them less credible in terms of character, or that they are having a hard time gathering their thoughts, in which case we find them less credible in terms of competence. Similarly, the more frequently a person looks at you, the more honest and qualified she or he seems.

Both frequency and directness of glance also affect attributions of status and power. People who are looked at more often in a group are assumed by others to be the most powerful, and they themselves conclude that they are regarded highly. This assumption is reasonable; research has repeatedly found that powerful individuals experience more eye contact and communication directed toward them than others.[21] (Interestingly, though, the highest-status person receives less contact than a person of moderately high status. The notion of deference may explain the tapering-off effect.) The use of a steady, direct gaze also connotes status and is a privilege of rank.[22] Low-status individuals are not supposed to sustain direct eye contact with superiors. We typically show deference to our elders and high-ranking officials by lowering our eyes, while they are free to look at us. Finally, the total avoidance of eye contact on the part of a listener can be a power cue: speakers attribute more authority and control to listeners who do not look at them.[23]

Posture and gestural activity influence status and power in much the same way that eye contact does. In any group, the individual who is faced by the most people or toward whom the most gestures are directed can probably be assumed to have the most influence. It is very easy to pick out a faculty member among a group of students at a social gathering; he or she is the person in the middle of a cluster of bodies, the one toward whom all eyes are pointed. In addition, people are more likely to mirror the posture and gestures of people with high status or power. Such individuals set the stage, so to speak. They are the ones who dictate in an interaction whether people sit in a relaxed fashion or not and how many gestures people use. However, if people are not of equal status, those of the lower status do not imitate body position and tension level completely but remain less relaxed and more formal. For instance, when aquanaut crews were observed, crew members of higher status were seen to be more relaxed than those of lower status; the more equal people were in status, the more relaxed they were; crew members were more likely to mirror the high-status leaders; and body congruency between people increased as they became more similar in status.[24] Watch any business meeting and you'll discover that higher-status people allow arms, legs, and posture to be relaxed; they are more likely to lean sideways, and they feel free to put their feet up on chairs and desks.[25]

As for the effects of posture and body movement on credibility, it is probably safe to assume that we attribute more confidence, competence, and sincerity to the individual who has good posture and a walk that effuses confidence, uses animated behavior (such as illustrative gestures), and lacks nervous habits (such as self-adaptor gestures).

Voices

Numerous vocal qualities affect our impressions about a person's credibility, status, and power. In general, an overall good delivery increases credibility.[26] A conversational speaking style—one that is calm, not intense, slow, and low in volume—creates more favorable judgments as to trustworthiness, honesty, soci-

ability, and likeableness than does a dynamic style, but it doesn't seem to affect judgments of competence.[27] Johnny Carson is a good example of a performer with a conversational style. By contrast, speakers in many commercials have a dynamic delivery style. Perhaps that is why we find the ads offensive.

Some features that affect credibility include rate, pitch level and variation, nonfluency, and dialect. For example, James Stewart's slow drawl typically conveys the image of a shy, good-natured bumbler. His slow rate of speaking communicates benevolence (humility, sincerity, honesty, and so on) and incompetence; if he were to speed up his delivery, he would lose his kindly image and would appear much more extroverted.[28] His use of pitch also contributes to his image. A voice with high pitch and little variation is less credible in terms of competence and benevolence than is a deep-pitched, varied voice.[29] Stewart's voice is usually high-pitched but varied. Finally, he frequently uses nonfluencies (repetitions, stutters, and er- and uh-filled pauses), which give an impression of incompetence and introversion.[30] But notice that these impressions never lower evaluations of Stewart's character.

One last feature of voices that significantly affects credibility is dialect. Some of the more interesting findings on the subject of dialect are:[31]

1. People don't have a preference for their own regional dialect; they don't consistently rate it highest.
2. General American speech (what Midwesterners speak) is generally viewed as more credible than southern or New England speech.
3. The speech of native-born speakers is rated as more dynamic, more aesthetically pleasing, and reflective of higher socio-intellectual status than that of speakers with foreign accents.
4. Both blacks and whites rate speakers of standard English higher than speakers using a

nonstandard dialect (including black dialect). Black speakers who use standard English are assumed to be white.

5. People with a New York accent are rated more dynamic but less sociable than those with a southern drawl.

6. People speaking with a New York accent or Central U.S. pattern (which is equivalent to General American speech) are rated as more competent than speakers with a New England or southern accent.

7. Finally, the effects of dialect on a receiver's judgment are short term.

From this evidence we can tentatively conclude that the voice most often judged credible is the voice that is fluent, low-pitched, varied, moderately paced, and General American in dialect. This is the voice that radio and television stations cultivate in their broadcasters. (No wonder Walter Cronkite has been voted the most credible man in America.) It will be interesting to observe whether this pattern changes with Jimmy Carter in the White House. Carter's rate and pitch qualify as credible, but his southern accent may cause some to doubt his competence. Maybe through his model, the South will rise again in the evaluation of others. We should point out, though, that Lyndon Johnson was unable to overcome the stigma attached to the southern dialect.

Vocal qualities also influence judgments of power and status. The low-pitched, fluent, nonaccented voice conveys self-confidence, authority, and education, which contribute to status. Studies done on teachers' ratings of children's voices illustrate the importance of such vocal cues.[32] A group of researchers took samples of speech from white, black, and Mexican–American children of middle- and lower-class backgrounds then asked teachers to evaluate the children on a wide range of characteristics. The results showed that the teachers recognized whether the children followed a standard or nonstandard intonation pattern. The voice can easily give away a lower-class,

mini-experiment

Tape-record voices of several friends who have different dialects. Then play the tapes for people who don't know your friends and have them rate the vocal features on a standard credibility-rating form. (You can make sure that the verbal element and your friends' differing dramatic abilities don't influence judgments by having everyone record the same relatively colorless passage.) Compare the responses to the research findings we've been discussing.

You may also want to note any differences in ratings of male and female voices with the same dialect. It has been suggested, for instance, that some consider a southern accent sexy in women, effeminate in men.

uneducated person. The teachers also noticed whether the children seemed eager and confident or not. A follow-up study found that the black children's voices were rated as nonstandard, and the lower-class black children were rated as less confident and eager than the others. In other words, even children are typecast by their voice as having high or low status. These judgments, in turn, undoubtedly influence predictions of success at school.

In addition to pitch, fluency, and dialect, the rate, volume, and resonance of a voice may affect perceptions of power. A moderately fast rate, high volume, and full resonance may carry the sound of a voice of authority, one that commands attention. Representative Barbara Jordan's voice exemplifies this pattern. People associate such voices with power. When a teenager tries to pass as an adult, all these vocal factors are brought into play.

Distance and Touch

Proxemics and haptics operate in very similar fashion in communicating credibility, status, and power. First, people of high status and power are given more space. Others keep a greater distance from them, and so do not touch them. When John F. Kennedy became president, even his closest friends began to accord him much greater distance even in social situations. The military has a penchant for using distance to reinforce status and power. The story is told of a regulation that was passed requiring privates to maintain a ten-foot distance as a sign of respect when addressing senior officers. Unfortunately, that distance is too great for normal conversation. The result was that the privates found themselves yelling at the officers. Finally, the military was obliged to retract the regulation in embarrassment.

The second way in which distance and touch signal status and power is in who defines the interaction distance and who initiates touch. The person of higher status or power usually determines the distance at which interaction takes place. Suppose you, as a student, go to interview a local banker. The banker's office probably offers several possible seating arrangements. Whether you are seated opposite the desk or at a more comfortable seat at a coffee table (allowing close interaction) may tell you what status the banker is willing to grant you.

Initiation of touch also signals who is the controlling member of an interaction. The person of higher status or power determines whether both parties touch and what forms of touch are acceptable. The individual of lower status does not have that prerogative. For example, you are not free to hug your dentist or your employer, especially if they have not initiated some form of contact first. Even if they did choose to touch you, the degree of contact they selected would limit the range of touch that you could use. If your employer limited touch to a handshake, for instance, you would not have the freedom to put your arm around her or pinch her.

As an observer of interactions, you can usually judge the relative status and power of two interacting individuals on the basis of how much distance is maintained, how much contact is permitted, and who is the initiator. Students in our classes have looked at films and photographs of pairs of people interacting. In one series, a man is standing in an office behind a desk and another man comes to the door. In one case, he hesitates at the door; in another, he enters the room and remains at a distance of eight feet, waiting; in yet another, he walks directly up to the desk and goes behind it. The students usually conclude that the man behind the desk is clearly of high status and that the first two men who approach the office are of lower status while the third is of equal or higher status. Why? Because the first two maintain a greater distance and wait for the man behind the desk to signal when they may approach while the last man himself defines the distance, which is very close. Similarly, given photos of people touching one another, observers conclude that the people involved are of relatively equal status.

Our knowledge of how touch and distance affect credibility is much more limited. Some initial research suggests that people may be able to increase credibility by reducing distance.[33] For instance, interviewers may make themselves appear more competent, composed, and dynamic by invading their interviewees' space. Judgments may depend on the nature of the person doing the moving in. If the initiator is attractive, of high status, or giving approval, then moving closer may increase judgments of competence, sociability, composure, character, and extroversion. If the initiator is viewed as unattractive, of low status, or critical, then moving closer may have negative consequences.

Time and Silences

People may also show control of a relationship by dictating meeting times, governing the length of interactions, and having the freedom to break silences. The more powerful party in a relationship is the one who dominates the chronemic patterns, deciding when the two get together, how long they talk, and even how much time they devote to each topic of discussion. A friend of ours was interviewed by a college dean, presumably so the dean could decide whether to grant our friend the right to work with doctoral students. Instead of asking questions, the dean chose to read aloud his original poetry. Since he was of high status and power, he had the freedom to do so. Our friend was not free to suggest that they spend the time discussing politics or even the intended topic—his academic credentials. Similarly, people of high status and power have the luxury of setting appointments and meetings for times that are convenient for them. They are also free to be late for such appointments, whereas a low-status person is expected to apologize if he or she is late.

The use of silence functions in much the same way. People in positions of authority are shown respect through silence; they have the privilege of deciding when to break silences by initiating conversation; and they may even choose to impose extended silences on people they wish to punish or keep in subordinate positions. Tom Bruneau explains:

Silence is used to show respect (or disrespect) for a socio-political position or station. For instance, when teachers, clergy, doctors, lawyers, judges and many others in authoritative positions enter rooms, a characteristic hush falls upon persons in that room. . . . Often, certain roles are protected by rules or obligatory norms imposed on persons to aid the established order. Hence, teachers operate in some schools with discipline codes, doctors operate with noise regulations preventing noise inside and outside hospitals, clergy are protected by unstated moral codes, and judges can enforce silence by issuing contempt of court charges. Silence can also protect power by aggravating those seeking to destroy or discredit persons in power. This can be done by forcing subordinates into awkward positions whereby they exhibit behaviors detrimental to their own cause —because their frustration is aggravated by silent response to their efforts. Silence as absence of response to or lack of recognition of subordinates may very well be the main source of protection of power in socio-political orders where physical restraint has lost repute.[34]

The relationship of time and silences to credibility is not as easy to pinpoint. Promptness is usually highly valued, but what are the effects of being either late or early? Communication researchers Leslie Baxter and Jean Ward asked eighty-four secretaries what their impressions would be if someone arrived fifteen minutes early, fifteen minutes late, or on time for an appointment. The responses indicated that some elements of credibility would be helped and others hurt by each arrival time. Late arrivers were regarded as highly dynamic but low on competence, composure, and sociability. Prompt arrivers were considered the most competent, composed, and sociable but not very dynamic. Early arrivers fared less well: they were rated low on dynamism and only moderate on the other three qualities.[35] If the secretaries' judgments can be considered typical, the moral seems clear—be punctual if you want to seem credible.

Physical Appearance

Every four years, when election time rolls around, the country is reminded of the importance of physical appearance in influencing judgments of power and credibility. John F. Kennedy's rapid ascent to power and popularity was due in part to his attractiveness and his Ivy League style. By contrast, Richard Nixon's face, with small eyes, bad complexion, heavy jowls, and five-o'clock shadow, doomed him to be distrusted. And in the 1976 presidential campaign, Jimmy Carter's popularity was attributed in part to his boyish good looks.

It appears that all facets of one's appearance can affect judgments of status, credibility, and power. Height seems to make a difference; the taller of the presidential candidates generally wins the election. Jimmy Carter is an exception. It is reported, though, that he was so concerned about his height disadvantage that, during the first campaign debate, he stretched his neck to look taller. The effect was odd, and Carter discontinued the practice. The importance of height is reflected in a study that found that we actually see higher-status people as taller.[36]

Body type is a factor, too. Kevin Toomb and Larry Divers investigated the relationship of body shape to credibility by attributing a message to an ectomorphic, mesomorphic, or endomorphic male or female pictured in a photograph accompanying the speech. (Heads were cropped off the pictures to rule out the effects of facial attractiveness.) Subjects who heard the speech and saw the pictures rated the female ectomorph as the most sociable, followed closely by the mesomorphic male.[37] The experimenters explained these results as reflecting our culture's preference for slender women and athletic men. Although Toomb and Divers did not find that body type affected other judgments of credibility, the somewhat artificial nature of the test may have been responsible. We suspect that in normal circumstances, body type does influence impressions of character, extroversion, and composure and may even affect judgments of competence.

Hair length, at least for males, and beards also make a difference. Peter Andersen, Tim Jensen, and Lyle King attempted to assess the role of hair length in creating credibility by having the same male speaker address two audiences wearing his hair at two different lengths. In one case, his hair was teased out from the head so that it appeared long; in the other case, it was combed close to the head. Surprisingly, the college audiences rated the short-haired speaker as more competent and dynamic. A more recent study similarly found that short-haired men were rated as more intelligent, moral, masculine, mature, wise, and attractive than long-haired men.[38] Interestingly, though, beards appear to produce better effects than the clean-shaven look. (See Figure 7.2.) Some studies have shown that college students attribute higher power and status to a bearded male.[39] For instance, when a picture of a bearded male is paired with a picture of an elderly man or woman, the bearded man is seen as the one in control of the relationship. When the same male is pictured without the beard, he is seen as more submissive.

This greater power and status may be granted only by women and people in the university community. John Pedersen writes that when he grew a beard and long hair, his reception among family, male friends, and business people cooled considerably.[40] The fact that many bearded, long-haired males still have difficulty in being hired for jobs suggests that they are still regarded as less trustworthy and perhaps less competent than others. A recent court ruling stands as further testimony that beards, mustaches, and long hair are still an issue. The court ruled that police forces could enforce grooming codes for their officers, that such standards were not a violation of freedom of speech. Apparently, many police forces still feel that too much hair on the head and face undermines a policeman's credibility.

Finally, apparel makes a difference. One of our students, Theresa Wicklin, who studied status and power cues among medical personnel, found that one of the ways doctors, nurses,

Figure 7.2 Which man appears more powerful?
What elements of the photos affected your decision?

and medical students reinforce their power position is through the conspicuous display of the badges of their profession. She noted that they were never without their white lab coats, stethoscopes, name tags, insignia, and beepers. Doctors wore their lab coats everywhere—to the cafeteria, the bookstore, to meetings, and even to their cars. They also wore them open, exposing the beeper, and when they walked, the coat flowed behind them, creating an image of energy and confidence.

Of course, medical people are not the only ones who use elements of apparel to heighten credibility and status. The research clearly indicates that people judge well-dressed individuals to be of high status. Astute trial lawyers have their clients dress so as to convey an impression of sincerity and innocence.

Ultimately, evaluations of credibility, power, and status also facilitate behavior changes. In Chapter 11, we shall look at some interesting cases in which dress, and especially uniforms, had a strong impact on the behavior of observers.

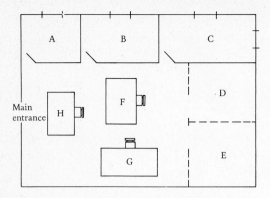

Figure 7.3

Artifacts

In the office layout pictured in Figure 7.3. the letters represent offices or desks assigned to employees. Offices A, B, and C are completely enclosed and have windows; Office C has two windows. Offices D and E have only half partitions for the dividing walls. F, G, and H are desks. If you were to rank the employees assigned to those spaces from highest status to lowest, how would you order them?

You probably assigned the highest status to the person in Office C. Because of the two windows, the larger enclosed space, and the distance from the main entrance to the office, that is the choicest spot. It is clearly the office of a boss or office manager. Office B is the next most desirable because it is farther from the entrance than A, which is the third best. D and E come next, because they offer at least some privacy, followed by G, which at least has a wall. H is worst; it is the most accessible to visitors and has the least amount of physical space and is also open to surveillance from almost everybody else.

The designation of status according to office size and location has become standard practice in most businesses. Employees can readily judge how much favor they have with their employer by such things as the amount of privacy they are afforded, the degree of proximity to other important employees, their access to secretaries, and even what floor of a building they are on. In some places, a rise in the organization is accompanied literally by a rise to an office on a higher floor. The employee assigned to an office in a broom closet on the first floor has a long way to go up the status ladder. Unfortunately, many employers are not sensitive to the meanings attached to office assignments and may never know the reason certain employees feel alienated. We witnessed a near insurrection among a group of graduate teaching assistants who had to be placed in a building apart from the rest of the staff. It was bad enough that they were segregated, which to them meant that they were low in status; but then the office turned out to have bats. They were sure that the message was intentional. One even left the program.

Of course, office location is not the only important consideration. Such factors as the size of a desk and the luxuriousness of the surroundings can also make a difference. The richness of decor tells us that we are in the office of someone of high position. The University of Florida policy manual actually specifies how expensive office furnishings may be at each professorial rank. Other objects also help to convey status. The kind of car a person drives and even one's choice of stationery can reveal relative status.

The use of features and objects in one's environment can work two ways in forming relational messages. They tell the occupants of an environment what their position is in the hierarchy, and they also tell visitors what status they are assigned. A young-looking student of ours called this fact to our attention when he related his experience with his insurance company. On several occasions, when he went to the insurance office to conduct some business, he was helped by a secretary at the counter. This would not have seemed strange to him except that he noticed that older men in business suits were ushered into the inner offices to be assisted by one of the agents. The same kind of status differential is apparent at banks. One's perceived importance determines whether one is helped by a loan officer seated in the middle of an open office area or welcomed into a vice president's suite.

The territory where disputes are negotiated can also have status and power implications. Sports tell us that the advantage is with the home court. We know of two otherwise reasonable, intelligent men who carried on a feud for months because neither one would agree to meet in the other person's office to discuss their differences. Going to the other person's office was a sign of submission. For the same reason, finding acceptable neutral territories for international diplomacy is critical. The strong connotations of power associated with the locale and features within it has extended to concern over such matters as the shape of the conference table and the number of doorways. During the Vietnam War, the Paris peace talks were held up for months while people battled over the shape of the table and who would sit at the head. The shape of a table can dictate who dominates negotiations, and the head of the table is always reserved for the leader. The story is also told that when Secretary of State Henry Kissinger carried on negotiations with one high-ranking Russian official, the official refused to convene the talks until a second doorway was cut into the conference room so that both men could enter at the same time.

Employing the accouterments of political office to the best advantage is an art that the most skillful and powerful politicians have successfully acquired. Unfortunately, for some the trappings of political power become a fetish. Richard Nixon dressed his staff in ornate costumes, took the presidential dinnerware with him on his travels, and refused to eat off anything but china with the presidential seal.

Summary

We have seen how relationships among people can be defined by the nonverbal messages they use. Nonverbal communication can signal attraction and liking between parties to a relationship or the degree of credibility, power, and status that exists among the parties involved. The whole gamut of nonverbal signals may be used by participants in an interaction or observers of it to determine how people regard each other and themselves. Attraction and liking are generally demonstrated through inclusion, confirmation, and affection messages, with kinesic, haptic, proxemic, appearance, and vocalic cues playing the predominant role. The same codes are used to reveal lack of attraction or dislike through messages of exclusion, disconfirmation, and disaffection. The degree of credibility, power, and status that exists in a relationship is generally signalled through control messages, although confirmation and affection messages from subordinates may help to indicate who is in the dominant position. Credibility messages make particular use of kinesic, vocalic, and appearance cues, whereas status and power messages draw heavily on proxemic, haptic, chronemic, and artifactual cues.

In Chapter 10, on the ways in which people intentionally manage their impressions, and Chapter 11, which examines the nonverbal strategies people use to influence the thinking and behavior of others, we shall see that many of the cues that function as relational messages may be employed as manipulative devices.

Suggested Reading

Addington, D. W. "The Effect of Vocal Variations on Ratings of Source Credibility." *Speech Monographs*, 38 (1971), 242–247.

Argyle, M. *The Psychology of Interpersonal Behaviour*. Baltimore: Penguin, 1967.

Bruneau, T. J. "Communicative Silences: Forms and Functions." *Journal of Communication*, 23 (1973), 32.

Burgoon, J. K., and Jones, S. B. "Toward a Theory of Personal Space Expectations and Their Violations." *Human Communication Research*, 2 (1976), 131–146.

Ellsworth, P. C., and Ludwig, L. M. "Visual Behavior in Social Interaction." *Journal of Communication*, 22 (1972), 375–403.

Fast, J. *Body Language*. New York: Pocket Books, 1970.

Goffman, E. *Frame Analysis*. New York: Harper and Row, 1974.

Goffman, E. *Interaction Ritual*. Garden City, N.Y.: Doubleday, 1967.

Knapp, M. L. *Nonverbal Communication in Human Interaction*. New York: Holt, Rinehart and Winston, 1972.

Mehrabian, A. "Significance of Posture and Position in the Communication Attitude and Status Relationships." *Psychological Bulletin*, 71 (1969), 365.

Mehrabian, A. *Silent Messages*. Belmont, Calif.: Wadsworth, 1971.

Scheflen, A. E. *How Behavior Means*. Garden City, N.Y.: Doubleday, 1974.

Watzlawick, P., Beavin, J. H., and Jackson, D. J. *Pragmatics of Human Communication*. New York: W. W. Norton, 1967.

Notes

1. B. Hawkins and C. Book, "Relational Communication: An Integration of Theory and Structure," paper presented at the International Communication Association Convention, New Orleans, April 1974.

2. Hawkins and Book (note 1); W. C. Schutz, *FIRO: A Three Dimensional Theory of Interpersonal Behavior* (New York: Holt, Rinehart and Winston, 1958); P. Watzlawick, J. H. Beavin, and D. D. Jackson, *Pragmatics of Human Communication* (New York: W. W. Norton, 1967), pp. 83–90.

3. H. Broch, *The Sleepwalkers: A Trilogy* (New York: Pantheon, 1964).

4. Z. Rubin, "Measurement of Romantic Love," *Journal of Personality and Social Psychology*, 16 (1970), pp. 265–273.

5. R. V. Exline and L. Winters, "Affective Relations and Mutual Glances in Dyads," in S. S. Tomkins and C. E. Izard (eds.), *Affect, Cognition and Personality* (New York: Springer, 1965), pp. 319–350; C. N. Goldberg, C. A. Kiesler, and B. E. Collins, "Visual Behavior and Face-to-Face Distance During Interaction," *Sociometry*, 32 (1969), pp. 43–53; R. P. Murray and H. McGinley, "Looking as a Measure of Attraction," *Journal of Applied Special Psychology*, 2 (1972), pp. 267–274; S. Thayer and W. Schiff, "Observer Judgement of Social Interaction: Eye Contact and Relationship Inferences," *Journal of Personality and Social Psychology*, 30 (1974), pp. 110–114.

6. Exline and Winters (note 5); Murray and McGinley (note 5).

7. E. H. Hess and J. M. Polt, "Pupil Size as Related to Interest Value of Visual Stimuli," *Science,* 132 (1960), pp. 349–350; M. P. Janisse and W. S. Peavler, "Pupillary Research Today: Emotion in the Eye," *Psychology Today*, 7, No. 9 (1974), pp. 60–73; A. S. King, "The Eye in Advertising," *Journal of Applied Communications Research,* 2, No. 1 (1974), pp. 1–12.

8. E. Hess, "The Role of Pupil Size in Communication," *Scientific American,* 222 (1975), pp. 110–119.

9. R. F. Haase and D. T. Tepper, "Nonverbal Components of Empathetic Communication," *Journal of Counseling Psychology*, 19 (1972), pp. 417–424.

10. A. L. Chaikin, E. Sigler, and V. J. Derlega, "Nonverbal Mediators of Teacher Expectancy Effects," *Journal of Personality and Social Psychology*, 30 (1974), pp. 144–149.

11. R. S. Mach, "Postural Carriage and Congruency as Nonverbal Indicators of Status Differentials and Interpersonal Attraction," dissertation, University of Colorado, 1972.

12. E. J. Charney, "Psychosomatic Manifestation of Rapport in Psychotherapy," *Psychosomatic Medicine*, 28 (1966), pp. 305–315; E. Mansfield, "Empathy: Concept and Identified Psychiatric Nursing Behavior," *Nursing Research*, 22 (1973), pp. 525–530.

13. A. E. Scheflen, "Quasi-Courtship Behavior of Psychotherapy," *Psychiatry*, 28 (1965), pp. 245–256.

14. T. J. Bruneau, "Communicative Silences: Forms and Functions," *Journal of Communication*, 23 (1973), p. 32.

15. M. G. King, "Interpersonal Relations in Preschool Children and Average Approach Distance," *Journal of Genetic Psychology*, 108 (1966), pp. 109–116; R. Kleck, "Physical Stigma and Task Oriented Interaction," *Human Relations*, 21 (1968), pp. 351–361; D. F. Lott and R. Sommer, "Seating Arrangements and Status," *Journal of Personality and Social Psychology*, 7 (1967), pp. 90–94; A. Mehrabian, "Relationship of Attitude to Seated Posture, Orientation and Distance," *Journal of Personality and Social Psychology*, 10 (1968), pp. 26–30; G. A. Norum, N. J. Russo, and R. Sommer, "Seating Patterns and Group Tasks," *Psychology in the Schools*, 4, (1967), p. 3; M. L. Patterson and L. B. Sechrest, "Interpersonal Distance and Impression Formation," *Journal of Personality*, 38 (1970), pp. 161–166; H. Rosenfeld, "Effect of Approval-Seeking Induction on Interpersonal Proximity," *Psychological Reports*, 17 (1965), pp. 120–122.

16. Kleck (note 15); R. Sommer, "Spatial Parameters in Naturalistic Social Research," in A. H. Esser (ed.), *Behavior and Environment* (New York: Plenum Press, 1971).

17. E. G. Beier, "Nonverbal Communication: How We Send Emotional Messages," *Psychology Today*, 8, No. 5 (1974), pp. 52–59.

18. G. Breed and J. Ricci, " 'Touch Me, Like Me': Artifact?" in Proceedings of the Eighty-First Annual Convention of the American Psychological Association, Montreal, 1973, pp. 153–154; T. D.

Burley, "An Investigation of the Roles of Imagery, Kinesthetic Cues and Attention in Tactile Nonverbal Communication," dissertation, University of Tennessee, 1972.

19. W. H. Watson, "The Meanings of Touch: Geriatric Nursing," *Journal of Communication,* 25 (1975), pp. 104–112.

20. R. M. Weisbred, "Looking Behavior in a Discussion Group," cited by M. Argyle and A. Kendon, "The Experimental Analysis of Social Performance," in L. Berkowitz (ed.), *Advances in Experimental Social Psychology* (New York: Academic Press, 1967), pp. 55–98.

21. B. E. Collins and H. Guetzkow, *A Social Psychology of Group Processes for Decision-Making* (New York: John Wiley & Sons, 1964); G. Hearn, "Leadership and the Spatial Factor in Small Groups," *Journal of Abnormal and Social Psychology,* 54 (1957), pp. 269–272; A. Mehrabian, "Significance of Posture and Position in the Communication of Attitude and Status Relationships," *Psychological Bulletin,* 71 (1969), p. 365.

22. H. T. Moore and A. R. Gilliland, "The Measure of Aggressiveness," *Journal of Applied Psychology,* 5 (1921), p. 98.

23. Argyle and Kendon (note 20).

24. Mach (note 11).

25. A. Mehrabian and M. Williams, "Nonverbal Concomitants of Perceived and Intended Persuasiveness," *Journal of Personality and Social Psychology,* 13 (1969), pp. 37–58; E. Goffman, *Encounters* (New York: Bobbs-Merrill, 1961).

26. J. C. McCroskey and W. Arnold, cited in J. C. McCroskey, *An Introduction to Rhetorical Communication* (Englewood Cliffs, N.J.: Prentice-Hall, 1972).

27. W. B. Pearce and B. J. Brommel, "Vocalic Communication in Persuasion," *Quarterly Journal of Speech,* 58 (1972), pp. 298–306; W. B. Pearce and F. Conklin, "Nonverbal Vocalic Communication and Perception of a Speaker," *Speech Monographs,* 38 (1971), pp. 235–241.

28. D. W. Addington, "The Effect of Vocal Variations on Ratings of Source Credibility," *Speech Monographs,* 38 (1971), pp. 242–247; B. L. Brown, W. J. Strong, and A. Rencher, "Fifty-four Voices from Two: The Effects of Simultaneous Manipulations of Rate, Mean Fundamental Frequency and Variance of Fundamental Frequency on Ratings of Personality from Speech," *Journal of the*

Acoustical Society of America, 55 (1974), pp. 313–318; B. L. Brown, W. J. Strong, and A. C. Rencher, "Perceptions of Personality from Speech: Effects of Manipulations of Acoustical Parameters," *Journal of the Acoustical Society of America,* 54 (1973), pp. 29–33.

29. Brown, Strong and Rencher, 1973 (note 28); Brown, Strong and Rencher, 1974 (note 28).

30. J. C. McCroskey and R. S. Mehrley, "The Effects of Disorganization and Nonfluency on Attitude Change and Source Credibility," *Speech Monographs,* 36 (1969), pp. 13–21; G. R. Miller and M. A. Hewgill, "The Effect of Variations in Nonfluency on Audience Ratings of Source Credibility," *Quarterly Journal of Speech,* 50 (1964), pp. 36–44; K. K. Sereno and G. J. Hawkins, "The Effects of Variations in Speaker's Nonfluency upon Audience Ratings of Attitude Toward the Speech Topic and Speaker's Credibility," *Speech Monographs,* 34 (1967), pp. 58–64.

31. A. D. Brooks, "Responses to Three American Dialects," paper presented at the AILA Congress, Stuttgart, Germany, 1975; J. F. Buck, "The Effects of Negro and White Dialectal Variations upon Attitudes of College Students," *Speech Monographs,* 35 (1968), pp. 181–186; J. G. Delia, "Dialects and the Effects of Stereotypes on Impression Formation," *Quarterly Journal of Speech,* 58 (1972), pp. 285–297; H. Giles, "Communicative Effectiveness as a Function of Accented Speech," *Speech Monographs,* 40 (1973), pp. 330–331; A. D. Marston, "The Effect of American Regional Dialects upon Speaker Credibility and Perceived Personality," dissertation, University of Illinois, 1973; A. Mulac, T. D. Hanley, and D. Y. Prigge, "Effects of Phonological Speech Foreignness upon Three Dimension of Attitude of Selected American Speakers," *Quarterly Journal of Speech,* 60 (1974), pp. 411–420; M. G. Ryan, "The Factor Structure of Credibility Reactions to Standard and Dialect English Speech," paper presented at the International Communication Association Convention, New Orleans, April 1974; and J. K. Toomb, J. G. Quiggins, D. L. Moore, L. B. MacNeil, and C. M. Liddell, "The Effects of Regional Dialects on Initial Source Credibility," paper presented at the International Communication Association Convention, Atlanta, April 1972.

32. F. Williams, J. L. Whitehead, and J. Traupmann,

"Teachers' Evaluations of Children's Speech," *Speech Teacher,* 20 (1971), pp. 247–254; J. L. Whitehead, F. Williams, J. M. Civikly, and J. W. Albino, "Latitude of Attitude in Ratings of Dialect Variations," *Speech Monographs,* 4 (1974), pp. 397–407.

33. J. K. Burgoon, "Further Explication and an Initial Test of the Theory of Violations of Personal Space Expectations," paper presented at the Speech Communication Association Convention, San Francisco, December 1976; J. K. Burgoon and S. B. Jones, "Toward a Theory of Personal Space Expectations and Their Violations," *Human Communication Research,* 2 (1976), pp. 131–146; P. H. Garner, "The Effects of Invasion of Personal Space on Interpersonal Communication," thesis, Illinois State University, 1972; Patterson and Sechrest (note 15).

34. Bruneau, p. 39 (note 14).

35. L. Baxter and J. Ward, cited in "Newsline," *Psychology Today,* 8, No. 8 (1975), p. 28.

36. P. R. Wilson, "Perceptual Distortion of Height as a Function of Ascribed Academic Status," *Journal of Social Psychology,* 74 (1968), pp. 97–102.

37. K. Toomb and L. T. Divers, "The Relationship of Somatotype to Source Credibility," paper presented at the International Communication Association Convention, Atlanta, April 1972.

38. P. A. Andersen, T. A. Jensen, and L. B. King, "The Effects of Homophilous Hair and Dress Styles on Credibility and Comprehension, paper presented at the International Communication Association Convention, Atlanta, April 1972; K. Peterson and J. C. Curran, "Trait Attribution as a Function of Hair Length and Correlates of Subjects' Preferences for Hair Style," *Journal of Psychology,* 93 (1976), pp. 331–339.

39. D. G. Freedman, "The Survival Value of the Beard," *Psychology Today,* 3 (1969), pp. 36–39.

40. J. M. Pedersen, "Change in Perception by Others Due to Growth of Hair and Beard," in L. B. Rosenfeld and J. M. Civikly (eds.), *With Words Unspoken* (New York: Holt, Rinehart and Winston, 1976), p. 67.

8

The Communication of Affect

Test Your Sensitivity

True or False?

1. The face is usually better than the voice at supplying evidence of emotions.
2. The area of the mouth provides the most reliable cues regarding emotion.
3. Through training, an individual can improve his or her ability to judge emotions accurately.
4. Pure emotional expressions never occur in our daily interaction.
5. Anger is the easiest emotion to identify.
6. Expressions of affection are learned before all other displays of emotion.

"He is the Napoleon of crime, Watson!" As my friend spun round from his position before the fireplace, the flames behind him and the shrill, unnatural quality of his voice lent his attitude a terrible aspect. I could see his nerves stretched to their highest limits. "He is the organizer of half that is evil and of nearly all that is undetected in this great city and in the annals of contemporary crime. . . ." And so he rambled on, sometimes incoherently, sometimes declaiming as if from the stage of the Old Vic. . . . I listened to this erratic recital with mounting alarm, though I did my best to conceal it. I have never known Holmes to be untruthful and I could see at a glance that this was not one of his occasional practical jokes. He spoke in deadly earnest, almost babbling with fear. . . . The tirade did not so much conclude as run down. From shrill statements Holmes gradually subsided into inarticulate mutterings and from thence to whispers. Accompanying this modulation in speech, his body, which had been striding energetically to and fro, now leaned up against a wall, then flung itself absent-mindedly into a chair and, before I realized what had happened, Holmes was asleep.[1]

By the end of the chapter, you should know the correct answer to all six questions and understand these concepts:

- affect blends
- universality of emotions
- dimensions of emotions
- role of body and gestures in expressing emotion
- facial regions responsible for increasing accuracy of interpretation for various cues
- difficulties in interpreting facial cues
- patterns of vocal cues expressing emotions
- factors influencing ability to send and receive emotional cues accurately
- ease of identifying various emotions
- research problems

Watson's description of master detective Sherlock Holmes illustrates the complexity of emotional expressions. Affective states, while subject to the most dramatic and momentary changes, are nevertheless detected by observers. The most subtle changes in voice, body, and facial expression are as important a feature of our learning to communicate as is the acquisition of language. The body can indeed be a mirror of the mind. It is nowhere else as obvious as with our ability to observe others and extract impressions (often quite accurate) of another's feelings and emotions.

In this chapter, we shall try to answer those questions about the communication of affect: What are some of the myths surrounding the study of emotional expression? How do we acquire the ability to express emotions? What dimensions underlie affect displays? How do the various parts of the body contribute to the communication of emotion? What factors influence our accuracy in sending and receiving both facial and vocalic cues of emotions? What problems surround research on the communication of affect?

Myths Surrounding the Study of Emotions

What we know about the communication of affect is sometimes clouded by misconceptions. Consider some of the problems that arise out of these myths regarding emotional expressions:

1. *Humans display pure emotions.* Untrue. No individual is so simple in psychological make-up that his or her emotional state and emotional expressions reflect only a single emotion. Plutchik has argued that emotional states overlap.[2] For example, anger is often accompanied by anxiety or fear.

Pure emotions are theoretical constructs not to be found in the real world. That doesn't mean that we wouldn't recognize an emotion if we were to see it. The silent films often presented exaggerated portrayals of certain emotions. Many emotional expressions fall into a category known as *affect blends,* which are actually a combination of the characteristics of two or more emotional expressions (for example, fear and anger or surprise and sadness).

More than any other channel, the voice illustrates how interrelated emotions are. Even expressions of love are fraught sometimes with doubt or curiosity or nervousness. Just as the human being is incapable of experiencing a single emotion, our nonverbal behaviors communicate complex human emotions.

2. *Emotional expressions are events.* Certainly not. Emotional expressions are processes, having both a beginning and an end. When we see someone express happiness, we don't see merely a frozen display; we see an

assortment of muscular changes over a short interval of time as the face and body develop an image that we have learned to associate with emotional states. While researchers often investigate emotions by relying on fixed images, such as sketches and photographs, those images represent nothing more than a single frozen moment within an interpersonal process.

By treating an emotion as if it were a fixed display, we lose a great deal of meaning. For example, the quickness with which emotions are expressed and then replaced by other expressions provides information about sincerity, intensity, and the control an individual has over the situation. Emotional expressions, like all other message systems, are an active process—a series of events that are organized into a message only to be replaced in time by other messages.

3. *We know what cues reveal emotions.* Again untrue. As members of a culture, we are able to identify a wide variety of emotional expressions, but we do not know what cues lead us to associate a display with a particular emotional state. Without saying a word, using only your body and face, try to show an emotion—contempt, say. Now think: What behaviors make up contempt? Most of us choose only the most obvious behaviors as the key to the emotional expression. In the next several pages, we shall explore some of these keys. You will be surprised to find that many emotions are communicated principally by behaviors that are very subtle and apparently unnoticed. But they aren't really unnoticed; time after time, we are able to pick up the signals whether we know consciously what those signals are or not.

Robert Plutchik, in *The Emotions: Facts, Theories, and a New Model,* surveyed the existing theories of emotion and reached six conclusions which summarize current thinking regarding emotions.[3] (1) "There is a small number of pure or primary emotions." (2) "All other emotions are mixed; that is, they can be synthesized by various combinations of the primary emotions." For example, love is actually a mixture of joy and acceptance. Aggression is no more than a combination of expectancy and anger. Pride is a mixture of anger and joy. (3) "Primary emotions differ from each other with regard to both physiology and behavior." Although this may seem obvious to many of us, it actually represents an important addition to any theory of emotions. Emotions and emotional expressions are interwoven, and certain behavioral cues allow us to determine the prevailing psychological state of the communicator. (4) "Primary emotions in their pure form are hypothetical constructs or idealized states whose properties can only be inferred from various kinds of evidence." Plutchik is making the point mentioned earlier— that it is impossible to conceive of a stimulus that would prompt only a pure emotion. Likewise, it is impossible to conceive of a human being who could respond to any condition with only one emotion. (5) "Primary emotions may be conceptualized in terms of pairs of polar opposites." Actually, primary emotions aren't states; they are dimensions within which we can pinpoint any given expression. In subsequent sections of this chapter, we shall explore some of the various dimensions that other researchers suspect underlie judgments of emotion. (6) "Each emotion can exist in varying degrees of intensity or levels of arousal." Individuals are different, and one of the ways that we differ is in terms of the intensity with which we feel and express emotions. Borrowing a point from the behaviorist tradition, Plutchik has suggested that the problem of detecting emotional states from expressions is much broader than merely determining which emotional expression is being communicated. One must assess the intensity of the expression as well.

Joel Davitz of Columbia University is one of the most highly respected researchers involved in the study of the communication of emotion. Davitz has added a final word regarding the nature of emotions. Emotions refer to experiences, and the labels we use for various emotions refer to a "range of experiences about which there is more or less consensus among members of the same language group."[4] Although there are individual and subcultural differences within a larger language group, a shared pool of experiences influences us when we speak of an emotional state or when we express it nonverbally. When a friend frowns and expresses sorrow, you are able to reflect upon past experiences of your own that allow you to understand the emotions and also to imagine situations that might have provoked your friend's behavior.

The Acquisition of Emotional Expressions

A persisting question for scholars who are interested in the study of emotional communication has been the issue of how this ability to display affect is acquired. Are emotional expressions all learned, or are they innate? How early in a child's development do they begin to appear?

Theoretical Positions

The *universalists* argue that there is good reason for believing that affect displays are consistent from culture to culture and are therefore innate. Work by Ekman, Sorenson, and Friesen has demonstrated that five specific emotional expressions function in other cultures.[5] Universalists have argued that there is a common core of behaviors that are characteristically human and are shared by all cultures. Some have argued that these behaviors are acquired because of their survival value, which explains their universality. Research by Darwin proposed the notion that certain affect displays serve instrumental survival-related functions for human beings.

On the other hand, the *cultural relativists* view emotional expression as specific to a given culture. Advocates of this position have argued that even when emotional expressions transcend culture, the rules for emotional expression and the social function associated with expressions are determined by the cultural context.

A third view sees emotional expression as both biologically and culturally determined. Ekman proposed a *neurocultural* position— while some muscular configurations are common to all members of the species because of our common neurophysiological make-up, culture affects the way in which people use expressions and their functions within the social context.[6] By no means should we presume that all emotional expressions are learned.

Nature–Nurture Evidence

For the moment, let's return to the nature–nurture controversy and specific evidence on emotional expressions. Observations of blind and deaf children reveal some universality in their affective behavior.[7] These youngsters exhibit many of the facial expressions and gestures used by normal children. Since they cannot be learning the behaviors by seeing or hearing, it is assumed that the behaviors are instinctual and therefore universal.

Yet another source of support comes from intracultural and crosscultural studies. One particularly important study was conducted by Ekman, Sorenson, and Friesen.[8] They eliminated the possibility that mass media and exposure to Western civilization might affect results, by selecting as subjects a group in New Guinea that had been isolated from the rest of the world. The subjects listened to stories that described various emotional behaviors and then picked from several pictures the one that best depicted the emotion that had been de-

scribed. The researchers found that, for the emotions of happiness, sadness, anger, and disgust, the subjects picked the same faces Westerners and Easterners had chosen. The only difficulty they had was in distinguishing fear from surprise, a common source of confusion. These results were taken as support for the existence of universal expressions. They also served to corroborate the observations of Darwin. His careful and wide-ranging survey of emotional expressions convinced him that most are innate or instinctual, a conclusion he was sure was accepted by everyone.

Darwin's observations did yield some persuasive evidence. His study of weeping led him to hypothesize that weeping originates from earnest attention to how one looks and, through association, to moral behavior.[9] Studying emotional displays in several countries, he found a high degree of commonality in expressions that could not be explained by learning or imitation alone. For instance, he reported that some British children used a shoulder shrug at a very early age despite the fact that their parents didn't use it and that it was a rarity in England. Shortly after the behavior occurred, it became extinguished, which offered a plausible explanation of why it doesn't appear among adults in the nondemonstrative British culture. The same children adopted a finger-rubbing gesture that was identical to that used by their Parisian grandfather whom they had never seen. This evidence led Darwin to conclude that most expressive behavior is inherited or the result of reflexes common to all humans. Here is how he explained it:

Actions, which were at first voluntary, soon become habitual, and at last hereditary, and may then be performed even in opposition to the will. Although they often reveal the state of mind, this result was not at first either intended or expected. Even such words as that "certain movements serve as a means of expression" are apt to mislead, as they imply that this was their primary purpose or object. This, however, seems rarely or never to have been the case; the movements having been at first either of some direct use, or the indirect effect of the excited state of the sensorium. An infant may scream either intentionally or instinctively to show that it wants food; but it has no wish to draw its features into the peculiar form which so plainly indicates misery; yet some of the most characteristic expressions exhibited by man are derived from the act of screaming, as has been explained.[10]

Thus, Darwin thought expressive acts arise initially from behaviors that gratify some need or relieve some physiological sensation and, through habitual use by the species, eventually become inherited. He also believed that the recognition of emotions could be explained by the same process.

Darwin did not completely rule out the influence of learning. He noted that even such innate behaviors as laughing and weeping have to be practiced before they are performed in an acceptable manner. And he admitted that such conventional gestures as folding the hands for prayer and kissing as a sign of affection have to be learned. Thus, he is not totally at odds with those who have found a multitude of cultural differences in body language. Such differences occur, Darwin could explain, either when a culture modifies innate behaviors (as in the case of the British suppression of the natural shoulder shrug) or when all the members of a culture take on a completely learned behavior that fits the needs of their culture. Such an explanation seems the most reasonable to reconcile the nature–nurture controversy.

Developmental Stages

At what ages and in what sequences are affective behaviors acquired? To the extent that there are some observable patterns, they may be taken as additional clues of universality

(regardless of whether those universal behaviors are inherited or learned by all humans).

The literature of child development reveals that most kinesic cues appear at a very early age and follow discernible patterns. Charlotte Wolff opens her study of children's body language with the statement that "gesture is a preverbal language which starts at birth. In the first years of life it is the most important means of expression, only receding into the background as speech develops, but remaining vivid and powerful in the child up to six years."[11]

Wolff proposes that children go through three stages in the development of kinesic behaviors. The first is the *instinctive phase*. This is the period immediately following birth during which babies use automatic, instinctive behaviors. They cry, smile, show startle reactions, and use gestures designed to maintain their balance. The mouth is an important source of activity in the form of sucking and tongue movements. Children also develop autistic gestures, those that are directed toward the self and discovering one's body. These are the kinds of behaviors that Ekman and Friesen labeled adaptors. Children as early as two months begin to imitate the movements and expressions of others. The imitation tendencies are apparently very strong. Birdwhistell's observations present two typical cases.[12] He filmed a 15-month-old girl who had already adopted the typical stance of southern, upper-middle-class females—the pelvis rolled forward and the insides of the legs touching—and a 22-month-old boy who had adopted the spread-legged stance with the pelvis rolled back.

The second phase in kinesic development is the *emotional phase*. (See Figure 8.1.) Infants begin displaying emotions as early as the second or third week after birth, but the expressions are not differentiated at that point. Perhaps the musculature is not yet able to show differences. Darwin noted, for instance, that newborn babies do not shed tears when they

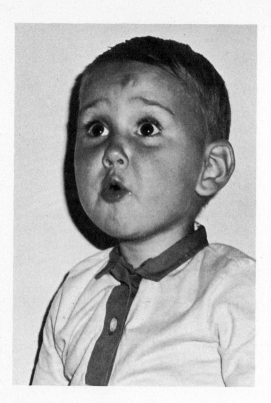

Figure 8.1 This child is well into the emotional phase of his kinesic development.

this transition takes place at age six. In this phase, the child finally develops gestures that are related to thought. If we apply this to Ekman and Friesen's functional categories of gestures, we conclude that in this phase illustrators, regulators, and emblems finally appear.

A further examination of the literature on nonverbal communication in children suggests that a fourth phase overlaps the emotional phase. According to the compilation done by Blurton Jones, children in the first three years develop many behaviors that are related to their interactions with other children and adults. We might therefore call this the *social-interaction phase*.[15] A common gesture among one-year-olds is arm-raising, which is a signal to adults that the child wants to be lifted. By the time children are two, they laugh and smile at play with other children. In fact, laughter, and often smiling, occur only in the presence of others. Children's gaze pattern with an adult is the same as that between two adults. By the time a child is three, waving is no longer a sign of general activity but is specifically a departure cue, and crying shifts from being associated with separation to being associated with quarrels or falls. Thus, behaviors that originate as reflex or autistic movements evolve a social meaning.

Although children acquire the ability to display affect very early, they seem to be somewhat slower at learning to interpret emotional cues. We noted in Chapter 1 that children often do not understand contradictions between verbal and nonverbal behaviors and are apt to believe the verbal meaning; but at least some interpretive ability is learned in the first several years.

The fact that some emotional cues are learned at such an early age implies that they play a major role in communication. We know

cry, and that it takes several months for the tear ducts to become functional. Nevertheless, certain emotional expressions become evident very quickly. Table 8.1[13] gives a sample of the ages at which various emotional gestures appear and a sample of the types of body language used.

An investigation conducted recently of three- to five-year-olds also found a good many behaviors that expressed aggression and escape. Altogether, eighty facial and head movements and fifty-five body and limb movements were observed to show aggressiveness and defensiveness.[14] By the time a child reaches kindergarten, he or she has a well-developed repertoire of emotional expressions.

The emotional phase leads to the third period, the *objective phase*. According to Wolff,

Table 8.1 The Development of Emotional Behaviors

Age	Emotion	Typical Behaviors Associated with Emotion
3 months	Rage	Trembling mouth; self-hitting; body rigidity
5 months	Disgust	Downturned, taut mouth; nostril movements
6 months	Passive joy	Relaxed, open mouth; rhythmic movements; opening and closing of fist
7 months	Fear	Tightened lips; startled eyes; recoiling gestures
1 year	Exuberant joy	Heightened activity and muscular tension
2 years	Jealousy	Combination of anger and fear gestures
2 years	Affection	Smiling, caressing, coquettish expressions

that they are the main means of communication for children before speech is acquired. And we suspect that the importance of affect displays carries over long beyond childhood. When we "intuitively" don't like someone but can't put our finger on what it is about the person that's bothering us, our reaction may be based on associations we learned in childhood but have since left to subconscious awareness.

Dimensions Underlying Affect Displays

Early researchers devoted much of their effort to debating the kinds of human emotions, but without a satisfactory result. Today estimations of the number of emotions range from six to approximately twenty. The issue is important because each researcher's answer can influence the kinds of research that are attempted and our ability to integrate the findings of different researchers. Without knowing the *primary affects,* it is impossible to decipher which channel is capable of transmitting which emotion. While Robert Plutchik has argued that there are eight emotions—fear, anger, grief, joy, acceptance, disgust, surprise, and expectation—Tomkins has listed what are thought by many to be the primary affects, that is, the universal emotions.[16] They are:

interest–excitement	fear–terror
enjoyment–joy	shame–humiliation
surprise–startle	contempt–disgust
distress–anguish	anger–rage

(See Figure 8.2.)

These are the emotions that research investigations have studied. Usually, subjects are asked to identify these emotions in photographs. Studies have usually found that humans cannot discriminate emotions without considerable error. We do much better if we are asked to judge emotions along two or three continuums, although researchers disagree as to which ones give the best results. Some investigations have turned up two or four such dimensions, but most have found three. In some cases, they are labeled pleasantness, control, and activation. *Pleasantness* includes such emotions as happiness, joy, anger, and sadness. *Control* refers to the degree of intentionality or deliberateness of an emotional display. Usually displays of rage show little control while an emotion such as interest is more under the conscious direction of the sender. *Activation* refers to how much arousal is revealed. Terror shows high activation while sleep shows none.

Other studies have varied these dimensions somewhat. One calls the dimensions pleasant–unpleasant, sleep–tension, and attention–rejection.[17] The first two dimensions are the same as those given above (the sleep–tension

(a) Interest–excitement

(b) Shame–humiliation

(c) Surprise–startle

(d) Distress–anguish

(e) Contempt–disgust

(f) Anger–rage

(g) Fear–terror

(h) Enjoyment–joy

dimension being the same as activation); but attention–rejection is different. It concerns whether the displayed emotion shows some interest in or rejection of the person toward whom it is directed. Yet another set of three contains the similar dimensions pleasant–unpleasant, irritated–calm, and receptive–nonreceptive.[18] In this case, emotions such as anger, fury, shyness, and calmness define the irritation factor, and such affects as curiosity, surprise, indifference, and sleepiness define the receptivity factor. All of these studies agree that pleasantness and tension or arousal are primary underlying dimensions. Any other factors concern the relationship of the sender to the receiver—whether the sender is consciously controlling emotions in the presence of others and whether the sender is interested in and open to the receiver.

The Roles of Body Parts

Research on emotions has tried to identify which body parts or regions can operate as meaningful transmitters on their own, independent of other areas, and whether clusters of similar messages are conveyed by different areas of the body. It appears that the body and touch play lesser roles in communicating affect than do the face and the voice. Let's consider exactly what those roles are.

The Lower Body

So far, researchers have concluded that the body trunk carries information about the *intensity* of an emotion, while the face reveals which emotion is being felt. There seems to be

some evidence that, by looking at body position and movement alone, we are able to reach some consensus as to the emotion being sent. But that is not how we decode emotions in our everyday interactions. We look at the face and listen to the voice to identify the emotion; the body is only an indicator of degree and a secondary source of confirmation, a crosscheck, on the face and voice.

Degree of muscle tension, body posture, rate of body movement, and overall *coordination* of body actions all help us judge the intensity of emotions. From these sources, we can begin to make judgments about level of arousal or excitement, involvement, spontaneity, and even the control or lack of control implied by an emotional state.

Touch

Since our culture is essentially a noncontact one, our ability to use touch as a means of communication is somewhat limited. Touch generally plays a lesser role than the other channels in communicating meaning. Our culture has evolved so many rules stipulating when we can't touch that we would hardly expect touch to play the same role in our culture as it might in a contact culture.

Nevertheless, the skin is highly sensitive and capable of sending and responding to messages of which most of us are unaware. We have looked already at an intriguing series of studies initiated by Alma I. Smith that explored the potential of touch to communicate and receive emotional meaning.[19] Smith's results indicated that, when given the task of encoding an emotion through touch, we are relatively stable in our patterns of touch (the length of touch and the amount of pressure) and that we are capable of making fine discriminations among emotions through the way we touch one another. Our capacity to receive and correctly interpret emotions by being touched by another is quite a different story. It is clear from Smith's research that our judgments based upon touch are highly varied and generally quite poor. We encode touch accurately enough, but we tend not to know how to interpret touch.

Nguyen, Heslin, and Nguyen attempted to determine whether the type of touch (pat, stroke, squeeze, and brush) or the location of touch (top and back of head, shoulders, face, back arms, chest, stomach, thighs and buttocks, genital area, legs, and hands) influence the kinds of judgments made by the people being touched.[20] Results of the study indicated that both factors contribute to meaning. In particular, subjects' responses confirmed the following associations of type and meaning of touch:

strokes = sexual desire
pats = friendliness, playfulness
squeezes, brushes = ambiguous interpretation

It is possible to suggest through touch some general emotional states, such as an inclination toward, say, aggression or interest. It is less possible to communicate a specific emotion such as fear through touch alone. Again, while it is possible to show a general tendency toward tenderness through touch, it is difficult to discriminate between sadness, love, and grief, since each might well involve similar caresses and strokes.

Take a look at some silent movies. They rely greatly on touch for communication. In fact, they give embraces, passionate kisses, and caresses a relatively specific and identifiable emotional meaning. Flicks, however, even current ones, aren't everyday social interaction. We use subtle and complex multichannel messages to convey emotion.

Voice

Now that we have mentioned the body and touch, let's consider how the voice contributes to the process of displaying affect. In Chapter 1, we mentioned estimates that the voice accounts for as much as 38 percent of the total meaning of a message. So, while we normally think of the face as the primary means of communicating emotion, the voice is also a powerful channel. In fact, the percentage of information carried by the voice alone may be much higher when we are dealing exclusively with messages of emotion.

One of the major questions facing researchers interested in studying how the voice communicates emotion has been how to determine which vocalic qualities are associated with which emotion. The voice is every bit as complex a channel as the face. The research method of determining judgments of facial expressions is rather straightforward—photographs containing the cues are used. But how do we construct a voice tape that contains the right properties when we are not sure what those properties are in the first place?

In 1972, Scherer conducted what many regard as the seminal work in this area.[21] He relied on a product of our electronic age—the Moog synthesizer. Scherer first identified five vocalic qualities fundamental to the display of affect. These qualities were *pitch variation* (moderate, extreme, up contour, down contour), *amplitude variation* (moderate, extreme), *pitch level* (high, low), *amplitude level* (high, low), and *tempo* (fast, slow). The Moog synthesizer allows one to produce artificial voices characterized by every possible combination of the vocal qualities listed above. Scherer submitted these voices to judges, who attempted to determine which emotion was being portrayed by which voice.

This pilot study was followed by another, more comprehensive study, the results of which are shown in Table 8.2. As you might have guessed, an emotion such as happiness involves large pitch variation, moderate amplitude variation, and fast tempo. Boredom is reflected by a voice that has little pitch variation, a generally low pitch level and a slow tempo.

Table 8.2 Vocal Cues of Emotion: Acoustic Parameters of Tone Sequences Significantly Contributing to the Variance in Attributions of Emotional States

Emotional State	Cues*
Pleasantness	Fast tempo, few harmonics, large pitch variation, sharp envelope, low pitch level, pitch contour down, small amplitude variation (salient configuration: large pitch variation plus pitch contour up)
Activity	Fast tempo, high pitch level, many harmonics, large pitch variation, sharp envelope, small amplitude variation
Potency	Many harmonics, fast tempo, high pitch level, round envelope, pitch contour up (salient configurations: large amplitude variation plus high pitch level, high pitch level plus many harmonics)
Anger	Many harmonics, fast tempo, high pitch level, small pitch variation, pitch contours up (salient configuration: small pitch variation plus pitch contour up)
Boredom	Slow tempo, low pitch level, few harmonics, pitch contour down, round envelope, small pitch variation
Disgust	Many harmonics, small pitch variation, round envelope, slow tempo (salient configuration: small pitch variation plus pitch contour up)
Fear	Pitch contour up, fast tempo, many harmonics, high pitch level, round envelope, small pitch variation (salient configurations: small pitch variation plus pitch contour up, fast tempo plus many harmonics)
Happiness	Fast tempo, large pitch variation, sharp envelope, few harmonics, moderate amplitude variation (salient configurations: large pitch variation plus pitch contour up, fast tempo plus few harmonics)
Sadness	Slow tempo, low pitch level, few harmonics, round envelope, pitch contour down (salient configuration: low pitch level plus slow tempo)
Surprise	Fast tempo, high pitch level, pitch contour up, sharp envelope, many harmonics, large pitch variation (salient configuration: high pitch level plus fast tempo)

*Single acoustic parameters (main effects) and configurations (interaction effects) are listed in order of predictive strength.
SOURCE: From "Cue Utilization in Emotion Attribution from Auditory Stimuli" by Klaus R. Scherer and James S. Oshinsky, *Motivation and Emotion,* 1, No. 4 (1977), p. 340. Reprinted, with slight modifications, with permission of Plenum Publishing Corporation and kind assistance of Dr. Scherer.

Face

Emotional expressions arise in each of us as we respond to our immediate environment, but this doesn't mean that we are merely reactors with no control over our expressions of emotion. Quite to the contrary, facial expressions are much more than automatic responses to stimuli. Norms called *affect display rules*[22] govern our use of facial cues of emotion. They reflect the impact our culture has on our willingness to make our feelings public. *Display rules* are those situational requirements that guide our facial communication in a particular context. Consequently, we know implicitly when it is appropriate (and inappropriate) to show fear, anger, sadness. Display rules allow members of a culture to be somewhat consistent in *what* emotion is expressed, *when,* for *how long,* and to what *degree.* We don't laugh at funerals. We don't direct anger toward a total stranger.

What happens when someone violates one of these unwritten regulations? Not much, except that we tend to make negative personal attributions toward such individuals. They are thought to be insensitive or irresponsible or overwrought or emotionally ill. A friend of ours illustrated just this kind of attribution process. The day after an important basketball victory at the University of Florida, our friend was recounting her experiences at the game. She remarked that, after the last-second, game-winning free throw, the stands went wild, with one notable exception. A very tall gentleman seated just below her stood very slowly and stared for a long time at the basket with a blank expression. He showed no identifiable emotion whatsoever. She concluded that he was "either mentally retarded or a preacher." We are not sure what aberration of logic led her to these two explanations. The moral to this episode is that when you violate norms regarding the expression of emotion, you may find that bizarre things are said about you.

Rules for displaying affect differ radically from culture to culture. According to Margaret Mead, "In Bali, all expressions of grief at a death—with the solitary exception of a mother whose infant dies at less than six months old— are culturally interdicted. The dead will be reincarnated; ritual acts are performed to ensure that an individual will be more beautiful in the next incarnation. Grief is inappropriate."[23]

While culture is an important factor in regulating the area of emotional expressions, the kinds of emotional cues provided by the face are common to all cultures. The face actually communicates three different types of signals: static, slow, and rapid.[24] *Static signals* are the permanent features of the face such as skin color and bone structure. *Slow signals* tend to alter gradually over time as is the case with skin texture and wrinkles. Our primary concern in studying the communication of emotion is the *rapid signals*. These provide the primary cues about affect, including all the kinesic movements usually associated with the face.

While static and slow signals usually function as sources of information about sex, age, and race, they can alter or complement the transmission of emotional cues. Norman Markel, a sociolinguist and communication researcher, is fond of telling a story about Hubert H. Humphrey during his campaign for the presidency on the Democratic ticket in 1968. Humphrey, so the story goes, was having trouble eliciting the kinds of responses from audiences that he had hoped for. Surveys indicated that people just weren't taking him seriously. Markel was supplied with a videotape of a speech and was implored by Humphrey's men to help determine the cause of the candidate's difficulties. Markel noticed that Humphrey had quite bushy eyebrows that extended high on the forehead, giving a rather comical, often surprised impression. He recommended trimming the brows. The result: Humphrey still didn't win the election, but audience response picked up—clear evidence, no doubt, that static and slow signals can influence the ability to transmit emotion.

Ekman and Friesen have developed a system for measuring the signals that contribute to emotional expression by dividing the face into three regions: area I, the brows and forehead; area II, the eyes, eyelids, and bridge of the nose; and area III, the cheeks, nose, mouth, chin, and jaw.[25] This system, referred to as the *Facial Affect Scoring Technique* (FAST), assumes that each of the three areas supplies cues that contribute to the emotional meaning of an expression. That doesn't mean that cues from all areas are *important* to the expression of all emotions. On the contrary, it is quite likely that we pay attention only to certain areas of the face in judging particular emotions. Although we don't ignore the other areas of the face, they are often viewed only as a check, to make sure that the emotion is ac-

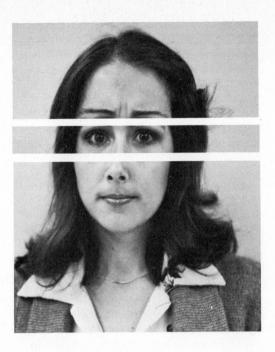

Figure 8.3 Facial Affect Scoring Technique: three regions of the face.

tually what we believe it to be. Figure 8.3 shows the three regions into which the FAST system divides the face.

Two studies in particular have examined how well each region of the face conveys the emotions of fear, disgust, anger, surprise, happiness, and sadness. In the first study, trained observers identified the emotions in the various facial regions and compared them with ratings for the entire face.[26] In the second study, photos depicting each emotion were cut up into the three regions.[27] Both the slices of the face and composites made up of a slice combined with a neutral expression in the remaining regions were judged. In almost all cases, disgust was best conveyed by the cheeks/mouth area, fear by the eyes/eyelids, sadness by both the brows/forehead and eyes/eyelids, happiness by both the cheeks/mouth and eyes/eyelids, anger by both the cheeks/mouth and brows/forehead, and surprise equally well by all three. In the second study, the only exception was anger, and even there, the trend was in the right direction.

If we attempt to integrate the findings of the studies we have mentioned, we come up with the summary in Table 8.3 (an asterisk denotes the regions that generally carry the emotion best).

Different parts of the face convey different elements of emotion. This has been demonstrated through a variety of research techniques. One study created a series of transparencies with different expressions for different facial features.[28] There were four eyebrow positions, three eye positions, and five mouth positions. Subjects were given lists of emotions representing the three dimensions of pleasant–unpleasant, irritated–calm, and receptive–nonreceptive and asked to put together combinations of eyebrow, eye, and mouth positions that best depicted the emotion. The investigator tried to determine how much uncertainty existed about which features convey emotions. High certainty meant that there were few options about which features could be used. According to the results, pleasant emotions were best revealed by the mouth, followed by a combination of the mouth with the eyes or the brows. Unpleasant emotions were much more difficult to decipher from a single feature or even a combination of features. The single best indicator was the eyebrow position, but certainty about the expression was improved when all three features were used. For expressions of irritation, about equal effectiveness was obtained with the brows alone and the brows and eyes combined, but neither yielded great certainty. People agreed least often about the correct element or combinations for expressing calm emotions. The mouth alone, the brows and mouth, and the combination of all three were equal in their

Table 8.3 Regions of the Face That Best Display the Dimensions of Emotion

	Eyes	Brows/Forehead	Mouth/Cheeks	Ease of Identification
Pleasant (e.g., happiness/joy)	*		*	Easy
Unpleasant (in general)		*	*	Hard
Fear	*			
Sadness	*	*		
Disgust			*	
Calm	*	*	*	Very hard
Irritated (in general)	*	*		Moderately hard
Anger		*	*	
Receptive (e.g., attentive/open)	*			Moderately easy
Nonreceptive (e.g., indifferent)	*	*		Moderately easy

ability (or inability) to clarify the emotions. For receptive and nonreceptive emotions, the eyes were the best single indicator, but greater certainty was achieved for receptive emotions if the eyes were combined with the mouth, and, on the nonreceptive emotions, if they were combined with the brows. Overall, the easiest emotions by far for subjects to put together were the pleasant ones.

Sending and Judging Vocalic Cues

Davitz and Davitz raised the question of how accurately we can transmit and interpret vocalic cues of emotion.[29] Their findings indicate that there is quite a range of accuracy both in the encoding and decoding of vocalic cues. When given the task of creating a vocal expression of a particular emotion, individuals varied somewhere between 23 and 55 percent accuracy. When given the task of associating an emotion with a tape recording of a voice, people varied somewhere between 20 and 48 percent accuracy. In other words, people vary dramatically in their ability to send and receive accurate vocalic cues of emotion. Two possible factors account for these differences: the nature of the emotion and people variables (such as sex, intelligence, experience, physiology of the communicator).

Nature of the Emotion

As Table 8.4 shows, of ten emotions, anger was most easily identified through the voice alone (a 65 percent accuracy rate). At the other extreme, pride generated the lowest accuracy level (21 percent). The emotion itself can account for much of the difficulty or ease with which expressions are understood.

The research by Davitz and Davitz also indicates that much of our difficulty in detecting

an emotional expression from the voice is due to the similarity between certain emotions. For example, while fear is correctly identified only 25 percent of the time, 20 percent of the time it is mistaken for sadness, and another 17 percent of the time it is thought to be nervousness. Love, which also had an accuracy rate of 25 percent, is misclassified as sadness 23 percent of the time and identified as sympathy 20 percent of the time. Furthermore, the researchers reported that pride, correctly identified in only 21 percent of the cases, was mistaken as satisfaction 20 percent of the time and thought to be happiness 15 percent of the time. Apparently, some emotions are consistently misclassified as some other emotion almost as often as they are correctly identified.

It is easy to see how some of these emotions can be mistaken for each other. You can see why, on a dimension ranging from irritated to calm, love, sadness, and sympathy would be confused; they probably cluster toward the calm end of the continuum. In other words, these emotions are *dependent;* they imply psychological qualities that overlap. If we were to develop a list of independent emotions (not overlapping) and submit voices to raters, limiting their choice to our list of independent emotions, we would improve the accuracy of judgments substantially. Research has also found that when subjects hear highly intense emotional messages, their scores are likely to improve.[30]

People Variables

In Chapter 5, we mentioned that in both sending and interpreting emotional expressions, females are slightly superior to males. This holds true for communicating and judging vocalic expressions of affect as well. Females are slightly more accurate than males.

Also, intelligence seems to be a factor in judging and transmitting vocalic expressions

Table 8.4 Percentage of Correct Judgments of Emotion Expressed Through Vocal Cues

Emotion	% Accuracy*
Anger	65
Nervousness	54
Sadness	49
Happiness	43
Sympathy	39
Satisfaction	31
Fear	25
Jealousy	25
Love	25
Pride	21

*Computed from J. R. Davitz and L. J. Davitz, "The Communication of Feelings by Content-Free Speech," *Journal of Communication*, 9 (1959), pp. 6–13.

of emotion, just as it influences the assessment of facial displays. [31] The more intelligent the individual, the more likely he or she is to be accurate in encoding and decoding emotional messages. Amount of experience has much the same impact. Research has demonstrated that individuals with greater experience simply do better on such tasks. With relatively little effort and exposure to the kinds of nonverbal cues that indicate emotion, you can significantly improve your ability to identify the emotional meaning of a message. In fact, simply by reading this chapter, you have probably already improved your sensitivity to and skill in encoding and decoding emotions.

Surprisingly enough, research on vocalic cues of emotion has revealed a consistency between overall encoding and decoding ability. Individuals who can transmit vocal expressions accurately also do quite well in judging emotions from voice tapes. Though we have suggested that some people are skilled at sending emotional cues while others are able to interpret emotional expressions but not to transmit them particularly well, this seems not

to be the case when the voice is the lone channel for communication. There also seems to be some grounds for believing that a person's encoding ability is relatively consistent for all nonverbal channels. Those who are able to display emotions accurately with the face also do well in transmitting vocal cues.

A final personal variable that influences the ability to handle vocalic cues of affect—especially the transmission of emotional cues—is the physiology of the speaker. Some people's vocal skills are limited by the inherent qualities or general inflexibility of their voice. The individual with a very raspy or gruff voice may have trouble sending certain cues and may well find that, even when these cues are sent accurately, they are not perceived accurately because the emotion seems inconsistent. For example, the orotund voice, which is consistently loud, masks many vocal cues necessary to communicate subtle emotions, especially those that require moderation in amplitude.

Sending and Judging Facial Cues

Factors that influence our accuracy in judging emotional expressions can be grouped into four categories: the social context, the physical environment, people variables, and the nature of the emotion being expressed.

Social Context

The social context includes all aspects of a situation that may provide information to help interpret the cues being transmitted. The norms of a given situation play a significant role. For example, the norm at football games is to be extremely expressive—to jump up, to yell, to wave arms and shake fists, and to screw up your face in anger or disappointment when the team loses ground. To an uninformed observer, that behavior could be mistaken as a sign of a fit or suffering. Knowing the norms, however, we understand that the fans are actually enjoying themselves. The role the individual holds in a given situation is also important. Saral conducted a clever study that demonstrated this principle.[32] He videotaped faces of individuals during an interaction and asked a number of observers to rate the emotions portrayed by the facial expressions. He told some of the observers that the face was that of a father talking to his son and told another set that they were seeing the face of the son. A third group thought they were watching a parole officer speaking to a parolee while a fourth group thought they were watching the parolee. A fifth group was told they were watching the son with the parolee. A final group was given no information about the role of the person being observed. The results supported the importance of knowing a person's role in interpreting expressions. Those who had no information marked the rating scales near neutral (that is, no discernible emotion). In the other five groups, the markings indicated greater emotional intensity and were consistent with the characteristics of the role the observers thought they were observing.

The norms and roles in a situation are important in interpreting kinesic cues because they provide a means of crosschecking our initial impressions. The more information there is available about the social situation, the more accurate our interpretations. When we know the cultural norms or the sets of behaviors that are appropriate for a situation, our guesswork is greatly reduced. Information can also be supplied by other nonverbal cues from the sender. If we think a person's eye behavior indicates that he or she is uncomfortable in our presence, we may observe hand and foot behavior for confirmation. Another source of information for checking cues is the behavior of others in the same situation. A relevant study asked people to evaluate facial expressions in different contexts provided by contrasting expressions.[33] Evaluations differed according

to what expressions shared the context with the one being rated. For instance, when a smiling face was seen with a frowning face, it was judged as friendly and good-natured. When it was seen with a glum face, it was judged as dominant and vicious. Other contextual sources of information include our familiarity with people's idiosyncrasies and our initial impressions of them, which serve as a standard of comparison for other behavior.

Physical Environment

Just as the social situation influences our judgment, so do the physical surroundings. Knapp has reported an experiment conducted by one of his students in which faces were placed against backgrounds of different colors and people were asked to judge the faces' emotions. Bright, warm colors produced positive judgments while dark, dull colors produced more negative responses.[34]

Although there is no direct evidence, it is likely that such a factor as heat or cold has an impact on our judgments of emotional cues. We probably associate pleasant emotions with moderate temperatures and less pleasant feelings with cold.

We don't need research to tell us that distance between individuals and lighting can alter our ability to judge and send emotions accurately if for no other reason than that they limit the kinds and number of cues that can be seen. If you have ever tried to coax a friend into smiling for the camera while facing into the sun, you know the kinds of contortions the face is likely to go through under the mandate to smile in those conditions.

The physical environment, like the social context, can be a kind of *noise* in the communication system whether or not the messages are related to emotion. Sounds, colors, temperature, lighting can distract and modify our perceptions, our moods, and our willingness to encode and decode emotion.

Table 8.5 Emotion Expressions: Specific Cues and Accuracy of Interpretation

Dimensions of Emotion and Specific Emotions	Kinesic Cues	Vocalic Cues	Accuracy of Interpretation
Pleasant	Single best indicator is mouth region (area III); also evident from combination of mouth and eyes (areas II and III) or mouth and brows[6,7]	Extreme pitch variation; down-contour pitch; combination of low amplitude and high pitch or high amplitude and low pitch[3]	High visual accuracy[1,11]
Happiness	Smiling[2]	Laughter[2]; extreme pitch variation; up- or down-contour pitch; moderate amplitude variation; high pitch level; fast tempo[3]	Highest kinesic accuracy[4,5]; high vocal accuracy[8]
Love		Peak pitch[9]	Vocally mistaken for sadness
Unpleasant	Single best indicator is brows[7]	Moderate pitch variation; extreme amplitude variation[3]	Most accurate visually when information is from brow region or all three facial regions[7]
Anger	Best indicated by areas I and III	Peak loudness[9]; moderate pitch variation; high pitch level; fast tempo; up pitch contour[3]; slower rate for men[10]	Highest vocalic accuracy[8]
Sadness, depression	Best indicated by areas I and II[6]	Moderate pitch variation; slow tempo[3]	Low accuracy visually[7]; high accuracy vocally[8]
Grief	Less eye contact; lower head angle; down in mouth	Peak pitch or peak loudness	
Fear, anxiety	Best indicated by area II[6]	Extreme amplitude variation; moderate pitch variation; up pitch contour; high pitch level; fast tempo; rhythmic[3]; speech errors	High visual accuracy[6]; low vocal accuracy[8]

Table 8.5   (cont.)

Dimensions of Emotion and Specific Emotions	Kinesic Cues	Vocalic Cues	Accuracy of Interpretation
Calm	Need information from all three regions[7]		Lowest accuracy visually[7]
Boredom		Moderate pitch variation; low pitch level; slow tempo; not rhythmic[3]	
Irritated	Best indicator is brows[7]	Moderate amplitude variation; extreme pitch variation; high pitch level; fast tempo[3]	Low visual accuracy[7]
Surprise	Areas I, II, and III equal in information provided[6]	Extreme pitch variation; up pitch contour; high pitch level; fast tempo; rhythmic[3]	High visual accuracy[11]
(Also see anger, fear)			
Receptive (e.g., interest, attention)	Best indicated by eyes and brows	Extreme pitch variation; fast tempo[3]	Moderate visual accuracy[7]
Nonreceptive	Best indicated by eyes or eyes and brows	Moderate pitch variation; slow tempo[3]	Low visual accuracy[7]
Disgust	Best indicated by area III[6]	Moderate pitch variation; slow tempo; atonal[3]	High visual accuracy as part of cluster[1]
(Also see boredom)			

1. C. E. Osgood, "Dimensionality of the Semantic Space for Communication via Facial Expressions," *Scandinavian Journal of Psychology*, 7 (1966), 1–30.

2. N. H. Frijda and E. Philipszoon, "Dimensions of Recognition of Emotion," *Journal of Abnormal Social Psychology*, 66 (1963), 45–51.

3. Scherer, "Acoustic Concomitants of Emotional Dimensions," in S. Weitz (ed.), *Nonverbal Communication* (New York: Oxford University Press, 1974).

4. R. M. Drag and M. E. Shaw, "Factors Influencing the Communication of Emotional Intent by Facial Expression," *Psychonomic Science*, 8 (1967), 137–138.

5. D. F. Thompson and L. Meltzer, "Communication of Emotional Intent by Facial Expression," *Journal of Abnormal Social Psychology*, 68 (1964), 125–129.

6. Ekman and Friesen, *Unmasking the Face* (Englewood Cliffs, N.J.: Prentice-Hall, 1975).

7. Cuceloglu, "Facial Code in Affective Communication," in Speer (ed.), *Nonverbal Communication* (Beverly Hills: Sage Publications, 1972).

8. Davitz and Davitz, "The Communication of Feelings by Content-Free Speech," *Journal of Communication*, 9 (1959), 6–18.

9. F. S. Costanzo, N. N. Markel, and R. R. Costanzo, "Voice Quality Profile and Perceived Emotion," *Journal of Counseling Psychology*, 16 (1969), 267–270.

10. Speer (ed.), *Nonverbal Communication* (Beverly Hills: Sage Publications, 1972).

11. J. Frois-Whitman, "The Judgment of Facial Expression," *Journal of Experimental Psychology*, 13 (1930), 113–151.

People Variables

Differences between people is the third class of factors affecting accuracy in sending and interpreting facial cues. One such element is the construction of the body part sending the cues. Fat-cheeked, heavy-jowled faces may not be able to display as many variations of emotions as a thin, more mobile face. We have a friend whose smile forces his eyes to close to a narrow slit, making it impossible to read variations in his eye expressions.

Body type and idiosyncracies aren't the only people variables that influence the communication of affect. We mentioned in Chapter 5 that sex seems to play a role. Recall that females are slightly superior to males in sending and interpreting certain emotions based upon facial expressions. What little evidence we have indicates that intelligence also makes a difference, that more intelligent individuals outperform less intelligent in both sending and receiving facial cues of emotion.[35] Earlier in this chapter, we mentioned that age, too, can influence a person's ability, especially in the first years of development.

Personality is also important, although its relationship to the communication of facial displays is difficult to describe. For some time, researchers have suspected that there are two distinct classes of individuals with respect to sensitivity and skill in dealing with cues of emotion: *externalizers,* who are particularly adept at portraying emotion, good actors and actresses capable of controlling the face and in command of the rules associated with the display of emotions; and *internalizers,* who are highly skilled at receiving and judging emotions but may be relatively unskilled in sending cues.[36] Whether these two categories are indeed legitimate personalities is a question that will have to be answered by future research.

One factor that explains differences in our ability to send emotional expressions accurately is the *style* of expression. Ekman and

Friesen have identified eight idiosyncratic styles for displaying affect in the face.[37] The *withholder* is someone who tends not to be very expressive. Withholders simply don't send the kinds of rapid signals that reveal emotion, and they know it. It isn't that they aren't emotional; it is just that their faces don't show emotion. They are often accused of lacking interest, of being placid, bored, or withdrawn. Of course, that isn't the case at all. The *revealer* is just the opposite. No matter how hard they try to control the face, to hide emotions, revealers seem automatically to reveal what they feel.

Unwitting expressors are much like the revealers, only they aren't aware of just how expressive they are. They are continually amazed that others are able to read their thoughts, but it is not the thoughts people are reading—it is the face. *Blanked expressors* think that they are expressing emotions, but they aren't. For some reason, their faces do not display the appropriate cues. They appear either expressionless or ambiguous.

Some of us may find ourselves continually thinking that we are communicating one emotion when we are actually communicating another. The *substitute expressor* may have a preemptive expression that occurs to the exclusion of other expressions. Unfortunately, such people are convinced that they are communicating what they feel. To the contrary, they are communicating a substitute expression. *Frozen-affect expressors* tend to have one predominant facial expression. It usually results from facial construction. These individuals seem locked into a particular emotion. Even when they express other emotions, traces of the primary expression remain.

An *ever-ready expressor* is someone who has an *initial* expression for almost any situation. No matter whether the emotion be surprise, anger, or fear, the initial expression is always the same. As time passes, other expressions may take its place. Last, the *flooded-affect expressor* is rare indeed. This individual has one or two expressions that continually flood the face. Ekman and Friesen have reported few instances of constant flooding and then only among individuals who are undergoing major trauma.

It is important to point out that, no matter what an individual's level of accuracy in judging emotions, improvement is quite possible. In other words, training can affect one's ability to interpret facial displays of emotion. Izard has reported evidence indicating that people can improve their accuracy level by at least 5.9 percent and by as much as 51 percent.[38]

Nature of the Emotion

The degrees of difference between messages also affect interpretation. The more similar an emotion is to another, the more difficult it is to interpret accurately. Thus, joy is hard to distinguish from happiness. Certain expressions are by their nature difficult to interpret, perhaps because they involve cues that have multiple meanings. Osgood classified emotions on the basis of the accuracy with which they can be interpreted. He found that glee, amazement, adoration, horror, quiet pleasure, and boredom were most accurately recognized, and cynical bitterness, acute sorrow, pity, despair, loathing, anxiety, and excitement were least accurately identified.[39]

An emotion can be especially difficult to interpret if it is shown on only some areas of the face or if it is actually a combination of emotions. Sometimes emotions may be displayed as *partials*—expressions using only part of the face. For example, the eyes alone may show fear while the rest of the face is neutral.

Emotions may also be expressed as *blends,* part of the face showing one emotion while another part shows a different one. The mouth may be turned up in a pleasant smile while the eyes are narrowed in anger producing a happiness–anger blend. Surprise–disgust, anger–

contempt, fear–surprise, and happiness–contempt are a few common blends. Now try your skill in determining in the photos in Figure 8.4 what parts of the face are communicating which emotion.

A final difficulty that results from the nature of the emotions being communicated arises from the fact that many emotions are actually categories of displays and not a single expression at all. Ekman and Friesen have identified four discrete types of surprise, each having different facial cues.[40] For example, *questioning surprise* involves cues of surprise in the eyes and brow but a neutral mouth, while *amazed surprise* involves a mouth open as if having just inhaled breath. One can achieve *dazed surprise* or *full surprise* by altering either the mouth or the eyes and brow. Thus, a range of different expressions can roughly approximate the same emotion, causing problems in the judgment of affect from facial cues.

Figure 8.4   The faces of some of these Beatles fans demonstrate affect blends. (Wide World Photos)

Problems of Research

By this time, you may be asking the question, "How do we know all this is true?" We posed this question as the last one to consider in this section. How much faith can we place in our observations? This is a critical concern. Researchers have not yet developed a method for studying emotions with which they are fully satisfied.

In studying facial displays, much research has employed photographs, some spontaneous and some posed, which are rated by observers. Critics claim that photos of spontaneous behavior may include idiosyncrasies of the individual that can mislead an observer who is unfamiliar with the sender. On the other hand, posed photos may be exaggerated, and laboratory studies may obtain higher agreement among judges than actually occurs normally. In addition, in some studies, judges supply the name of the emotion they are judging, and in others, they mark one from a list supplied by the researcher. Both procedures have pitfalls. If two observers look at a picture and one calls it *terror* and the other *horror*, are they in agreement? Suppose instead they have to mark a list supplied by the investigator. If both words appear on the list, the same problem exists. If only the word *fear* is on the list, one individual may mark it and the other may not. Or several photos representing a range of emotions from mild fear to absolute horror may all be labeled the same if only one suitable term is given.

Photographs have the added problem of excluding the context, which, as we pointed out earlier, is a critical factor affecting the accuracy of interpretation. Research using videotapes and films has overcome this particular problem; but it has picked up some new ones. Suppose you are asked to observe a gesture on film and decide what it means. If you watch it in motion, other behaviors and contextual features provide a crosschecking, but you may have difficulty deciding when the gesture begins or ends. It may actually be a part of a series of behaviors that are meaningful only in their entirety. Or it may change in meaning through the sequence. Another individual asked to observe the same behavior may select a different beginning and ending point and give a different interpretation. In other words, it is difficult to isolate units of behavior from the mainstream of an interaction. If the film is slowed down or even frozen at each frame, then the judge must analyze the tree without knowing its forest. Furthermore, by freezing individual film frames, one may end up looking at minute behaviors that are not meaningful. A micro facial expression can take as little time as one-fifth of a second. If we identify all the microexpressions in a small sequence, what do we have?

Studying how the voice contributes to the communication of affect presents a somewhat different set of problems. Every time you hear a voice that signals some emotion, you are not only hearing that particular signal but hearing it in the context of a number of vocal characteristics. How important is the information supplied by the vocal context? If it is valuable, how do we go about studying it?

Complex emotional messages are particularly difficult to investigate from vocal cues alone. Can the voice communicate a *vocal blend* or *partials*? Research has not even considered these possibilities. Even if we wished to, how would we go about investigating the structure of these complex messages? The face is visually observable, and blends can be created by integrating a dominant cue from one area of the face associated with one emotion with a cue in another area of the face associated with another emotional expression. How do we accomplish this with the voice? Many important vocal features associated with the expression of certain emotions have never been investigated, since most research in this area has been confined to the study of a very few cues. The use of sophisticated electronic equipment has permitted the study of artificially created voices that omit the idiosyncracies cluttering both spontaneous vocal and facial messages; but how artificial are these creations? Can we reasonably apply these findings to spontaneous informal interaction?

Additional difficulties confound investigations into the use of the body and touch as a means of communicating emotion. The body, even more than the face, is a multichannel message system capable (as we indicated in Chapter 3) of thousands of movements. The sheer number of body movements presents an obstacle to the study of emotional displays.

Perhaps the greatest handicap facing those who are interested in studying the function of the body in displaying emotion is the peculiar role of the body in signalling intensity. We know very little about how this is accomplished. Are there different cues for indicating extremes of happiness and fear, or are the cues for intensity similar for all emotions? The current research doesn't provide many answers.

Because of the difficulties that exist with the methods of researching the communication of emotion, all the findings we have reported must be viewed somewhat tentatively. As techniques become more sophisticated and findings with one method are validated with other methods, we shall develop more confidence in what we know about affect.

Summary

The communication of emotion is not a simple and direct process. Some codes, particularly voice and facial expression, are well suited to the communication of affect, while other codes are not in themselves highly informative. Our success in sending and interpreting emotional displays is due to a number of factors, including the kind of emotion, the sex of the sender and receiver, and the social and physical environment. The study of emotional messages is particularly difficult because of the human tendency to blend or compound emotions, revealing nonverbal cues of two or more emotional displays. Finally, a number of problems plague scholars interested in the communication of emotions, problems that cloud our understanding of all the factors that facilitate and obstruct the transmission of emotional displays.

Suggested Reading

Alloway, T., Krames, L., and Pliner, P. (eds.). *Communication and Affects: A Comparative Approach.* New York: Academic Press, 1972.

Darwin, C. *The Expressions of Emotions in Man and Animals.* New York: Philosophical Library, 1955.

Davitz, J. R. (ed.). *The Communication of Emotional Meaning.* New York: McGraw-Hill, 1964.

Davitz, J. R., and Davitz, L. J. "The Communication of Feelings by Content-Free Speech." *The Journal of Communication,* 9 (1959), 6–13.

Davitz, J. R., and Davitz, L. J. "Correlates of Accuracy in the Communication of Feelings." *The Journal of Communication,* 9 (1959), 110–117.

Ekman, P. "Universals and Cultural Differences in Facial Expression of Emotion." *Nebraska Symposium on Motivation,* Lincoln: University of Nebraska Press, 1972. (pp. 207–283).

Ekman, P., Ellsworth, P., and Friesen, W. V. *Emotion in the Human Face: Guidelines for Research and an Integration of Findings.* New York: Pergamon Press, 1971.

Ekman, P., and Friesen, W. V. *Unmasking the Face.* Englewood Cliffs, N.J.: Prentice-Hall, 1975.

Frijda, N. H. "Recognition of Emotions" In L. Berkowitz (ed.), *Advances in Experimental and Social Psychology.* New York: Academic Press, 1969. (pp. 170–179).

Izard, C. *The Face of Emotion.* New York: Appleton-Century-Crofts, 1971.

Knapp, P. (ed.). *Expression of the Emotions of Man.* New York: Holt, Rinehart and Winston, 1968.

Plutchik, R. *The Emotions: Facts, Theory and a New Model.* New York: Random House, 1962.

Wood, B. S. *Children and Communication: Verbal and Nonverbal Language Development.* Englewood Cliffs, N.J.: Prentice-Hall, 1976.

Notes

1. J. H. Watson, *The Seven-Per-Cent Solution*, N. Meyer (ed.) (New York: Ballantine, 1976), p. 16. Originally published by E. P. Dutton, New York, 1974. Copyright © 1974 by Nicholas Meyer. Reprinted by permission of the publishers, E. P. Dutton.
2. R. Plutchik, *The Emotions: Facts, Theories, and a New Model* (New York: Random House, 1962).
3. Plutchik, pp. 41–42 (note 2).
4. J. R. Davitz, *The Language of Emotion* (New York: Academic Press, 1969), p. 141.
5. P. Ekman, R. Sorenson, and W. V. Friesen, "Pan-Cultural Elements in Facial Display of Emotion," *Science*, (April 4, 1969), pp. 86–99.
6. See P. Ekman, "Face Muscles Talk Every Language," *Psychology Today* (September 1974), pp. 35–39.
7. F. L. Goodenough, "The Expression of the Emotions in a Blind Child," *Journal of Abnormal and Social Psychology*, 27 (1932), pp.328–333.
8. Ekman, Sorenson, and Friesen, *Science*, 1969, pp. 86–88 (note 5).
9. C. Darwin, *The Expression of the Emotions in Man and Animals* (Chicago: University of Chicago Press, 1965).
10. C. Darwin, 1965, p. 356 (note 9).
11. C. Wolff, *A Psychology of Gesture* (New York: Arno Press, 1972).
12. R. Birdwhistell, *Kinesics and Context* (Philadelphia: University of Pennsylvania Press, 1970).
13. K. Bridges, "Emotional Development in Early Infancy," *Child Development*, 3 (1932), pp. 324–341.
14. C. Brannigan and D. Humphries, "I See What you Mean . . . ," *New Scientist* (May 22, 1969), pp. 406–408.
15. N. G. Blurton Jones, "Non-Verbal Communication in Children," in R. A. Hinde (ed.), *Non-Verbal Communication* (Cambridge: Cambridge University Press, 1972), pp. 271–295.
16. S. S. Tomkins, *Affect, Imagery, Consciousness* (New York: Springer, 1962).
17. R. P. Abelson and V. Sermat, "Multidimensional Scaling of Facial Expressions," *Journal of Experimental Psychology*, 63 (1962), pp. 546–554; T. Engen and N. Levy, "Constant-Sum Judgments of Facial Expressions," *Journal of Experimental Psychology*, 51 (1956), pp. 396–398; T. Engen, N. Levy, and H. Schlosberg, "The Dimensional Analysis of a New Series of Facial Expressions," *Journal of Experimental Psychology*, 55 (1958), pp. 454–458; H. Schlosberg, "Three Dimensions of Emotion," *Psychological Review*, 61 (1954), pp. 81–88; H. C. Triandis and W. W. Lambert, "A Restatement and Test of Schlosberg's Theory of Emotion with Two Kinds of Subjects from Greece," *Journal of Abnormal and Social Psychology*, 56 (1958), pp. 321–328.
18. D. Cuceloglu, "Facial Code in Affective Communication," in D. C. Speer (ed.), *Nonverbal Communication* (Beverly Hills: Sage Publications, 1972).
19. A. I. Smith, "Non-Verbal Communication through Touch," unpublished Ph.D. Dissertation, Georgia State University, 1970.
20. T. Nguyen, R. Heslin, and M. Nguyen, "The Meanings of Touch: Sex Differences," *Journal of Communication*, 25 (Summer 1975), pp. 92–103.
21. K. Scherer, "Acoustic Concomitants of Emotional Dimensions: Judging Affect from Synthesized Tone Sequences," in S. Weitz (ed.), *Nonverbal Communication* (New York: Oxford University Press, 1974), pp. 105–111.
22. P. Ekman and W. V. Friesen, *Unmasking the Face* (Englewood Cliffs, N.J.: Prentice-Hall, 1975), pp. 137–139.
23. M. Mead, untitled book review, *Journal of Communication* (Winter 1975), p. 212.
24. Ekman and Friesen, pp. 10–11 (note 22).
25. P. Ekman, W. V. Friesen, and S. S. Tomkins, "Facial Affect Scoring Technique: A First Validity Study," *Semiotica*, 3 (1971), pp. 37–58.
26. J. D. Boucher, "Facial Areas and Emotional Information," *Journal of Communication*, 23 (1975), pp. 21–29.
27. Ekman, Friesen, and Tomkins, 1971 (note 25).
28. Cuceloglu (note 18).
29. J. R. Davitz and L. J. Davitz, "The Communication of Feelings by Content-Free Speech," *Journal of Communication*, 9 (1959), pp. 6–13.
30. Davitz and Davitz (note 29).
31. R. Tagiuri, "Person Perception," in G. Lindzey and E. Aronson (eds.), *The Handbook of Social Psychology*, 2nd edition (Reading, Mass.: Addison-Wesley, 1969), Vol. III, pp. 395–449.
32. T. B. Saral, "A Study of the Effect of Role Infor-

mation on Interpretation of Facial Expressions," dissertation, University of Illinois, 1969.

33. M. Cline, "The Influence of Social Context on the Perception of Faces," *Journal of Personality,* 25 (1956), pp. 142–158.

34. M. L. Knapp, *Nonverbal Communication in Human Interaction* (New York: Holt, Rinehart & Winston, 1972), pp. 125–126.

35. R. Tagiuri (note 31).

36. R. W. Buck, V. J. Savin, R. E. Miller, and W. F. Caul, "Communication of Affect through Facial Expressions in Humans," *Journal of Personality and Social Psychology,* 23 (1972), pp. 362–371.

37. Ekman and Friesen, pp. 155–157 (note 22).

38. C. E. Izard, *The Face of Emotion* (New York: Appleton-Century-Crofts, 1971).

39. C. E. Osgood, "Dimensionality of the Semantic Space for Communication via Facial Expressions," *Scandinavian Journal of Psychology,* 7 (1966), pp. 1–30.

40. Ekman and Friesen (note 22).

9

The Regulation of Interaction

Test Your Sensitivity

True or False?

1. By looking away from the person to whom you are speaking, you can signal that you have not finished speaking.
2. Establishing eye contact is an important factor in determining whether you will initiate verbal interaction with a person.
3. When there are a number of silences in a conversation, the people talking probably dislike each other.
4. One of the least supportive, least reinforcing stages in a conversation comes when it is about to end.
5. Students sitting near the front of a classroom are more likely to interact with the instructor than those at the back.

The body has a great deal to do with how we communicate as well as *what* we communicate. Communication among several individuals is roughly analogous to the flow of traffic through a busy intersection. Communication, like traffic, is not random; it has a purpose, and there are rules to guide its flow. To ensure efficiency in communication, societies have developed norms that regulate the initiation, flow, and termination of interaction.

In this chapter, we shall explore the regulatory functions of nonverbal communication, including the use of nonverbal cues to affect the orderly exchange of speaking turns, the role of backchanneling and silence in the social interaction, the breaking up of conversations into themes and episodes, and the nonverbal messages involved in initiating and terminating a conversation.

By the end of this chapter you should know the correct answer to all five questions and understand these concepts:

- determinants of initiating interaction
- sequencing
- turn
- turn-suppressing cues
- turn-yielding cues
- backchanneling
- turn endings
- episodes and positions
- environmental factors in regulation
- preclosings and closings
- signature

Initiating Interaction

In our culture, communication encounters do not happen without forethought. We survey the setting, seeking cues indicating that an encounter is likely to be satisfying and rewarding. If the cues are not there, or if cues suggest that the encounter will not be successful, we avoid interaction. Many of the signals by which we calculate the potential success of an encounter are nonverbal messages. Unfortunately, investigations of such nonverbal factors have been neither systematic nor thorough. Some of the research is scientific, while other studies are more anecdotal. Here is a brief discussion of three behavioral cues that make the initiation of interaction likely.

Physical Attraction

Physical attraction between strangers is an important factor in determining satisfaction with an encounter. Appearance is an obvious source of information for forming initial impressions about and projections for a relationship. The first few minutes of an encounter bring out the amateur psychologist in all of us. When we meet an individual for the first time, we experience what Berger and Calabrese call *uncertainty*.[1] We are unsure how to behave toward the stranger, how she or he will react, what the person wants; we are uncertain of the prospects for liking and acceptance. We resolve uncertainty by inventing information or inferring it from limited physical data, constructing a basis for relating to this *other*.

Physical appearance is important because it implies certain things about the social talents of the individual, his or her occupational status, happiness, and personality traits. Although a number of studies have been conducted to determine exactly what traits we suppose highly attractive persons to possess, one particular finding illustrates the point. Arthur Miller, a psychologist at the University of Miami in Ohio, asked both male and female students to rate, with a variety of adjectives, photographs of individuals who were approximately the same age.[2] The results indicated that very attractive people were rated as being significantly more curious, complex, outspoken, flexible, serious, candid, amiable, happy, active, assertive, confident, and perceptive than unattractive persons. It seems clear that one's physical attractiveness influences the perception of other traits that may in turn influence the initiation of interaction.

A more direct test of the importance of physical attraction is the computer date experiments that we mentioned in Chapter 6.[3] Results of the study indicated that both males and females prefer attractive partners, although males tend to rely more than females on attractiveness as the basis for overall evaluation. The personality of the people involved played a minor role in affecting preferences.

A similar test was performed at the University of Texas.[4] Experimenters paired students with members of the opposite sex, gave them fifty cents for a Coke at the student union, and told them to get to know one another. Follow-up interviews indicated that the students preferred partners who were either similar in physical attractiveness to themselves or who were very attractive.

Physical attractiveness is only a limited advantage. As time goes on, other bases for developing impressions become available to us. Eventually, we learn to depend on more reliable but more elusive sources of information. Berscheid and Walster[5] have noted that physically attractive people often prefer one-time encounters to lasting relationships simply because their beauty makes it easy for them to give good first impressions.[6]

Eye Contact

There are a lot of myths about eye contact or gaze, many of which have actually been borne out in the research laboratory. In most social contexts, eye contact is a sign of approachability,[7] of being available for interaction. Gaze accompanies other positive cues such as smiling and waving. Our society has evolved rules about how and when one gazes at a stranger. Goffman has recognized that, in much of our *unfocused* social action (passing others on the street, sitting across from others in a restaurant or store), where there is no intention of initiating conversation, our gaze behavior is governed by the rule of *civil inattention*.[8] In other words, we may look at another person, but we must not stare. Goffman notes, "Where the courtesy is performed between two persons passing on the street, civil inattention may take the special form of eyeing the other up to approximately eight feet, during which time sides of the street are apportioned by gesture, and then casting the eyes down as the other passes—a kind of dimming of lights."[9] Greater scrutiny than that amounts to suspicious behavior.

Research has shown that people who look at

other people as part of their overall social style are generally viewed as less formal and less nervous than others, and are chosen more often as partners in interaction. Perhaps Georg Simmel said it best in his *Soziologie:*

Of the special sense-organs, the eye has a uniquely sociological function. The union and interaction of individuals is based upon mutual glances. This is perhaps the most direct and purest reciprocity which exists anywhere. This highest psychic reaction, however, in which the glances of eye to eye unite men, crystallizes into no objective structure; the unity which momentarily arises between two persons is present in the occasion and is dissolved in the function. So tenacious and subtle is this union that it can only be maintained by the shortest and straightest line between the eyes, and the smallest deviation from it, the slightest glance aside, completely destroys the unique character of this union. No objective trace of this relationship is left behind, as is universally found, directly or indirectly, in all other types of associations between men, as, for example, in interchanging of words. The interaction of eye and eye dies in the moment in which directness of the function is lost. But the totality of social relations of human beings, their self-assertion and self-abnegation, their intimacies and estrangements, would be changed in unpredictable ways if there occurred no glance of eye to eye. This mutual glance between persons, in distinction from the simple sight or observation of the other, signified a wholly new and unique union between them.[10]

Proximity

Nearness has a mixed impact on initial interaction. Closeness (within 12 feet) seems to pressure individuals into interaction.[11] Studies have shown that, in business and medical offices, when workers are seated within 12 feet of each other, they seek interaction. Closeness also provides an overall impression of friendliness. A study of distances between an interviewer and interviewee and their impact on first impressions showed that closeness, but not too much closeness, gives the most favorable impression, suggesting that extremely close personal distances, especially among strangers, is uncomfortable.[12]

Structuring Interaction

> *Silence is one great art of conversation.*
> —William Hazlitt

Sequencing in Conversational Interaction

The *segmentation of interaction roles* is a distinctive feature of interaction in our culture. Though in some cultures the norm is for more than one individual to speak at a time—this being done with no loss of comprehension—Western cultures distinguish between the roles of speaker and listener. We have developed the notion that the most efficient means of communicating is to exchange opportunities to speak and not to speak simultaneously. This pattern is known as *sequencing.*

Taking Turns All social encounters can be thought of as an extended series of speaking opportunities shared by all who are present and to whom cultural custom grants the opportunity to speak. The term used to describe these intervals during which a person has the chance to speak without interruption is *speaking turn.* Jaffe and Feldstein define a speaking turn as "possession of the floor,"[13] while Wiemann and Knapp call it "floor apportionment."[14] Whatever the label, they are referring to that period of time during which an individual engages in solo speaking bounded by the speech of others. The average speaking turn in normal social conversation is approximately six seconds in duration. A number of different channels, both verbal and nonverbal, come into play as we attempt to achieve the smooth, orderly exchange of these generally brief turns without loss of information.[15]

Turn-taking Cues: The Speaker Once an individual has captured the conversational floor, two broad categories of turn-taking cues can be used to ensure the orderly exchange of turns. These are called *turn-suppressing cues* and *turn-yielding cues*.[16] As the terms suggest, the former indicate that the speaker wishes to continue speaking without interruption, while the latter signal the termination of a turn and the opening of the floor to others.

Research has identified five behavioral cues that function to suppress attempts by others to capture the floor:[17] (1) an *audible inhalation* by the speaker; (2) a *continuation of gesture*; (3) a *facing away*, that is, a diverting of the eye from the auditor; (4) a *sustained intonation* pattern, cueing the auditor that more speech will follow (a sustained intonation pattern occurs when a speaker maintains a similar pitch level for several spoken words; in English, a declarative statement ends with a falling intonation and an interrogative with rising intonation); and (5) *fillers* (also called *vocalized pauses* or *filled pauses*), utterances, such as *uh*, which fill a pause in the speaking turn so that the auditors will not mistake the silence for a turn-yielding cue. In theory, the proper transmission of one or any combination of these cues should be sufficient to permit the speaker to retain the turn without interruption. (See Figure 9.1.) In practice, of course, this is not always the case.

In many instances, turn-yielding cues are simply a matter of terminating a turn-suppressing behavior: facing the receiver, maintaining an unfilled or sustained silence, or terminating hand or arm movement. A speaker may also signal the intention to relinquish the floor by using a falling intonation pattern at the end of a phonemic clause (or a rising intonation pattern in the case of a question). You can achieve much the same effect by drawling

out either the last syllable or a stressed syllable immediately preceding the termination of speech. These cues, of course, exist only at the nonverbal and paralinguistic level. At the verbal level, syntax, certain forms of idiomatic expression, and speech rate can function either to sustain or yield the speaking turn.

Starkey Duncan examined the relationship between turn-yielding and turn-suppressing signals and attempts by an auditor to capture the conversational floor and initiate a speaking turn. Duncan found that an orderly exchange of speaking turns occurred when an auditor's attempt at taking a turn followed some turn-yielding signal. Also, the greater the number of paired turn-yielding cues transmitted, the greater the probability that an auditor would initiate a turn. On the other hand, even a single turn-suppressing cue was sufficient to offset simultaneous turn-yielding cues and prevent unwanted interruption by the auditor.[18]

Turn-taking Cues: The Auditor Although much of what we know about turn taking is the result of studies that have focused primarily on the speaker and speaking signals, it is reasonable to assume that an auditor does not simply sit motionless, awaiting a turn-yielding cue. There are also signals that indicate a desire to speak.

John Wiemann, while at Purdue University, investigated behaviors that might help an auditor gain the conversational floor. Results indicated that gaze directed at the speaker, nods, and forward leans are nonverbal cues that fit in this category.[19] Wiemann and Knapp have also identified a number of cues that may play some role in the turn-taking process but for about there is insufficient or inconclusive data. These behaviors include a raised index finger and an inhalation of breath coupled with a straightening of the back.[20]

The Backchannel Not all behavior on the part of an auditor is an attempt to wrest the floor from the speaker. Much of the nonverbal

Figure 9.1 Turn-suppressing cues being used, apparently to good effect. (Harvey Stein)

Table 9.1 Forms of Backchannel Behavior

Focal Behavior	Researcher	Accompanying Behavior
"M-hm," "yeah," "right," "surely," "I see," "yes, quite," "that's right"	Duncan (1972) Kendon (1967)	
Sentence completions	Yngve (1970) Duncan (1972)	
Request for clarification	Duncan (1972)	
Brief restatement	Duncan (1972)	
Head nods/shakes	Duncan (1972) Dittmann (1972)	
"Yes," "uh-hunh," "yeah"	Fries (1952)	Rising intonation
"I see," "good," "oh"	Fries (1952)	Rising intonation
"That's right," "yes, I know," "oh-oh"	Fries (1952)	Falling intonation
"Fine," "so"	Fries (1952)	Rising intonation
"Oh, my goodness"	Fries (1952)	
Simple acceptance ("yeah," "right")	Snyder (1945)	
Change in direction of gaze	Dittmann (1972)	
Smiling	Dittmann (1972)	

SOURCE: A. Dittmann, "Developmental Factors in Conversational Behavior," *Journal of Communication*, 22 (1972); S. Duncan, Jr., "Some Signals and Rules for Taking Speaking Turns in Conversations," *Journal of Personality and Social Psychology*, 23 (1972), pp. 283–292; C. C. Fries, *The Structure of English* (New York: Harcourt, Brace, 1952); A. Kendon, "Some Functions of Gaze-Directions in Social Interaction," *Acta Psychologica*, 26 (1967), pp. 22–63; W. U. Snyder, "An Investigation of the Nature of Non-Directive Psychotherapy," *Journal of General Psychology*, 33 (1945), pp. 193–223; and V. H. Yngve, "On Getting a Word in Edgewise," in M. A. Campbell (ed.), Papers from the Sixth Regional Meeting, Chicago Linguistics Society, Chicago, Ill., 1970, pp. 567–577.

behavior of an auditor may function as feedback directed at the speaker. Many researchers refer to this as *backchanneling*.[21] There seems to be agreement that, even when the backchannel takes a verbal form, this should not be considered a speaking turn. Instead, certain vocalizations are an integral part of the auditor's role. (For a list of some of these vocalizations, see Table 9.1.)

Backchannels, however, do more than let the speaker know how the speaking turn is going; they *confirm* the speaker in the role, indicating that the speaking turn should continue and that the auditor is intent (at least for the moment) on listening. (See Figure 9.2.) Backchannels also provide information about the auditor, often signalling recognition of a topic or person by use of a nod or smile or indicating agreement with a position or idea. Backchanneling may also function as a form of *pacing*, or what Ekman and Friesen have called a *regulator*.[22] In other words, by nodding one's head at regular intervals in response to the speaker's words, the auditor can actually pace the speaking turn. Thus, backchannels can take the form of feedback, relational messages, or regulators.

How much or how little an auditor uses the backchannel will change from conversation to conversation and from individual to individual; but the degree to which the backchannel is used is never determined entirely by the auditor. Since the backchannel provides valuable information to a speaker, the speaker may pressure the auditor to provide feedback. For example, by pausing after the mention of a name or object, a speaker can, in effect, demand a signal of recognition from the auditor, the pause functioning as an indication that the continuation of the turn depends on a response from the auditor. Also, the speaker may have to adapt the turn to accommodate either underuse or overuse of backchanneling on the part of the listener. The backchannel and the speaking turn are interdependent; each influences the other. The chronology of a conversation shown in Table 9.2 should suggest this interdependence.

Dittmann has used the phrase *listener responses* to refer to the behaviors occurring in the backchannel of conversations.[23] Although many take the form of vocalized behaviors, he claims that listener responses are neither clearly verbal nor nonverbal but lie somewhere in between. Listener responses are not symbolic—that is, they do not imply a specific referent. Even though they may take linguistic forms, the conventional meanings associated with the linguistic forms do not necessarily apply. Dittmann has argued that "they do not qualify as a 'language,' but are perhaps best described as specific signals that the listener is paying attention to the speaker, is keeping up with him, or that he has understood what was just said."[24]

Dittmann's research has suggested that responses from the auditor, whether verbal or nonverbal, are more likely to occur during the interval (usually a brief silence) following a phonemic clause than at other points in the conversation. Also, nodding and vocalizations by an auditor are correlated, suggesting that

Figure 9.2 Backchanneling working in conjunction with turn-taking cues. The direction of a gaze can indicate whose turn it is to speak, while a gaze itself can support the speaker.

Table 9.2   Chronology of a Conversation

Time	Person A	Person B	Function of Behavior
000:02.2	Facing start		
000:02.8	Smile start	Facing start	
000:03.8	Smile stop		
	Starts turn		
000:05.1		Smile start	Backchannel (BC)
000:05.6	Left-hand (LH) gesture start	Smile stop	
000:06.0	LH gesture stop		Turn-yielding cue
000:06.1		Head nod start	BC
000:07.3		Head nod stop	
000:07.9	LH/RH gesture		
000:08.5		Vocalization start	Simultaneous speech/BC
000:08.9		Vocalization stop	
000:09.3	Gesture stop		Turn-yielding cue
000:09.9		Mouth open	Turn-taking cue
000:10.4	Turn stop		
000:10.8		Turn start	Open turn switch
000:11.3	Body shift		Juncture
000:12.0		RH gesture start	
000:12.7	Head tilt		
000:13.9		RH gesture stop	Turn-yielding cue
000:14.1		Facing stop	Turn-maintaining cue
000:14.5	Touching start		
000:16.1	Touching stop		
000:16.8		Facing start	Turn-yielding cue
000:17.9		LH gesture start	Turn-maintaining cue
000:18.9	Vocalization start		Start attempting interruption
000:19.4		RH gesture start	Turn-maintaining cue
000:19.7	RH gesture start		Turn-maintaining cue
000:20.6	RH gesture stop		Turn-yielding cue
000:21.0	Vocalization stop		Stop attempting interruption
000:21.8		Facing stop	Turn-maintaining cue
000:22.9	Head nod start	Facing start	BC
000:23.6		LH/RH gesture stop	Turn-yielding cue
000:24.4	Head nod stop	Turn stop	
000:24.5	Turn start		Closed turn switch

they may in fact make up a package or multi-channel message. Dittmann feels that the non—vocalization package may function as a signal designed to indicate a desire for the floor or as a means of responding to the speaker's desire for feedback.

Silence   Silence is a particularly interesting conversational event. First, it represents an interval of time during which the verbal channel is not in operation; nonverbal behavior becomes the sole mechanism for communicating meaning. Second, many researchers have viewed silence as a symptom of a breakdown in the procedures governing the conversation. In other words, silence, like simultaneous speech, may indicate that the system devised to regulate the flow of interaction between speaking turns is in some kind of jeopardy. For example, if a speaker suddenly stops speaking, looks at the ceiling as if to retrieve some lost thought, and then continues to talk after a couple of seconds of silence, most researchers would agree that the interval of silence was a significant event in the conversation. The literature on the subject of silence points to a number of different conditions that may cause the breakdowns in conversation that we refer to as silences.

There is, however, more than one kind of silence. The term is often used to refer to a number of different types of pauses in interaction. First, there is the *hesitation* or *pause,* which is a short interval of silence within a turn. Second, a *switch pause* is the period of silence between turns. An *imposed silence* can be either a hesitation or switch pause; it is an intentional silence on the part of either speaker or receiver and may come out of deference to cultural norms or as part of some overall speaking strategy. Imposed silences are often limited to specific environments (churches, hospitals, funeral parlors) or in response to specific roles (president, teacher, a high-ranking military officer).[25] Within a turn, an imposed silence may function to dramatize a

point or to prompt a favorable backchannel response from the receiver.

Isolating the causes of silence can be very difficult indeed. Not only are there several different types of silence, but scholars have evolved a number of different ways of looking at their causes. The literature on silence suggests three different models for explaining its occurrence. The *speaker model* looks at the behavior of the speaker as the primary source of silence. The speaker can do a number of things to increase the likelihood that silence will occur between turns or within a turn. First, the more unfamiliar the ideas or topic of interaction is to the speaker, the greater is the likelihood that the speaking turns will be broken by hesitation.[26] Second, Goldman-Eisler suggests that complex ideas cause hesitations within speaking turns. Third, a number of researchers contend that various forms of stress perceived by the speaker can result in periods of silence.[27] Stress interferes with normal cognitive processes, and the ensuing breakdowns in thought are reflected in silence. Black demonstrated that upward or downward shifts in the level of abstraction can precipitate silence as the other participants in the conversation take time to adjust to the new level of thought.[28] For instance, if you are discussing your choice of color for a car and then, without warning, shift up the abstraction ladder to a statement about the nature of color perception, it may take a few seconds for the listeners to connect the two points in some logical fashion. A better strategy is to move up the ladder gradually, looking for evidence of a receiver's comprehension through the backchannel. Fourth, research on turn taking has shown that failure on the part of a speaker to send turn-yielding cues prior to ending a turn, thereby forewarning an auditor of a new speaking opportunity, may result in a brief silence.[29]

There is also a *receiver model* of silence. A receiver can contribute to the occurrence of silence by failing to perceive turn-yielding cues transmitted by a speaker or by unintentionally transmitting turn-taking cues. Such violations of the rules governing the exchange of speaking turns heightens the chance that silence will result. A receiver can also prompt a breakdown of the structure by abusing or failing to use the backchannel. By refusing to give either verbal or nonverbal response, the receiver may actually force the speaker to ask directly for feedback or lapse into silence, hoping to elicit a response. Since the backchannel is a communication mechanism negotiated between the participants in the conversation, an auditor who uses the backchannel early in a conversation and then ceases to use it may be unintentionally violating a norm. Such violations can foster breakdowns.

Some researchers have been dissatisfied with models that place responsibility for silences (and the breakdowns that result in silence) on one individual (or role) in the conversation. They have cast a new model, best thought of as a *relational model*. The relational model views silence not as a feature of any single role nor as an event caused by one individual but as a property of the communication system as a whole. Silence is produced jointly; it is a product of the way people behave together and how behaviors fit together, both at the verbal and nonverbal level. Organized, unified, and coordinated actions lower the likelihood of breakdowns or violations in the rules governing a conversation.

One of your authors has identified two competing relational models for viewing the occurrence of silence: the *synchronous* and the *concatenous models*.[30] The synchronous model proposes, in effect, that the more similar the behaviors of speaker and listener are within a given speaking turn, the less chance there is of a breakdown that precipitates silence. Synchronous nonverbal behavior refers to what we usually think of as *mirroring*.[31] Individuals who are "in sync" with one another are usually attracted to, or are in agreement with, one another, and this simultaneous movement is a way of demonstrating their solidarity. An interesting example from an unrelated research project may illustrate the point. Several years ago, we were engaged in a series of experiments involving video-taping dyads of unaware subjects as they were awaiting the arrival of a third party. The subjects were seated in large, cushioned swivel chairs. In one case the two subjects (who were strangers) were probing one another for information and discovered that they were from the same small town in Florida. Immediately, they began to swivel their chairs in a synchronous fashion, smiling and laughing about common experiences and mutual friends. One asked, "Do you know so-and-so?" Immediately the second individual stopped swiveling and began to move the chair in a way that no longer mirrored the movement of the first. The second person replied, "Yeah, but I never did like her." The first agreed, "Yeah, well, neither did I." The two resumed synchronous swiveling.

The concatenous model assumes a linear rather than a simultaneous perspective.[32] Since dyadic conversations are comprised of speaking turns alternating from person A to person

Table 9.3 Sources of Silence

	Type of Silence
Speaker model	
Unfamiliar material	Hesitation
Complex material	Hesitation
Stress	Hesitation
Shifts in abstraction	Switch pause
Cue violation	Switch pause
Receiver model	
Cue violation	Switch pause
Failure to backchannel	Hesitation
Failure to perceive cue	Switch pause
Relational models	
General factors	
Strangers	Switch pauses
Age differences	Switch pauses
Cultural differences	Switch pauses
Synchronous model	
Dysynchronous nonverbal behavior	Switch pause
Concatenous model	
Stylistic differences	Both
Content differences	Switch pause
Differences in positions	Switch pause

B and then back again, it is possible to compare any two speaking turns that are adjacent in time. In other words, how is A's speaking turn similar to or different from the subsequent speaking turn of B? The greater the similarity in both the verbal and nonverbal features of the two adjacent turns, the greater, we might assume, is the similarity between the two individuals and, therefore, the less likely is the dissolution of speaking turns into silence. The concatenous model provides a number of ways of looking at the relationship between any two people. How similar is their vocabulary? How similar in duration are the two adjacent turns?

Are the nonverbal behaviors of A similar in length and frequency to those of B?

For a summary of what the three different models have to say about the sources of silence, see Table 9.3.

Turn Endings Regardless of which model you use, it is likely that in any given conversation you will find wide variations in the number of hesitations within turns and the length of silences between turns. How does one know how much silence between turns is too much? Jaffe and Feldstein among others have pointed out there are a number of types of *turn endings*.[33] Many of these turn endings are defined in terms of the length of silence prior to the next speaking turn. An *interruption* is a turn ending precipitated by the simultaneous speech of an individual not owning the speaking floor, but in fact wresting it from another. Interruptions, of course, do not allow for silence. A second type of turn ending is called the *closed* turn and occurs when one individual ceases to speak and a second individual initiates a turn after .1 seconds or less of silence between the turns. An *open* turn ending is one in which there is an interval of silence ranging from .1 seconds to 2.9 seconds. An *overlong* turn ending is one in which silence exceeds 2.9 seconds. (See Table 9.4.)

What do these turn endings indicate about the adherence to rules governing the conversation? Most scholars agree that both interruptions and overlong turn endings reflect some violation or breakdown in the rules governing turn taking. On the other hand, open and closed turn endings often fall well within an acceptable range of silence. Not all researchers agree with the Jaffe and Feldstein criteria for distinguishing among the silences. Some argue that the kind of turn endings used in a particular conversation is negotiated by the participants.[34] In other words, communicators develop a norm for the amount of silence between adjacent turns. There are no ranges for

Table 9.4 Turn Endings

Type	Silence Interval
Interruption	No silence
Closed turn	.0 to .1 seconds
Open turn	.1 to 2.9 seconds
Overlong turn	3.0 seconds and up

what is acceptable or unacceptable; interactants determine how silences are to be used.

Episodes and Positions

Scholars have been fumbling for some time for terms to describe what is in reality a fairly simple concept—the notion of an *episode* within the larger conversation. *Episode* refers to behaviors initiated as part of the interaction surrounding a particular topic or theme being discussed. Lengthy conversations may involve several episodes, while a short encounter may embrace a single topic. The term *position* is a little more difficult to understand. *Position* is Albert Scheflen's term for a segment of an interaction during which a person maintains a fairly consistent disposition toward the topic of conversation and toward other participants.[35] An episode is likely to contain several positions as participants gain or lose interest, identify or reject, pursue or avoid ideas. A position, then, reflects an attitude toward the interaction.

Nonverbal cues are important means of signalling changes of position within an episode and changes of episode within a conversation. In this way, certain nonverbal behaviors help to break up the conversation into stages or segments, partitioning the major intervals of unified thought. Research has shown that at least four nonverbal boundary markers occur in normal interaction: postural or proxemic shifts, extrainteractional activities, silences, and paralinguistic markers.

Frederick Erickson, a Harvard anthropologist, has found that *proxemic shifts*—which include such postural changes as leaning forward or back as well as changes in distance between communicators—are the most consistent markers of episodes in conversation.[36] Blom and Gumperz, in their analysis of the speaking styles of a group of Norwegian villagers, observed that proxemic shifts indicated not only topical shifts but situational shifts as well.[37] *Situational shifts* are "momentary changes in the mutual rights and obligations between speakers."[38] This theory implies that the responsibilities of the participants change with shifts in topic or theme and these, in turn, are noted by changes in distance and posture.

Erickson observed conversations between and within ethnic groups and found that proxemic shifts consistently indicate the end of one segment and the beginning of a new one. Furthermore, proxemic shifts are a more accurate index of episodes than eye contact, paralinguistic cues, or simultaneous speech. Finally, Erickson's data showed that tense or uncomfortable moments invariably produce shifts.

Researchers occasionally cite behaviors that seem to serve the function of marking boundaries to either episodes or positions but that defy standard classifications of nonverbal behavior. Many of these actions fit a category that we have called *extrainteractional activities*. Pittinger and his associates noted instances in therapeutic interviews when a subject lit a cigarette, took a deep breath, and then exhaled.[39] In many instances, the actions coincided with the termination of a specific subject of discussion. Other extrainteractional activities might include reaching for a drink, adjusting the cushion of a chair, removing an article of clothing, or rearranging books, purse, and so on.

As we have mentioned, silence often acts as a natural marker in conversations by indicating the termination of a topic. Schegloff and

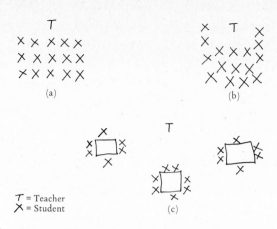

T = Teacher
X = Student

Figure 9.3 Which seating arrangement is conducive to high classroom participation?

Sacks observed that silences often function as *topic closings*—signals that participants are no longer interested in pursuing a specific theme of conversation.[40] Silences often function as transitions between themes, allowing the participants the time to relax both physically and mentally before engaging in a divergent line of discussion.

Evidence indicates that we also use paralinguistic cues to mark the end of segments of conversation. Pittinger et al. found that interviewees denoted larger episodes and positions within episodes with sighs, gasps, and other nonverbal utterances.[41] They suggest that these sounds—which in reality are little more than vocalized explosions of breath—may permit a change in speaking style. Sighs and gasps release air from the lungs, thereby permitting a person to change rate and volume of vocalization for the ensuing exchange. These nonverbal utterances also function to release body tension developed in the preceding exchange, in a sense renewing and restoring the body.

Environment and Regulation

Factors in the environment also govern the flow of communication. Seating patterns, furniture arrangement, room size, number of interactants are all part of the geography of communication. Consider some of the ways in which the setting can affect patterns of interaction.

1. *The environment can affect the amount of communication.* Something as simple as the arrangement of furniture in a room can significantly influence the total amount of participation (see Fig. 9.3). Sommer and his students have looked at various arrangements in different contexts.[42] They found that, for classroom seating, a laboratory setting with lab tables and equipment produced more instances of participation than did a standard classroom or seminar room with a central table surrounded by chairs. However, those who actually participated in the seminar arrangement participated to a greater degree than did those who participated in the other arrangements. In the seminar room, greatest participation usually came from those directly opposite the instructor, while in the standard classroom or auditorium, greatest participation came from the center and front or along the aisles. Heston and Garner found that, when given the opportunity to assemble chairs in a classroom in such a way as to facilitate interaction, people formed an

inverted U.[43] The one common element seems to be the ability to maintain eye contact with the instructor. The more opportunity to meet the teacher's eye, the greater the participation.

This also may explain some of the problems that have been encountered in other environments. Recall Sommer's rearrangement of furniture in the lounge of the women's ward of a state hospital (Chapter 4).[44]

2. *The environment can influence who talks to whom.* The setting can alter not only whether you communicate and how much you are likely to contribute to a conversation but also to whom you speak. Research has shown that when people are seated in a circle, they tend to direct more messages to people seated directly opposite them than to other members of the group *if* there is weak leadership in the group.[45] When there is a strong leader, individuals interact with people adjacent to them. Sommer has reasoned that "since it is impermissible to look directly at a dominant individual at close quarters, the individual restricts his gaze to his immediate neighbors when a strong leader is close by."[46] However,

when leadership is *group centered* (shared equally by all group members), distance or seating arrangement has no impact on whom you are likely to speak to.

Generally, proximity is an important factor, especially in highly structured environments such as offices, planes, theaters, and so on. In these settings, individuals are controlled by the environment. It becomes impossible to communicate with someone who is not seated near you. In many cases, there is a *least effort* phenomenon at work. In other words, it is possible to walk down the hall and converse with individuals who are several offices away, but it requires less effort to strike up a conversation with the person in the office next door. A substantial amount of research backs up this point. Festinger found, in studies of dormitory and apartment life, that the closer someone lives to you, the more likely you are to interact with and be attracted to him or her.[47]

3. *The environment can influence the role of nonverbal messages in interpersonal communication.* We have mentioned that many kinesic behaviors are useful in determining who speaks, but some settings can alter the kinds of nonverbal messages that can be used. Obviously, tasks requiring two individuals to use their hands for purposes other than gesticulation limit or eliminate altogether the role that gesture might play in turn taking. When you are washing dishes with a friend, or when two mechanics are working on an engine, a limited number of nonverbal signals are available for regulating interaction. The telephone is a feature of the communication environment that renders useless all kinesic messages. In telephone conversations, regulation is governed by ritual (the order in which individuals are supposed to speak), by verbal instructions, and by vocalic cues.

4. *The environment can influence one's role in regulating interaction.* Research has shown that people who by chance or design find themselves seated centrally (at the head of a table, in the center of a group, at the crest of a

mini-experiment

Keep a record over four or five class meetings of the seat location of each individual who interacts with the instructor. Keep a tally of how many times the individual interacts. You might try this in a class where the seats are not assigned and where seating seems to change with each class session. What do your notes tell you about seating and teacher–student interaction? Draw a diagram that shows where the greatest participation tends to come from.

semi-circle) are assigned higher status, are perceived by others as being higher in status, have more messages directed to them, and enjoy the interaction more than those located in more peripheral seats.[48] Also, research has shown that when shy individuals are seated in central places, they increase their interaction. By contrast, being seated outside a group makes entering the conversation difficult. For one thing, the ability to send and receive turn-taking cues is severely restricted. Others may have trouble seeing cues and knowing when an "outsider" wishes to participate. Thus, the environment can increase one's role or responsibility in regulating interaction or it can minimize one's function in the communication system.

5. *The environment can influence the content of verbal communications.* It may seem strange, but what we say to someone is influenced in part by where that person is in relation to us. People seated across a circle from one another tend to verbalize their disagreements with each other. On the other hand, individuals who are seated side-by-side tend to converse on a more intimate, personal level. Sommer has pointed out that the task at hand and the kinds of messages we want to send influence how we arrange ourselves. We position ourselves in relation to others so as to minimize the friction of space and increase the efficiency with which we can send and receive the kinds of messages that brought us into the encounter in the first place.[49] Given a particular task or situation requiring certain kinds of communications, we structure our environment accordingly.

Terminating Interaction

Just as nonverbal behaviors are important in regulating aspects of social interaction, the body and voice provide a mechanism for getting out of an encounter. As we have seen (Chapter 2), Knapp and his associates have

referred to this process of signalling the closing of interaction as the "rhetoric of goodbye."[50]

Although it is not frequently investigated, leave-taking is as important an aspect of interaction as are the other ingredients that help to build a conversation. The process by which we terminate interaction is a crucial interval in the overall interaction ritual. For one thing, unsuccessful or premature cessation of communication is likely to evoke a number of negative interpretations in the abandoned party. Feelings are often hurt; friends are disappointed or confused; prior commitments may be jeopardized. If nothing more, the departing individual may feel awkward or embarrassed by this failure to coordinate a properly timed exit.

Knapp et al. have identified three functions fulfilled by conversational closings.[51] First, by drawing a conversation to a close, conversers can *signal inaccessibility,* indicating that they are no longer available. Greetings, on the other hand, may signal availability. In social settings in which it is possible to enter into more than one conversation, inaccessibility implies a temporary condition. For example, the host or hostess at a cocktail party may feel compelled to move from one cluster of people to another, lingering for a few minutes of interaction, then closing and moving on.

A second function of human leave-taking is the *signalling of supportiveness.* Traditionally, closings are intervals of mutual support and reinforcement, as the participants reflect on points of agreement and their overall satisfaction with the encounter, and exchange promises for renewal. Knapp found that "the anecdotal rule of thumb seems to be that if our interaction has been mutually reinforcing, our leave-taking will be supportive—in spades! Indeed, even when an interaction has been dull or distasteful, leave-taking is still often seen as a 'special time' for being supportive to others."[52]

A last function of leave-taking is *summarization.* The final moments of a conversation or group discussion are often used to highlight the particular achievements of the encounter. In some cases, decisions reached during the discussion are mentioned again. In other instances, summarizing may be less specific, as when two drinking companions remark, "We must have finished off a case apiece." The final series of acts, then, may serve to symbolize achievements, providing a closing testimony to the combined talents of the parties involved.

If these are the functions of leave-taking, exactly *how* is termination accomplished? And what role do nonverbal cues play in the process? In order to answer these questions, Knapp et al. recorded the nonverbal and verbal behavior of interviewees during the forty-five seconds prior to their leaving their seats. These nonverbal behaviors (ranked from most to least frequent) were found to accompany conversational closings:[53]

1. breaking of eye contact
2. left positioning (pointing of interviewee's hands or feet toward the proposed exit)
3. forward lean (leaning of interviewee toward partner with a minimum trunk angle of 45°)
4. nodding behavior
5. major leg movement
6. smiling
7. sweeping hand movement
8. explosive foot movement (the striking of foot against floor)
9. leveraging (use of the hands to assist in rising from chair)
10. trunk movement (straightening posture, leaning back)
11. handshake
12. explosive hand contact (striking of hand either on other parts of the body or on objects)

Of course, some of these behaviors may seem more typical than others of traditional closings. That is because some behaviors are simply more apparent. They are more direct or explicit forms of communication. Also, the fact that these behaviors are used in some fashion by people attempting to part company doesn't imply that all the behaviors perform the same functions. Even though two behaviors (say, nodding and major leg movement) are initiated simultaneously, they may contribute to different functions. Knapp et al. have classified the nonverbal behaviors associated with closings into *subtle* and *direct* cues and into cues that signal *inaccessibility* and those that signal *supportiveness*.[54] (See Table 9.5.)

When Emanuel Schegloff and Harvey Sacks concentrated their research efforts on the study of conversational closings, they brought a very definite research bias: an interest in identifying the *structure of closing*.[55] Schegloff and Sacks agree with Knapp and his associates on at least two points. First, they feel that closing is not an isolated event or a single instance within a conversation but a process involving several determinable stages. Second, they agree that closings are cued on both verbal and nonverbal channels—although Schegloff and Sacks have focused their investigations on the verbal exchanges that precede and accompany the termination of interaction. The central difference between the two groups of researchers is that Knapp et al. have concentrated on identifying the specific behaviors that contribute to closings, while Schegloff and Sacks have been more interested in the steps by which people end a conversation than in the specific signals that are given at each step.

In other respects, Schegloff and Sacks have made a unique contribution to our understanding of conversational closings. First, they have suggested that the *process of reaching conversational closing is a "porous" one*. There is no invariable course that leads to closing. Repeated observations of numerous groups suggest that any party to a conversation can veto attempts to close at any stage up to and including the act of physically parting company. One

Table 9.5 Functions and Cues for
Leavetaking

	Cueing Inaccessibility	Cueing Supportiveness
Subtle	Major leg movement	Forward lean
	Forward lean	Major nodding movement
	Major trunk movements	
	Major nodding movement	
	Smiling behavior	
	Breaking eye contact	
Direct	Sweeping hand movements	Smiling
	Left positioning	Handshake
	Explosive hand contact	
	Explosive foot contact	
	Handshake	

SOURCE: Abbreviated from Knapp et al., "The Rhetoric of Goodbye: Verbal and Nonverbal Correlates of Human Leave-Taking," *Speech Monographs*, 40 (1973), p. 197.

does not merely signal an end to a conversation but instead negotiates it. Without consensus, the conversation has merely broken down rather than terminated.

Second, Schegloff and Sacks point out that *not all conversations require closings*. In some cases, the context and the relationship between the parties either eliminate the need for closing or provide for other (possibly externally established) boundaries to the communication. For example, students conversing before class need not negotiate an end to their conversation, since the instructor's introductory remarks may automatically signal a temporary limit to interaction. Likewise, members of a family need not achieve closure with each subsequent discussion over the course of an evening but are free to leave a topic while performing certain chores (preparing food,

cleaning, answering the door) and renew the interaction later.

Last, *conversational closings are typically composed of at least two elements:* preclosing exchanges and terminal exchanges. *Preclosings* are a minimum of two adjacent turns by which participants signal that the conversation has lost its earlier interest. While preclosings may involve nonverbal markers, it is easier to illustrate the concept with verbal exchanges:

Al: "There is no way to tell about Cindy. She's just crazy!"
Zeke: "Sure is."
[**Al:** "We——ll . . ."]
[**Zeke:** "So——oo . . ."]
Al: "I better get to class. See ya."
Zeke: "Take care."

In the segment above, the two bracketed turns are examples of preclosings. They function much like passes in playing cards. A preclosing is a way of signalling one's reluctance to continue contributing to the topic of conversation; it is a way of checking with the partner to determine whether he or she wishes to continue contributing to the theme. If preclosing statements are exchanged, then the interactants are ready for termination. Termination need not occur, but it may occur. A preclosing appears to be a minimal turn—a brief, nonsubstantive statement—after which the floor is offered to the other participant.

As is the case with preclosings, *terminal exchanges* usually involve a minimum of two adjacent turns that signal the intention to part company. The terminal exchange is traditionally the final feature of conversation and embraces what Schegloff and Sacks refer to as a *signature*. A signature is a set of behaviors chosen by individuals as their distinctive (although not unique) method of signing off. In the conversation between Al and Zeke, the

Alf: "We——ll, I guess . . . if . . ." (Breaks eye contact)

Zoe: "Good!" (Smiles)

Alf: "That's it, huh?" (Major leg movement; left positioning)

Zoe: "I guess, but don't. . . ." (Eye contact gestures)

Alf: "That wasn't so bad, I guess. . . ." (Leveraging; trunk movement)

Zoe: "Weren't we supposed to . . . say somethin' about . . . whether we liked it or not?" (Head tilt; stops gesture)

Alf: "Well, yeah. . . . But we kinda . . . I thought we agreed that . . . yeah we liked it. OK?" (Eye contact; major leg movement)

Zoe: "Yeah, I guess you're right. We all seemed to like it." (Nodding; breaks eye contact; major leg movement)

Alf: "All right?" (Smile; explosive hand contact; forward lean)

Zoe: "OK." (Smile)

Alf: "See ya tomorrow." (Leverage; left positioning; breaks eye contact; forward lean)

Zoe: "OK. Take care." (Smile; leverage; major leg movement; forward lean)

final two turns make up the terminal exchange and suggest their respective signatures.

Figure 9.4 is a typical "casual" leave-taking exchange. See if you can tell how the speakers' turns are serving to structure this termination of interaction.

Summary

Nonverbal messages can work in a number of different ways to determine who should speak, when speech is appropriate, to whom speech may be directed, and even what speakers should say. Our culture shares with many others a notion of interaction that presents a special problem—the notion of turn taking. We rely heavily on nonverbal cues to determine when we should speak. Of course, breakdowns in the system are numerous, but we are never comfortable with the course of a conversation until we negotiate a way to exchange speaking opportunities in a smooth and efficient manner.

Listeners can help out in the negotiation process. Listeners do not remain immobile while another person is speaking. They can provide important feedback through the backchannel. A listener can pace, confirm, acknowledge, or reject a speaker.

The environment, too, plays an important role in the regulation of communication. Seating, the arrangement of furniture, and room size can all influence whom we choose to interact with, when we communicate, and what we say. Nonverbal cues are also important in determining whether we initiate interaction with others and how we get out of conversations, bringing them to a close. We rely especially on trunk movements to communicate positions or attitudes and to segment conversations into episodes or themes.

Suggested Reading

Berger, C., and Calabrese, R. "Some Explorations in Initial Interaction and Beyond: Toward a Developmental Theory of Interpersonal Communication." *Human Communication Research*, 1 (1975), 98–112.

Berscheid, E., and Walster, E. "Physical Attractiveness." In L. Berkowitz (ed.), *Advances in Experimental Social Psychology*. New York: Academic Press, 1973.

Bruneau, T. "Communicative Silences: Forms and Functions." *Journal of Communication*, 23 (1973), 17–47.

Duncan, S. "Interaction Units During Speaking Turns in Dyadic, Face-To-Face Conversations." In A. Kendon, R. Harris, and M. Key (eds.), *Organization of Behavior in Face-To-Face Interaction*. The Hague: Mouton, 1975.

Goffman, E. *Behavior in Public Places*. New York: Bobbs-Merrill, 1963.

Knapp, M., Hart, R., Friedrich, G., and Schulman, G. "The Rhetoric of Goodbye: Verbal and Nonverbal Correlates of Human Leave-Taking." *Speech Monographs*, 40 (1973), 182–198.

Scheflen, A. *How Behavior Means*. New York: Doubleday, 1974.

Schegloff, E., and Sacks, H. "Opening Up Closings." *Semiotica*, 8 (1973), 289–327.

Notes

1. C. Berger and R. Calabrese, "Some Explorations in Initial Interaction and Beyond: Toward a Developmental Theory of Interpersonal Communication," *Human Communication Research*, 1 (1975), pp. 98–112.

2. A. Miller, "Role of Physical Attractiveness in Impression Formation," *Psychonomic Science*, 19 (1970), pp. 241–243.

3. E. Walster, V. Aronson, D. Abrahams, and L. Rottmann, "Importance of Physical Attractiveness in Dating Behavior," *Journal of Personality and Social Psychology*, 4 (1966), pp. 508–516; R. Brislin and S. Lewis, "Dating and Physical Attractiveness: Replication," *Psychological Reports*, 22 (1968), p. 976.

4. D. Byrne, C. Ervin, and J. Lamberth, "Continuity Between the Experimental Study of Attraction and Real-Life-Computer Dating," *Journal of Personality and Social Psychology*, 16 (1970), pp. 157–165.

5. E. Berscheid and E. Walster, "Physical Attractiveness," in L. Berkowitz (ed.), *Advances in Experimental Social Psychology*, Vol. 7 (New York: Academic Press, 1973).

6. In light of the evidence supporting the role of physical attractiveness in initial interactions, one discrepant finding should be mentioned: see C. Berger and M. Larimer, "When Beauty is Only Skin Deep: The Effects of Physical Attractiveness, Sex, and Time on Initial Interaction," paper delivered at the International Communication Association Convention, New Orleans, 1974.

7. C. Goodwin, "The Construction of the Utterance in Natural Conversation as a Communicating Process," paper delivered at the International Communication Association Convention, Portland, 1976.

8. E. Goffman, *Behavior in Public Places* (New York: Free Press of Glencoe, 1963), p. 84.

9. E. Goffman, p. 84 (note 8).

10. From *Soziologie,* cited in R. Parks and E. Burgers, *Introduction to the Science of Sociology* (Chicago: University of Chicago Press, 1924), p. 358.

11. E. Goffman, p. 84 (note 8).

12. M. Patterson and L. Sechrest, "Interpersonal Distance and Impression Formation," *Journal of Personality,* 38 (1970), pp. 161–166.

13. J. Jaffe and S. Feldstein, *Rhythms of Dialogue* (New York: Academic Press, 1970), p. 19.

14. J. Wiemann and M. Knapp, "Turn-Taking in Conversations," *Journal of Communication,* 25 (1975), p. 75.

15. Jaffe and Feldstein (note 13).

16. S. Duncan, Jr., "Some Signals and Rules for Taking Speaking Turns in Conversations," *Journal of Personality and Social Psychology,* 23 (1972), pp. 283–292.

17. Duncan, p. 185 (note 16).

18. Duncan (note 16).

19. J. Wiemann, "An Exploratory Study of Turn-Taking in Conversations: Verbal and Nonverbal Behavior," unpublished M.S. thesis, Purdue University, 1973.

20. Wiemann and Knapp (note 14).

21. See S. Duncan, Jr., "Interaction Units During Speaking Turns in Dyadic, Face-To-Face Conversations," in A. Kendon, R. Harris, and M. Key (eds.), *Organization of Behavior in Face-to-Face Interaction* (The Hague: Mouton, 1975).

22. P. Ekman and W. Friesen, "The Repertoire of Nonverbal Behavior: Categories, Origins, Usage, and Coding," *Semiotica,* 1 (1969), pp. 49–98.

23. A. Dittmann, "Developmental Factors in Conversational Behavior," *Journal of Communication,* 22 (1972), p. 404.

24. Dittmann, p. 405 (note 23).

25. T. Bruneau, "Communicative Silences: Forms and Functions," *Journal of Communication,* 23 (1973), pp. 17–46.

26. F. Goldman-Eisler, *Psycholinguistics: Experiments in Spontaneous Speech* (London: Academic Press, 1968).

27. Goldman-Eisler (note 26).

28. E. Black, "A Consideration of the Rhetorical Causes of Breakdown in Discussion," *Speech Monographs,* 22 (1955), pp. 15–19.

29. Duncan (note 21).

30. T. Saine, "Synchronous and Concatenous Behavior: Two Models of Rule-Violation in Conversational Interaction," paper delivered at the Southeastern Psychological Association Convention, New Orleans, 1976.

31. W. Condon and W. Ogston, "A Segmentation of Behavior," *Journal of Psychiatric Research,* 5 (1967), pp. 221–235.

32. M. Argyle, *Social Interaction* (Baltimore: Methuen, 1967), p. 171; E. Rogers and R. Farace, "Analysis of Relational Communications in Dyads: New Measurement Procedures," *Human Communication Research,* 1 (1975), pp. 222–239; W. Soskin and U. John, "The Study of Spontaneous Talk," in R. Barker (ed.), *The Stream of Behavior* (New York: Appleton-Century-Crofts, 1963).

33. Jaffe and Feldstein (note 13).

34. Duncan (note 21).

35. A. Scheflen, *How Behavior Means* (New York: Doubleday, 1974).

36. F. Erickson, "One Function of Proxemic Shifts in Face-to-Face Interaction," in A. Kendon, R. Harris, and M. Key (eds.), *Organization of Behavior in Face-to-Face Interaction* (The Hague: Mouton, 1975), pp. 175–188.

37. J. Blom and J. Gumperz, "Social Meaning in Linguistics Structure: Code Switching in Norway," in J. Gumperz and P. Hymes (eds.), *Directions in Sociolinguistics: The Ethnography of Communication* (New York: Holt, Rinehart and Winston, 1972).

38. Erickson, p. 176 (note 36).

39. R. E. Pittinger, C. F. Hockett, and J. Darehy, *The First Five Minutes* (Ithaca, N.Y.: P. Martineau, 1960), p. 45b.

40. E. Schegloff and H. Sacks, "Opening Up Closing," *Semiotica,* 8 (1973), p. 304.

41. Pittinger, p. 255 (note 39).

42. R. Sommer, *Personal Space* (Englewood Cliffs, N.J.: Prentice-Hall, 1969).

43. J. K. Heston and P. Garner, "A Study of Personal Spacing and Desk Arrangement in a Learning Environment," paper presented at the International Communication Association Convention, Atlanta, Georgia, 1972.

44. Sommer, 1969 (note 42).

45. B. Steinzor, "The Spatial Factor in Face to Face Discussion Groups," *Journal of Abnormal and Social Psychology,* 45 (1950), pp. 552–555.

46. R. Sommer, "Small Group Ecology," *Psychological Bulletin,* 67 (1967), p. 146.

47. L. Festinger, S. Schacter, and K. Back, *Social Pressures in Informal Groups: A Study of Human Factors in Housing* (New York: Harper and Row, 1950).

48. H. J. Leavitt, "Some Effects of Certain Communication Patterns in Group Performance," *Journal of Abnormal and Social Psychology,* 46 (1951), pp. 38–50; F. L. Strodtbeck and L. H. Hook, "The Social Dimensions of a Twelve Man Jury Table," *Sociometry,* 24 (1961), pp. 397–415.

49. Sommer, 1967, p. 147 (note 46).

50. M. Knapp, R. Hart, G. Friedrich, and G. Schulman, "The Rhetoric of Goodbye: Verbal and Nonverbal Correlates of Human Leave-Taking," *Speech Monographs,* 40 (1973), pp. 182–198.

51. Knapp, pp. 184–186 (note 50).

52. Knapp, p. 185 (note 50).

53. Knapp, p. 191 (note 50).

54. Knapp, p. 197 (note 50).

55. Schegloff and Sacks, pp. 289–327 (note 40).

10

The Presentation of Self

Test Your Sensitivity

True or False?

1. A successful performer segregates his or her audiences.
2. Cosmetics, cologne, and contact lenses are items that might be found in one's *identity kit.*
3. Hair color or freckles can be a source of role stigmatization.
4. The face is the best area for providing cues that signal deception.
5. We frequently rely on micro facial expressions for information about people with whom we interact.

What were my feelings then and now about Ali? What kind of man, at bottom, did I find him to be?

He is a chameleon—a man of many moods. Open, expansive, gay and charming. Full of fun and mischief. Gregarious. Born to perform. But sullen, petulant and sometimes cruel. Without formal education but with native brightness and vocally quick. A very short attention span. A practical joker. A man of inordinate courage; how else to explain the willingness to have a career destroyed, to give up millions of dollars, to defy the authority of the United States, to risk the abuse of multimillions of people? A man of unquestioned sincerity in his religious belief. A man with an inborn need for that belief. . . . A mercurial man, impenetrable, a man who will always puzzle and confuse me. But, always, a salesman.

I was present at what I would regard as his denouement, against Ken Norton, when in the throes of inexplicable defeat and humiliation and pain, his only words to me were a final attempt at humor. To the end, he played a part.[1]

By the end of the chapter, you should know the correct answer to all five questions and understand these concepts:

- self-presentation
- kinds of social roles
- front regions and personal front
- back regions and backstage language
- stage, wings, and specialist roles
- elements of a successful performance
- performance violations
- frames, keys, and negative experiences
- stigmatized roles
- leakage, microexpressions, and deception cues

What Howard Cosell has recognized about Muhammad Ali is that he is a master performer; he is capable of controlling and manipulating his image. In a way, we are all performers, attempting day by day and minute by minute to make others see us as we want to be seen. We are impression managers, actors, chameleons.

In this chapter, we shall explore some of the ingredients necessary for successful self-presentation and the role nonverbal behavior plays in our various performances. We shall investigate those performances that require special nonverbal skills and discuss research on deceptive performances and ways of gleaning evidence that someone is concealing or distorting information.

The notion of self-presentation is certainly not new. For many years, sociologists have been explaining human behavior by reference to social *roles*, which are clusters of behaviors, attitudes, responsibilities, and opportunities appropriate to a certain position in a social structure. In many instances, roles require negotiation among individuals. Roles such as husband or wife, best friend, confidant, secretary, or legal adviser generally require the parties involved to clarify their expectations and determine their ability and willingness to perform the various roles. Persons seeking out these roles are probably doing some self-analysis to determine how prepared or willing they are to act in a way that is fully consistent with the roles.

Some roles, of course, are not open to negotiation, such as sex roles, brother or sister, uncle or aunt. Biological factors are the basis of eligibility for these roles. When the prevailing expectations for a role are inconsistent with one's values, one may choose either to avoid the role, to modify and redefine the role to suit his or her concept of self, or to present him- or herself in ways that are consistent with the role and suppress or change accompanying feelings of guilt and frustration.

Regardless of the kind of role being assumed or one's satisfaction with the prevailing definition of the role, an investigation of social roles invariably raises questions concerning one's performance in that role. The way in which we choose to present ourselves to others is based on our choice of social roles, our understanding of the role, and the performing skills that can be brought to bear in executing the role.

Three Theories of Role Playing

Role theory has generally failed to explain how a person goes about consciously preparing to assume a role. Three theoretical perspectives have contributed greatly to our understanding of how a communicator conveys impressions through nonverbal behaviors. E. E. Jones has advanced *ingratiation theory* as an explanation of how people give a favorable impression of themselves.[2] Jones has focused on a specific set of *ingratiatory* behaviors—that is, behaviors that bring one into the good graces of another. As a general strategy, ingratiation is an attempt to increase one's attractiveness to another by generating an appreciation for certain personal qualities. The primary motive underlying self-presentation, according to Jones, is the desire to be seen as attractive. A person can, through subtle nonverbal and verbal actions, maximize another's feelings of attraction. And attraction is power. We tend not to jeopardize or criticize those to whom we are attracted. Consequently, by increasing our attractiveness to others, we make it possible to act without fear of reprisal.[3]

Impression management theory provides a second perspective on self-presentation. Impression management advocates have argued that individuals consciously conduct themselves in ways that enlarge their impact and influence upon others.[4] We tailor our self-presentations to the audience at hand, building our presentation on the kinds of prior information about us that an audience may have and adapting our communications to their needs, attitudes, and values. Therefore, we can study a leader's success with a group, a speaker's success with an audience, or a teacher's success with a class by investigating the kinds of impressions constructed, the verbal and nonverbal behaviors employed, and the suitability of the impression to the audience.

Dramaturgic analysis combines elements of both ingratiation theory and impression management theory. It is this theory with which we shall concern ourselves throughout the rest of this chapter. Dramaturgic analysis explores how the performer goes about "staging" the performance of his or her role. Erving Goffman has done much to advance our understanding of the various techniques, strategies, problems, and verbal as well as nonverbal skills that may be necessary to the successful enactment of a role—the successful presentation of self.

As Goffman has explained the term, *self-presentation* is more than the staging of a socially or biologically determined role. It is a process whereby we constantly attempt to communicate impressions of ourselves to others.[5] In most instances, these impressions transcend a specific role. Roles are just scenes within a larger dramatic performance, having as its goal the selling of ourselves to others.

Goffman's theory of dramaturgic analysis reflects much of the functional approach to the study of nonverbal communication that we described in Chapter 2. His theory is known as *dramaturgic* because of the analogy it draws between self-presentation and theater. Of course, control over and the effective use of various nonverbal codes are important to any successful dramatic presentation whether it takes place on a theater stage or on the many informal stages where we carry out social, interpersonal encounters.

Elements of Dramaturgic Analysis

Aspects of the Dramatic Setting

In *Presentation of Self in Everyday Life*, Goffman develops the analogy between social encounters and the theater, describing the various factors involved in self-presentation in theatrical terms. Goffman uses the term *performance* to refer to the total range of behaviors displayed by an individual in the presence of a specific group of observers and upon whom the behaviors are designed to achieve some impact. In this respect, we are all actors, capable of playing many parts and having to give various performances during the course of each day. Observers—people not directly involved in the dramatic performance—constitute the audience.

Each performance is staged at a particular location, or stage, within which there is a specific region where the performer conducts the dramatic action. For example, classrooms are often the staging areas for a certain type of dramatic production referred to as instruction. The physical boundaries of the classroom are also the physical boundaries of the staging area; but within the physical expanse of the classroom, only certain areas are used by the teacher in conducting the performance. These areas are often referred to as the *front region*. For many instructors, this encompasses the open area between the seats and the blackboard.

Goffman has used the term *front* to embrace all forms of expressive equipment that assist the performer in defining the dramatic situation for the audience. This includes objects associated with the setting (chairs in a room, blackboard, dining table, napkins) that provide information about the kinds of dramatic action that are likely to follow, as well as the expressive equipment intimately associated with the performer. This equipment he calls the *personal front*. A performer's personal front includes both physical appearance—which primarily indicates the performer's social status—and manner. *Manner* may involve facial expression, posture, rate of movement—any action that forewarns the audience of either the interaction role to be taken by the performer in subsequent performances or the performer's attitude toward the role.

Clothing is an important aspect of personal front. Clothes provide a major means of defining the situation for the audience (see Fig. 10.1). John Molloy, who refers to himself as a "wardrobe engineer," has served as a clothing consultant to a number of prominent national and international figures. Clothes, Molloy has contended, speak for the wearer, letting others know who one is and how one is to be treated. Molloy observed that former President Gerald Ford learned a good deal about how clothes can project the impression of leadership: "If you have a man who is running for the presidency of the United States, he must say 'I am leader.' One of the things Jerry Ford . . .

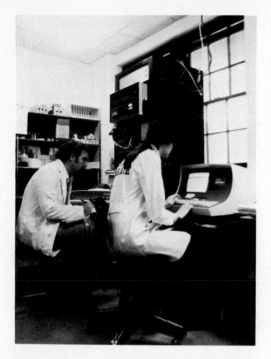

Figure 10.1   Compare the two photos. How are setting and personal front altered to suit two different performances?

learned is how to dress like a president. When he first got into office he wore some of the wildest-looking ties you ever saw. He said, 'I'm good old Jer. Follow me to the golf course.'"[6]

Clothes serve not only to distinguish an actor from his or her audience but also to create the appearance of similarity between performer and audience. In this respect, one can dress down or up to one's audience. According to Molloy, George Wallace's appearance is reassuring to middle-class Southerners, but to upper-middle-class Northerners it says, "I am a southern rube."

Just as there is a front region on which performances take place, there is a backstage area as well. It has physical as well as psychological features. The backstage is that area beyond

the sight and hearing of the audience in which the performer feels free to escape the constraints of the role and to act and speak in a more informal, less consistent, and more spontaneous way. The psychological advantage of a backstage area is that it allows a performer the opportunity to relax, to rehearse lines, and to prepare for future interaction. A professor's office is an example of a backstage area.

Goffman has pointed out that performers often use the backstage as a private forum for expressing dissatisfaction with their own performances, derogating the audience, and generally engaging in behaviors that contradict the performance, including smoking, undressing, swearing, and grooming. For example, dancers may slump, move awkwardly, cough, belch, cry, or indulge in any number of behaviors that must be suppressed on stage for the sake of a successful performance.

In a theater, the regions to either side of the stage are referred to as the *wings*. In Goffman's scheme, the wings are any areas away from the stage in which are located either people or equipment that may assist the performer in the execution of the role. At a party, the kitchen may fulfill the function of the wings, providing storage for equipment, various utensils, and accessories that are important to the performance of host or hostess.

It is important to understand that our performances are seldom totally independent productions. We often rely on others to perform simply services either prior to or during a performance—services we cannot, or choose not to, perform by ourselves. These supporting individuals fulfill *specialist roles*. They are not considered to be a part of the actual dramatic scene, but they do facilitate the actor's preparation. The two specialist roles are *technical* and *training* specialist. The technical specialist can be thought of as someone who provides a skill or performs a function required by the nature of the performance (a cook at a restaurant, a hairdresser, a tailor). The training specialist is someone who *instructs* the performer in the various actions that make up the performance itself. Anyone who functions as an adviser, teacher, or counsel can be considered a training specialist. Often our parents, brothers and sisters, roommates, and friends find themselves fulfilling the training functions for us.

Elements of a Successful Performance

There are a number of principles that are basic to the successful presentation of self.

1. *A performer must segregate audiences.* In the course of a day, each of us may find it necessary to perform contradicting parts. If a performance is to seem credible to an audience, the audience must not have the opportunity to witness the performer in some obviously inconsistent role.

2. *A performer should be aware of and adhere to requirements of decorum that accompany dramatic action.* Our society has established a number of rules governing civilized social and interpersonal encounters. It is important to the successful presentation of self that the performer be aware of and avoid intentionally or accidentally violating the rules of conduct. (In some situations, as in Figure 10.2, the rules allow behavior that in other situations would appear very indecorous.) Goffman distinguishes between *moral* and *instrumental* requirements of decorum: "Moral requirements are ends in themselves and presumably refer to rules regarding non-interference and non-molestation of others, rules regarding sexual propriety, rules regarding respect for sacred places, etc. Instrumental requirements are not ends in themselves and presumably refer to duties such as an employer might demand of his employees—care of property, maintenance of work levels, etc."[7] Violations of rules regarding decorum may invalidate a performance, showing the performer to possess socially undesirable traits.

3. *A performer must coordinate verbal and nonverbal codes to create an impression.* It is a mistake to assume that if you have mastered the rhetoric of an impression, then the body language is under control. Goffman argues that, though verbal behavior is relatively easy to monitor and control, it is very difficult for us to know precisely what message our face and body are conveying. He calls these behaviors the *ungovernable aspects* of expressive behavior.[8] Most people are unaware of the uncontrollable nature of facial expressions and body movements. Later in this chapter, we shall explore the kinds of cues to deception that leak out through our nonverbal behavior.

4. *For a performance to be accepted by an audience, the actor must be judged to be sincere.* In many cases, the voice and body betray our words and create suspicions of insincerity.

Figure 10.2 In performance: Billy Sunday, famous evangelist of the first third of the twentieth century. (Wide World Photos)

5. *An actor must appear satisfied with the role.* Goffman has referred to this as the "impression of sacred compatibility" between an individual and the job. Whatever the action demanded of a performer, the presentation will not be successful if the audience does not sense a coordination between actor and role. For example, a doctor who appears to be too young may not seem suited to a position of such responsibility. Kenneth Burke refers to much the same condition as *actor–act ratio.*[9] If an action is not appropriate to an actor, then the credibility of the performance must be in doubt.

It is characteristic of successful performances that the action reveals an idealized actor—an actor performing an idealized version of the role. Goffman points out that most of us have an ideal self that usually departs in some significant respect from our self-concept. Since we seldom desire others to sense our self-doubt, confusion, and insecurity, we portray our skills and strengths and conceal the aspects of self that are not respectable and, if known, might jeopardize the outcome of the interaction.

Performance Violations

Just as there are ingredients that go into the development of a successful performance, there are important nonverbal sources of *invalidity*—actions that may contradict the impression one wishes to present to others. First, "a performer may accidentally convey incapacity, impropriety, or disrespect by momentarily losing muscular control of himself."[10] An actor may suffer temporary loss of coordination or may stutter, cough, sneeze, stumble, or otherwise divert the audience's attention away from the performance and raise questions about his or her self-control. Consider the effect that developing the hiccups would have on the prospects for carrying on a serious romantic encounter.

Second, an actor may jeopardize a performance by appearing too little or too much involved in the part. Each actor is expected to demonstrate a certain *attitude toward the role*. Individuals who do not show the proper attitude can achieve undesired dramatic effects. Excessive involvement or interest in or concern for a role can result in tension, anxiety, feelings of stress, breakdowns in behavioral patterns, perspiration, hesitations in speech, wrenching of hands, exaggerated gestures, and the like.

Last, a presentation may "suffer from inadequate dramaturgic direction."[11] Failure on the part of the actor to be aware of props, lighting, and provisions for comfort such as temperature and seating can invalidate a performance. By not taking into consideration the special architectural features of the staging area, the actor may develop a script that does not fit the setting. Inadequate dramaturgic direction may occur when a performer is unaware of the available equipment, unaware of how to use the equipment, or has failed to arrange equipment properly prior to a performance. The following incident illustrates lack of dramaturgic control and direction:

Another drunken occasion. . . . [A] group of New Yorker writers has been invited up to Bennington. We have been asked to conduct a panel discussion on the current state of magazine journalism. . . . [T]here is reason to suppose that something informative may emerge from the discussion. Unfortunately, the hospitality provided by the Bennington girls at a cocktail party held in our honor before the discussion proves far too lavish for our good. We reach the auditorium in a state of total obfuscation. Making matters worse is the fact that we must rely on a public-address system to make ourselves heard and there is only a single microphone to be passed up and down

---

mini-experiment

Ask a number of people to pose for individual photographs. Instruct them to pose in a way that reflects how they would like to be seen by others, paying special attention to dress, lighting, environmental objects. Note their use of nonverbal codes. How did each person use nonverbal behaviors to create an impression? What features make up each one's personal front? What kinds of attributes are suggested by the setting?

---

the length of a trestle table. In the course of being fumbled over and shoved back and forth by unsteady hands, the mike quickly falls to pieces. We all babble on more or less inaudibly, often laughing with delight at the good points we are scoring. An intermission has been scheduled, after which the plan is for the audience to return and put questions to the panelists. When the intermission is over and we resume our seats on the platform, there is no audience. It is literally the case that not a single person has returned to ask a question. A few days later, I receive a small check from the bursar of the college, thanking my colleagues and me for our "performance."[12]

Frames and Performances

Every successful performance is made possible in part by the audience's willingness to interpret dramatic action in the way in which it is intended. In many cases, a skillful actor takes deliberate precautions to cue the audience as to how action should be interpreted; in other instances, the situation itself or some aspect of the situation indicates to the audience the frame of mind in which the action should be viewed. This attitude or perspective for viewing performances is what Goffman has referred to as *frame*. [13] A difference in frames can dramatically change the viewer's understanding of the event. Consider this situation: you walk into a building and find a naked woman seated atop a desk. The proper frame becomes evident when you learn that you have walked into an advanced art class and the woman is a professional model. To understand the significance of the action properly, one must acquire a professional frame (as have the students in the class) for interpreting the event. Any other frame might distort the action. A frame helps answer the question "What is going on here?" It implies rules for assigning meaning; it defines what is important; it structures and organizes behavior so that certain actions make sense.

Nonverbal behaviors perform a crucial role in communicating frames. First, by the judicious arrangement of objects, clothing, and so on, an actor can let the audience know what kind of performance they can expect to view. Nonverbal messages are often the primary source of information for an audience as to the appropriate frame for viewing an interaction. For example, when you go to a doctor for a physical examination, you expect the doctor to have a certain frame and to demonstrate it to your satisfaction. Seldom, though, does a doctor actually have to indicate verbally what that frame is. The decor of the office, the sanitary, almost sterile nature of the environment, the presence of other patients, the array of medical journals, the display of medical degrees all contribute to your expectations regarding a doctor's professional performance.

The body can also serve the function of *frame maintenance*. [14] In *Frame Analysis*, Goffman illustrates the importance of frame maintenance with a reference to male gynecologists: "The gynecological examination is even today a matter of some concern, special effort being taken to infuse the procedure with

terms and action that keep sexual readings in check." [15] Or, as Henslin and Biggs say, "Body posture, the use of equipment, indifferent expressions, and a systematic procedure which does not vary from one examination to the next are necessary to avoid sexual interpretation of the action." [16]

Goffman acknowledges a third role the body can perform with respect to the communication of frames. The body can be used as a *key* to indicate that a frame traditionally associated with a particular action is not the appropriate frame for understanding what is going on. Keying involves a kind of *transformation of meaning*. When changing frames, we usually send a number of keys to indicate when the new frame takes effect and when it is no longer appropriate. Make-believe situations (situations in which some fantasy or fabrication is consciously being enacted), contests (boxing, sparring, fox hunting, fencing, and so on), ceremonials (weddings, coronations, ordinations), technical reenactments (performances undertaken with the understanding that the consequences are not the typical ones and that the purpose behind the performance is instructional) are examples of types of performances that rely on certain keys to indicate to observers that the meaning intended by the action departs in some way from traditional interpretations.

For example, during a football game, a great deal of physical contact occurs between opposing linemen. The prevailing frame entails rules indicating that certain aggressive physical behaviors are permissible. Occasionally aggression gets out of hand, and one player indicates to another that the action has approached the limits allowable in the contest. A cheap shot (a late hit, an excessively hard tackle, or an unnecessary blow to the head) keys others to interpret the action as personal, dangerous, and illegal.

A variety of social *simulations* (games in which individuals use role-playing situations that simulate actual social issues) are used as classroom exercises to illustrate the dynamics of a problem. In these cases, provisions are often taken to prevent accidental keyings that might indicate that the action is real instead of simulated. In the same way, children playing at fighting provide a number of keys to demonstrate that their intentions are not serious, such as the avoidance of hard blows, the interjection of laughter, and the use of exaggerated movements.

Dimensions of Self-Presentation

As we have seen, in the course of a day, each of us is involved in a number of different performances, some quite contradictory. Our performances may differ because one role requires that we present ourselves in a way that is entirely the opposite of some other role. Most of us attempt to keep these differences to a minimum because of the risks involved in maintaining two diametrically opposed impressions of ourselves. Nevertheless, we must often present ourselves in ways that stress different qualities or emphasize different dimensions of our presentational self.

Marc Reiss, Dorothy Fieldbinder, and Harvey Abrams have explored the dimensions underlying self-presentations.[17] Their research has indicated that at least six dimensions underlie the impressions we attempt to sell to others. These dimensions are: (1) *attraction*, (2) *depth*, (3) *expertise*, (4) *status*, (5) *prestige*, and (6) *believability*.

It is easier to understand the concept of *dimension* in terms of *goals* or *judgments*. When we set out to construct an impression for others, we usually have in mind certain goals that we wish to achieve, such as appearing attractive or believable. In other words, we are trying to get others to judge us in particular ways. We shall consider briefly each dimension and the kinds of nonverbal behaviors that Reiss, Fieldbinder, and Abrams have found to be em-

ployed to achieve that particular judgment. Table 10.1 summarizes the role of nonverbal codes in conveying these impressions.[18]

Promoting Attraction

There are many ways to make oneself attractive to others through nonverbal behavior. Forward lean, relaxed posture, and fluid gestures have been shown to increase feelings of friendliness in others.[19] By contrast, leaning closer than normal, gesturing aggressively, or staring gives an impression of unfriendliness.

We can also use proxemic and haptic cues to signal attractiveness and to encourage reciprocal feelings. Research has shown that closeness and brief contact are perceived as friendliness and can promote liking.[20] For example, library clerks receive more positive evaluations when they briefly touch people at the check-out counter.

As for vocal messages, we can contribute to our attractiveness to others by showing *immediacy* (directness and attention).[21] Utterances that confirm a speaker (*um hum, yeah*) stimulate attraction. We can do the same thing through the face by using eye contact to show attentiveness; by changing facial expressions in response to a speaker's content, we can indicate approval, involvement, and sincerity. On the other hand, extremes in the rate, pitch volume, and pauses in our speaking behavior can lower our attractiveness to others.[22]

Communicating Depth

Every relationship can be described in terms of *depth*, although a better word might be *familiarity*. In other words, how well do the individuals know one another? We convey familiarity through body movements that show we are at ease. Some evidence indicates that there is a simple, positive correlation between amount of facial and gestural expressiveness

Table 10.1 Nonverbal Impression Management: Key Words

Nonverbal Channel	Dimension of Impressions					
	Attraction	Depth	Expertise	Status	Prestige	Believability
Kinesics	Immediacy Relaxation Familiarity	Familiarity Emotion	Appropriate performance skills	Body orientation	Reinforcement	Reinforcement
Proxemics	Interpersonal distance	Interpersonal distance		Seating arrangements Violations of space	Territorial markers	Interpersonal distance
Vocalics	Immediacy	Familiarity Emotion	Appropriate performance skills	Interruptions	Reinforcement	Reinforcement
Haptics	Presence of touch Mutual touching	Pressure Location		Presence of touch		
Physical appearance	Somatype Preening behavior	Adornment	Adornment Uniform	Clothing Uniform Props	Uniform	Physical attractiveness
Environment and objects	Material aspects (regulatory)		Furnishings	Furnishings Props Scenes	Ownership Props	
Chronemics	Promptness	Concession and sacrifice time	Task completion time Promptness	Waiting time	Reinforcement Latency	Reinforcement

and the depth of a relationship.[23] Similarly, we can communicate intimacy through close interpersonal distance.[24]

Emotional displays can do much to define the level of intimacy between two people. Our willingness to show certain emotions and convey certain feelings can indicate a level of familiarity that one would not wish to show to a stranger.

Research by Sidney Jourard has emphasized the role of touch in conveying familiarity and intimacy.[25] Jourard found that *where* we touch others and the *number* of touches clearly indicate intimacy.

Showing Expertise

As we mentioned earlier, the appearance of competence is often crucial to a performance. It is difficult to pinpoint specific kinesic behaviors that suggest expertise, but researchers generally agree that behaviors that accompany task-related verbal messages tend to portray the individual as competent for the task. One can show competence vocally in several ways. Recall from Chapter 7 that General American dialect communicates more competence than, say, southern or New England dialect. Fluent speech can also contribute to the overall impression that you know what you are saying. Fast rates of speech and loud speech tend to increase another's judgment of one's expertise, but they usually lower perceptions of attractiveness.

There is little empirical research to clarify the role of touch in promoting the impression of competence. (We shall discuss later in this chapter how touch, specifically by doctors during examinations and interviews, can generate confidence—or distrust—in patients.) There are right and wrong ways to touch in order to give a certain impression. For example, touch is a crucial factor in a surgeon's conveying an impression of competence. The hands are such an important feature of the surgeon's profession that the slightest suggestion of awkwardness or insensitivity could jeopardize the impression.

Perhaps the most obvious way in which physical appearance communicates expertise is through the use of uniforms and insignia. From medals for marksmanship awarded in the military to black belts for karate instructors, dress and insignia separate the expert from the novice.

Time also plays a role in conveying competence. Assignments, tests, attendance all require students to be on time. A student who does not operate within the limits of the allotted time is judged to be less competent than others. People who are perpetually late or tardy are generally thought of as less competent than those who are punctual.

Reflecting Status

Research has shown that, if you want to communicate an elevated status, you should maintain a rigid posture, touch others more than they touch you, smile less than others, and gaze less at them than they look at you.[26] You might also want to sit at the head of a table, assume the right to violate others' interpersonal space, interrupt others, and keep others waiting for you. While these behaviors would certainly lower your attractiveness to others, they are nevertheless correlates of status and position.

Status, like expertise, is easily communicated through apparel (see Fig. 10.3). An interesting experiment reflects the change in status that dress can make. Hoult asked people to rank faces and clothing in terms of social status. He then placed the low-ranked faces with the high-ranked clothes and vice versa.[27] The results indicated that people's perceptions of the status of a face depended greatly on the clothing associated with the face. (See Chapter

7 for other cues associated with status that may be manipulated to create the proper impression.)

Promoting Prestige

Prestige is the value placed on what a person does or can do or the resources available for use by that person. Behaviors that reinforce others tend to elevate prestige. By nodding, smiling, and encouraging others, we can increase their judgments of our importance and value. We can also convey importance by showing independence from others. Often we

use *territorial markers* to indicate ownership of property and resources that distinguish what we have from what others have. Simply by leaving your books at a table in the library, you can communicate temporary ownership or control of property. Although the library is public territory, people will ask if they can sit at *your* table.

Bolstering Believability

If you want to be believed and have what you say accepted as truth, then make sure that you never unintentionally convey inconsistency or

Figure 10.3

Hiroji Kubota/Magnum

signal deception. In other words, synchronize your verbal and nonverbal behaviors. Too little or too much expressiveness can cause suspicion. In the next section of this chapter, we shall explore some of the behaviors that can lead others to suspect you of deception.

Special Types of Self-Presentation

By circumstance or choice, an actor may find him- or herself involved in a situation that demands a special performance, one requiring specific dramaturgic skills and consideration and posing new implications for the use of nonverbal codes. Four roles in particular can be said to represent special forms of self-presentation: the team performance, institutional roles, stigmatized roles, and negative experiences.

Team Performances

In many situations, one actor alone cannot achieve as successful and convincing a performance as two or more actors working together. Sometimes the demands are simply too great for one actor to meet. In other instances, an actor chooses to involve others in order to heighten action, enliven the performance, and create the impression of a spontaneous, authentic encounter. Improving one's own self-presentation is not the only reason for team performances. In some cases, the impression being communicated is not of an individual but of a larger unit. For example, husbands and wives often work together to achieve a successful performance, communicating an impression of the happily married couple. This team performance may be contradictory to the individual goals of specific team members; but personal goals that are not consistent with the team performance must be suppressed. Goffman has defined a *team* as "a set of individuals whose intimate cooperation is required if a given projected definition of the situation is to be maintained. A team is a grouping, but it is a grouping not in relation to a social structure or social organization but rather in relation to an interaction or series of interactions in which the relevant definition of the situation is maintained."[28] The co-performers, then, are not necessarily friends, nor are they of equal social status. Their interaction with one another merely helps the members of the audience establish an understanding of the situation.

Two friends may portray themselves as enemies for the purpose of staging a performance. Howard Cosell recalls an encounter with Muhammad Ali:

Driving across the Seventy-ninth Street Causeway to Miami, Ali said, "I'm going to take you to the ghetto to meet my people. You'll see what life is really like." His first stop was at a pool parlor. We jumped out of the car and went in, with Ali yelling. "Here he is, here's the white guy who gives me all that trouble on television." It was a dingy, smelly place filled with what were doubtless habitues. The shades were drawn, the only lights those above the tables. The scene looked like one of those dust jackets on books about junkies. "Knock it off," I whispered. "These guys might take you seriously." But nothing would contain him. He kept on egging them on as they gathered around him and me, and I began to get more and more nervous. Then abruptly, in that manner so characteristic of him, he threw an arm around my shoulder and said, "I'm only kidding. He's my friend." And then he leaned into my ear and said, "Call me nigger." No way, I may have a few years left.[29]

A variety of factors may converge to pressure an individual into teaming with another in order to communicate a believable impression. In some cases, the needs are professional (see Fig. 10.4), while in other instances, the forces may be biological or sexual. Here are some of the more obvious partnerships:

dance partners
husband—wife
musicians
news commentators
twins
roommates
romantic couples

lawyer—client
secretary—boss
team teachers
bridge partners
mountain climbers
doctor—patient

Team performances and individual performances require different kinds of dramaturgic controls. Teams must initially convince the audience that they are in fact a team and that their individual performances should be viewed as part of a larger dramatic production.

Nonverbal behavior plays an important part in creating and sustaining this impression. Clothes are an important factor in fostering the illusion of a team. By wearing similar clothes, teammates give the appearance of partnership. A fad of the early sixties was matching his-and-her sweaters, shirts, and so on—all of which fostered the impression that two people were intimately related to one another and that they should be viewed in terms of their togetherness. Much the same effect can be achieved by the use of emblems indicating membership. Some *symbols of membership* take the form of apparel (insignia, numbers or names on jackets,

Figure 10.4   Team performance. Here the teaming-up is required by the demands of the profession. (Jean Claude Lejeune/Stock Boston)

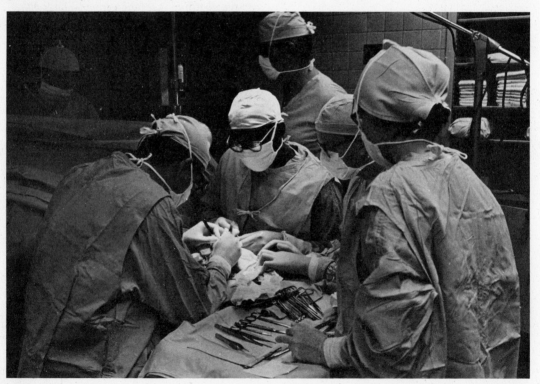

sorority or fraternity pins, tattoos) while others may involve the display of equipment (knapsacks, books). In many cases, such symbols of membership are the result of general conformity to social norms for dress, but in some instances, they represent conscious attempts to signal inclusion in team performances.

A second way in which nonverbal behavior may assist in creating the impression of a team is through the appearance of *symbols of possession*. One individual may move or dress in ways that indicate subordination to and possession by another. Remember when identification bracelets and class rings were exchanged as symbols of possession?

Symbols of membership and symbols of possession also develop in the members of a team a feeling of commitment and loyalty to the team. Some symbols, such as tattoos, are relatively permanent forms of public commitment to a group. A symbol may demonstrate to the team and to oneself that team membership is important.

Leadership is an important feature of team productions. Because of the need for tight dramatic controls, teams often evolve *directors* — leaders who are responsible for the quality of the performances. Any number of factors may warrant changes in either the composition of team or in the type of performance to be presented. Graduation, loss of a roommate, birth or adoption of a child, divorce, remarriage, death all may alter the composition of teams, often placing upon the director the burden of soliciting and training new team members.

Families are an interesting source of material on the responsibilities and functions of team directors. Direction of family performances is often divided between father and mother. Children, depending on their ages, present special problems of dramaturgic control. In many instances, parents may not trust the children to behave in a manner consistent with the team line. In the early 1960s, Art Linkletter's television show, *People Are Funny*, featured interviews with small children. In many cases, the parents had obviously taken great pains to prepare the children for the performance, cautioning them what to do and what *not* to do. Linkletter had a knack of cutting through the dramaturgic controls by asking the children, "What did your mommy and daddy tell you not to do on the show?" The children's responses were often spontaneous, truthful, and amusing.

A director may find that the preparation of teammates is only one of the responsibilities he or she faces; an equally important function is the *cueing* of dramatic action. In other words, a director may take responsibility for initiating, scheduling, and terminating the actions of the various participants. Teammates may look to the director for cues that they should begin their part, that it is appropriate to communicate on a particular topic, that their performance is adequate, or that they have achieved their goals. A teacher conducting classroom discussion often signals speaking turns by a simple nod of the head or a movement of the hand in the direction of a student. As teammates become more and more sensitive to the subtle nonverbal signals that coordinate performances, the *directive dominance* by one individual becomes less apparent. Surgical teams who have worked together for a long time know just what to do and when to do it without verbal signals from the chief surgeon. In such cases, teammates take cues from the performance of the director.

The effective director is not always unobtrusive. Often a director will distinguish him- or herself from team members by developing a distinctive personal front. A director may dress differently or may be positioned more centrally or closer to the audience than others. Consider the positioning of gang members in relationship to their leader. His stance, clothing — in general, his manner — distinguish him from his subordinates. The lead singers of vocal groups often dress in ways that distinguish them from other group members and stand at the front of the stage, between the band and the audience.

Several ingredients are necessary for an effective team performance. First, teammates must share an understanding of the *performance goals*. When members of a team are divided in their interests to the point of pursuing different goals, then the performance ceases to be a team performance and becomes several competing individual performances. Second, team members must have a common understanding of the *dramaturgic effects* of certain actions. Third, there must be no hint of inconsistency or dissatisfaction among the team members. It is inevitable that in team performances some disagreements will arise, but these must be settled in private if the actors wish to maintain the credibility of their performance.

Institutional Performances

Institutions, whether social, academic, governmental, religious, or commercial, pose special challenges and obstacles to formulating and communicating a favorable impression of self. Institutions are sustained and vitalized by the allegiance, involvement, and energies of the members. Without their support, whether willing or otherwise, the influence and resources of an organization cannot long be maintained. This is especially the case for universities, boarding schools, military units, convents and monasteries, camps, mental hospitals, penal institutions—what Goffman has referred to as *total institutions* because of the degree of control they maintain over the lives of their members.[30] Such settings have a direct bearing on the kinds of nonverbal behaviors an individual can use in communicating an impression of self.

Institutions have developed a number of operational procedures that violate many of the conditions necessary for successful individual and team performances. First, institutions promote *self-distantiation*, alienation or disaffection from oneself. Most people, in developing an impression of self, attempt to portray a distinctive, unique person, possessing special talents and worthy of special interest and attention. However, individuality is not consistent with most institutional goals. Individuality challenges discipline and the existing methods of control in an organization; it makes the calculation of resources difficult, and it lessens the appearance of authority, the perceived credibility of the institution. Institutions promote distance from oneself in a number of ways. For instance, many organizations relieve members of their names, substituting numbers or titles. In many large university classes, students are reduced to a number on a seating chart, a social security number, or a student I.D. number. Thus, the symbols by which one is known in an institution are not the traditional symbols of self.

Some institutions make a practice of *reinforced property dispossession* as one means of restricting self-presentational behavior. Many of the props used in preparing one's personal front—including wardrobe, make-up, cigarettes—are replaced by institutional equipment designed to create the appearance of uniformity. The military provides what is known as "army issue," replacing personal equipment with military provisions. A particularly restricting practice is the institutional confiscation of what Goffman calls one's "identity kit."[31] Each of us, Goffman observes, either carries with us or has stored at a convenient location an accumulation of items that assist us in preparing and repairing our personal front, such as cosmetics, shaving utensils, cologne, contact lenses, hair spray and dye, and jewelry. To ensure that members of certain institutions do not acquire these tools illegally, administrators conduct searches of personal quarters, seizing unauthorized items. Locker inspections in high school and barracks inspections in the military constitute forms of reinforced property dispossession.

The consequences of these restrictions in the available means for attending to one's personal front is a general feeling of frustration, inadequacy, and ultimately self-distantiation. Consider the imprisoned prostitute:

First, there is the shower officer who forces them to undress, takes their own clothes away, sees to it that they take showers and get their prison clothes—one pair of black oxfords with cuban heels, two pairs of much-mended ankle socks, three cotton dresses, two cotton slips, two pairs of panties, and a couple of bras. Practically all the bras are flat and useless. No corsets or girdles are issued.

There is not a sadder sight than some of the obese prisoners who, if nothing else, have been managing to keep themselves looking decent on the outside, confronted by the first sight of themselves in prison issue.[32]

Self-distantiation can also be achieved by forcing people to engage in *self-degrading behaviors*. Many institutions have rites of membership requiring new members to perform self-demeaning actions in order to demonstrate their allegiance to the organization. Fraternity and sorority pledging typically involve humiliating and painful experiences. These activities, of course, are possible only with the cooperation of the initiate. One must be willing to pay a price for membership, and that price is self-degradation. In other institutional settings, volition is not required. "An extreme here, perhaps, is the situation of a self-destructive mental patient who is stripped naked for what is felt to be his own protection and placed in a constantly lit seclusion room, into whose Judas window [a small window for viewing patients] any person passing on the ward can peer."[33]

Institutions often force individuals to undertake *disidentifying roles*—that is, any pattern of behaviors that forces the individual to accept as reality his or her subservience to the institution, recognizing one's own worthlessness and doubting one's own capacity to function properly independent of the institutional community.[34] Often work schedules in institutions require members to serve others, to perform menial or tedious tasks. These tasks are accompanied by nonverbal behaviors that convey disaffection from self. "Given the expressive idiom of a particular civil society, certain movements, postures, and stances will convey lowly images of the individual and be avoided as demeaning. Any regulation, command, or task that forces the individual to adopt these movements or postures may mortify his self."[35]

In many institutional settings, individuals, for a variety of reasons, may be denied the right to speak, thereby limiting the performance of roles to nonverbal methods. Forms of public embarrassment are designed to humiliate the individual as a method of punishment for role violations; standing in the corner and standing at attention are examples.

A second method of disrupting traditional means of self-presentation is *role desegregation*. As we mentioned earlier, an important ingredient in successful self-presentation is the ability to control audiences effectively, permitting only those for whom the performance is intended to see the performance and avoiding exposing oneself in contradictory presentations. Geography and control over the stage and backstage areas have a great deal to do with role segregation. In most social situations, rules of privacy allow us time away from others during which we can avoid the psychological strain of certain roles, rehearse performances, and so on. In institutions, however, privacy is a luxury not to be taken for granted. In many cases, people are housed so as to eliminate backstage regions. Few partitions exist to provide a backstage area. Inmates must sleep, bathe, dress, and relax in public territory. In most total institutions, there is no concept of home territory. There is little chance for an individual to segregate audiences.

How, then, does one go about adapting to an institutional environment designed to disrupt the typical methods of self-presentation? Goffman has called one method of coping with the problem *situational withdrawal*.[36] One adopts a trancelike state in which the mind avoids focusing on institutional pressures; one *regresses*, "withdraws apparent attention from everything except events immediately around his body. . . ."[37] The senses, like the mind, become dull. One no longer perceives what is happening. Things cease making sense.

A second method of adapting to the institutional environment is the adoption of the *intransigent line*.[38] One may defy institutional norms, including an accommodating perception of self, which cooperative inmates acquire. One remains independent, presenting him- or herself as rebellious, defiant, and possessing inner strength and will power. Nonverbal behavior is one of the few tools available for constructing this impression. People often develop facial expressions, hand gestures, and postures that indicate defiance. For example, smiling while performing a particularly difficult task may demonstrate a strength not broken by institutional pressures.

Third, one may *colonize*;[39] that is, a member may choose to accept the fact of institutional existence and give the appearance of cooperation, thereby accruing the maximum benefits permissible in that setting. This is often the case in prisons, where inmates cooperate, giving the appearance of having accepted their role, but at the same time develop a social and work hierarchy in which some are privileged and others are suppressed. Reports on Mexican prisons indicate that often new prisoners are forced to pay other prisoners for the right to work and earn money. Objects or opportunities easily accessible on the outside often take on a special value because of their illicit nature. Goffman used the phrase *kitchen strata* to refer to illegally obtained items that provide a kind of monetary system for the inmates.[40] These items may include candy bars, weapons, special clothing, extra blankets, food, soft drinks, or privileges such as recreation time, laundry privileges, and so on. These objects and opportunities help define a kind of informal social structure. Who an individual is often is defined by what he or she possesses.

A last method of adaptation to the institutional environment is called *conversion*. One can cope with the pressures of an institution simply by succumbing, by coming to believe in his or her inadequacy, by accepting the concept of self developed by the institution. By converting, one accepts a negative self-image, adopting the nonverbal behaviors that signify dependence. One willingly engages in self-degrading postures, self-criticism, and self-abuse.

Stigmatized Performances

It would be a mistake to assume that everyone is capable of performing all kinds of dramatic action. Most of us are limited in the ways in which we can present ourselves to others by such factors as our sex and age. For the most part, these limitations do not seriously restrict the kinds of performances we are likely to attempt. Some people, however, possess characteristics that severely limit performances crucial to the kinds of social impressions that they desire others to form. These people are *stigmatized* by some feature or characteristic that makes certain performances unconvincing. Goffman has examined such problems in *Stigma: Notes on the Management of a Spoiled Identity*. There are a number of causes of stigmatized performance, such as race, body structure, physical disability, facial features, dialect to name a few. The stigma may be physically evident, such as race or nationality; it may be psychological, including such conditions as personality disorders, reticence, introversion, and forms of mental retardation. Stigmatization may be temporary, as with some forms of illness and injury, or it may be permanent.

Figure 10.5 Some nonverbal sources of stigmatization

Poor eyesight	Broken limb
Somatype	Illness
Hair color	Nose size
Baldness	Height
Accent	Shortness
Race	Braces
Sex	Freckles
Age	Speech disorders
Extremes in physical attractiveness	Physical coordination
	Skin complexion

In most cases, stigmatization, however temporary, has a severe negative effect on the performer and his or her attempts to achieve socially stable and meaningful interpersonal relationships. First, the stigma is often a source of embarrassment to the actor, who may continually attempt to mask the nature or severity of the stigma. The actor may avoid situations that demonstrate the deficiency or weakness or performances that rely on a particular communication skill impaired by the stigma. The more physically evident the stigma, the more difficult it becomes to ignore or disguise the source of embarrassment. Physical stigma may require elaborate modifications in behavior. Obese people may attempt to dress so as to hide their form; they may avoid social situations that make noticeable the lack of coordination that often accompanies obesity.

Second, an actor may develop feelings of guilt, especially when the stigma is thought to be controllable, although it may not actually be so. The overweight child may not be sufficiently in control of the home environment to choose and stick to a reducing diet.

Third, prolonged stigmatization invariably leads the performer to adjust his or her self-concept. Goffman has contended that part of being socialized in our culture is sharing standards for identity. In other words, we learn to have certain expectations regarding our ability to function socially (the ability to make and maintain friendships, to converse with others, to maintain control over our bodies). These standards are applied regardless of the nature of the stigma. The result is a feeling of disaffection from self.

Of course, not all kinds of stigma are thought of as liabilities. Physical beauty, for example, can impose limitations on the kinds of performance others view as credible. Beautiful people may be considered unapproachable or unintelligent. When a performance demands that the actor appear physically undistinguished, physically attractive individuals may find that dressing down for the part is insufficient.

Obvious types of stigmatization are likely to influence the criteria others use in evaluating your performances. Many kinds of stigma result in a form of *role release* whereby the performer, because of the stigma, is relieved of the traditional responsibilities associated with the performance. Role release is not always a positive feature of stigmatization; release can be disparaging. Disabled people, for example, are often viewed as *nonpersons* incapable of tending to personal needs. You may have heard others refer to disabled individuals in the third person as if they were not actually present, only to turn around the next minute to express concern over their personal comfort. Similarly, to be released from certain job-related responsibilities because of race, age, or sex can be a demoralizing experience.

Negative Experiences

Some kinds of performances are intended to create *negative experiences* for others.[41] A performer may deem it essential to his or her act that another be embarrassed, humiliated, frightened, or similarly exposed before members of the audience. Obviously, people try to avoid threatening encounters. Therefore, most negative experiences involve some violation of expectations. This is called *breaking frame.*[42] One breaks frame by altering either the goals of the performance, the rules of conduct that govern the action, or the importance and meaning of the behaviors. Consider this situation: Two married couples are out on the town for an evening of dinner and dancing. One of the men invites the other man's wife to dance, an action that is quite permissible and falls well within the prevailing definition of the situation. However, while dancing, he holds the woman in what might be considered a romantic embrace. Whether intentionally or otherwise, he has communicated a key that indicates that the original frame is no longer in effect (dancing with the friend's wife is not merely a social courtesy). The frame has been broken, perhaps without the actor's knowledge. At best, the action is subject to ambiguous interpretations; at worst, his behavior is seen as constituting inappropriate conduct. If the action was intentional and motivated, say, by the desire of the actor to demonstrate to his own wife that he is attractive to members of the opposite sex, then the situation is most certainly a negative experience.

One can create negative experiences for others in a number of ways. By involving a person bearing a certain stigma in an encounter that, unknown to that person, may publicize the stigma and thereby cause embarrassment, an actor can violate expectations and generate a negative experience.

A second means of manufacturing a negative experience involves altering the importance of an action or series of behaviors. A child becomes dirty during play after school. While the dirty clothing does not go unnoticed by the child's mother, she gives no indication that the grass stain and mud are of serious concern. Then one day, Grandmother comes to visit. The child appears after school dirty as usual. The mother, in an effort to appear to be a good parent, scolds and punishes the child. In such an instance, the importance of the child's actions have been changed for the sake of a new audience (Grandmother). The frame has been broken, and the child may rightly feel betrayed.

Third, one can create negative experiences by denying the agreed-upon frame for interpreting behavior. Not laughing at statements made in jest is a way of denying that the appropriate and understood frame for interpreting the behavior is one of humor. The communicator may be embarrassed, confused, or frustrated by his or her apparent inability to communicate.

Finally, a negative experience may result when certain behaviors, which are expected and understood in moderation, occur in excess. One can use touching as a means of comforting another, but excessive touching alters the definition of the situation, often suggesting a sexual motivation.

Deceptive Performances

We have all been guilty of deception at one time or another, however minor the incident. We exaggerate reality; we screen information, often presenting only that which is favorable to us; we deceive. It would be a mistake to assume that communication based upon deceit is no different from messages that have sincere intentions. On the contrary, messages intended to deceive are fundamentally different from our other communications. The key to deception is our nonverbal behavior. Recent studies have attempted to determine how deception messages differ from others and which nonverbal clues signal deceit.

As we have seen, verbal behavior is primarily conscious and self-monitored. Verbal behavior in itself rarely provides much information about deception, but nonverbal behavior is another story. As Freud has pointed out: "He that has eyes to see and ears to hear may convince himself that no mortal can keep a secret. If his lips are silent, he chatters with his fingertips; betrayal oozes out of him at every pore."[43] Since we cannot monitor all our nonverbal signals at the same time, and since many signals are unconsciously motivated, the movements of our body belie our thoughts. Ekman has used the term *leakage* to refer to the process whereby our body betrays our speech.[44]

Leakage and clues of deception may differ depending on what kind of deception is taking place. *Interpersonal deception* refers to an individual's conscious attempt to mislead others. *Intrapersonal deception* is a little more difficult to conceptualize; it involves the attempt to deceive oneself.[45] Instances of the latter happen all the time, but we tend not to label them as deception. We try to convince ourselves that we really aren't nervous before giving a speech, that an unsuccessful political candidate wasn't impressive to us anyway, or that someone else was responsible for an argument. Whether we label it rationalization, self-persuasion, or deception, it boils down to the same thing—we are telling ourselves something that (at least initially) we don't believe to be the case.

Whatever the type of deception, we attempt to suppress leakage and the clues to our deception. Even in cases of intrapersonal deception,

Ekman has argued, the ego (unconscious mind) is sensitive to signals that the conscious mind ignores. When we suspect that leakage is occurring and our deception is in jeopardy, we may attempt to salvage our performance either by *curtailing* it, thereby eliminating the possibility of leakage, or by attempting to *simulate* normal interaction.[46] Curtailing the interaction has the limited advantage of reducing the risk of failure through continued deception, but it also carries with it some additional disadvantages. By aborting the performance, one may actually insinuate deception or otherwise indicate that something has gone amiss. Simulation, on the other hand, carries its own risks, since one must continue the deception throughout the performance.

Emotional expressions often play an important role in deceit. Many deceptions involve the portrayal of an emotion that is not genuine. (See Figure 10.6.) Depending on the situation, we may choose to *underintensify* an emotional feeling—that is, to send nonverbal cues indicating that emotion is felt to a lesser degree than is the actual case. The student who had professed all the confidence in the word of being admitted to law school may underintensify the feelings of joy (and surprise) at receiving a letter of acceptance. We may also *neutralize* our expressions, showing no detectable trace of the emotion that we actually feel. We may choose to *overintensify* an emotional expression, exaggerating actual feelings. Finally, we often *substitute* emotions; that is, we display an emotion we do not feel at all. The problem of leakage is different with each of these strategies.

Substitution of emotions is especially difficult to carry off convincingly. Research has shown that no matter how skillful we are at controlling emotional expressions, the face and body are quick to show our true feelings. When we must portray an emotion we do not actually feel, our face often responds by displaying what is known as a *micro facial* expression.[47] A *microexpression* is a momentary display of the actual emotion. It lasts only a fraction of a second and is usually so brief that it goes undetected by the human eye. Using slow-motion film or videotape equipment, we can identify these clues to deception. However, we aren't able to recognize them in everyday interaction.

What behaviors signal deceit? Ekman has theorized that the face, which is generally the best source of kinesic cues for information about the individual, is not a particularly good source of cues for deception. Since we tend to rely on the face to express emotions, we have learned to exert a great deal of control over facial expressions. So, except for micro facial expressions, the face provides little information about deception.

On the other hand, the legs and feet, which provide little intended information, are therefore least under the control of the communicator. Feet and legs are the regions most susceptible to leaking cues regarding deception. "Leakage in the legs/feet could include aggressive foot kicks, flirtatious leg displays, auto-

erotic or soothing leg squeezing, abortive restless flight movements. Deception clues can be seen in tense leg positions, frequent shift of leg posture, and in restless or repetitive leg and foot acts."[48]

The regions of the hands, fingers, and arms convey less information, and they are easily controlled. Consequently, we pay only moderate attention to what our hands are doing. We assume that unconscious gestures won't expose our deception. Although the hands do not provide clues to deception to the degree that the legs and feet do, hand gestures still leak more information about deception than do facial expressions. "Major forms of leakage in the hands are the adaptors, particularly the self-adaptors. While facially smiling and pleasant, ego [the unconscious mind] may be tearing at a fingernail, digging into his cheek, protectively holding his knees, and so forth. Self-adaptors can also serve as deception clues, betraying discomfort about the deception."[49] From the drumming of fingers to the tapping of objects to the gripping of an armrest, the hands can signal that something is

Figure 10.6   Charles Van Doren answers correctly question after question on the quiz show "Twenty-One" in 1956. Van Doren's accomplishments are later discovered to be a hoax—and his performance a master job of deception. (Wide World Photos)

being concealed. Emblems may also play a role. One interesting one that has been uncovered is the *hand shrug*, a rotation of the hands outward, palms exposed, that signals helplessness. People attempting deception use this behavior frequently.[50]

In order to test the thesis that the face provides fewer clues of deception than the rest of the body, Ekman and Friesen filmed patients at a mental hospital—patients for whom differing diagnoses had been given and who provided ample evidence of contradiction between verbal and nonverbal ones. The patients often attempted to disguise symptoms of illness, protesting that the problem had been resolved. Films were taken of psychiatric interviews and shown to observers. Some observers were shown only a film of the head, while others viewed only the body minus the head; a third group were shown both head and body. After observing the films, observers provided adjectives to describe the patients. Those who saw the head alone judged the patient to be cheerful, cooperative, affectionate, warm, and often honest. Those who saw only the body concluded that the patient was confused, defensive, tense, and cautious—quite a different picture. Those observers who looked at both body and head judged the patient to be changeable, active, emotional, and defensive. In this instance, clues of deceit were shown in the hands, feet, and legs.[51]

Albert Mehrabian investigated the nonverbal features of truthful and deceitful messages.[52] Results of three experiments indicated that an individual engaged in deception talks less, more slowly, and with more disfluencies than someone telling the truth. The rate of body movement also tends to be slower in transmitting deceptive messages.

McClintock and Hunt undertook a similar investigation of the nonverbal correlates of deception.[53] Their research showed that deception is accompanied by an increase in postural shifts, self-manipulations (touching of the body, face, hands), and gestures over other communications.

Finally, a study conducted by Knapp, Hart, and Dennis broached the same question: What are the nonverbal features of a deceptive message?[54] Their findings revealed that people engaged in deception spoke for less time than nondeceivers, displayed more self- and object adaptors (self-touching, touching of objects such as glasses or a shirtsleeve), paused more often, and engaged in fewer and briefer glances.

These studies tell us that the body is the major source of leakage, although it seems clear that the role of the voice has been insufficiently investigated. In spite of our ability to monitor our voices for content, we are rela-

mini-experiment

Devise three broad topics of communication. The first should be relatively unimportant to most people (what they wore to class on a given day); the second topic should be moderately important to most individuals (how old they are, things they like or dislike in others); and the third topic should be highly important (religious beliefs, feelings about their body, embarrassing moments). Ask a number of people to tape-record two messages for each topic—one truthful and one a lie. Play the messages for another group of people and calculate the percent who succeed in distinguishing the lie from the truth. Are there vocal cues that indicate deception? How does the deception on the highly important topic differ from deceptions on topics of lesser importance?

Table 10.2 Summary of Deception Cues

Function	Cues
Shows underlying anxiety or nervousness	Hand shrug emblems (signifying helplessness, inability, uncertainty), face manipulation (scratching bridge of nose), blushing, perspiring, voice tremors, gulping, shaking, increase in speech errors, self- and object adaptors (random self-touching, playing with pencils, glasses, creasing trousers)
Shows underlying reticence or withdrawal	Fewer words, shorter messages, more pauses
Shows that actual feelings are more moderate than overt behavior indicates	Fewer head nods, fewer gestures, less leg and foot movement, less immediacy (proximity, eye contact, touching, body orientation), talks slower, more pleasant faces
Shows external behavior to contradict actual feelings	Contradictory verbal and nonverbal cues, micro facial expressions, failure to emphasize remarks with natural accompanying gestures, inconsistent verbal statements
Shows underlying vagueness and uncertainty	Restricted verbal code, more silences, fewer factual statements, tendency toward nonspecific statements, less nonverbal immediacy
Shows underlying unpleasantness	Fewer mutual glances, fewer group references, more limited eye contact, more disparaging remarks

tively unsuccessful in managing some of the other features of the voice, including rate of speaking, pauses, and pronunciation.

Also, eye behavior appears to be an important exception to Ekman's argument regarding our inability to conceal deception through facial expressions. In several cases, the eye behavior of people attempting to deceive was noticeably different from that of nondeceivers. One study in particular investigated the phenomenon of pupil dilation. The conclusions indicated that the "eyes do not lie. While the mouth may express an unfelt smile, true feelings usually reveal themselves in the depth of a person's eyes."[55] Generally, dilated pupils accompanied lying. For a summary of deception cues, see Table 10.2.

One individual variable—*machiavellianism*—may portend success in deception.[56] A *high mach* is an individual who is extremely manipulative when the situation permits. Some evidence suggests that when high machs are lying, their eye behavior closely resembles that of most people when they tell the truth. Beyond this scant evidence, little is known about who succeeds at deceiving.[57]

These studies and other research on clues to deception don't tell us how people go about detecting deception. Theoretically, a person who knows what behaviors signal deception could simply watch for them. Of course, detection is not that easy. For one thing, most people do not know what behaviors signal deception. When they suspect that things are not on the up and up, they cannot readily identify the source of their suspicions.

Researcher Donald Lombardi has proposed a two-stage model that, while it doesn't address fully the problem of the source of an observer's suspicions, nonetheless outlines the general process of detecting deception[58] In Stage One, the observer perceives nonverbal *signals of state*—signals that provide information about the communicator's attitude toward the interaction—that seem inconsistent with other verbal and nonverbal messages related to the topic at hand. At this point, the receiver must make a decision. He or she may conclude that deception is occurring, in which case the goal of the interaction shifts from the initial, topic-related goal to a goal of determining the truthfulness of the communicator's messages. In this instance, the receiver takes on the role of detector and monitors the communicator for evidence of deception. Other conclusions are possible. For example, one might decide that the apparent inconsistencies are nothing more than idiosyncracies of the communicator. One may also conclude that the discrepancies are accidental. With either of these last two explanations, the receiver rejects (at least for the moment) the possibility of deception and returns to the original goal of the interaction.

In Stage Two, continued monitoring of the communicator yields additional inconsistencies. The choices faced in Stage One again present themselves. If the receiver concludes that deception is occurring, then leakage has indeed taken place. At this point, the receiver reevaluates his or her goal for the interaction, possibly choosing to continue the role of detector while scanning the communicator for continued inconsistencies. The receiver may decide to ignore the deception, confront the deceiver, withdraw from interaction, or modify future interaction with the deceiver.

Lombardi has argued that a similar process occurs for the deceiver. "The deceiver's initial goal, of course, is deception. If, however, he begins to suspect counter-deception or discovery, he may change his goal, increase masking behaviors or combine other defensive strategies. In Stage Two, the deceiver may become certain that he has been discovered and may 'confess' or engage in still more defensive kinds of behavior." So, both the deceiver and the deceived engage in an ongoing process of scanning, interpretation, goal modification, more scanning, more interpretation, and more revision of goals.

Summary

Nonverbal behavior is a crucial element in how we present ourselves to others. Our success in conveying an impression depends, to a great degree, on how we manage our nonverbal actions, on our ability to stage our performances, on our skill in exerting dramaturgic control over the production area, and on our ability to eliminate inconsistencies in our nonverbal behavior or cues that contradict the impression we want to communicate.

Goffman's dramaturgic method breaks down the components of a presentation into an understandable collection of elements, each of which influences the other. Goffman's terminology, drawn from the theater, provides a structure from which a performance can be analyzed.

Of course, all performances are not alike. Goffman has recognized that certain types of self-presentation require a special understanding of the situation and of the factors involved in the performance. They are team, institutional, stigmatized, negative, and deceptive performances.

Suggested Reading

Ekman, P., and Friesen, W. V. "Detecting Deception from the Body or Face." *Journal of Personality and Social Psychology*, 29 (1970), 288–298.

Ekman, P., and Friesen, W. V. "Nonverbal Leakage and Clues to Deception." *Psychiatry*, 32 (1969), 88–106.

Ekman, P., and Friesen, W. V. *Unmasking the Face.* Englewood Cliffs, N.J.: Prentice-Hall, 1975.

Goffman, E. *Asylums.* Garden City, N.Y.: Doubleday, 1971.

Goffman, E. *Frame Analysis.* New York: Harper and Row, 1974.

Goffman, E. *Presentation of Self in Everyday Life.* Garden City, N.Y.: Doubleday Anchor Books, 1959.

Goffman, E. *Stigma: Notes on the Management of Spoiled Identity.* Englewood Cliffs, N.J.: Prentice-Hall, 1964.

Notes

1. H. Cosell, *Cosell* (New York: Pocket Books, 1974), p. 200.
2. E. E. Jones, *Ingratiation: A Social Psychological Analysis* (New York: Wiley, 1964).
3. E. E. Jones and C. Wortman, *Ingratiation: An Attributional Approach* (Morristown, N.J.: General Learning Press, 1973).
4. J. T. Tedeschi, "Impression Management Theory," in L. Berkowitz (ed.), *Advances in Experimental Social Psychology* (New York: Academic Press, in press); J. T. Tedeschi, B. R. Schlenker, and T. V. Bonoma, *Conflict, Power, and Games* (Chicago: Aldine, 1973).
5. E. Goffman, *The Presentation of Self in Everyday Life* (Garden City, N.Y.: Doubleday Anchor Books, 1959).
6. Associated Press release, Gainesville *Sun,* October 19, 1975.
7. Goffman, p. 107 (note 5).
8. Goffman, p. 7 (note 5).
9. K. Burke, *A Grammar of Motives* (Berkeley: University of California Press, 1969).
10. Goffman, p. 52 (note 5).
11. Goffman, p. 52 (note 5).
12. B. Gill, *Here at the New Yorker* (New York: Random House, 1975), pp. 248–249. Published in England by Michael Joseph Ltd. Copyright © 1975 by Brendan Gill.
13. See, for detailed definitions, E. Goffman, *Frame Analysis* (New York: Harper and Row, 1974), pp. 1–20.
14. Goffman, p. 36 (note 13).
15. Goffman, pp. 35–36 (note 13).
16. J. M. Henslin and M. A. Biggs, "Dramaturgic Desexualization: The Sociology of the Vaginal Examination," in J. M. Henslin (ed.), *Studies in the Sociology of Sex* (New York: Appleton-Century-Crofts, 1971), pp. 243–272.
17. M. Reiss, D. Fieldbinder, and H. Abrams, "Toward a Self-Presentational Theory of Nonverbal Communication," unpublished manuscript, University of Florida, 1976. We would like to acknowledge the valuable contribution of these authors to this section of the chapter.
18. From Reiss, Fieldbinder, and Abrams (note 17).
19. A. Kendon, "Movement Co-ordination in Social Interaction: Some Examples Described," *Acta Psychologica,* 32 (1970), pp. 100–125; A. Mehrabian, "Significance of Posture and Position in the Communication of Attitude and Status Relationships," *Psychological Bulletin,* 71 (1969), pp. 359–372; A. Mehrabian, "Nonverbal Communication," in J. K. Cole (ed.), *Nebraska Symposium on Motivation* (Lincoln: University of Nebraska Press, 1971), pp. 107–161; A Scheflen, *Body Language and Social Order: Communication as Behavioral Control* (Englewood Cliffs, N.J.: Prentice-Hall, 1972); M. Weiner and A. Mehrabian, *Languages Within Language: Immediacy and Channel in Verbal Communication* (New York: Appleton-Century-Crofts, 1968).
20. E. Bottheil, J. Corey, and A. Parades, "Psychological and Physical Dimensions of Personal Space," *Journal of Psychology,* 69 (1968), pp. 7–9; J. D. Fisher, M. Rytting, and R. Heslin, "Hands Touching Hands: Affective and Evaluative Effects of an Interpersonal Touch," *Sociometry,* 39 (1976), pp. 416–421; J. L. Kuethe, "Social Schemas," *Journal of Abnormal and Social Psychology,* 64 (1962), pp. 31–38; K. B. Little, "Personal Space," *Journal of Experimental Social Psychology,* 1 (1965), pp. 237–247.
21. Weiner and Mehrabian, p. 3 (note 19).
22. F. Goldman-Eisler, *Psycholinguistics: Experiments in Spontaneous Speech* (London: Academic Press, 1968).
23. Reiss, Fieldbinder, and Abrams (note 17).
24. Kuethe (note 13d); Gothell, Corey, and Parades (note 20); Little (note 20).
25. S. M. Jourard, "An Exploratory Study of Body Accessibility," *British Journal of Social and Clinical Psychology,* 5 (1966), pp. 221–231.
26. A. Mehrabian and J. T. Friar, "Encoding of Attitude by a Seated Communication via Posture

Cues," *Journal of Consulting and Clinical Psychology*, 33 (1969), pp. 330–336; H. Rosenfeld, "The Experimental Analysis of Interpersonal Influence Processes," *Journal of Communication*, 22 (1972), pp. 424–442.

27. T. F. Hoult, "Experimental Measurement of Clothing as a Factor of Some Social Ratings of Selected American Men," *American Sociological Review*, 19 (1954), pp. 324–328.

28. Goffman, p. 104 (note 5).

29. Cosell, pp. 239–240 (note 1).

30. E. Goffman, *Asylums* (Garden City, N.Y.: Doubleday and Company, 1961), p. 4.

31. Goffman, p. 20 (note 30).

32. J. M. Murtagh and S. Harris, *Cast the First Stone* (New York: Pocketbooks, 1958), pp. 239–240.

33. Goffman, pp. 24–25 (note 30).

34. Goffman, p. 23 (note 30).

35. Goffman, pp. 21–22 (note 30).

36. Goffman, p. 61 (note 30).

37. Goffman, p. 62 (note 30).

38. Goffman, p. 55 (note 30).

39. Goffman, p. 63 (note 30).

40. See, for thorough discussion, E. Goffman, *Stigma: Notes on the Management of Spoiled Identity* (Englewood Cliffs, N.J.: Prentice-Hall, 1964).

41. Goffman, pp. 378–438 (note 13).

42. Goffman, pp. 345–377 (note 13).

43. S. Freud, "Fragment of an Analysis of a Case of Hysteria (1905)," *Collected Papers*, Vol. 3 (New York: Basic Books, 1959), p. 94.

44. P. Ekman and W. V. Friesen, "Detecting Deception from the Body or Face," *Journal of Personality and Social Psychology*, 29 (1974), pp. 288–298.

45. P. Ekman and W. V. Friesen, "Nonverbal Leakage and Clues to Deception," *Psychiatry*, 32 (1969), pp. 84–106.

46. Ekman and Friesen, pp. 88–106 (note 45).

47. Ekman and Friesen, pp. 88–106 (note 45).

48. Ekman and Friesen (note 45).

49. Ekman and Friesen (note 45).

50. P. Ekman and W. V. Friesen, "Hand Movements," *Journal of Communication*, 22 (1972) pp. 353–374.

51. Ekman and Friesen, pp. 88–106 (note 45).

52. A. Mehrabian, "Nonverbal Betrayal of Feeling," *Journal of Experimental Research in Psychology*, 5 (1971), pp. 64–73.

53. C. McClintock and R. G. Hunt, "Nonverbal Indicators of Affect and Deception in an Interview Setting," *Journal of Applied Social Psychology*, 5 (1975), pp. 54–67.

54. M. L. Knapp, R. P. Hart, and H. S. Dennis, "The Rhetoric of Duplicity: An Exploration of Deception as a Communication Construct," unpublished manuscript, Purdue University, 1975.

55. M. P. Janisse and W. S. Peavler, "Pupillary Research Today: Emotion in the Eye," *Psychology Today*, 7 (1974).

56. R. Exline, J. Thibaut, C. B. Hickey, and P. Gumpert, "Visual Interaction in Relation to Machiavellianism and an Unethical Act," in P. Christie and F. Geis (eds.), *Studies in Machiavellianism* (New York: Academic Press, 1970), pp. 53–75.

57. Knapp, Hart, and Dennis (note 54).

58. D. Lombardi, "A Model of the Process of Recognition of Nonverbal Leakage from Deception Clues," unpublished manuscript, University of Florida, 1976.

11

Manipulating Others

Test Your Sensitivity

True or False?

1. People are most likely to comprehend a person's true meaning the slower that person talks.
2. Vocal nonfluencies hurt learning and attitude change.
3. A physically attractive woman is less persuasive than an unattractive one.
4. A threatening stare usually provokes verbal aggression.
5. A person discloses more about him- or herself if a listener smiles and nods a lot.
6. A high-status person may increase his or her credibility by violating personal space norms.

In this last chapter, we shall consider ways in which we use nonverbal communication, either consciously or unconsciously, to alter the thinking and behavior of others. In Chapter 10, we examined the ways in which we use nonverbal cues to manipulate how others view us, how we manage our behaviors so that they find us attractive, interesting, and sincere. In this chapter, we shall discuss the ways we manipulate *their* behavior, modifying what others learn, think, do, and say.

Nonverbal messages may be coupled with behavior modification techniques to engineer the behavior of others. People who have achieved power have long recognized this fact. Consider some well-known examples of situations in which such techniques have been applied:

Item: During World War II, the German populace was persuaded by a previously unknown man named Adolph Hitler to commit atrocities against vast numbers of Jews and other people, atrocities so horrible that many Germans later denied any knowledge or responsibility. Yet the people were thoroughly responsive to Hitler's edicts at the time.

Item: During the Korean War, American prisoners of war were brainwashed. Hard-nosed, well-trained military men learned the basic tenets of the Communist Manifesto and publicly espoused them, renouncing the United States. Their change in attitude and behavior was not a charade put on for the benefit of their captors; the men retained their new views when they returned to the United States.

Item: Charles Manson, a drifter, burglar, forger, and pimp, managed to mold a hapless group of young people into a cult of cold-blooded murderers. Even behind bars, this self-styled Jesus figure continues to exert immense control over his growing family.

Item: In recent years, another cult has triggered alarm among many parents and religious groups—the rise of the Unification Church of the Reverend Sun Myung Moon. Numbers of

By the end of the chapter, you should know the correct answer to all six questions and understand these concepts:

- positive reinforcement
- negative reinforcement
- punishment
- nonverbal cues that affect comprehension through
  reinforcement
  attention arousal
  distraction
- effects of the following nonverbal strategies on persuasion:
  affiliation appeals
  attractiveness appeals
  credibility appeals
  distraction
  violations of expectations
- effects of the following nonverbal strategies on overt behavior and communication patterns:
  threat cues
  dominance, power, and status appeals
  positive regard and interest appeals
  pleasure and pain
  modeling
  violations of expectations
  experimenter expectancy effects

young people have abandoned their families to join the church. The "Moonies" are reputed to live in abject poverty, to suffer ordeals during the conversion process, and to work exhaustingly at menial tasks to raise money for the church, while Reverend Moon lives in the utmost luxury.

In all of these instances, certain psychological and physiological influences must be credited in part for the mass conversions. Verbal messages also wielded significant influence. However, nonverbal cues played a powerful role as well. In fact, their very subtlety may have made them the most effective influence. It is to such nonverbal cues that we shall turn our attention in this chapter.

Some scholars wonder whether it is ethical to expose students to this kind of information, feeling that it may teach them to become better manipulators. We feel that, since everyone uses these techniques to some degree without even realizing it, we might as well bring them under conscious control. Manipulating others is not inherently bad. After all, manipulation includes teaching children new concepts, social rules, and cultural values; persuading a friend to go to a lecture; helping a spouse show more affection. The therapist, salesperson, politician, teacher, and priest are openly dedicated to influencing others. We are all the target of endless persuasion campaigns in the mass media. The fact that we all consume manipulative techniques is in itself the most compelling reason for familiarizing ourselves with the research on the subject. If we become better informed, we can resist subtle influences that we consider inappropriate.

Analysis of nonverbal techniques in this area is complicated by several factors. One is that research comes from such a variety of approaches and disciplines—speech, mass communication, sociology, psychology, marketing—that no one has integrated the materials in one source. Another is that researchers on the various aspects of manipulation have operated independently of each other. This makes it difficult to identify similar principles operating in each area. A third problem is that the nonverbal factors have not always been carefully identified. For instance, a researcher may simply report having observed "friendly" behavior. We have tried to use only those studies that specify which nonverbal cues are responsible for the results. Finally, the subjects of the research range from the intentional manipulation of nonverbal cues to the accidental, unconscious use of nonverbal means in the process of manipulating some other variable. Some of the more interesting research comes from the second category. For instance, experimenters frequently bias the outcome of a research project accidentally by communicating nonverbally to the subjects what responses they expect. These subtle messages, once discovered, can supply a key to the way in which powerful individuals exert influence over others without appearing to do so. They may also offer clues as to how we unconsciously control those who are close to us.

Comprehension and Retention

Sara is attempting to explain to her fifth-grade classmates how Egyptians mummified their dead. As she begins her explanation, the teacher looks at her expectantly and nods frequently as Sara proceeds correctly. When Sara begins to make an error, the teacher cocks her head and narrows her eyes. Sara revises her statement, the teacher smiles and Sara continues. At the conclusion of Sara's presentation, the teacher gives another reassuring smile and warmly praises Sara for her informative talk. That night, Sara delightedly repeats without error her new-found knowledge to her parents.

German researchers decide that color has an effect on mental abilities. To test their hunch, they place one group of children in brightly colored rooms to play and another group in rooms painted white, black, or brown. They discover that the children playing in the "happy" (bright) colored rooms show an immediate increase in IQ of twelve points, while those children playing in the "ugly" rooms show a drop of fourteen points![1]

These are just two illustrations of the ways in which nonverbal cues can facilitate or hinder learning and remembering. The first example, a hypothetical situation, demonstrates the use of kinesic cues to shape an accurate understanding of a new concept and to reinforce its continued retention. The second, an actual research finding, highlights the potential impact of environmental features in stimulating or depressing mental processes, thereby affecting learning. Every day we learn new facts and principles, and that learning takes place in the presence of a host of nonverbal stimuli. The question is how those nonverbal elements can be harnessed to assist understanding. There appear to be at least three general strategies for using nonverbal messages to ease, encourage, or interrupt the learning process.

Reinforcement Cues

Suppose you are trying to teach your younger brother the names of colors. You show him a colored object and ask him, "What color is this?" Every time he answers correctly, you say, "Right," and you also signal your approval nonverbally with smiles, nods, and positive vocal tones. In other words, you employ the process of *reinforcement* to accelerate your brother's learning. According to learning theory, the presentation of verbal and nonverbal positive feedback should increase the likelihood of your brother's giving the correct response next time you present the same colored object. You can further facilitate his learning if you reward him whenever he gives a nearly correct answer. If he says "Red" when you present orange, you reinforce him by smiling

expectantly and replying "Almost" until he arrives at the correct answer. This process of reinforcing progressively closer approximations of the right answer is called *shaping*. As the learner tries out various answers, he or she is nudged in the right direction through various methods of reinforcement.

Reinforcement may take the form of providing rewards after the desired behavior occurs—*positive reinforcement*—or presenting some kind of negative consequence that the learner tries to escape or avoid through exhibiting the desired behavior—*negative reinforcement*. The key consideration in both cases is that the desired behavior *increases*. If something negative results in a *decrease* in behavior, that something is called *punishment*. Research has overwhelmingly demonstrated that reinforcement encourages learning while punishment is less predictable in its effects.

Although the general principle of reinforcement is known to work, it is not clear yet what specific nonverbal cues or combinations of cues work best as reinforcers. It has generally been assumed that smiles, nods, forward leaning, increased eye contact, touching, approving vocal cues, and so on serve as positive reinforcers, while frowns, scowls, knitted brows, reduced eye contact, neutral facial expressions, angry or cold vocal tones, and silence serve as negative reinforcers.

Research on the role of these cues in cognitive learning is sparse. A study by Kleinfeld offers some support. Groups of Caucasian and Eskimo children received either a nonverbally warm teaching style or a nonverbally impersonal one. Both styles included a broad range of kinesic, vocalic, and haptic cues. Kleinfeld found that both sets of children learned more under the warm style.[2] Another related study used approval cues—in this case, smiles and physical contact—to reinforce attentiveness in the classroom and found that the cues effectively increased overall attention for eleven out of twelve students.[3] (The greater attention level is assumed to facilitate learning.)

Nonverbal reinforcers do not always work in expected ways, however. For instance, one of the authors conducted an experiment in which she expected learning to be greatest when subjects were approached at a closer-than-normal distance and received positive nonverbal feedback. Instead, recall was highest when the positive feedback was coupled with a greater-than-normal conversational distance.[4] Albert Furbay, another researcher who expected proximity to have a reinforcing effect, similarly failed to find support for his predictions. He thought that a compact seating arrangement would facilitate learning and persuasion better than a scattered one. He based his prediction on the observation that members of a mob seem to reinforce each other. However, his study found recall to be the same in both arrangements.[5] His finding should not be taken as evidence that distance isn't a factor. His audience started out initially opposed to his topic and may not have been excited enough about the topic (nuclear disarmament) to arouse each other. Numerous social psychologists and rhetoricians still hold the position that a compact audience can serve a reinforcing function. The results of these two studies demonstrate simply that the relationship between nonverbal and verbal variables may be more complex than had been anticipated.

Although we may not know which codes are most effective, educators argue that positive cues are preferable to negative cues. Positive cues, they claim, act as a reward and inform the learner that he or she has succeeded; negative feedback may retard rather than aid the learning process. Unfortunately, many people fail to realize how often they communicate negative evaluations to others who do not learn a new concept as quickly as they would like. We know a graduate student who alienated many of his peers whenever he tried to help them with a computer programming problem, by condescending and sneering at their mistakes. Needless to say, most of them felt they learned very little from him. Some parents are guilty of communicating the same message to their children. Many children who fail at school report that their teachers and parents make them feel stupid.

American Airlines recently recognized the counterproductiveness of such negative approaches to learning. They actually issued to their management and training personnel guidelines for providing reinforcement to other employees. Two of the main points were to look for the good and reward the good. Means of reward included praise, recognition, and giving feedback, all of which may take nonverbal forms. These methods can improve learning and interpersonal relations, especially if the nonverbal cues are alternated with verbal recognition and tangible rewards.

Attention Arousal

Most learning theorists agree that you have to pay attention to something before you can learn it. At a job interview, you must attract the prospective employer's attention if all your qualifications are to be remembered. The nonverbal codes of vocalics and artifacts have been investigated as attention-arousers. Public-speaking texts teach that a good speaker uses a lot of vocal variety, that is, variation in pitch, rate, intensity, tonal quality, and so on. As early as 1920, Woolbert tested this prescription and found that variety in the pitch, tempo, intensity, and voice quality in a public presentation did indeed produce more retention than unvaried versions of the readings.[6] Two similar studies found that skilled speakers produced more comprehension than unskilled speakers, especially of difficult or disorganized material.[7] The skilled speakers probably used more variety and were more fluent. Pitch alone may make a difference. One experiment found less comprehension of prose and poetry when they were read in a "mono-pitch" than when they were read with varied pitch; another investigation failed to find that comprehension improved with pitch variety but did find that listeners preferred the presentation that used maximum pitch interval and inflection.[8] Perhaps the fairest conclusion is that vocal variety may improve comprehension and retention, and lack of variety may have negative effects, but this is not always the case. Other factors may be more important.

A second factor that has received considerable attention is the general rate of a presentation. The average rate of speaking ranges from 125 to 195 words per minute (wpm). Usually public-speaking teachers admonish speakers who exceed that rate, claiming that a listener cannot easily follow too rapid a presentation. Numerous research projects, however, have arrived at a different conclusion. A sample study illustrates the point. Fairbanks, Guttman, and Miron used a method called *compressed speech* to determine at what rate comprehension begins to decline. The method of compressing speech involves removing tiny segments from a tape-recorded speech so that the words are all intelligible in themselves but such things as the length of vowel sounds and pauses are shortened. Two technical messages on meteorology were recorded at 141 wpm then compressed by various amounts. At 282 wpm, comprehension was slightly less than 90 percent; at 353 wpm, comprehension dropped to 50 percent.[9] If listeners could understand a technical message at double the normal speed, it seems likely that the average listener can decipher less difficult material at a faster-than-normal rate. Another investigator reports that both comprehension and retention of an accelerated speech remained equivalent to that of a normally paced speech until the accelerated speech reached 275 to 300 wpm. Moreover, when given a choice, subjects typically preferred a rate one-and-a-half times the normal speed.[10] The explanation seems to lie in the fact that the faster pace forces the audience to listen more carefully. As an attention-arousal strategy, then, acceleration may be successful. One word of caution, however. You should not indiscriminately begin increasing the rate of your speaking on the assumption that people will attend more closely to what you say. People will listen more carefully only if they are motivated to do so. The teacher confronting a bored class might lose the students completely by speaking more rapidly, but Peace Corps seminar leaders educating new volunteers might prosper from it.

The other class of nonverbal factors that has a clear impact on attention arousal is environmental features. Noble has written:

Normal consciousness, perception and thought can be maintained only in a constantly changing environment; when there is no change a state of "sensory deprivation" occurs. Experiment has shown that a homogeneous and unvarying environment produces boredom, restlessness, lack of concentration and reduction in intelligence.... Office blocks in which each floor has the same layout, color, materials and climate are just asking for trouble.... The sort of variation that we often demand instinctively on aesthetic grounds has a sound physiological and psychological basis. A change in environment stimulates our built-in devices to perceive and respond rapidly to significant events and efficiency is thereby increased.[11]

The German study cited at the opening of this section is evidence of this point. The environment is responsible in part for stimulating the senses so that information is easily comprehended and retained. This is why classrooms use hard, straight-backed chairs and churches use uncomfortable wooden pews. This is also why new classrooms and office buildings are being designed with a variety of colors, lines, textures, and materials. The color and intensity of lighting may also affect comprehension. In one study, subjects achieved the highest scores on a multiple-choice test after interacting in a room with either low-intensity red lighting or medium-intensity blue lighting. Interestingly, test scores were lowest when high-intensity white light was used,[12] which makes one wonder about most classroom lighting. Finally, music seems to make a difference. An elementary-school teacher, Susan McEvoy,

Figure 11.1 Although the people in this office apparently are working busily, to outsiders this environment could well appear to offer the ultimate in distraction. What environmental features might cause us to make such a judgment? (Elliot Erwitt/ Magnum)

communicator selects an environment that is conducive to comprehension (when that is the desired outcome) or manipulates the environment to produce the hoped-for results. (See Figure 11.1.) Companies training people to work on electrical lines or dangerous assembly lines, police academies training new recruits in rescue techniques, medical schools teaching their students sophisticated surgical methods, insurance companies instructing agents in sales strategies—all could benefit from paying careful attention to the environment in which instruction takes place. We know of one firm that likes to train its people at resort hotels. We would like to recommend the same accommodations for our college classes, but we don't think our Dean will go for it.

Distraction Cues

The cues that arouse attention may also become sources of distraction, thereby hurting comprehension and retention. Researchers have been interested in determining which features are harmful and at what point attention-arousing stimuli become a negative influence rather than a positive one.

Many vocal characteristics once thought to be a distracting influence do not have a harmful effect. For instance, it has always been assumed that nonfluencies (such as repetitions, mispronunciations, hesitations) hamper comprehension. However, one dissertation studying a range of fluency from four to sixty-four breaks in two minutes found no loss of comprehension. Another dissertation found that stuttering did not hurt comprehension.[14]

conducted an informal study of the effects of music by taping thirty commercials, some of which included musical jingles, some of which had musical background, and some of which had no musical accompaniment. Adults and children listened to the tape and then answered recall questions such as "Which product gets out greasy, grimy dirt?" Her results showed an overwhelming superiority in recall for the ads with musical jingles, followed by the ones with musical background.[13] Some schools are experimenting with the effects of background music on classroom performance.

The findings regarding the effect of environment on attention suggest that the prudent

Although listeners find such vocal disruptions unpleasant, they are apparently not sufficiently distracted by them to lose comprehension. In fact, some researchers have argued that, in the case of stuttering, the listener, in the process of trying to anticipate and understand what the stutterer is saying, may actually pay closer attention. In other words, stuttering may serve an attention-arousing function. Researchers have yet to establish consistently bad effects for unpleasant voice qualities as well. Diehl and McDonald have confirmed that simulated nasal or breathy voices interfere with comprehension but simulated harsh and hoarse voices do not.[15] Whether real rather than simulated voices would have the same effect, we do not know.

Research on the distracting features of space and the environment is equally inconclusive. Environments can be so busy that they distract rather than arouse attention, but no one seems to know when that point is reached. As for distance, Stuart Albert and James Dabbs thought that comprehension and persuasion would be greatest when an audience was seated at a moderate distance (four to five feet) from a speaker. They reasoned that a closer distance (one to two feet) would be threatening and therefore distracting and a greater distance would be distracting by virtue of being inappropriate. (Actually, Albert and Dabbs didn't use the term *distracting*, but it seems consistent with their analysis.) Although the recall scores were highest at the middle distance, they were not superior enough for the investigators to claim definite support for their prediction.[16] Thus, their study does not reveal to us how much or how little distance is disruptive.

General Principles

From the evidence and ideas we have covered, what conclusions can be drawn? We believe that the following principles can be extracted:

1. Reinforcement is a generally recognized strategy for improving comprehension and retention of information.
2. Nonverbal cues such as smiles, nods, increased eye contact, forward body lean, pats, hugs, and approving vocal cues may act as positive reinforcement; frowns, threatening looks and gestures, neutral facial expressions, reduced eye contact, hostile or cold vocal cues, and silences may act as negative reinforcement. (Not all of these relationships have been individually supported with evidence. Also, while distance is probably a factor, just how it operates is not clear.)
3. Positive reinforcement is preferable to negative reinforcement.
4. Nonverbal cues may improve comprehension and retention by arousing attention. Vocal cues and environmental factors in particular may serve this function.
5. Nonverbal cues may hinder comprehension and retention by serving to distract, but very few cues have been shown to have this effect. Many suspected vocal elements have yet to be established as harmful.

Attitude Change

A long-haired speaker and a seminarian each present the same anti-marijuana speech to two different audiences. Then they each give a pro-marijuana speech to two new audiences. The anti-marijuana audiences are more persuaded by the long-haired speaker than by the seminarian.[17]

An actor is paid to act confidently as he mimes a prerecorded tape of a legal argument. His presentation is viewed by a group of students. He then alters his presentation to be neutral for a second group of students and doubtful for a third group. Consistent with predictions, students viewing the confident presentation are most persuaded and those viewing the doubtful manner are least persuaded.[18]

These examples represent two manipulative strategies that we use to change people's attitudes. The first reflects the positive effects that may result when expectations are violated; the second illustrates the power of credibility cues. Altogether there are five basic strategies, three of which may also be classified as reinforcement. We will begin with these approaches first. They are the use of affiliation, attractiveness, and credibility cues.

Affiliation Appeals

To the extent that people have a need or desire to affiliate with others, affiliation cues may be considered reinforcing. Because affiliation cues carry connotations of liking, acceptance, and approval, people usually find such messages rewarding. We should not be surprised, therefore, to find that these nonverbal messages may be enlisted in persuasion. If you want to persuade your parents that you should be treated as an adult, you may reinforce them with affection when they let you make your own decisions; if you want to persuade the local butcher to give you a special cut of meat, you may turn on the charm.

Kinesic, proxemic, and vocalic cues have received the bulk of attention. Albert Mehrabian and Martin Williams undertook three experiments to discover which nonverbal cues are persuasive or associated with persuasiveness.[19] In the first experiment, subjects gave a highly persuasive speech on one position, a fairly neutral speech on another, and a completely neutral presentation of a third topic. The speeches were all videotaped and then scored by three trained judges. Mehrabian and Williams expected that as *intended* persuasiveness increased, they would observe the following changes in the nonverbal cues: (1) smaller distances to the listener, (2) more eye contact with the listener, (3) a smaller reclining angle, (4) more direct body orientation by

females and more indirect orientation by males, (5) a shift to a moderate rather than high or low degree of relaxation, (6) more smiles, (7) more positive nods, (8) fewer self-manipulations, (9) more verbal reinforcers, (10) more gestures by females, (11) longer messages, and (12) a higher rate of speech disturbances. These predictions were all based on previous evidence that these cues are signals of liking, attraction, approval, or comfort. The results of their first experiment supported their hypotheses for eye contact, reclining angle, nodding, and gesturing (which increased for both sexes). They also found that as intended persuasiveness increased, so did facial activity (aside from pleasant expressions), speech volume, speech rate, intonation, and fluency. The fluency finding was unexpected. Untrained subjects were then asked to rate how persuasive they *perceived* the messages to be. They rated speeches as more persuasive if the presentations involved more eye contact, gesturing, facial activity, vocal volume, fluency, intonation, a faster rate, and less self-manipulation. The vocalic factors were first in order of importance.

In the second experiment, the subjects who encoded the messages gave either a persuasive or an informative talk. Mehrabian and Williams also manipulated the audience to give positive or negative feedback. Again *intended* persuasiveness was highly related to *perceived* persuasiveness. The speakers who intended to be persuasive used more eye contact, and females exhibited less trunk swivel; speakers showed a higher rate of self-manipulation if their audience was receptive. Those who were perceived by observers to be persuasive used the same vocal, facial, gestural, and eye-contact patterns. The final experiment manipulated specific cues and determined whether observers judged them to be more persuasive. Since the first two studies had not found any effects for distance, relaxation, or shoulder orientation, these were controlled, as was eye contact, in thirty-two new video recordings. This time, all of the factors made a

Figure 11.2   Persuasive nonverbal cues

difference. Speakers were seen as more persuasive at closer distances, with a moderate degree of relaxation, and with an indirect body orientation for males. Eye contact had an effect only at greater distances, and even then it depended on the sex of the speaker; females did better with more eye contact and males with less. Finally, the sex of the speaker made a difference for the relaxation factor; women were better off being either slightly tense or slightly relaxed while men were better off being slightly relaxed.

Three other research findings reinforce the Mehrabian and Williams conclusions.[20] Interviewers instructed to use affiliative cues are rated as more persuasive by observers. Second, subjects in a role-playing situation change their attitude according to the eye contact that an accomplice uses. Finally, body position can be a source of influence. Subjects in an experiment by McGinley, LeFevre, and McGinley were asked to read a questionnaire completed by a female student then look at pictures taken of her as she expressed her attitudes in an interview. Those subjects who saw her photographed with an open (limbs outward) body position changed their attitudes more in the direction of hers than those who saw her photographed in a closed (limbs inward) position. This finding reveals how even minor nonverbal cues can influence attitudes. (See Figure 11.2.)

We have summarized these research findings in Table 11.1. The research clearly supports the dictum that sugar goes down easier than vinegar.

Attractiveness Appeals

We have already made the case for the importance of physical attractiveness in the development of first impressions. Attractiveness also contributes to persuasion. Mills and Aronson designed an experiment in which a woman gave the same speech to two different audiences, altering only her appearance. In one case, she was made to look unattractive. Her hair was messy, her skin oily, she wore no make-up, and her clothing was loose and ill-fitting. The researchers even drew a faint mustache on her lip. Before the other audience, the woman wore attractive clothing, her face was made up, and her hair was clean and neat. Men were significantly more persuaded by the attractive female.[21] In another study, Singer predicted that women would use their appearance to manipulate male teachers into giving them good grades. He asked forty male faculty members to rate photographs of 192 freshman women on attractiveness. He then compared the ratings to the grades the women received. Consistent with his hypothesis, the more attractive women received higher grades, but only if they were first-borns. Observations and interviews revealed that these women were more likely to talk to the professor after class, make appointments with him, and sit in the front of the room—in other words, to be more manipulative. A follow-up study established that first-born women were also more likely to

be concerned with their appearance, more accurate in describing themselves, more accurate in describing the ideal body, and more likely to distort their measurements toward the ideal when they knew that no one would be checking on them.[22] From this, we can conclude that the relationship between grades and appearance is not due to chance. Singer's closing statements are telling: "The results imply that the poor college professor is a rather put-upon creature, hoodwinked by the male students (later born) and enticed by the female students (first born) as he goes about his academic and personal responsibilities. He is seemingly caught in a maelstrom of student intrigue and machination."[23] The question that has yet to be answered is whether attractive males use the same strategies with female professors.

Both the Mills and Aronson and the Singer studies demonstrate that attractiveness is related to persuasiveness and that it can be manipulated by the speaker. Just why it leads to more attitude change is not clear, but it is

Table 11.1   Nonverbal Cues Associated with Persuasiveness

	Cues Used by a Speaker Who Intends to Persuade Others	Cues Seen by Receivers as Persuasive
Kinesics	More eye contact	More eye contact (especially for females)
	More positive head nods	
	More gesturing by females	More gesturing
	More facial activity	More facial activity
	Moderate relaxation	Moderate relaxation (slightly more tense for females)
	Smaller reclining angle	
	Direct body orientation for females	Indirect body orientation for males
	Indirect body orientation for males	Open body position
	Less trunk swivel	
Vocalics	Higher volume	Higher volume
	More intonation	More intonation
	Faster rate	Faster rate
	More fluency	More fluency
Proxemics		Closer distances
Haptics		Fewer self-manipulations

possible that receivers find it reinforcing to listen to attractive individuals and to agree with them. Credibility may play a role, too. In the chapter on relational messages, we presented evidence that attractive individuals are seen as more credible. This heightened credibility should lead to more attitude change.

Credibility Appeals

There are other nonverbal cues that seem to derive their effectiveness from the fact that they make the speaker appear more credible. Consider, for example, a public speaker's use of either bad or good delivery (bad delivery includes poor use of voice, limited eye contact, poor use of gestures, bad posture, too rapid a rate and frequent nonfluencies; good delivery is the opposite of these things). If the speaker has a weak message to begin with, delivery won't make a difference; but if the verbal message is strong, good delivery produces much more attitude change than does poor delivery. If both vocal and visual delivery are weak, the effects are particularly detrimental.[24] Good delivery also produces significantly higher ratings of credibility, thus providing support for our assumption that these cues communicate credibility.

One of the ways in which nonverbal cues enhance credibility is by conveying confidence. In the study cited at the opening of this section, Maslow, Yoselson, and London examined kinesic cues associated with a confident, a doubtful, and a neutral manner. The confident manner was most persuasive. When the tapes of the speeches were analyzed, they revealed that the confident speaker used rhythmic, forceful gestures, continuous eye contact (with the camera), and a relaxed posture. By contrast, the doubtful speaker fidgeted with a piece of paper, twirled a pencil, brought his hand to his mouth, pulled at his shirt collar, avoided eye contact with the camera, and sat in a tense, erect position.[25] Timney and

London tried to replicate these findings by designing an experiment in which subjects played jurors and tried to persuade one another about the correct verdict. The researchers hoped that the successful persuaders would display the same cues: high rate of gesturing, less self-manipulation, and high eye contact. Unfortunately, they found only the eye-contact pattern to be consistent—persuasive speakers spent more time looking at their partners.[26] The differences in the two studies might be accounted for by the fact that, in the second study, everyone was trying to be persuasive. The gesturing and self-manipulation might, therefore, be more of a sign of intent to persuade than actual effectiveness. It should be noted that many of the findings here are consistent with those found by the Mehrabian and Williams study discussed in connection with affiliation cues. It is probably safe to conclude that eye contact and relaxation do contribute to persuasiveness, that gesturing and self-manipulation may be signs of intent to persuade, and that these may be successful when coupled with the other vocalic and kinesic cues that have been established as persuasive.

Overall, a good delivery does appear to increase the speaker's credibility and thereby improve his or her persuasiveness. These credibility cues may be viewed as part of the larger reinforcement strategy, since the information and opinions offered by a competent, trustworthy source are appealing to a receiver. Or it may just be rewarding to listen to and agree with a credible speaker.

Distraction Cues

As in the case of comprehension, it has been assumed that certain nonverbal messages may hurt persuasion by distracting the listener. However, two studies on vocal nonfluencies failed to find a detrimental effect on attitude change (although credibility was hurt).[27] Similarly, the proxemic studies by Albert and Dabbs and by Furbay, cited earlier, found that attitude change was greatest when the audience sat in a scattered arrangement or at a considerable distance from the speaker.[28] Perhaps too much proximity to the speaker or other audience members is distracting. Limited support for this interpretation comes from a thesis by Pat Garner, who found that attitude change decreased when an interviewee's space was invaded by the interviewer.[29] Beyond these findings, little evidence suggests that nonverbal factors hurt persuasion by acting as distractions.

Violations of Expectations

The study cited at the opening of this section suggests that people may be more persuaded when their expectations are violated. In that instance, listeners probably did not expect a hippie to speak against marijuana. Consequently, they were open to his presentation. A similar experiment found that householders were more persuaded on a tax issue by a hippie advocate than by a speaker of conventional appearance.[30] In this case, people were probably surprised that an apparent deviant was well-informed on such a topic. Thus, we may increase our persuasiveness if we violate people's expectations in a positive way. The slouching, unassuming student who lucidly argues a position in class may be more effective than the stereotypical student politician. The appearance cues set up a negative expectation which is then violated in a positive way by the verbal presentation.

General Principles

We have seen that one can manipulate many nonverbal cues to improve one's persuasive impact. All of the strategies can be employed in day-to-day conversations as well as in more formal presentations. Even personal attractiveness can be manipulated to some degree.

We can summarize the nonverbal strategies that improve persuasion in the form of the following principles:

1. Kinesic, vocalic, and proxemic cues that signal affiliation, liking, or approval increase perceived and actual persuasiveness.
2. Physical attractiveness enhances persuasiveness.
3. General good delivery increases credibility and attitude change.
4. Vocalic and kinesic cues that communicate confidence, poise, and energy are persuasive and are perceived as persuasive. These cues include authoritative vocal tone, fluent delivery, rapid rate, high volume, varied intonation, slightly relaxed posture, eye contact, varied facial expression, gestures, nods, and little self-manipulation.
5. Extremely close proximity between speaker and listener or among audience members may hurt persuasiveness, possibly because it is distracting.
6. Nonverbal violations of expectations may enhance persuasiveness if they do so in a positive way.

Changes in Communication and Overt Behavior

"On your knees!" "Strip!" In these statutory orders of the convoy lay the basic power one could not argue with. After all, a naked person loses his self-assurance. He cannot straighten up proudly and speak as an equal to people who are still clothed. . . . Naked prisoners approach, carrying their possessions and the clothes they've taken off. A mass of armed soldiers surrounds them. It doesn't look as though they are going to be led to a prisoner transport but as though they are going to be shot immediately or put to death in a gas chamber—and in that mood a human ceases to concern himself with his possessions. The convoy does everything with intentional brusqueness, rudely, sharply, not speaking

one word in an ordinary human voice. After all, the purpose is to terrify and dishearten.[31]

Alexander Solzhenitsyn's chilling description of how Russian prisoners were treated enroute to prison camps during the 1940s demonstrates some of the ruthless ways in which nonverbal cues have been used to shape behavior. One can picture the guards in their authoritative uniforms, ordering around the prisoners who have been robbed of their last symbol of identity and dignity—their clothing. The compelling contrast in dress, coupled with the harsh manner and voices of the guards, are all guaranteed to reinforce the menacing message of power and to produce fearful docility. These methods of engendering compliance, well-known to such manipulators as Adolf Hitler and Charles Manson, are only a few of the ways in which the behavior of masses of people has been molded. In this section, we shall look at some of the strategies commonly used to induce behavior change, including both communication behavior and overt behavior.

Many of the strategies are extensions of the principle of reinforcement. Those that act as actual threats, implied threats, or forms of physical discomfort may be classified as *negative reinforcers*. Those that offer some positive inducement such as affiliation or physical pleasure may be classified as *positive reinforcement*. In fact, much of the research in this field originated as research on reinforcement in learning. Many of the principles now carry the label of *behavior modification techniques*. Of the seven categories we shall examine, the first four most appropriately fall under that heading. The remaining three involve reinforcement in a more limited or indirect fashion.

Threat Cues

The excerpt from Solzhenitsyn's account of prison life is a prime example of the effective use of nonverbal threat cues to elicit desired behavior. The brusque movements and threatening voice are very familiar to us as the stock repertoire of film dictators, military men, and gangsters. Of course, these methods are not just media fantasies. They exist in real life; and they need not be blatant to work. A slight innuendo in a voice can make a child stop whining or an assembly-line worker buy an unwanted lottery ticket from his supervisor. Battered wives have reported that they knew when their husbands intended to beat them by their tone of voice.

Like the voice, the eyes are powerful instruments for molding behavior. The infamous Rasputin was alleged to have gained his great command over men and women through his penetrating, almost hypnotic stare. Charles Manson's eyes were the subject of much comment and apprehension during his trial; even his lawyer, Vincent Bugliosi, said that he found something frightening in Manson's steady gaze. If a stranger has ever held eye contact with you too long, you know how uncomfortable and disconcerting that can be.

Staring is a commonly used threat display among most primate species and often precedes an actual attack. The strength of its impact on humans has recently been demonstrated by a series of experiments on the effects of prolonged gazing. Phoebe Ellsworth, who is well known for her work on eye behavior, along with Merrill Carlsmith and Alexander Henson, decided to see how people waiting for a traffic light would respond to being stared at. They were specifically interested in how quickly people who were stared at would cross the intersection after the light changed compared to those at whom they did not stare. The experimenters picked pedestrians and motorists as subjects and either stood on the street corner or approached the subjects on a motorcycle. In all five versions of the experiment, subjects crossed the intersection much faster when they were stared at.[32]

Several other studies have found similar avoidance or flight reactions to prolonged eye

mini-experiment

Stand near a public pay phone or water fountain. Stare at half the people who approach. Compare their behavior to that of the people you don't stare at.

contact.[33] In one experiment, a researcher carrying a cumbersome shopping bag stared at people in the subway then dropped a stack of papers, apparently by accident. Regardless of whether the stare was straight or broken, unsmiling or smiling, fewer people who had been stared at offered to help pick up the papers than people who had not been stared at. In a similar experiment, subjects working on a puzzle in a room with the experimenter were much more reluctant to help the experimenter with a computer problem if he or she had stared at them. In other studies, people who thought they were applying shocks to others delivered fewer shocks when their supposed victims stared at them. Interestingly, victims with enlarged pupils were also given fewer shocks, and the shockers looked at them less. Large pupils are apparently threatening in themselves. However, when the victim vacillated between continuous and averted gazing instead of maintaining a constant stare, those giving the shock actually delivered more when the victim looked at them. All these experiments imply that people go to extremes to avoid or eliminate excessive eye contact.

While threatening stares usually evoke avoidance responses, they may at times prompt approach behavior. Ellsworth and Langer designed a study in which a person in distress stared at some bystanders but not at others. In some cases, the remedy to the problem was evident and in other cases ambiguous. When the plight and remedy were clear, sub-

jects who had been stared at gave more assistance.[34] The stare was apparently seen as more an entreaty than a threat, singling out the bystander from the anonymous crowd and probably heightening his or her sense of social responsibility. This finding demonstrates that both the timing and the purpose of a stare are important in determining the kind of response it will achieve. Evidently staring must be unprovoked and have no apparent purpose, other than a display of aggressiveness, if it is to be interpreted as threatening.

One last kinesic cue indicates that one wants to be left alone. It is tongue showing, the slight (or exaggerated—see Figure 11.3) protrusion of the tongue between the teeth. A research team recently made observations in Philadelphia, Panama, and the Canal Zone, and reported that all age groups in each of the locations exhibited the tongue when they were about to enter or were already involved in a situation from which they wanted to withdraw. The researchers interpreted the behavior as a signal for others to keep their distance.[35] The same behavior appears among apes and monkeys.

While it is evident from the research cited in this section that threat cues are often effective in influencing others' behavior, the reported estimate that 20 percent of the population resort at one time or another to actual violence in their interpersonal relations is an alarming reminder that threats alone do not always work.

Dominance, Power, and Status Appeals

Cues of dominance, power, and status are a two-sided coin: they may operate as negative reinforcement by implicitly threatening the application of negative sanctions or as positive reinforcement by implying the capacity to supply positive consequences. Either way, they have profound effects on attitudes and behavior. The use of uniforms is a good example. On the one hand, we typically react apprehensively to people in uniform, fearing that they

Figure 11.3

may catch us doing something wrong and punish us or that they may use their power against us. For example, people generally tense up when they find themselves being followed by a highway patrol car on the interstate. On the other hand, uniforms mean status and control of resources—the ability to bestow favors and rewards. The headwaiter in a fine restaurant has the power to give the best or worst table in the house. Therefore, if we comply with the wishes of a uniformed person, we may be helped; if we disobey, we may be harmed.

The power of the uniform to evoke blind obedience was forcefully demonstrated in the studies conducted by Stanley Milgram. In his studies, Milgram used a method, briefly described earlier, in which subjects were told to administer shocks to other subjects when they gave wrong answers on a learning task. In reality, the victims were confederates of the experimenter and were not actually hooked up to an electrical current; but they could be heard to moan and groan after each "shock" was delivered. They even pleaded with the subject to stop because they had a heart condition. Subjects nevertheless consistently increased the shock level up to and beyond a

danger level when told to do so by the white-coated experimenter. Even after the victim became silent, subjects continued to apply shock.[36] While this experiment was not directly designed to test the effects of dress on compliance—Milgram was investigating whether Americans could behave as inhumanly as the German people did under Hitler—the aura of authority created by the white coat and the trappings of the laboratory setting certainly reinforced the subjects' willingness to submit to the requests of the experimenter and transfer responsibility to him. This finding, which was replicated through several variations of the experiment, provoked other researchers to consider just how far people would go in submitting to the commands of someone who had no legitimate authority but merely the appearance of authority.

Leonard Bickman, for one, became curious about this question. For answers he went to the street.[37] He had male accomplices dress either as a civilian (wearing a sport coat and tie), a milkman, or a guard (wearing a uniform similar to a policeman's but with different insignia and badge and no gun). The accomplice then approached passersby on a Brooklyn street with one of three requests. In one case, he stopped a person, pointed to a small paper bag lying on the ground, and requested that the person pick it up. If the subjects first refused, he told them he had a bad back. He kept track of how many people actually picked up the bag. In another case, he stopped pedestrians, pointed to another accomplice near a parked car, and said, "This fellow is overparked at the meter but doesn't have any change. Give him a dime!" If the subject didn't comply, the experimenter said he didn't have any change himself. In the third case, the experimenter walked up to people waiting at a bus stop, pointed to the BUS STOP—NO STANDING sign and told them it meant they had to stand on the other side of the sign. (Of course, it actually means that no one can park in the bus-stop zone.) If the subject did not move, the accomplice explained that it was a new law and that the bus would not stop where they were standing. In all three cases, what the accomplice was wearing made a difference as to whether the subjects complied: when he wore the guard uniform, they were much more likely to obey his orders; the milkman uniform and civilian dress were equal in their effects.

Bickman also conducted a study which examined how just the implied status of a per-

son's clothing would affect the behavior of others. This time he picked John F. Kennedy Airport and Grand Central Station as the locales for his investigation. He had three males and three females serve as his confederates. Half the time they were dressed to appear of high status—the men wore suits and ties and the women wore neat dresses and carried a dress coat—and half the time they were dressed to appear of low status—the men wore working clothes and carried such things as a lunchpail or flashlight, while the women wore inexpensive skirts and blouses and looked generally unkempt. Bickman was interested in whether people would be more honest with a high- or low-status individual. He devised the following test: His accomplices first placed a dime in an obvious spot in a telephone booth. After an unsuspecting subject entered the phone booth to make a call, the confederate waited two minutes and then approached the subject and said, "Excuse me, I think I might have left a dime in this phone booth a few minutes ago. Did you find it?" When the results were tallied, Bickman discovered that, regardless of the sex, race, age, and status of the subject, more people returned the dime to the person of apparent high status (77 percent for the high-status attire compared to 38 percent for low-status dress).

Bickman made some follow-up studies. People answering a questionnaire said that they did not think that the status level of dress or the presence of a uniform would influence their responses to various trivial requests. Clearly, we don't recognize how susceptible we are to the influence of clothing on our behavior. People may claim that dress doesn't affect them, but the results of Bickman's field studies, using ordinary people in commonplace settings, reveal that clothing can be used to manipulate other people's behavior by signalling power and status.

Kinesic, vocalic, appearance, proxemic, chronemic, and environmental cues can also be manipulated to reinforce the message of dominance, power, and status. The confident

mini-experiment

To test the effects of clothing and appearance, alter your own appearance from highly informal and sloppy to highly formal and neat, approach salespeople in a department store, and note whether they offer to help, how much eye contact they give you, and how much time they spend with you in each appearance condition. You may want to have a friend make observations from a distance.

posture of the business executive, the orotund voice of the politician, and the lavish home furnishings of the socialite are a few examples of cues that can be used to exert pressure. An issue of *New Woman* magazine carried an article listing thirty-five tricks powerful people use. Here is a sample:[38]

1. Physical signs hint at power. "A certain immobility, steady eyes, quiet hands, broad fingers, above all a solid presence [suggest] that one belongs where one is, even if it's somebody else's office or home."
2. Use a small calendar that is easily filled up (write large if need be)—it gives the appearance of frenetic activity.
3. Sit still while others fidget. "The main thing is to be silent, impassive, alert in appearance and yet at the same time *visible.*"
4. Wear noneccentric clothing that makes you look solid, conservative, and reliable.
5. Avoid swinging the feet. Plant them firmly on the ground when trying to gain maximum power during a serious discussion; turn toes outward rather than inward while sitting (inturned toes show deference). A good pair of shoes conveys a lasting positive image.
6. Speak in hushed whispers so people have to lean forward to hear you.
7. Dim the lighting in your office. Bright lights mean less power.
8. Be theatrical, dramatic, hysterical when necessary.
9. Tempt people from behind their desks to sit on a chair or sofa, or if that doesn't work, put a hat or briefcase on their desk to pierce their barrier.
10. Allow a half hour for meetings that are bound to last an hour, or make people stand by for a meeting so that their schedule has to revolve around yours.

We leave it to you to decide for yourself which of these strategies are most likely to succeed.

Positive Regard and Interest Appeals

Common sense tells us that if people's attitudes can be changed by showing them that they are liked and accepted, so can their behaviors. The band director who encourages and praises novice musicians will turn out better performers than the one who yells at them and insults their efforts. Numerous applications of this principle of rewarding people through displays of approval, interest, and concern have attested to its validity in changing people's actions.[39] Children increase their play activity when they are reinforced with approval cues; delinquents respond better to rehabilitation efforts when instructions and feedback are delivered in a positive manner; library users show more positive evaluations of the library environment and the desk clerk when they are briefly touched by the clerk; and doctors even receive more referrals from alcoholic patients when their voices convey concern for their patients. A significant finding is that job interviewers are much more impressed by and likely to hire interviewees who adopt direct, affiliative seating positions.

Communication is also significantly influenced. First, people increase the length or amount of verbal communication when they receive such positive immediacy cues as head nods, touches, smiles, and direct eye contact, all cues that signal warmth.[40] Nurses, for example, find that their patients tell them more when they touch them. Second, rapport is increased. When an interviewer leans forward during an interview, the interviewee's expressive behaviors, emotional reactions, and speech patterns reveal a sense of rapport.[41] Third, interest and approval cues can be used to elicit self-disclosure, the degree to which people reveal information and feelings about themselves that may be potentially risky. Touch, nods, smiles, and other positive cues may lead a person to disclose more, especially if the cues are presented in combination.[42] Encounter groups recognized this possibility very early and have typically relied on touch as one of their chief means of getting people to open up about themselves.

Finally, these cues may influence intimacy.[43] Miles Patterson, who has developed a theory about intimacy, thinks that acting in an intimate way (say, decreasing interpersonal distance and increasing eye contact and touch) has an arousal effect. Whether that arousal leads to a reciprocal response depends on such things as the nature of the relationship and the setting. If two people already like each other and the setting is appropriate for such behavior, intimate behaviors by one party should lead to equally intimate behaviors by the other party. The reality may be more complex than that. Under the guise of studying encounter groups, Ellsworth and Ross conducted an experiment in which accomplices either maintained continuous eye contact or averted their gaze while another person talked. Observers, listeners, and speakers then rated the intimacy level of each person's communication. The results revealed a sex difference. Females became more intimate under continuous direct eye contact and less intimate under gaze aversion. The males became less intimate under continuous eye contact; but oddly, they thought they were more intimate. When given direct eye contact, men also increased their liking for the gazer and were satisfied with the task, two effects that didn't occur with women. These results suggest that males may simply be less able than females to match their behavior to their feelings of intimacy. Perhaps the direct eye contact made them more self-conscious and inhibited. At any rate, the results should be of interest to females trying to detect the true feelings of their husbands or boyfriends. In this case, the proof may be not in a man's behavior but in what he professes to feel.

One additional consideration in the use of positive cues as reinforcement is their timing. Behavior modification experts claim that picking up a screaming baby ensures constant screaming. The time to pick up and cuddle a baby is when the crying subsides, not while it is at its worst. Otherwise, the approval and affection cues implicit in the cuddling may reinforce misbehavior. The trick is to present the reinforcement cues immediately after a behavior you want to encourage. The child who constantly interrupts conversations should be ignored until he or she waits patiently to be recognized then rewarded for behaving well. Unfortunately, most parents succumb after the child has continued to tug and is whining loudly, thereby assuring that the show of interest will reinforce whining and interruption. Children learn quickly that a tantrum is the quickest route to getting attention. The same principle applies to any other kind of behavior we want to influence. This is one strategy you should be able to test for yourself.

Pleasure and Pain

In the category of pleasure and pain fall those forms of nonverbal reward and punishment that directly translate into physical pleasure, discomfort, or pain. Proxemics and environmental considerations are most relevant. Robert Sommer, a specialist in the area of proxemics, writes that the pleasurable effects of carpeting a school building influence for the better the way students behave.[44] The carpet gives them the impression that school is a desirable place to be by making it comfortable and aesthetically appealing. As a result, students behave well. They are quiet in the halls, less rowdy and restless in class. As we mentioned earlier, music also has positive effects. Besides soothing students in the classroom, music can calm jittery nerves in the doctor's office or stimulate buying in the supermarket. Soft music is a traditional part of the American male's seduction routine.

On the other hand, the absence of comfort and aesthetically pleasing qualities or the presence of physically noxious stimuli can also influence behavior. Prisons make extensive use of this strategy. Solzhenitsyn writes that one of the more insidious ways in which Russian prisons maintained submissive behavior among the prisoners was to deny them

adequate physical space. Prisoners had no territory to call their own. They frequently began
their internment by being placed in a box so
small that they could only stand up, squeezed
against the door. Later, when they were moved
to larger quarters, they would find themselves
in an extremely cramped cell, which caused
discomfort and anxiety. The prisoners became
compliant, willing to do anything to escape
the intolerable conditions.

Similar tactics are used in American prisons.
Sheila Ramsey, discussing the Pennsylvania
correctional system, says:

*An integral part of the punishment procedure
is the control of space. . . . Inmates have no
control over who they will live next to and
little control over who they will socialize with.
New inmates in the clinic live in cells half
the size of the regular population and are
kept from interaction with those in the
population.*[45]

She further notes that prisoners who display
antisocial behavior are placed in smaller cells
or solitary confinement, the idea being to remove them from the mainstream.

Because space is at such a premium, prisoners develop informal means of staking out
individual territories. One example is claiming
auditorium seats. When the auditorium is full,
there is usually a seat between each man. One
prisoner reports how inviolable those boundaries become and how they influence inmates'
behavior:

*The auditorium was getting really crowded; I
saw one dude who had to move three times
because he sat in somebody else's territory.
Finally he came over by me and sat down,
leaving one chair between us. The chair he
was sitting on was all busted up; there was no
back and only half the bottom left. I was gonna
tell him to move over by me. It would be a lot
more comfortable, but I thought he might take
it the wrong way. He was pretty flustered by
now anyway. So he watched the whole movie
sitting in this broken chair.*[46]

Some authorities on prisons believe that space
deprivation is one of the greatest causes of
prison riots. There is little private space. The
cement and tile buildings produce intolerable
noise levels. There is little or no natural lighting, and the environment is visually monoto-
nous with no variety in color or architecture to
relieve the sterility. Such an environment typically depresses behavior, but occasionally, because it is bleak and it denies the humanity of
the inmates, it can cause violence to erupt.

Some of these features take their toll outside
the prison environment as well. Researchers,
recognizing that many dormitories possess
characteristics similar to those of prisons, have
begun to investigate how crowding affects behavior. As we have mentioned, students who
live in dormitory rooms off a long corridor feel
more crowded and are less apt to help others
than those who live in dorms with a suite
arrangement.[47] They have been shown to be
less likely to mail a letter that appears to have
been accidentally dropped in a hallway, and
they are less likely to save milk cartons for a
charitable cause.

Group interactions are similarly affected by
crowding.[48] Subjects in one study seated close
together in uncomfortable chairs interacted
less, showed less interest, made fewer relevant
comments, were more tense, and evaluated the
environment more negatively than subjects
who had more space and comfortable chairs.
Sometimes, as we noted in Chapter 4, there is a
sex difference. All-male groups placed in a
small room for a jury deliberation became hostile and competitive, delivering stringent verdicts; all-female groups became friendlier,
found the environment pleasant, and delivered
lenient verdicts. (Mixed-sex groups showed no
negative effects from crowding.) The explanation for these conflicting findings may lie in
the nature of other environmental factors and
in the definition of crowding. The first study
included the element of comfort. Discomfort
might have magnified the effects of proximity.
Second, *crowdedness* was defined in the first
study as extremely close distance and in the
other studies as a small volume of space. This

variable may explain the sex difference. We know that men require more personal space than women; they may, therefore, have found the small room threatening while the women found it intimate. The principal investigator in the second group of studies ultimately concluded that the best definition of crowding might be based not on amount of space or distance but on how many others one has to interact with, a suggestion that is consistent with the findings of the dormitory studies.

The controlling effect of unpleasant environments is evident in the typical public high school. Craig Haney and Philip Zimbardo, in an article entitled, "It's Tough to Tell a High School from a Prison," write:

Inside the average high school, the drab and depressing interiors clearly show that they have been designed for efficiency, security and surveillance rather than beauty or the comfort of their inmates. The dulling uniformity of identical classrooms and endless hallways emphasize the anonymity and insensitivity of the place, and the regimentation it imposes on its inhabitants. . . . To the extent that a message can be translated from the high school's architectural medium, the language is clear: this place values regularity, order and control over creativity, spontaneity and freedom.[49]

Most high school teachers will attest that the regularity surpasses the creativity, even if the environment doesn't yield order as often as the administration would like. The dullness and disorder that so frequently occur are further evidence that punishment—in the form of unpleasant surroundings—produces unpredictable effects.

Modeling

Another method by which we can influence the behavior of others is to provide them with a model of the behavior we want. The phenomenon of *behavioral contagion* is common among children. One child, the leader, develops a unique behavior or dress style which the other children all mimic. We have witnessed, for instance, a case at a summer camp where one popular child became hoarse. Before the end of the week, over half the children were talking in hoarse tones. Behavioral contagion is also the explanation given for mob behavior. We mentioned in the section on attitude change a study that tried to produce imitative behavior among members of an audience. That effort didn't succeed, but the history books are full of instances of contagious reactions that had disastrous results. The riots in Watts and Washington, D.C., in the 1960s are an example.

On a smaller scale, one individual's behavior can be significantly influenced by the behavior of a model. A number of experiments on modeling, many conducted by the learning expert Albert Bandura, have produced conclusive evidence that children and adults adopt behaviors they see modeled (see Fig. 11.4).[50] Children who watched an adult display aggressive behavior toward a doll later exhibited the same behavior in free play and were more violent than children who did not witness the model's behavior. Black and white children who watch black and white adolescents interacting on film adopt the interaction style they see modeled. Those who observe the adolescents playing in a warm fashion later play closer together, facing each other more directly and using more eye contact than those who witness, and mimic, a cool interaction pattern. Adults similarly match the pattern of eye contact, and length of pauses, and utterances of an interviewer.

A study on infants drinking juice showed that modeling is influenced heavily by nonverbal cues. The infants, who were fed orange juice and tomato juice on alternate days by several women, frequently showed a definite preference for one juice over another. However, when they changed feeders, they often reversed their preferences. It turned out that the women doing the feeding had definite preferences themselves, which they somehow communicated nonverbally to the infants and the infants modeled.[51]

Modeling as a response may in itself also

manipulate behavior. In one study, some children were asked to model and others not to model the behavior of male college students trying to teach them basketball moves. The students who were imitated gave the children more positive verbal and nonverbal responses than those who were not.[52] Modeling may therefore be an effective form of flattery.

Several factors influence the use of modeling, one of which is the presence of reinforcement. Bandura's research has shown that people may learn a behavior from modeling but not exhibit it until they have an incentive for doing so. Some people may know good table manners but refuse to use them until, say, a job assignment or a pay raise depends upon it.

Whether the model is rewarded or punished for a given behavior also determines whether the observer adopts the same behavior. Other factors that make a difference are the nature of the model, the forms of reinforcement, and the skills of the learner. Nonverbal cues clearly play a role in the identification of these factors. The age, sex, and status of the model and the nature of the reward or punishment may all be signalled nonverbally. Door-to-door salesmen who want to sell you encyclopedias may show you pictures of people obviously of high status who have bought the books, to act as behavior models. If you comply, you may then be reinforced with nonverbal and verbal messages of approval.

Figure 11.4   The process by which children become adults involves modeling. Observation of yourself and of others should verify that adults, too, use modeling extensively in presenting themselves to others. (Frank Siteman/Stock Boston)

Violations of Expectations

We raised the issue earlier as to whether it is profitable to violate expectations in a given situation. With regard to appearance, if nonverbal cues are used to create a negative expectation that is then violated in a positive way by the verbal message, it may be a good persuasion strategy. But if the purpose is to get some kind of assistance from others, the best strategy is to conform to the dress and grooming norms. A host of studies[53] have verified this proposition by having experimenters of both conventional and unconventional appearance make a request. In a sample experiment, a man and a woman dressed in hippie attire with beads, bellbottoms, headbands, and so forth. The man had long hair and a beard, the woman wore her hair long and straight. They approached people at a shopping center and asked them to sign an innocuous petition. The following day, they changed their appearance. The man cut his hair short, shaved his beard, and put on a suit and tie. The woman wore a dress, high heels, and make-up and wore her hair on top of her head. They collected significantly more signatures for their petition.

Findings from other studies suggest that conventional attire produces more signing of antiwar petitions than does hippie attire; well-dressed hitchhikers (socks, shoes, pressed slacks, shirt, tie and jacket, well-groomed hair) are given more rides than those wearing bellbottoms, sandals, peace symbols, beads, bandanas, and shoulder-length hair (what are the implications of this finding for the travelers in Figure 11.5?); campaigners in unconventional dress have more difficulty distributing campaign leaflets than their counterparts in straight dress, and their candidate is assumed to be more radical; conventionally dressed black and white males have more luck exchanging a dime for two nickels outside a supermarket than when they dress like hippies or black nationalists.

However, when it comes to other purposes and other nonverbal codes, conformity isn't always the best policy. One of the authors and

Steve Jones have come up with a theory that predicts that violating expectations can sometimes produce a positive outcome. The theory, which is restricted to proxemics, argues that people who are highly regarded can create more positive effects by violating norms—specifically, by moving closer than is expected—but that individuals who are not highly regarded are better off conforming to the normative distance.[54] Preliminary research has established that people who are viewed as unattractive, critical, of low status, and so on achieve their best effects by conforming to the normative distance, while people who are physically attractive, give praise, are high status, and so forth are viewed as more attractive and credible if they violate expectations by adopting a distance that is either farther than or nearer than the norm, so long as they are not so close that they become threatening. If the deviation from the norm is so close as to be an invasion of personal space, it can have negative consequences. A person whose territory is invaded may talk more but disclose less, be less flexible in his or her views, and show more tension through increased nonfluencies, arm movements, or total body movement. The invader may also lose credibility.[55]

Whether the same kinds of relationships between type of violation and nature of the violator hold for other nonverbal codes has yet to be determined. But we think the notion is a provocative one—that we can manipulate the reactions of others in a predictable way by behaving in an unexpected way ourselves.

Experimenter Expectancy Effects

This final means of manipulating other people's behavior has only recently been discovered. Perhaps it shouldn't even be called manipulation, since the person doing it isn't aware that he or she is doing it. Nonetheless, the action alters someone else's responses. Simply put, experimenters nonverbally signal to subjects how they want them to respond and the subjects comply. Evidence of this effect can be traced back to 1911 to the remarkable feats of Clever Hans, a horse who could spell, read, and solve mathematical problems simply by tapping out the answers with his hoof. At least, that's what everyone thought. A committee even certified that Hans received no clues from his questioners. However, a man named Pfungst was able to demonstrate that Hans was using minute head and eye movements from the questioners as cues. When a question was posed, the questioner looked at Hans's hoof, since that was where the answer would appear. When Hans approached the correct answer, the questioner would inadvertantly move his head or eyes upward, or simply flare his nostrils. This was all Hans needed to know when to stop tapping.[56] The scientific community did not recognize until the 1960s that the same thing was happening in psychological research on human subjects.

One of the first experiments to test the experimenter expectancy hypothesis was conducted not with human subjects but with rats. The question was, Would experimenters unwittingly bias the outcome of the research if they thought they knew its purpose? Two groups of rats from the same litter were given to two different sets of experimenters. One set was told that their rats had been specially bred to be very bright and should perform well at running mazes. The other group was told that their rats were from dull stock and should perform poorly. That is exactly how the rats performed, even though they came from the same litter. Researchers led by Robert Rosenthal undertook to discover what an experimenter might do to bias responses.

Figure 11.5

The researchers employed a *person perception* task for observing the behavior of experimenters toward human subjects. Subjects were given a series of photographs of people and asked to judge whether they were successful or not. The observations revealed that experimenters used both auditory and visual cues to signal their expectations. If, when they read the instructions, they emphasized the success option, subjects rated more photographs as successful; if the failure alternative was emphasized, more photographs were rated as failures. Experimenters who were more likeable, dominant, warm, relaxed, and self-assured during the first few seconds and who used fewer leg movements later were also much more likely to bias the subject toward the results they expected. Most surprising, the expectations were communicated in the first thirty seconds, even before the subject had made any kind of response. Before instructions were given, visual cues were very important; during the reading of instructions, vocal cues also began to exert influence.[37] Some of the specific cues found to be important were amount of eye contact, vocal volume, vocal stress, and length of interaction. More eye contact from the experimenter produced more positive ratings of photos; increased volume or stress on key words determined which response pattern subjects favored; and longer interactions between experimenters and subjects of opposite sex produced more biased results.[58] Such factors as sex, age, and race of the experimenter also made a difference. For instance, male experimenters were more friendly overall to subjects than were female experimenters, but females were more friendly visually than males and males were more friendly vocally.[59]

The implications of these findings are twofold. First, they indicate that we are unconsciously able to shape other people's behavior by signalling our expectations. The alarming power of this form of influence has been illustrated in schools through what has been called the *pygmalion effect*. Children of equal ability have been randomly labeled as having either high potential (so as to merit the name *bloomers*) or low potential. Like Eliza Doolittle in George Bernard Shaw's *Pygmalion*, the children behaved according to what was expected of them in study after study. By the end of the experimental period (lasting anywhere from two months to two years), children who had been tagged as bright showed significant intellectual gains while those tagged as dull were failing. Average students became high achievers when their teachers thought they had high IQ's. Children who began to show progress counter to the teacher's expectations were evaluated negatively.[60] This *self-fulfilling prophecy* effect has also been demonstrated in interracial interaction. Word, Zanna, and Cooper conducted an experiment with an interesting twist. They asked white interviewers to interact with white and black interviewees, but the interviewees were actually confederates and the real subjects were the interviewers. Observations revealed that the interviewers made more speech errors, gave shorter interviews, and used less immediacy cues with the black interviewees. The researchers then trained two white confederates to approximate the interview styles used with the white and black interviewees and had them interview a new group of white subjects. Those subjects who received the style that had been addressed to blacks were judged to perform less well, to be more nervous, and to remain more distant than those receiving the style used for whites; the interviewers were also judged to be less adequate and friendly when they used the former style.[61] The results suggest that whites signal low expectations to blacks, who then fulfill those expectations. This bias probably operates at a subconscious, nonverbal level.

Clearly, this study and the previous ones are testimony to a general sensitivity to expectancy cues. Because such cues usually operate outside the awareness of the parties involved, they may be one of the most potent methods by which people engineer the behavior of others.

General Principles

From the research presented on strategies to change behavior, the following conclusions can be drawn:

1. Threat cues such as brusque movements, harsh voices, staring, and tongue showing produce avoidance responses or reduce aggressiveness on the part of the recipient.
2. Cues of dominance, power, and status increase compliance to requests from apparent authority or status figures, even to the point of endangering others. Uniforms and other clothing, posture, body movement, vocal volume and quality, and the manipulation of time, space, and environment may all be effective as cues.
3. Kinesic, proxemic, haptic, and vocalic cues signalling positive regard and interest may increase acceptable social behavior, length of interactions, rapport, self-disclosure, and intimacy of interactions.
4. Environmental factors that produce physically pleasant conditions may be used to reinforce socially desirable behavior, better learning performances, and so on. Environmental factors that produce uncomfortable conditions are less predictable; they may produce compliance, or they may reduce helping behavior, or result in avoidance of interaction, aggression, and hostility.
5. Behavior and communication are influenced by models; nonverbal cues may be used to model behavior, to identify the nature of the model, to indicate what rewards or punishments accompany the behavior, or to act as the rewards and punishments themselves.
6. Norm violations may have positive or negative effects on behavior, depending on what kind of norm is violated, what form that violation takes, and who does the violating. Violating dress norms produces negative consequences; people are less willing to listen to or help an unconventionally dressed person than a conventionally dressed one. Violating proxemic norms may have positive effects, but only if the person doing the violating is seen as powerful and does not invade personal space.
7. Actions and communication may be manipulated by vocalic and kinesic signals of expectations.

Summary

In this last chapter, we have examined the ways in which nonverbal cues may be used in intentional and controlled ways to affect what and how others learn, what attitudes they acquire, what communication patterns they develop, and what overt actions they display. Successful strategies generally involve some form of reinforcement. Nonverbal cues of affiliation, positive regard, interest, credibility, dominance, power, and status may be used as effective reinforcers. Additionally, nonverbal cues that arouse attention or distract, that provide direct pleasure or pain, or that threaten such outcomes may have reinforcing or punishing effects. Finally, modeling approaches, violating expectations, and nonverbally signalling expectations may significantly influence the way others think and act.

Suggested Reading

Bickman, L. "Social Roles and Uniforms: Clothes Make the Person." *Psychology Today*, 7, No. 11 (1974), 49–51.

Burgoon, J. K., and Jones, S. B., "Toward a Theory of Personal Space Expectations and Their Violations." *Human Communication Research*, 2 (1976), 131–146.

Darley, J. M., and Cooper, J., "The 'Clean for Gene' Phenomenon: The Effect of Students' Appearance on Political Campaigning." *Journal of Applied Social Psychology*, 2 (1972), 24–33.

Finkelstein, J. C. "Experimenter Expectancy Effects." *Journal of Communication,* 26 (1976), 31–35.

Krasner, L., and Ullman, L. P. (eds.). *Research in Behavior Modification.* New York: Holt, Rinehart and Winston, 1965.

Mehrabian, A., and Williams, M. "Nonverbal Concomitants of Perceived and Intended Persuasiveness." *Journal of Personality and Social Psychology,* 13 (1969), 37–58.

Patterson, M. L. "An Arousal Model of Inter-personal Intimacy." *Psychological Review,* 83 (1976), 235–245.

Proshansky, H. M., Ittelson, W. H., and Rivlin, L. G. (eds.). *Environmental Psychology: Man and His Setting.* New York: Holt, Rinehart and Winston, 1970.

Rosenthal, R., and Rosnow, R. L. *Artifact in Behavioral Research.* New York: Academic Press, 1969.

Sommer, R. *Personal Space.* Englewood Cliffs, N.J.: Prentice-Hall, 1969.

Notes

1. Cited in I. Silden, "Psychological Effects of Office Planning," *Mainliner* (December 1973), pp. 30–34.

2. J. S. Kleinfeld, "Effects of Nonverbal Warmth on the Learning of Eskimo and White Students," *Journal of Social Psychology,* 92 (1974), pp. 3–9.

3. A. E. Kazdin and J. Klock, "The Effect of Nonverbal Teacher Approval on Student Attentive Behavior," *Journal of Applied Behavior Analysis,* 6 (1973), pp. 643–654.

4. J. K. Burgoon, "Further Explication and an Initial Test of the Theory of Violations of Personal Space Expectations," paper presented at the Speech Communication Association Convention, San Francisco, December 1976.

5. A. L. Furbay, "The Influence of Scattered Versus Compact Seating on Audience Response," *Speech Monographs,* 32 (1965), pp. 144–148.

6. C. Woolbert, "The Effects of Various Models of Public Reading," *Journal of Applied Psychology,* 4 (1920), pp. 162–185.

7. K. C. Beighley, "An Experimental Study of the Effect of Four Speech Variables on Listener Comprehension," *Speech Monographs,* 19 (1952), pp. 249–258; K. C. Beighley, "An Experimental Study of the Effect of Three Speech Variables on Listener Comprehension," *Speech Monographs,* 21 (1954), pp. 248–253.

8. G. M. Glasgow, "A Semantic Index of Vocal Pitch," *Speech Monographs,* 19 (1952), pp. 64–68; C. F. Diehl, R. C. White, and P. H. Satz, "Pitch Change and Comprehension," *Speech Monographs,* 28 (1961), pp. 65–68.

9. G. Fairbanks, N. Guttman, and M. Miron, "Effects of Time Compression Upon the Comprehension of Connected Speech," *Journal of Speech and Hearing Disorders,* 22 (1957), pp. 10–19.

10. D. B. Orr, "Time Compressed Speech—A Perspective," *Journal of Communication,* 18 (1968), pp. 288–292.

11. J. Noble, "The How and Why of Behavior: Social Psychology for the Architect," *Architects' Journal* (March 1963), cited in H. M. Proshansky, W. H. Ittelson, and L. G. Rivlin (eds.), *Environmental Psychology: Man and His Physical Setting* (New York: Holt, Rinehart and Winston, 1970), p. 464.

12. G. A. Sadesky, "The Effects of Lighting Color and Intensity on Small Group Communication," paper presented at the International Communication Association Convention, New Orleans, April 1974.

13. S. McEvoy, "Music and Advertising," unpublished manuscript, University of Florida, 1976.

14. H. N. Klinger, "The Effects of Stuttering on Audience Listening Comprehension," dissertation, New York University, 1959; V. A. Utzinger, "An Experimental Study of the Effects of Verbal Fluency upon the Listener," dissertation, University of Southern California, 1952.

15. C. F. Diehl and E. T. McDonald, "Effect of Voice Quality on Communication," *Journal of Speech and Hearing Disorders,* 21 (1956), pp. 233–237.

16. S. Albert and J. M. Dabbs, Jr., "Physical Distance and Persuasion," *Journal of Personality and Social Psychology,* 15 (1970), pp. 265–270.

17. R. W. McPeek and J. D. Edwards, "Expectancy Disconfirmation and Attitude Change," *Journal of Social Psychology*, 96 (1975), pp. 193–208.

18. C. Maslow, K. Yoselson, and H. London, "Persuasiveness of Confidence Expressed via Language and Body Language," *British Journal of Social and Clinical Psychology*, 10 (1971), pp. 234–240.

19. A. Mehrabian and M. Williams, "Nonverbal Concomitants of Perceived and Intended Persuasiveness," *Journal of Personality and Social Psychology*, 13 (1969), pp. 37–58.

20. G. Breed and M. Porter, "Eye Contact, Attitudes and Attitude Change Among Males," *Journal of Genetic Psychology*, 120–122 (1972), pp. 211–217; M. B. LaCrosse, "Nonverbal Behavior and Perceived Counselor Attractiveness and Persuasiveness," *Journal of Counseling Psychology*, 22 (1975), pp. 563–566; H. McGinley, R. LeFevre, and P. McGinley, "The Influence of a Communicator's Body Position on Opinion Change in Others," *Journal of Personality and Social Psychology*, 31 (1975), pp. 686–690.

21. J. Mills and E. Aronson, "Opinion Change as a Function of the Communicator's Attractiveness and Desire to Influence," *Journal of Personality and Social Psychology*, 1 (1965), pp. 73–77.

22. J. E. Singer, "The Use of Manipulative Strategies: Machiavellianism and Attractiveness," *Sociometry*, 27 (1964), pp. 128–151; J. E. Singer and P. F. Lamb, "Social Concern, Body Size and Birth Order," *Journal of Social Psychology*, 68 (1966), pp. 143–151.

23. Singer, p. 150 (note 22).

24. J. C. McCroskey, *An Introduction to Rhetorical Communication* (Englewood Cliffs, N.J.: Prentice-Hall, 1972), pp. 243–244; R. L. Rosnow and E. J. Robinson, *Experiments in Persuasion* (New York: Academic Press, 1967) pp. 2–5.

25. Maslow, Yoselson, and London (note 18).

26. B. Timney and H. London, "Body Language Concomitants of Persuasiveness and Persuasibility in Dyadic Interaction," *International Journal of Group Tensions*, 3, Nos. 3–4 (1973), pp. 48–67.

27. G. R. Miller and M. A. Hewgill, "The Effect of Variations in Nonfluency on Audience Ratings of Source Credibility," *Quarterly Journal of Speech*, 50 (1964), pp. 36–44; K. K. Sereno and G. J. Hawkins, "The Effects of Variations in Speaker's Nonfluency upon Audience Ratings of Attitude Toward the Speech Topic and Speaker's Credibility," *Speech Monographs*, 34 (1967), pp. 58–64.

28. Albert and Dabbs (note 16); Furbay (note 5).

29. P. H. Garner, "The Effects of Invasions of Personal Space on Interpersonal Communication," thesis, Illinois State University, 1972.

30. J. Cooper, J. M. Darley, and J. E. Henderson, "On the Effectiveness of Deviant- and Conventional-Appearing Communicators," *Journal of Personality and Social Psychology*, 29 (1974), pp. 752–757.

31. A. Solzhenitsyn, *The Gulag Archipelago* (New York: Harper and Row, 1973) p. 570. Published in England by William Collins and Company Ltd.

32. P. C. Ellsworth, J. M. Carlsmith, and A. Henson, "The Stare as a Stimulus to Flight in Human Subjects," *Journal of Personality and Social Psychology*, 21 (1972), pp. 302–311.

33. P. Ellsworth and J. M. Carlsmith, "Eye Contact and Gaze Aversion in an Aggressive Encounter," *Journal of Personality and Social Psychology*, 28 (1973), pp. 280–292; P. Horn, "Newsline," *Psychology Today*, 7, No. 12 (1974), p. 27; R. F. Kidd, "Pupil Size, Eye Contact and Instrumental Aggression," *Perceptual and Motor Skills*, 41 (1975), p. 538.

34. P. Ellsworth and E. J. Langer, "Staring and Approach: An Interpretation of the Stare as a Nonspecific Activation," *Journal of Personality and Social Psychology*, 33 (1976), pp. 117–122.

35. See P. Horn, "Newsline," *Psychology Today*, 7 (1973), p. 92.

36. See, for example, S. Milgram, "Behavioral Study of Obedience," *Journal of Abnormal and Social Psychology*, 67 (1963), pp. 371–378.

37. For reports of several studies, see L. Bickman, "Social Roles and Uniforms: Clothes Make the Person," *Psychology Today*, 7, No. 11 (1974), pp. 49–51; L. Bickman, "The Effect of Social Status on the Honesty of Others," *Journal of Social Psychology*, 85 (1971), pp. 87–92; L. Bickman, "The Social Power of a Uniform" *Journal of Applied Social Psychology*, 4 (1974), pp. 47–61.

38. M. Korda, "Learn These 35 Signs of Power," *New Woman*, 6, No. 4 (1976), pp. 30–33, 41–42.

39. J. D. Fisher, M. Rytting, and R. Heslin, "Hands Touching Hands: Affective and Evaluative Effects of an Interpersonal Touch," *Sociometry*, 39 (1976), pp.. 416–421; A. S. Imada and M. D. Hakel, "Influence of Nonverbal Communication

on Impressions and Decisions in Simulated Employment Interviews," *Journal of Applied Psychology*, 62 (1977), pp. 295–300. M. Jacuńska-Iwińska, "An Experimental Modification of the Young Child's Level of Activity," *Polish Psychological Bulletin*, 6 (1975), pp. 27–35; S. Milmoe, R. Rosenthal, H. T. Blane, M. E. Chafetz, and I. Wolf, "The Doctor's Voice: Postdictor of Successful Referral of Alcoholic Patients," *Journal of Abnormal Psychology*, 72 (1967), pp. 78–84; E. L. Phillips, E. A. Phillips, D. L. Fixsen, and M. M. Wolf, "Behavior Shaping for Delinquents," *Psychology Today*, 7, No. 1 (1973), pp. 74–79.

40. D. C. Agulera, "Relationships Between Physical Contact and Verbal Interaction Between Nurses and Patients," *Journal of Psychiatric Nursing*, 5 (1967), pp. 5–21; S. M. Jourard and R. Friedman, "Experimenter–Subject 'Distance' and Self-Disclosure," *Journal of Personality and Social Psychology*, 15 (1970), pp. 278–282; A. Mahrabian, "Communication Length as an Index of Communicator Attitude," *Psychological Reports*, 17 (1965), pp. 519–522; M. Reece and R. Whitman, "Expressive Movements, Warmth, and Verbal Reinforcement," *Journal of Abnormal and Social Psychology*, 64 (1962), pp. 234–236.

41. M. H. Bond and D. Shiraishi, "The Effect of Interviewer's Body Lean and Status on the Nonverbal Behavior of Interviewees," *Japanese Journal of Experimental Social Psychology*, 13 (1973), pp. 11–21.

42. C. L. Cooper and D. Bowles, "Physical Encounter and Self-Disclosure," *Psychological Reports*, 33 (1973), pp. 451–454; H. Hackney, "Facial Gestures and Subject Expression of Feelings," *Journal of Counseling Psychology*, 21 (1974), pp. 173–178; Jourard and Friedman (note 40); A. E. Woolfolk and R. L. Woolfolk, "Student Self-Disclosure in Response to Teacher Verbal and Nonverbal Behavior," *Journal of Experimental Education*, 44 (1975), pp. 36–40.

43. M. L. Patterson, "An Arousal Model of Interpersonal Intimacy," *Psychological Review*, 83 (1976), pp. 235–245; P. Ellsworth and L. Ross, "Intimacy in Response to Direct Gaze," *Journal of Experimental and Social Psychology*, 11 (1975). pp. 592–613.

44. R. Sommer, *Personal Space* (Englewood Cliffs, N.J.: Prentice-Hall, 1969).

45. S. J. Ramsey, "Prison Codes," *Journal of Communication*, 26 (1976), p. 44.

46. Ramsey (note 45).

47. A. Baum and S. Valins, "Residential Environments. Group Size and Crowding," proceedings of the American Psychological Association, 1973, pp. 211–212; L. Bickman, A. Teger, T. Gabriele, C. McLaughlin, M. Berger, and E. Sunaday, "Dormitory Density and Helping Behavior," *Environment and Behavior*, 5 (1973), pp. 464–491; D. Stokols, "The Experience of Crowding in Primary and Secondary Environments," *Environment and Behavior*, 8 (1976), pp. 49–85.

48. J. P. Daley, "The Effects of Crowding and Comfort in Interaction Behavior and Member Satisfaction in Small Groups," paper presented at the International Communication Association Convention, Montreal, April 1973; J. L. Freedman, "The Crowd: Maybe Not So Madding After All," *Psychology Today*, 4 (1971), pp. 58–61, 86.

49. C. Haney and P. G. Zimbardo, "It's Tough to Tell a High School From a Prison," *Psychology Today*, 9 (1975), p. 29.

50. A. Bandura, "Behavior Modifications through Modeling Procedures," in L. Krasner and L. P. Ullmann (eds.), *Research in Behavior Modification* (New York: Holt, Rinehart and Winston, 1965), pp. 310–340; Breed and Porter (note 20); J. D. Matarazzo, A. N. Wines, and G. Saslow, "Studies in Interviewer Speech Behavior," in Krasner and Ullmann (note 50); B. J. Zimmerman and G. H. Brody, "Race and Modelling Influences on the Interpersonal Play Patterns of Boys," *Journal of Educational Psychology*, 67 (1975), pp. 591–598.

51. S. K. Escalona, "Feeding Disturbances in Very Young Children," *American Journal of Orthopsychiatry*, 15 (1945), pp. 76–80.

52. J. Bates, "The Effects of a Child's Imitation Vs. Nonimitation on Adults' Verbal and Nonverbal Positivity," dissertation, University of California at Los Angeles, 1973.

53. P. Crassweller, M. A. Gordon, and W. H. Tedford, Jr., "An Experimental Investigation of Hitchhiking," *Journal of Psychology*, 82 (1972), pp. 43–47; J. M. Darley and J. Cooper, "The 'Clean for Gene' Phenomenon: The Effect of Students' Appearance on Political Campaigning," *Journal of Applied Social Psychology*, 2 (1972), pp. 24–33; C. B. Keasy and C. Tomlinson-Keasy, "Petition Signing in a Naturalistic Setting," *Journal of Social Psychology*, 89 (1973), pp. 313–314; L. MacNeil and B. Wilson, "Effects of Clothing and

Hair Length on Petition-Signing Behavior," unpublished manuscript, Illinois State University, 1972; B. J. Raymond and R. K. Unger, "The Apparel Oft Proclaims the Man: Cooperation with Deviant and Conventional Youths," *Journal of Social Psychology*, 87 (1972).

54. J. K. Burgoon and S. B. Jones, "Toward a Theory of Personal Space Expectations and Their Violations," *Human Communication Research*, 2 (1976), pp. 131–146.

55. Burgoon (note 4); J. K. Burgoon, D. W. Stacks, and G. Woodall, "Violations of Personal Space Expectations and Reward as Predictors of Recall, Credibility and Attraction," paper presented at the Speech Communication Association Convention, Washington, D.C., December 1977; J. Dietch and J. House, "Affiliative Conflict and Individual Differences in Self-Disclosure," *Representative Research in Social Psychology*, 6 (1975), pp. 69–75; Garner (note 29); J. K. Heston, "Effects of Anomia and Personal Space Invasion on Nonperson Orientation, Anxiety and Source Credibility," *Central States Speech Journal*, 25 (1974), pp. 19–27.

56. O. Pfungst, *Clever Hans (the Horse of Mr. Von Osten): A Contribution to Experimental, Animal, and Human Psychology* (New York: Holt, 1911).

57. J. G. Adair and J. Epstein, "Verbal Cues in the Mediation of Experimenter Bias," *Psychological Reports*, 22 (1968), pp. 1045–1053; Cooper, Darley, and Henderson (note 30). S. D. Duncan and R. Rosenthal, "Vocal Emphasis in Experimenters' Instruction Reading as Unintended Determinant of Subjects' Responses," *Language and Speech*, 11 (1968), pp. 20–26; R. A. Goldblatt and R. A. Schackner, "Categorizing Emotion Depicted in Facial Expressions and Reaction to Experimental Situation as a Function of Experimenter 'Friendliness,'" paper presented at the meeting of the Eastern Psychological Association, Washington, D.C., April 1968; R. Rosenthal, "Interpersonal Expectations," in R. Rosenthal and R. L. Rosnow (eds.), *Artifact in Behavioral Research* (New York: Academic Press, 1969), pp. 181–277.

58. Duncan and Rosenthal (note 57); S. D. Duncan, Jr., M. J. Rosenberg, and J. Finkelstein, "The Paralanguage of Experimenter Bias," *Sociometry*, 33 (1969), pp. 207–219; R. A. Jones and J. Cooper, "Mediation of Experimenter Effects," *Journal of Personality and Social Psychology*, 20 (1971), pp. 70–74; K. R. Scherer, R. E. Rosenthal, and J. Kaivumaki, "Mediating Interpersonal Expectancies Via Vocal Cues: Differential Speech Intensity as a Means of Social Influence," *European Journal of Social Psychology*, 2 (1972), pp. 1963–1976.

59. D. F. Anderson and R. Rosenthal, "Some Effects of Interpersonal Expectancy and Social Interaction on Institutionalized Retarded Children," proceedings of the American Psychological Association, 1968, pp. 479–480; W. V. Beez, "Influence of Biased Psychological Reports on Teacher Behavior and Pupil Performance," proceedings of the American Psychological Association, 1968, pp. 605–606; L. K. Conn, C. N. Edwards, R. Rosenthal, and D. Crowne, "Perception of Emotion and Response to Teachers' Expectancy by Elementary School Children," *Psychological Reports*, 22 (1968), pp. 27–34; C. E. Flowers, "Effects of an Arbitrary Accelerated Group Placement on the Tested Academic Achievement of Educationally Disadvantaged Students," dissertation, Teachers College, Columbia University, 1966; R. Rosenthal and L. Jacobson, *Pygmalion in the Classroom: Teacher Expectation and Pupils' Intellectual Development* (New York: Holt, Rinehart and Winston, 1968.)

60. Rosenthal (note 57).

61. C. O. Word, M. P. Zanna, and J. Cooper, "The Nonverbal Mediation of Self-Fulfilling Prophecies in Interracial Interaction," *Journal of Experimental Social Psychology*, 10 (1974), pp. 109–120.

Author Index

Subject Index

Action language, 53
Adaptor gestures, 58, 64, 177
Affect, 195–218
   accuracy of judgment of, 209–216
   acquisition of, 197–201
   blends, 196, 215–216
   body displays of, 62–64, 203–209
   cultural differences in displays of, 55,
     197–198, 206
   display rules, 205–206
   displays of, as category of kinesic behavior,
     58
   facial displays of, 205–209, 210–216
   haptic cues of, 203–204
   myths surrounding, 196–197
   primary, 201
   research problems, 217–218
   underlying dimensions of, 201–203
   vocal cues of, 204–205, 209–210
   see also Emotional expression; Haptics;
     Vocalics
Affiliation appeals
   kinesic cues, 280–281
   proxemic cues, 280–281
   vocalic cues, 280–281
Age
   communicated by apparel, 149, 150(table)
   and environmental preferences, 106
   estimates of, by kinesic cues, 150
   and first impressions, 148–149
   and personal space, 94
Ali, Muhammad, 245, 257
Analogic coding system, 18
Androgyny, 135–136
Apparel, 78–80
   and communication of age, 149, 150(table)
   and communication of attitude, 158–160, 180,
     294
   and communication of sex, 150–151

and communication of status, 153–154, 186–
   187, 255, 286–288
   and cultural differences, 154
   and first impressions, 148–149
   norms, 79–80, 156–157
   and personality, 162–164
Approaches to field of nonverbal communication, 27–50
   body language, 29–32
   defined, 27–29
   ethological, 32–35
   functional, 48–49
   linguistic, 36–41
   physiological, 44–47
   psychoanalytic, 41–44
Artifacts, 104–115
   and attention arousal, 277–278
   and color, 109–110
   communications potential of, 111
   defined, 105
   dimensions of, 107–111
   and distraction, 279
   and personal space, 96
   and regulation of interaction, 235–237
   and self-presentation, key words in,
     254(table)
   and specific communication contexts,
     111–115
   and status, 188–189, 288–289
   see also Color; Environment
Attention arousal, 276–278
   artifact cues, 277–278
   and comprehension and retention, 276–278
   vocalic cues, 276–277
Attitude, communication of and apparel,
   158–160, 180, 294
Attitude change, 279–284
   by affiliation appeals, 280–281
   by attractiveness appeals, 281–283

Manson, Charles, 273, 285
Marx, Groucho, 12
Meaning-centered approach
  assumptions of, 40–41
  limitations of, 41
Mesomorph, 76–77. *See also* Body type
Micro facial expression (microexpression), 217,
  265–266
Mini-experiments, list of, 4, 14, 23, 49, 63, 79,
  96, 102, 106, 132, 136, 153, 154, 167, 177,
  182, 183, 208, 214, 231, 236, 251, 267, 286,
  288
Modeling, 292–294
Monochronism, 103
Monroe, Marilyn, 164
Moods, 95
  effect of colors on, 110(table)
Moon, Sun Myung, 273–274

Nature–nurture controversy, 14–17, 198–199
Negative, lack of in nonverbal communication,
  19–20
Negative reinforcement, 275. *See also*
  Reinforcement cues
Neurophysiological approach
  assumptions of, 45–46
  limitations of, 46
Neurophysiological processing, 17–18
Nixon, Richard M., 55, 186, 189
Noncontact culture, 127
Nonverbal communication
  and attitude change, 282(table)
  brain functioning in, 17, 46
  criteria for, 10(table)
  defined, 9–10
  functions of, 10–13
  language characteristics of, 18–20
  limitations of, compared with verbal
    communication, 18–20
  message characteristics of, 20–23
  origins of, 14–17
  relationship of, to verbal communication,
    10–23

Object language, 53

Pain and pleasure, 290–292
Paranoia, 137–138
Performances
  deceptive, 264–269
  elements of, 249–250
  and frames, 251–253
  institutional, 260–262
  and negative experiences, 264
  stigmatized, 262–264
  team, 257–260
  violations, 250–251
Personality differences
  and apparel, 162–164
  and colors, 163(table)
  deviant conditions, 136–138
  and environmental preferences, 106
  externalizers vs. internalizers, 214
  in need for personal space, 94–95
  and personality types, 138–139
  as stigma, 262
Personality traits
  and apparel, 162–164
  and body types, 161(table)
  and vocal cues, 166(table)
Personal space, 92–96, 294
Persuasion, *see* Attitude change
Physical appearance, 73–80
  and attitude change, 281–283
  and attraction, 180
  communication potential of, 80
  and credibility, 185–187
  defined, 73–74
  and dominance cues, 286–289
  and first impressions, 150–164 *passim*
  and initiating of interaction, 223–224
  norms, 76–80
  and power, 185–187, 286–289
  and relational messages, 180, 185–187
  and self-presentation, key words in,
    254(table)
  as sociocultural indicator, 153
  and status, 153–155, 185–187, 286–289
  see also specific physical features
Physical attractiveness, 74–76
  and attitude change, 281–283
  and first impressions, 224

Physical attractiveness (*cont.*)
    norms, 74
    as stigma, 162, 263
Physiological approaches, 44–47. *See also*
    Neurophysiological approach; Sensory
    approach
Pleasure, *see* Pain and pleasure
Population, density of, 96
Positions
    in conversation, 234–235
    in courtship behaviors, 177
Positive reinforcement, 275
Posture, 124–125(illus.)
Power
    and artifacts, 188–189, 288–289
    and behavior change, 286–289
    and chronemics, 288–289
    and eye contact, 181–182
    and haptics, 184, 288–289
    and kinesic behaviors, 181–182
    and physical appearance, 185–187, 286–289
    and proxemics, 184, 288–289
    as reinforcer of behavior, 286
    and silences, 185
    and vocalics, 155–156, 182–183, 185, 288–289
Preclosings, 239
Presentation of self, *see* Self-presentation
Prestige, 256. *See also* Power; Status
Primary affects, 201
Proxemics, 89–98
    and attraction, 94, 179–180, 253
    communication potential of, 97–98
    and credibility, 184
    and cultural differences, 94, 126–127
    defined, 89–90
    and distraction, 279, 283–284
    and first impressions, 150, 151
    and initiation of interaction, 225
    norm violations, 96–97
    and power, 94–95, 184, 288–289
    and reinforcement cues, 276
    and relational messages, 179–180, 184, 279,
        288–289
    and self-presentation, key words in,
        254(table)
    and sex differences, 93–94, 135, 291

    subcultural differences in, 130–131
    see also Personal space; Territoriality
Proxmire, Senator William, 74
Psychoanalytic approaches, 41–44
    assumptions of, 42–43
    limitations of, 43–44
Psychological features, 160–167
    conveyed by body type and body
        attractiveness, 160–162
    conveyed by dress and adornment, 162–164
    conveyed by hair and beards, 162
    conveyed by vocal cues, 164–167
Public territory, 92
Punctuality, 102
Punishment, 275
Pupil dilation, 175–176

Quasi-courtship behaviors, 176–178. *See also*
    Courtship behaviors

Race, 151–152
    and interviewer expectancy, 296
    and personal space, 94
    and physical appearance cues, 151–152
    and proxemics, 94
    as stigma, 262
    and vocalic differences, 152
    see also Subcultural differences
Rasputin, 285
Redundancy, and nonverbal cues, 10
Referencing the negative, 19–20
Regulation, of interaction, 13, 222–243. *See*
    also Interaction; Leave-taking; Turn-taking
    cues
Regulators, 58, 64–65, 200, 228
Reinforcement cues, 256, 274–276
    and comprehension and retention, 274–276
    see also Negative reinforcement; Positive
        reinforcement
Relational messages, 172–193
    and chronemics, 179, 185
    defined, 173–174
    and haptics, 179–180, 184
    and kinesics, 176–179, 181–182

Relational messages (*cont.*)
   and personal appearance, 180, 185–187
   and proxemics, 179–180, 184, 288–289
   silence as, 179, 184
   see also Attraction; Courtship behaviors;
      Credibility; Power; Status
Research
   experimenter expectancy in, 294–296
   problems of, 217
Retention, *see* Comprehension and retention
Rickles, Don, 12
Rituals, symbolic, 128–129(table)
Role theory, 246–247. *See also* Dramaturgic
   analysis; Self-presentation
Rule structure, 18–19

Sarcasm, and contradiction of cues, 12–13
Schizophrenia, 136–137
Self-presentation, 245–247, 253–257
   and bolstering believability, 256–257
   and chronemics, 254(table), 255
   and communicating depth, 253–255
   deceptive, 264–269
   key words in, 254(table) and promoting at-
      traction, 253 and promoting prestige, 256
   and reflecting status, 255–256
   role-playing theories of, 246–247
   and showing expertise, 255
   types of, 257–269
   see also Dramaturgic analysis
Self-reflexiveness, 19
Sensory approach
   assumptions of, 44–45
   limitations of, 45
Sequencing
   backchannel, 226–231
   turn endings, 233-234
   turn-taking, 225–226
Sex differences, 132–136
   and androgyny, 135–136
   and apparel, 150–151
   in encoding facial expressions, 133
   in environmental preferences, 106
   and eye contact, 133–134, 290
   haptic, 135

   in inflection patterns, 134–135
   in interruptions, 134
   in judging facial expressions, 132–133
   in kinesic behavior, 132–133
   and personal space, 93–94
   proxemic, 93–94, 135, 291
   in smiling, 134
   vocalic, 132–133, 134–135, 151
Signature, in conversation, 239
Sign language, 53
Signs, 7-8
Silence, 179, 185, 231–233
   and credibility, 185
   function of, in conversation, 231–232,
      234–235
   and power, 185
   as relational message, 179, 184
   and turn-taking, 231–232
   see also Vocalics
Skin color, 77. *See also* Race
Sociocultural features, and first impressions,
   153–160. *See also* Status
Somatype, 77. *See also* Body type
Staring, 285–286
Status
   and apparel, 153–154, 186–187, 255,
      286–288
   and artifacts, 188–189, 288–289
   and behavior change, 286–289
   and chronemics, 185, 288–289
   and eye contact, 181–182
   and haptics, 184, 255, 289–289
   and kinesic behavior, 181–182, 255
   and personal space, 94
   and physical appearance, 153–155, 185–187,
      286–289
   and proxemics, 94, 95, 184, 288–289
   as reinforcer of behavior, 286
   and self-presentation, 255–256
   and silences, 185
   and vocalics, 155–156, 182–183, 185,
      288–289
Stereotypes
   of body types, 160–162
   and first impressions, 146–147
Stigmatized performances, 262, 264